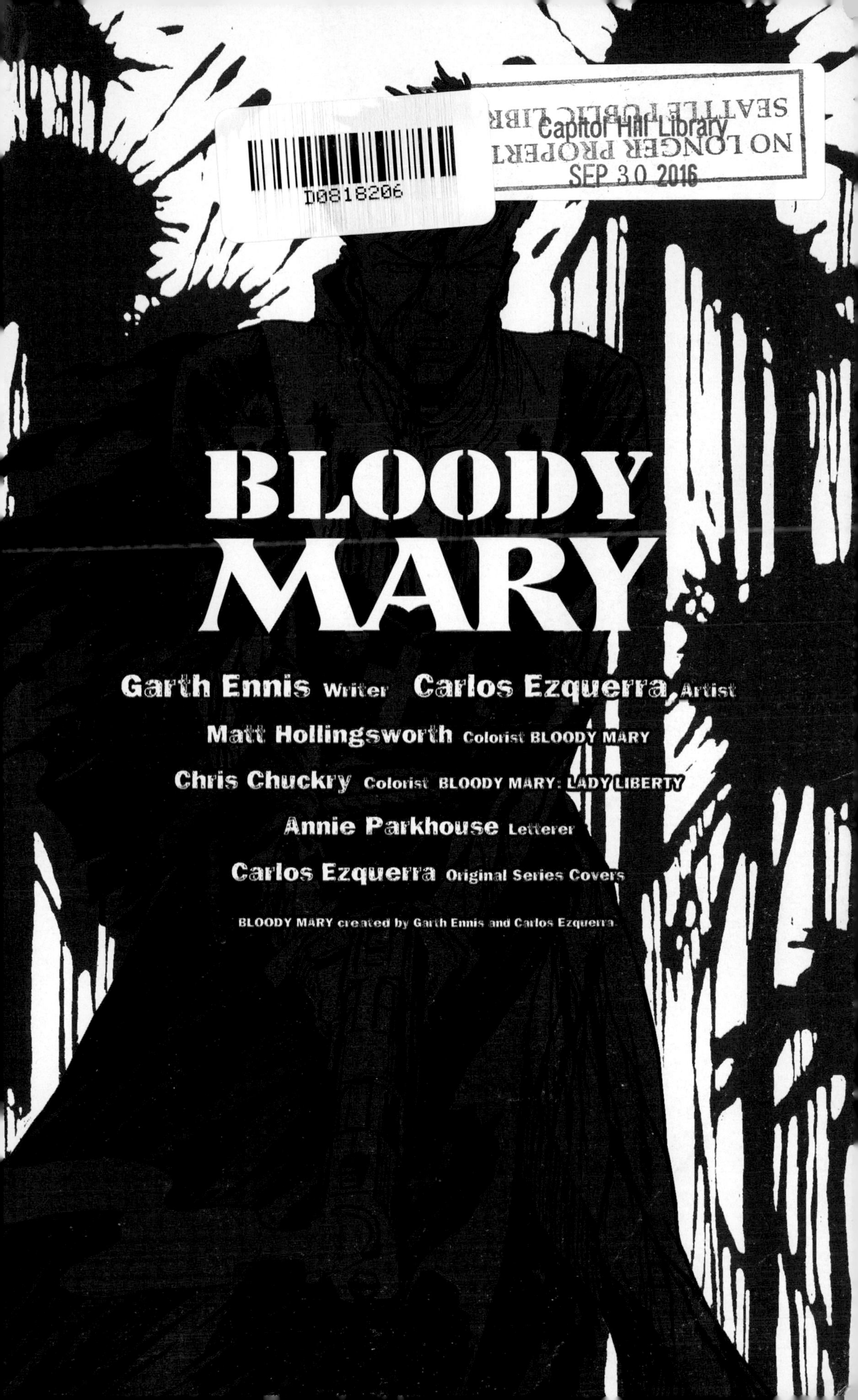

BLOODY MARY

Garth Ennis Writer **Carlos Ezquerra** Artist

Matt Hollingsworth Colorist BLOODY MARY

Chris Chuckry Colorist BLOODY MARY: LADY LIBERTY

Annie Parkhouse Letterer

Carlos Ezquerra Original Series Covers

BLOODY MARY created by Garth Ennis and Carlos Ezquerra.

IMAGE COMICS, INC.

Robert Kirkman – Chief Operating Officer
Erik Larsen – Chief Financial Officer
Todd McFarlane – President
Marc Silvestri – Chief Executive Officer
Jim Valentino – Vice-President

Eric Stephenson – Publisher
Corey Murphy – Director of Sales
Jeff Boison – Director of Publishing Planning & Book Trade Sales
Jeremy Sullivan – Director of Digital Sales
Kat Salazar – Director of PR & Marketing
Emily Miller – Director of Operations
Branwyn Bigglestone – Senior Accounts Manager
Sarah Mello – Accounts Manager
Drew Gill – Art Director
Jonathan Chan – Production Manager
Meredith Wallace – Print Manager
Briah Skelly – Publicity Assistant
Sasha Head – Sales & Marketing Production Designer
Randy Okamura – Digital Production Designer
David Brothers – Branding Manager
Ally Power – Content Manager
Addison Duke – Production Artist
Vincent Kukua – Production Artist
Tricia Ramos – Production Artist
Jeff Stang – Direct Market Sales Representative
Emilio Bautista – Digital Sales Associate
Leanna Caunter – Accounting Assistant
Chloe Ramos-Peterson – Administrative Assistant
IMAGECOMICS.COM

BLOODY MARY. First Printing. March 2016. Copyright © 2016 Garth Ennis & Carlos Ezquerra. All rights reserved. Published by Image Comics, Inc. Office of publication: 2001 Center Street, Sixth Floor, Berkeley, CA 94704. Contains material originally published in single magazine form as Bloody Mary #1-4 and Bloody Mary: Lady Liberty #1-4. "Bloody Mary," its logos, and the likenesses of all characters herein are trademarks of Garth Ennis & Carlos Ezquerra, unless otherwise noted. Image Comics and its logos are registered trademarks of Image Comics, Inc. No part of this publication may be reproduced or transmitted, in any form or by any means (except for short excerpts for journalistic or review purposes), without the express written permission of Garth Ennis, Carlos Ezquerra, or Image Comics, Inc. All names, characters, events, and locales in this publication are entirely fictional. Any resemblance to actual persons (living or dead), events, or places, without satiric intent, is coincidental. Printed in the USA. For information regarding the CPSIA on this printed material call: 203-595-3636 and provide reference #RICH–668844. For international rights, contact: foreignlicensing@imagecomics.com. ISBN: 978-1-63215-761-4.

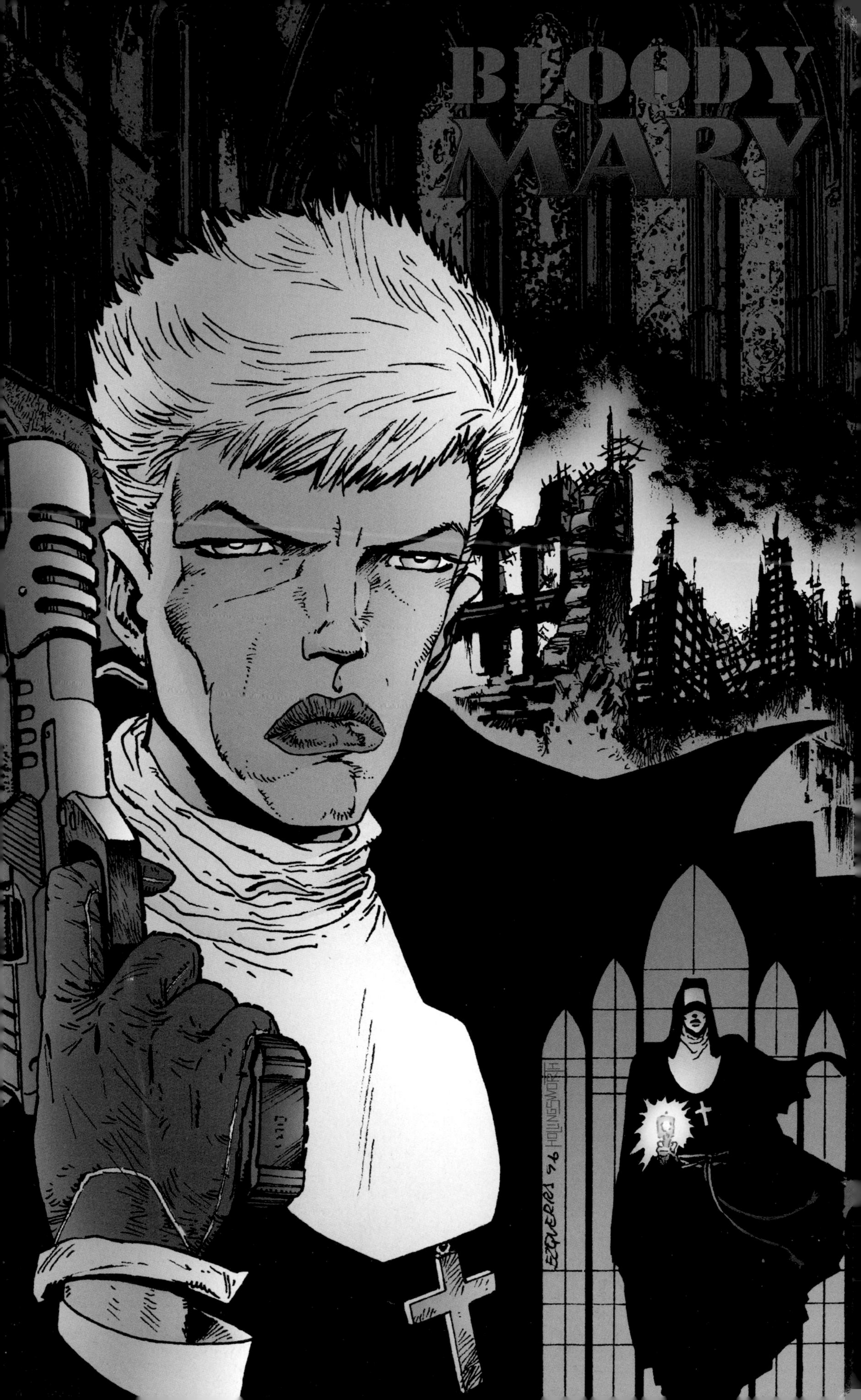
BLOODY
MARY
EZQUERRA '96 HOLLINGSWORTH

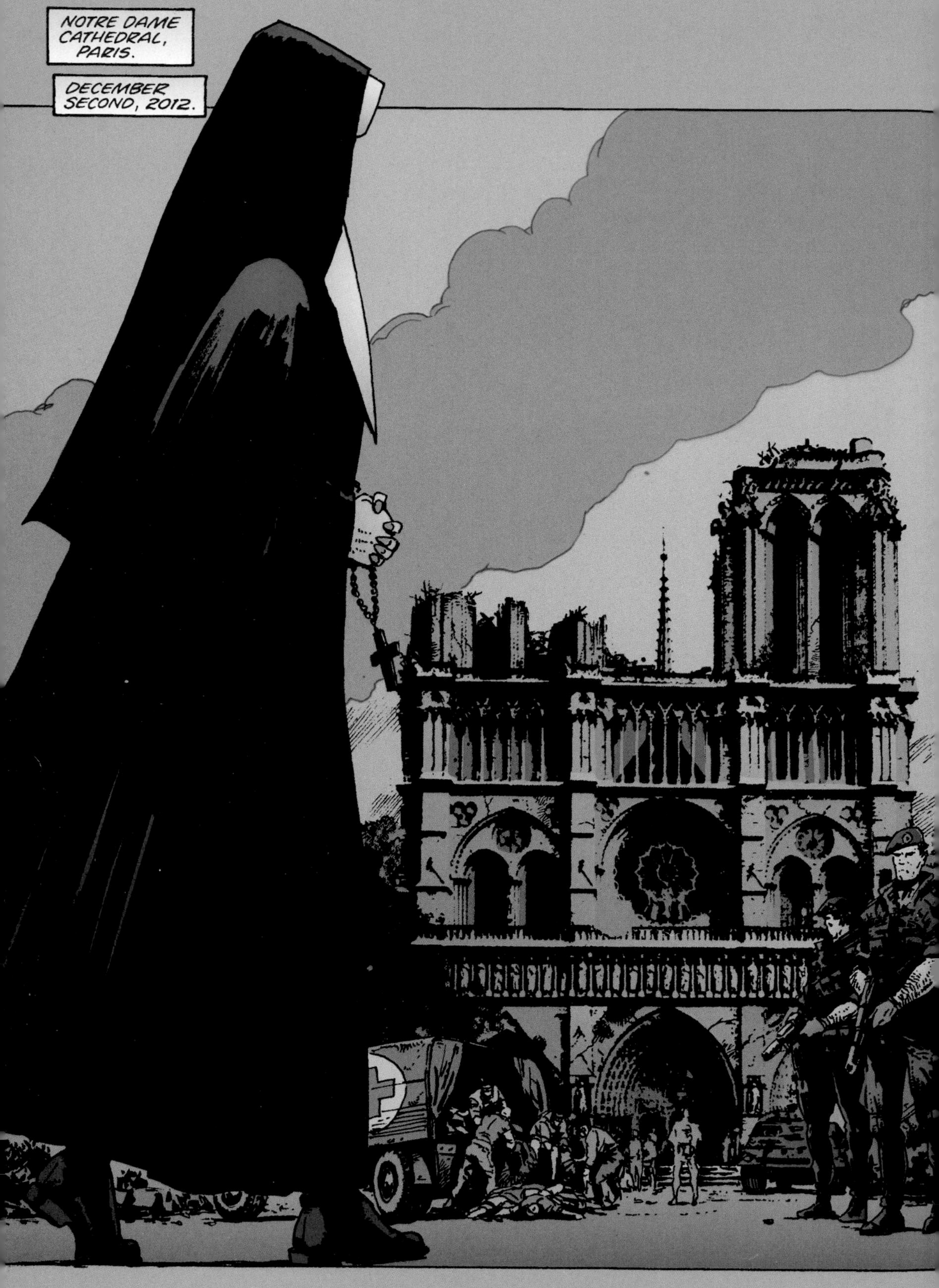
NOTRE DAME CATHEDRAL, PARIS.
DECEMBER SECOND, 2012.

IN GOD'S NAME, IF YOU HAVE TO USE THAT BLOODY SCALPEL, *CUT MY THROAT*

YOU THINK I WANT TO LIVE LIKE THIS?

AAAAAHHHH!

IF YOU CANNOT HOLD HIM STILL THEN BREAK HIS ARMS, NURSE—

MOTHER—!

WE HAVE NO MORPHINE! WE HAVE NO ANESTHETIC! *WE USED IT ALL!*

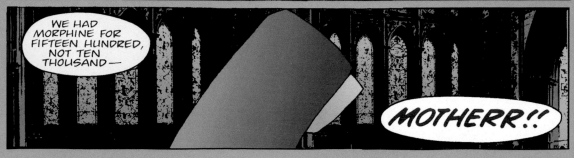

WE HAD MORPHINE FOR FIFTEEN HUNDRED, NOT TEN THOUSAND—

MOTHERR!!

5

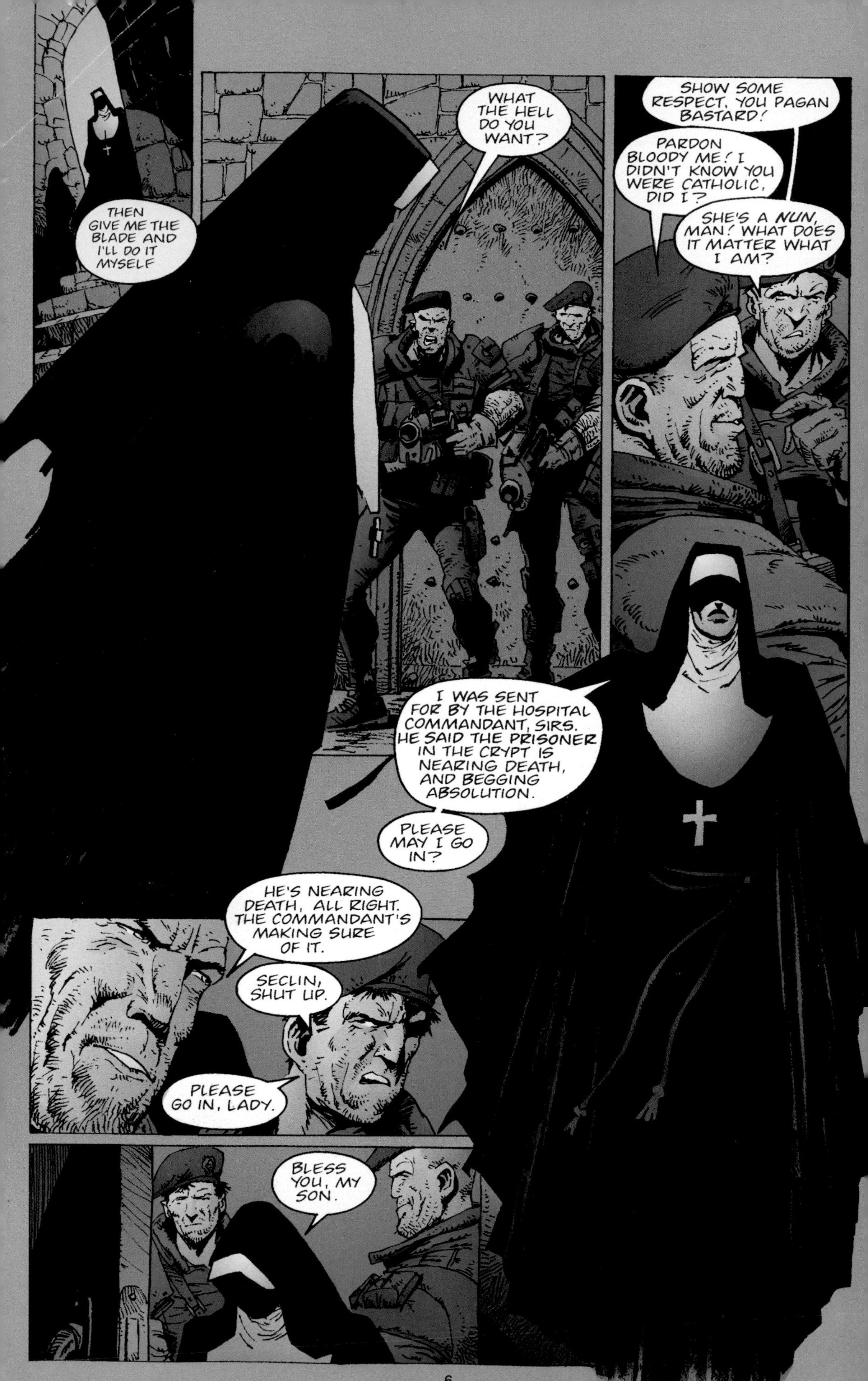
THEN GIVE ME THE BLADE AND I'LL DO IT MYSELF
WHAT THE HELL DO YOU WANT?
SHOW SOME RESPECT, YOU PAGAN BASTARD!
PARDON BLOODY ME! I DIDN'T KNOW YOU WERE CATHOLIC, DID I?
SHE'S A NUN, MAN! WHAT DOES IT MATTER WHAT I AM?
I WAS SENT FOR BY THE HOSPITAL COMMANDANT, SIRS. HE SAID THE PRISONER IN THE CRYPT IS NEARING DEATH, AND BEGGING ABSOLUTION.
PLEASE MAY I GO IN?
HE'S NEARING DEATH, ALL RIGHT. THE COMMANDANT'S MAKING SURE OF IT.
SECLIN, SHUT UP.
PLEASE GO IN, LADY.
BLESS YOU, MY SON.

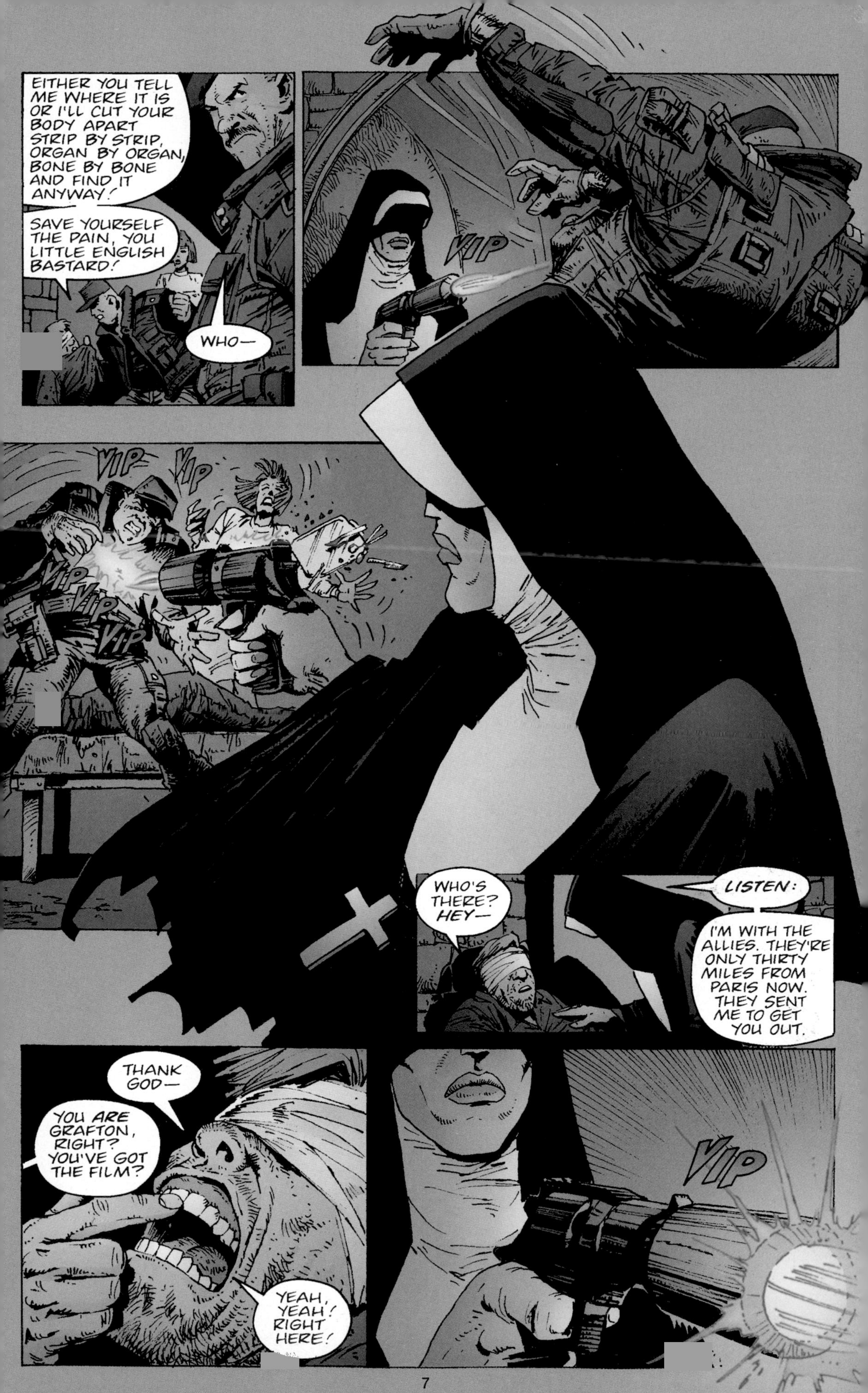
EITHER YOU TELL ME WHERE IT IS OR I'LL CUT YOUR BODY APART STRIP BY STRIP, ORGAN BY ORGAN, BONE BY BONE AND FIND IT ANYWAY!
SAVE YOURSELF THE PAIN, YOU LITTLE ENGLISH BASTARD!
WHO—
VIP
VIP
VIP
VIP
VIP
VIP
WHO'S THERE? HEY—
LISTEN:
I'M WITH THE ALLIES. THEY'RE ONLY THIRTY MILES FROM PARIS NOW. THEY SENT ME TO GET YOU OUT.
THANK GOD—
YOU ARE GRAFTON, RIGHT? YOU'VE GOT THE FILM?
YEAH, YEAH! RIGHT HERE!
VIP

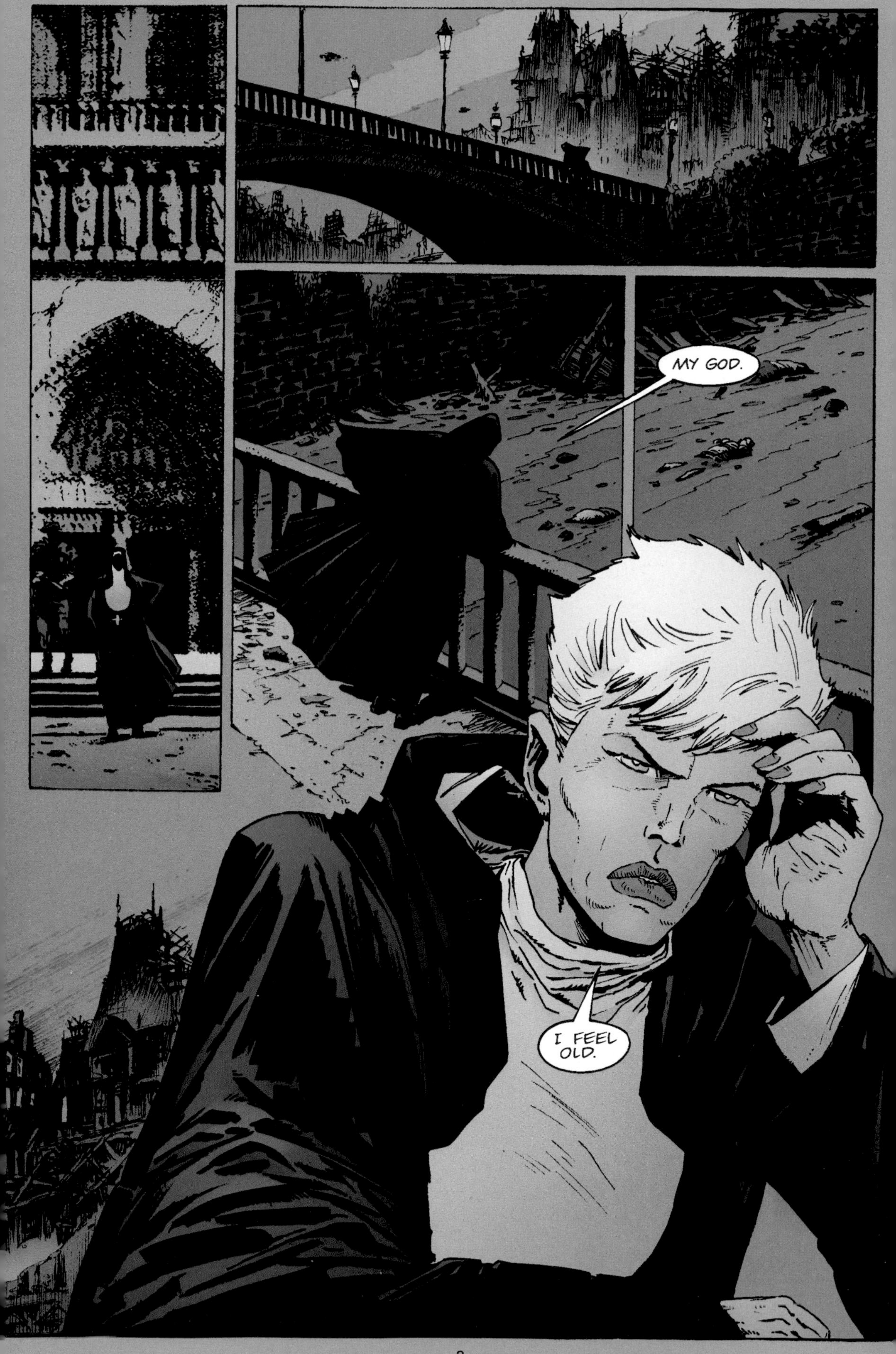
MY GOD.
I FEEL OLD.

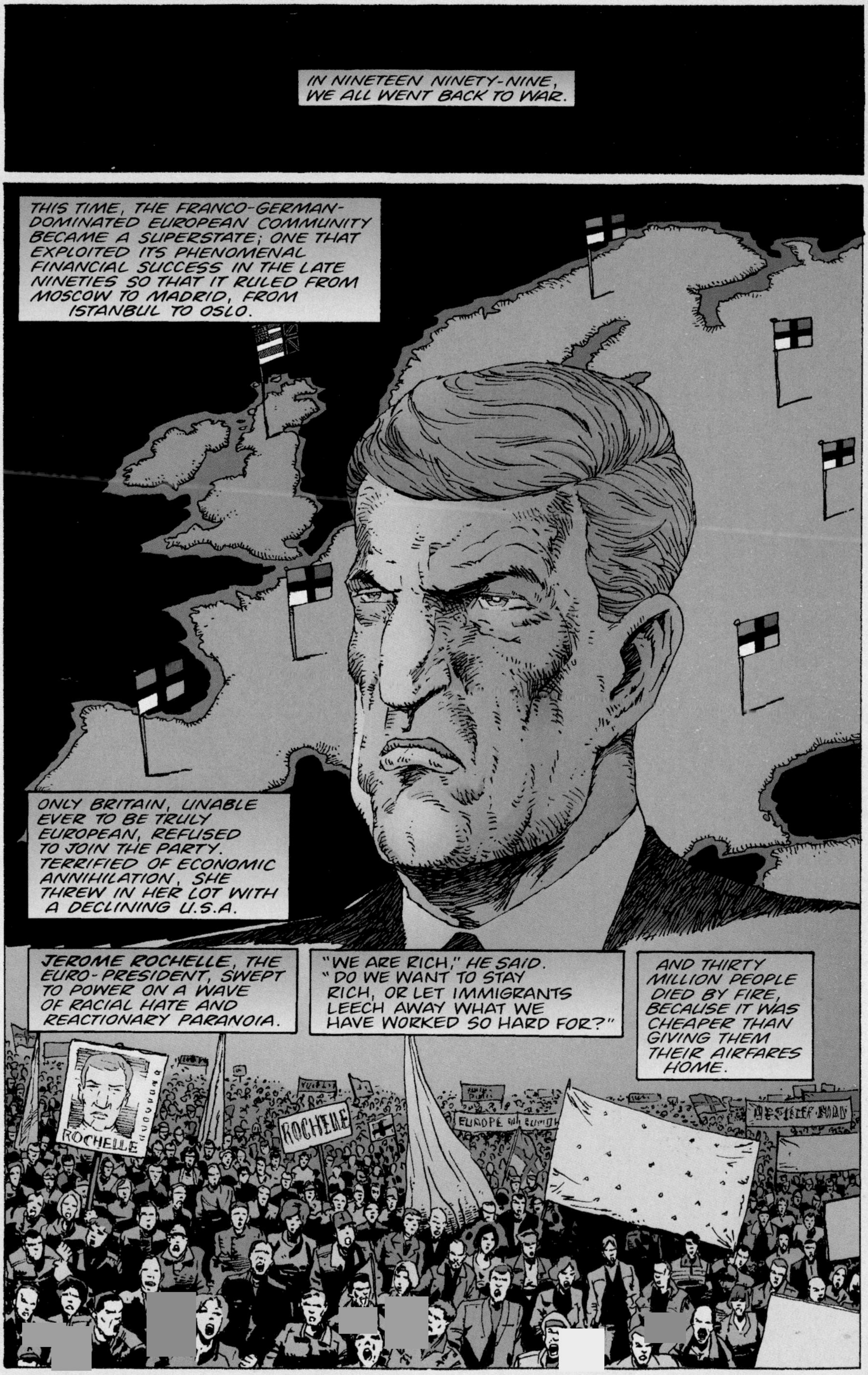
IN NINETEEN NINETY-NINE, WE ALL WENT BACK TO WAR.
THIS TIME, THE FRANCO-GERMAN-DOMINATED EUROPEAN COMMUNITY BECAME A SUPERSTATE; ONE THAT EXPLOITED ITS PHENOMENAL FINANCIAL SUCCESS IN THE LATE NINETIES SO THAT IT RULED FROM MOSCOW TO MADRID, FROM ISTANBUL TO OSLO.
ONLY BRITAIN, UNABLE EVER TO BE TRULY EUROPEAN, REFUSED TO JOIN THE PARTY. TERRIFIED OF ECONOMIC ANNIHILATION, SHE THREW IN HER LOT WITH A DECLINING U.S.A.
JEROME ROCHELLE, THE EURO-PRESIDENT, SWEPT TO POWER ON A WAVE OF RACIAL HATE AND REACTIONARY PARANOIA.
"WE ARE RICH," HE SAID. "DO WE WANT TO STAY RICH, OR LET IMMIGRANTS LEECH AWAY WHAT WE HAVE WORKED SO HARD FOR?"
AND THIRTY MILLION PEOPLE DIED BY FIRE, BECAUSE IT WAS CHEAPER THAN GIVING THEM THEIR AIRFARES HOME.
ROCHELLE
ROCHELLE

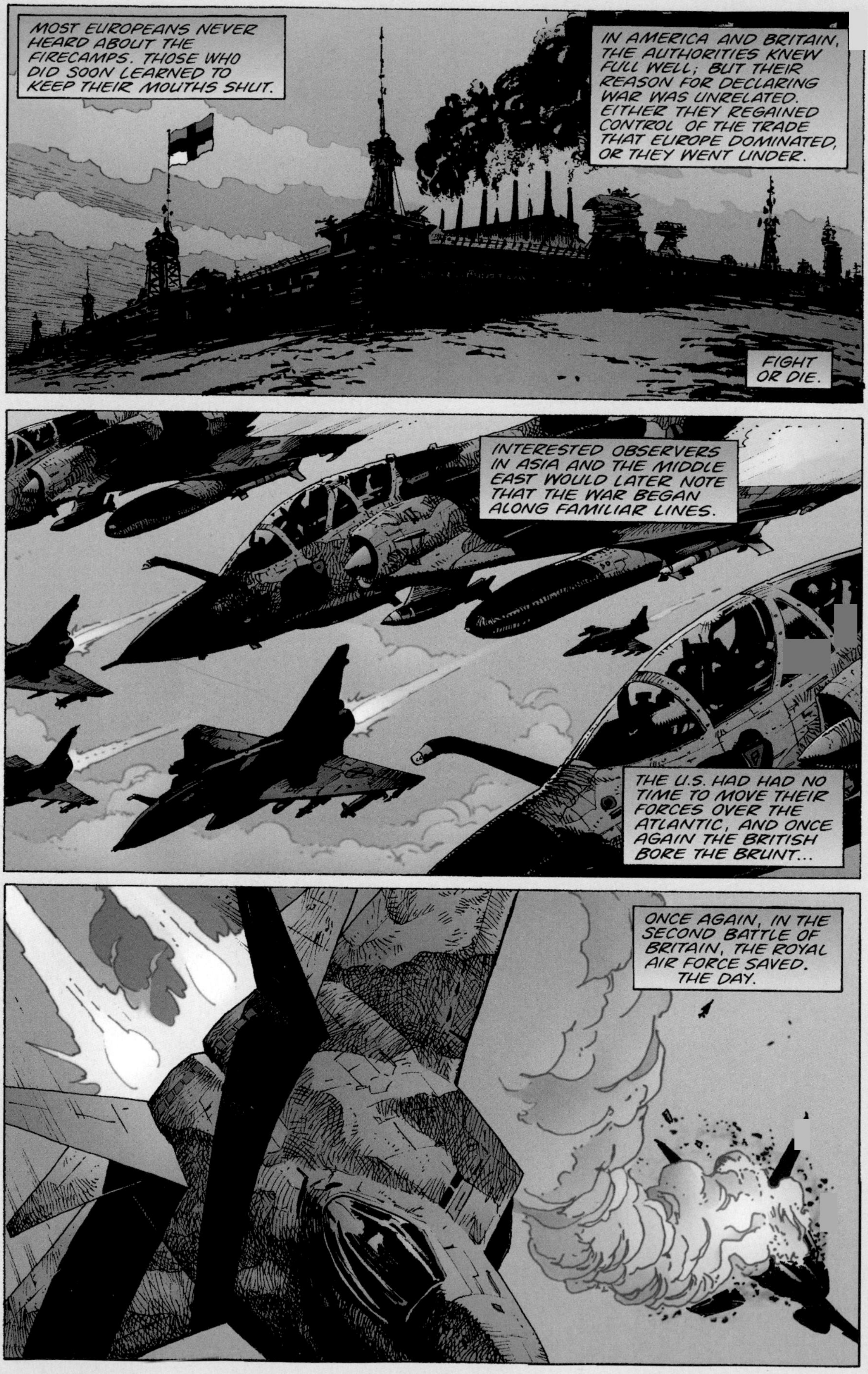
MOST EUROPEANS NEVER HEARD ABOUT THE FIRECAMPS. THOSE WHO DID SOON LEARNED TO KEEP THEIR MOUTHS SHUT.
IN AMERICA AND BRITAIN, THE AUTHORITIES KNEW FULL WELL; BUT THEIR REASON FOR DECLARING WAR WAS UNRELATED. EITHER THEY REGAINED CONTROL OF THE TRADE THAT EUROPE DOMINATED, OR THEY WENT UNDER.
FIGHT OR DIE.
INTERESTED OBSERVERS IN ASIA AND THE MIDDLE EAST WOULD LATER NOTE THAT THE WAR BEGAN ALONG FAMILIAR LINES.
THE U.S. HAD HAD NO TIME TO MOVE THEIR FORCES OVER THE ATLANTIC, AND ONCE AGAIN THE BRITISH BORE THE BRUNT...
ONCE AGAIN, IN THE SECOND BATTLE OF BRITAIN, THE ROYAL AIR FORCE SAVED. THE DAY.

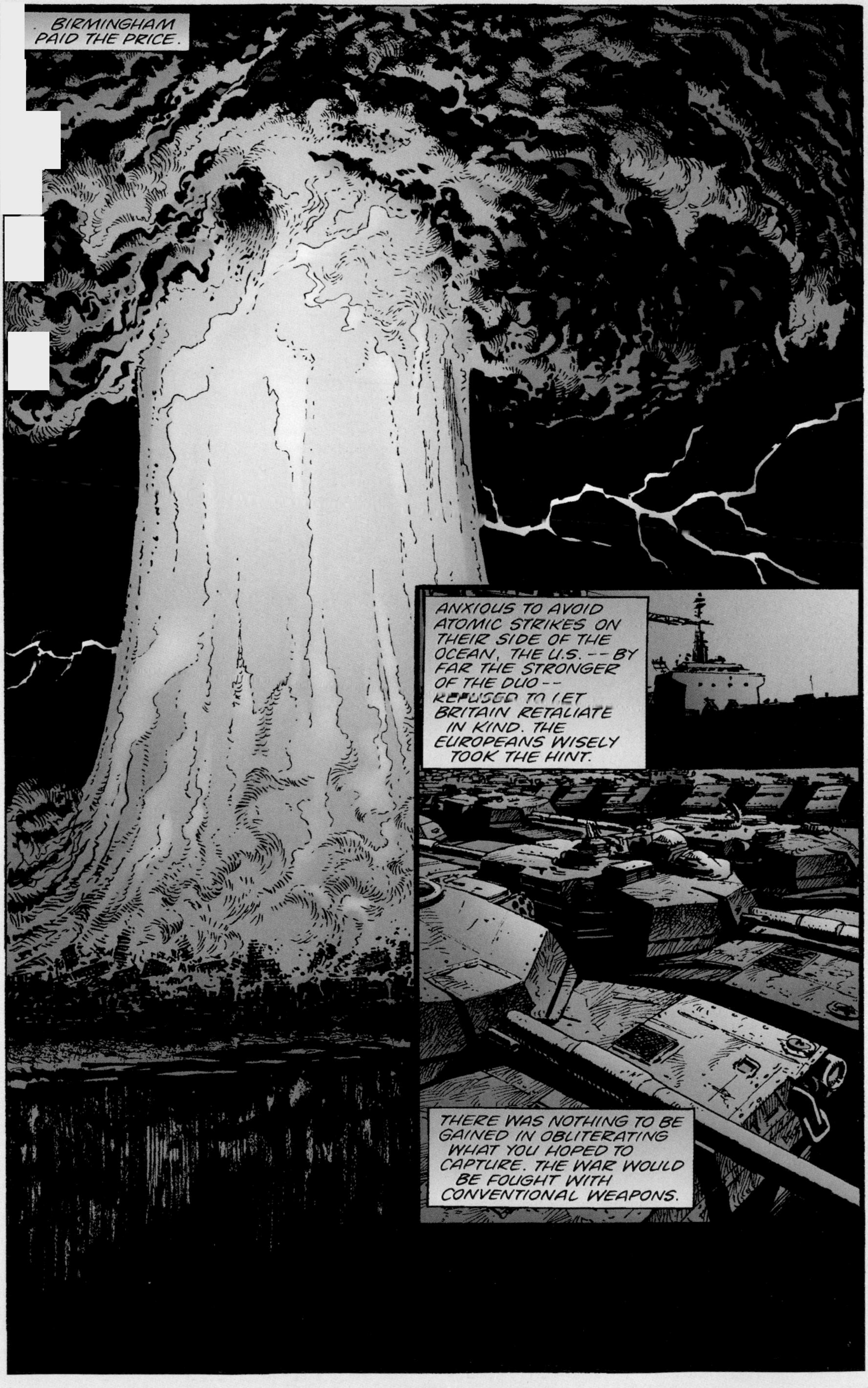
BIRMINGHAM PAID THE PRICE.
ANXIOUS TO AVOID ATOMIC STRIKES ON THEIR SIDE OF THE OCEAN, THE U.S. -- BY FAR THE STRONGER OF THE DUO -- REFUSED TO LET BRITAIN RETALIATE IN KIND. THE EUROPEANS WISELY TOOK THE HINT.
THERE WAS NOTHING TO BE GAINED IN OBLITERATING WHAT YOU HOPED TO CAPTURE. THE WAR WOULD BE FOUGHT WITH CONVENTIONAL WEAPONS.

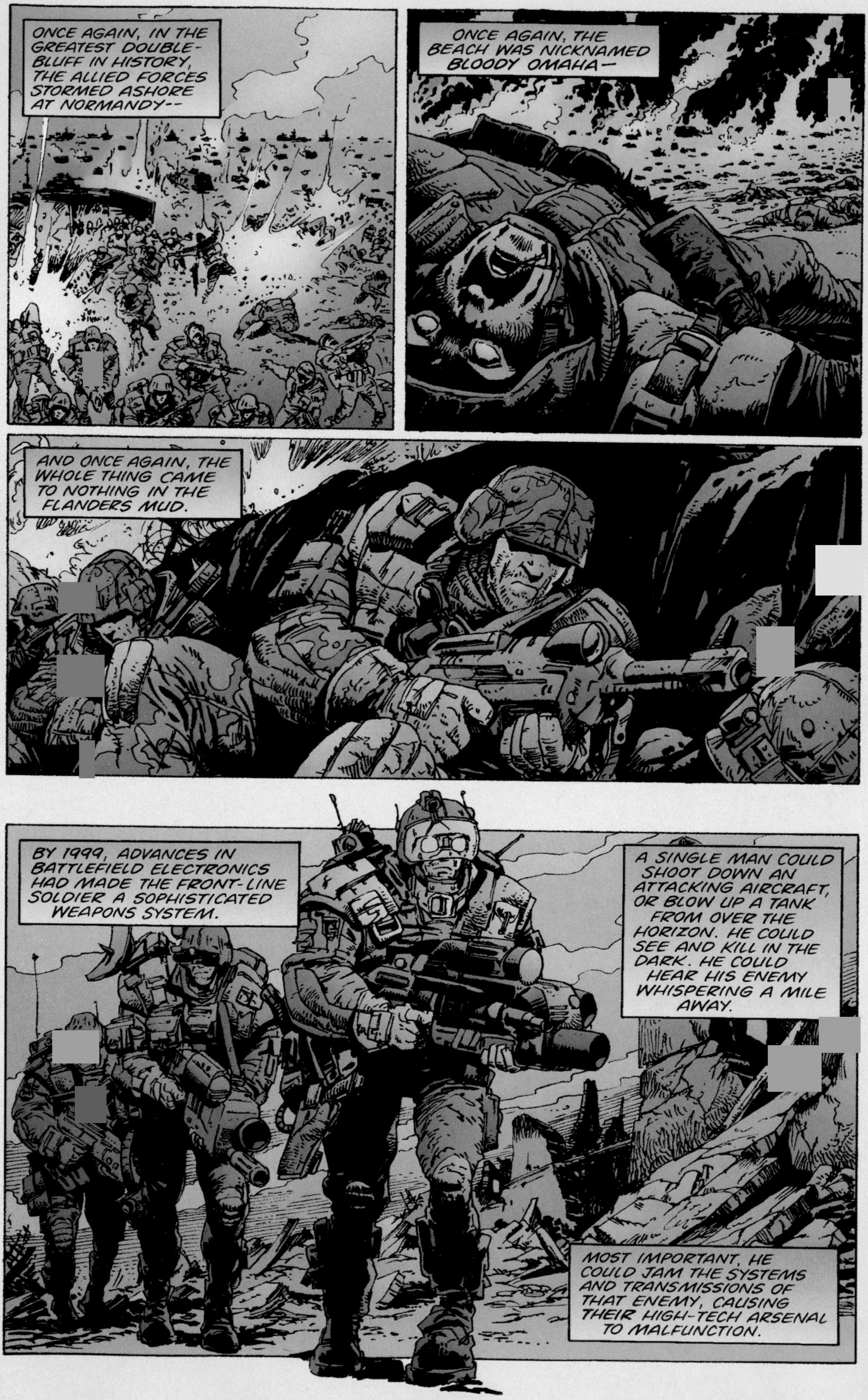
ONCE AGAIN, IN THE GREATEST DOUBLE-BLUFF IN HISTORY, THE ALLIED FORCES STORMED ASHORE AT NORMANDY--
ONCE AGAIN, THE BEACH WAS NICKNAMED BLOODY OMAHA—
AND ONCE AGAIN, THE WHOLE THING CAME TO NOTHING IN THE FLANDERS MUD.
BY 1999, ADVANCES IN BATTLEFIELD ELECTRONICS HAD MADE THE FRONT-LINE SOLDIER A SOPHISTICATED WEAPONS SYSTEM.
A SINGLE MAN COULD SHOOT DOWN AN ATTACKING AIRCRAFT, OR BLOW UP A TANK FROM OVER THE HORIZON. HE COULD SEE AND KILL IN THE DARK. HE COULD HEAR HIS ENEMY WHISPERING A MILE AWAY.
MOST IMPORTANT, HE COULD JAM THE SYSTEMS AND TRANSMISSIONS OF THAT ENEMY, CAUSING THEIR HIGH-TECH ARSENAL TO MALFUNCTION.

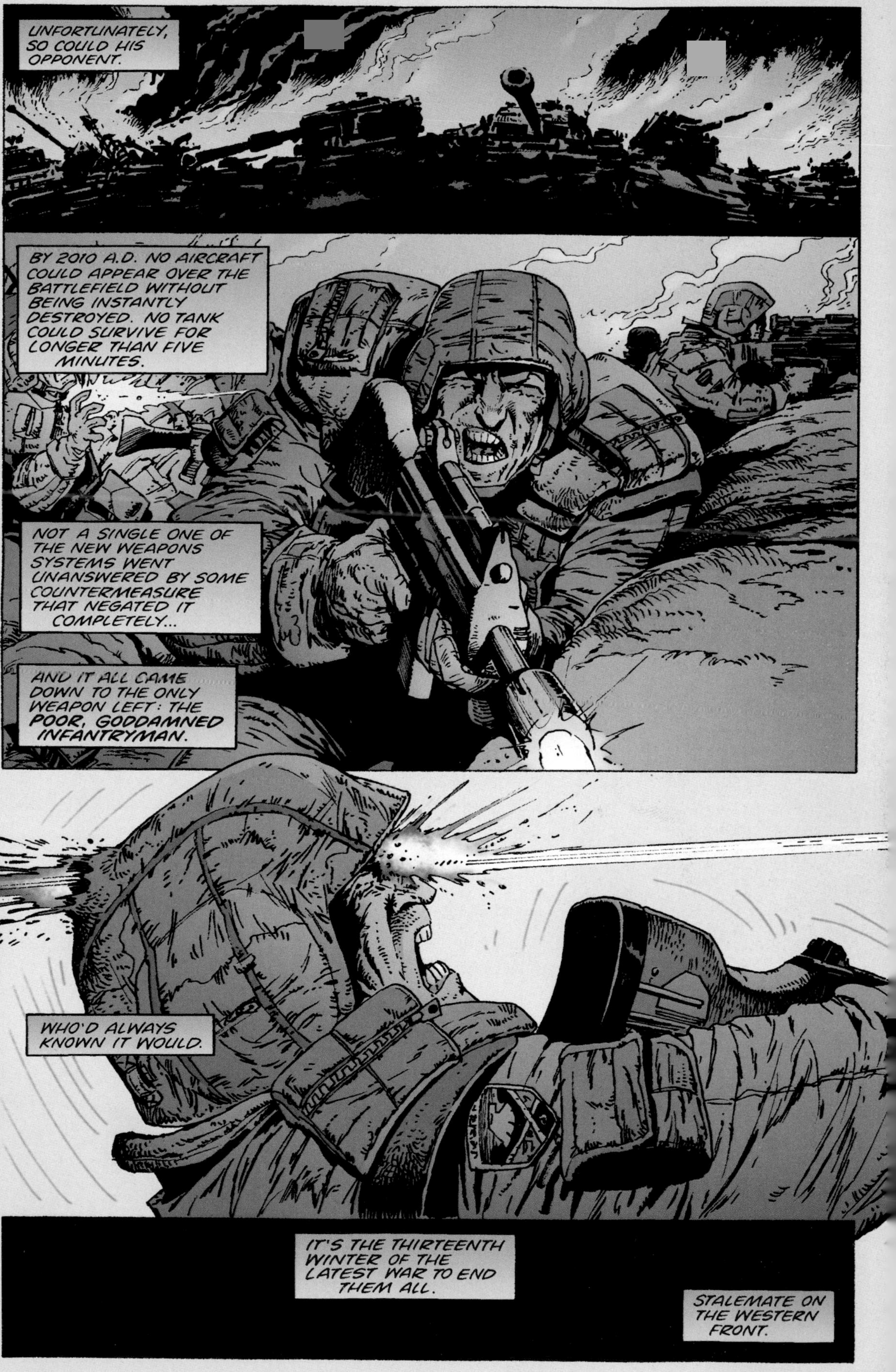

UNFORTUNATELY, SO COULD HIS OPPONENT.
BY 2010 A.D. NO AIRCRAFT COULD APPEAR OVER THE BATTLEFIELD WITHOUT BEING INSTANTLY DESTROYED. NO TANK COULD SURVIVE FOR LONGER THAN FIVE MINUTES.
NOT A SINGLE ONE OF THE NEW WEAPONS SYSTEMS WENT UNANSWERED BY SOME COUNTERMEASURE THAT NEGATED IT COMPLETELY...
AND IT ALL CAME DOWN TO THE ONLY WEAPON LEFT: THE POOR, GODDAMNED INFANTRYMAN.
WHO'D ALWAYS KNOWN IT WOULD.
IT'S THE THIRTEENTH WINTER OF THE LATEST WAR TO END THEM ALL.
STALEMATE ON THE WESTERN FRONT.

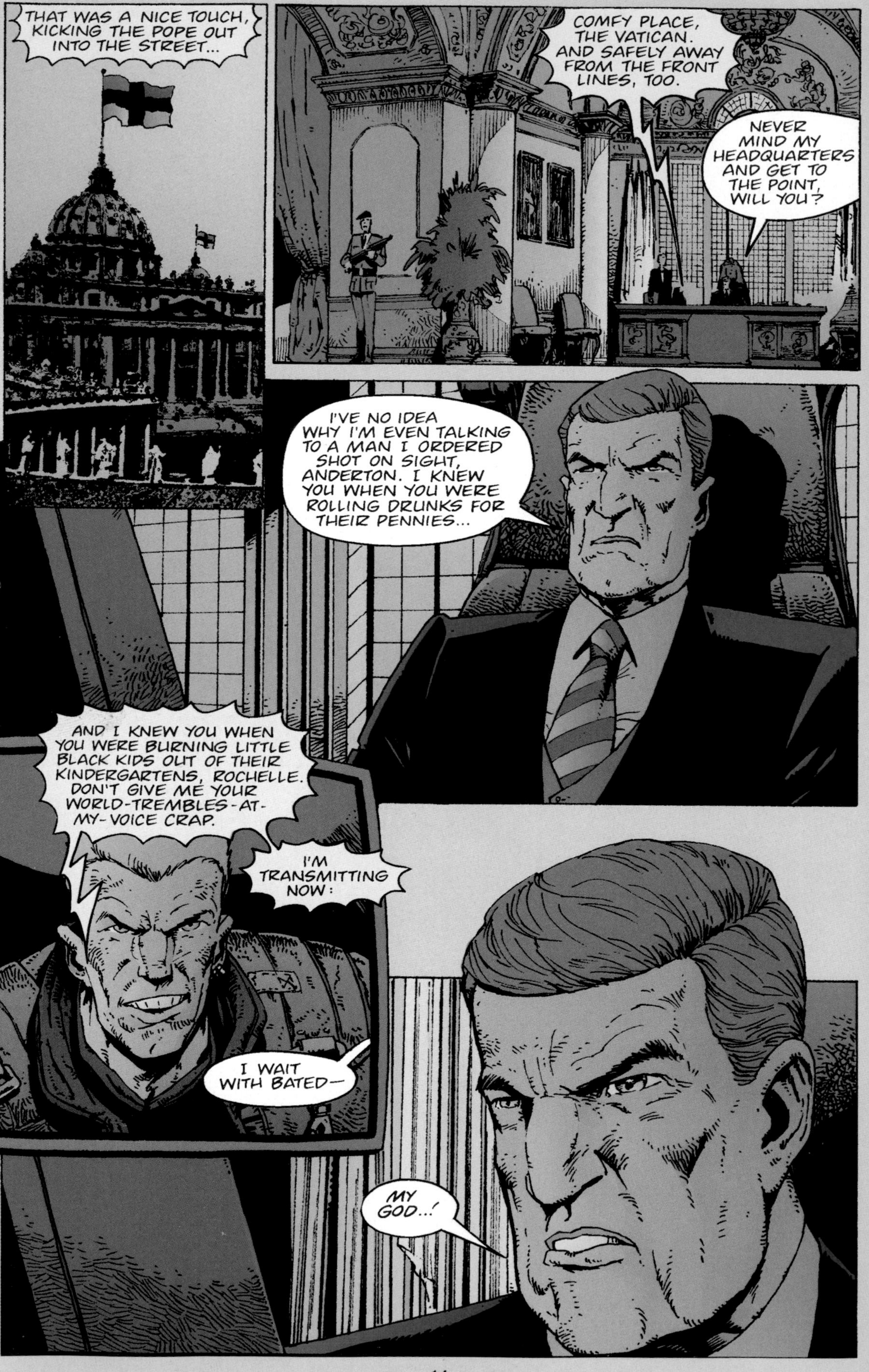
THAT WAS A NICE TOUCH, KICKING THE POPE OUT INTO THE STREET...
COMFY PLACE, THE VATICAN. AND SAFELY AWAY FROM THE FRONT LINES, TOO.
NEVER MIND MY HEADQUARTERS AND GET TO THE POINT, WILL YOU?
I'VE NO IDEA WHY I'M EVEN TALKING TO A MAN I ORDERED SHOT ON SIGHT, ANDERTON. I KNEW YOU WHEN YOU WERE ROLLING DRUNKS FOR THEIR PENNIES...
AND I KNEW YOU WHEN YOU WERE BURNING LITTLE BLACK KIDS OUT OF THEIR KINDERGARTENS, ROCHELLE. DON'T GIVE ME YOUR WORLD-TREMBLES-AT-MY-VOICE CRAP.
I'M TRANSMITTING NOW:
I WAIT WITH BATED—
MY GOD...!

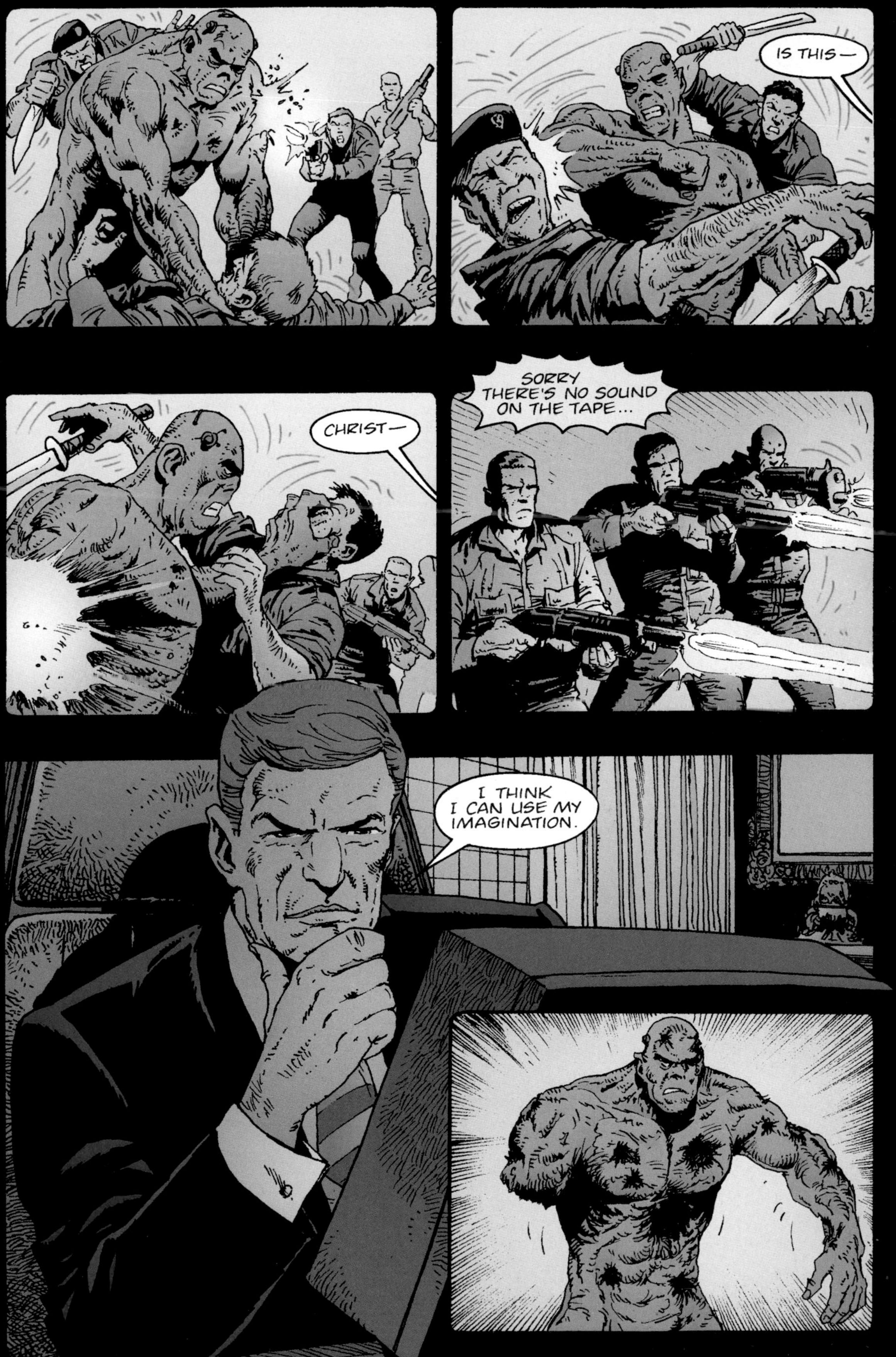
IS THIS—
CHRIST—
SORRY THERE'S NO SOUND ON THE TAPE...
I THINK I CAN USE MY IMAGINATION.

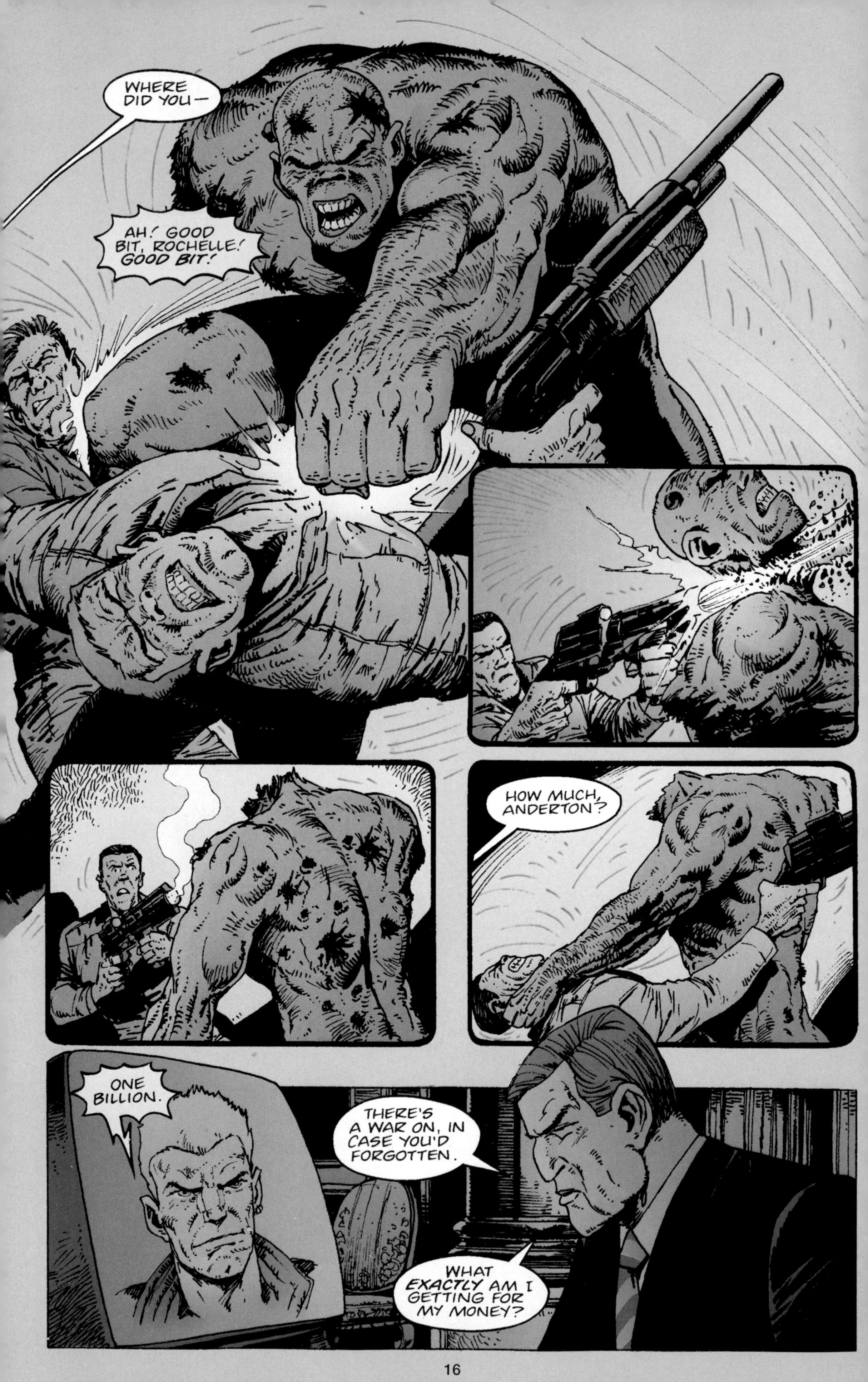
WHERE DID YOU—
AH! GOOD BIT, ROCHELLE! GOOD BIT!
HOW MUCH, ANDERTON?
ONE BILLION.
THERE'S A WAR ON, IN CASE YOU'D FORGOTTEN.
WHAT EXACTLY AM I GETTING FOR MY MONEY?

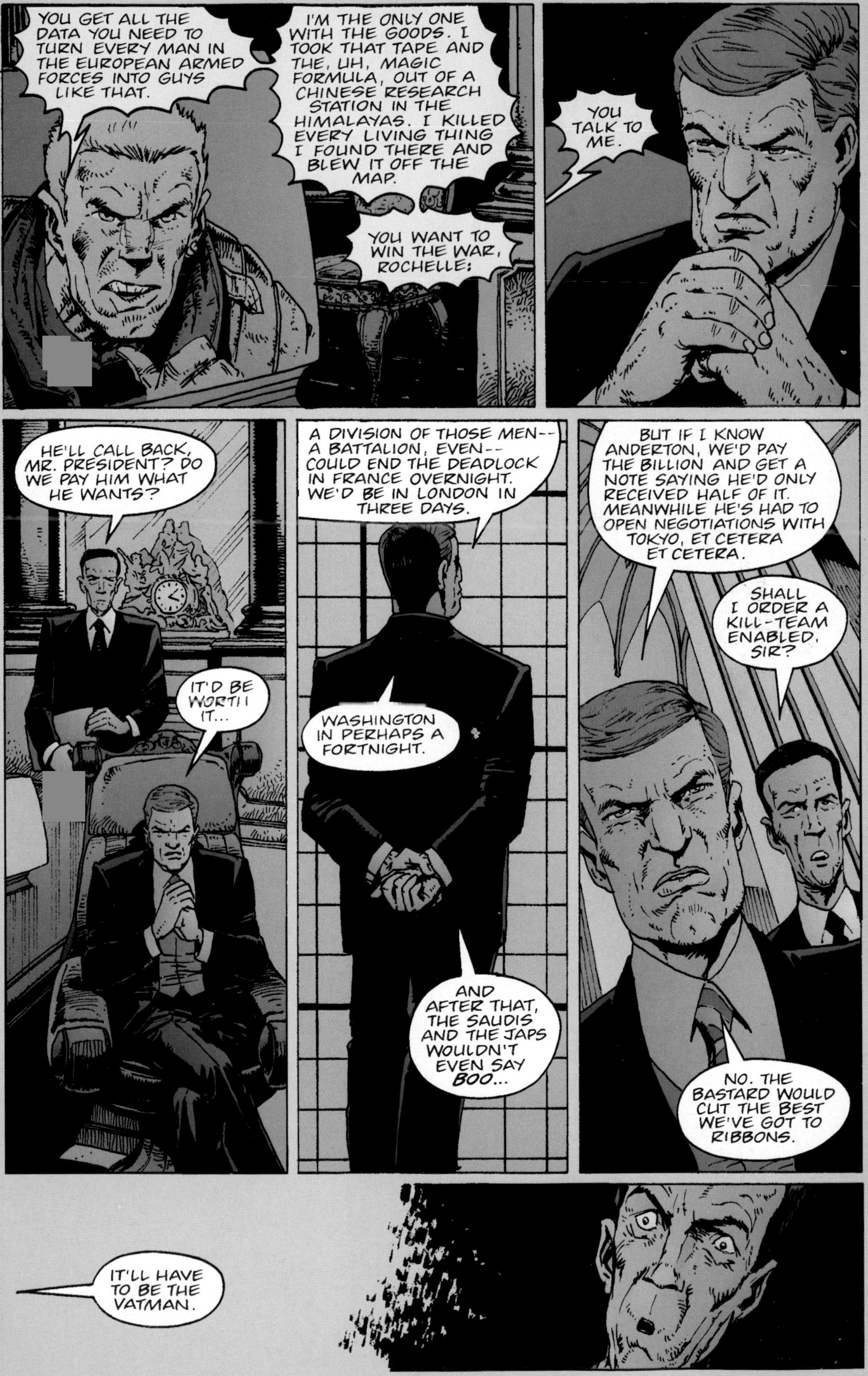
YOU GET ALL THE DATA YOU NEED TO TURN EVERY MAN IN THE EUROPEAN ARMED FORCES INTO GUYS LIKE THAT.
I'M THE ONLY ONE WITH THE GOODS. I TOOK THAT TAPE AND THE, UH, MAGIC FORMULA, OUT OF A CHINESE RESEARCH STATION IN THE HIMALAYAS. I KILLED EVERY LIVING THING I FOUND THERE AND BLEW IT OFF THE MAP.
YOU WANT TO WIN THE WAR, ROCHELLE:
YOU TALK TO ME.
HE'LL CALL BACK, MR. PRESIDENT? DO WE PAY HIM WHAT HE WANTS?
IT'D BE WORTH IT...
A DIVISION OF THOSE MEN-- A BATTALION, EVEN-- COULD END THE DEADLOCK IN FRANCE OVERNIGHT. WE'D BE IN LONDON IN THREE DAYS.
WASHINGTON IN PERHAPS A FORTNIGHT.
AND AFTER THAT, THE SAUDIS AND THE JAPS WOULDN'T EVEN SAY BOO...
BUT IF I KNOW ANDERTON, WE'D PAY THE BILLION AND GET A NOTE SAYING HE'D ONLY RECEIVED HALF OF IT. MEANWHILE HE'S HAD TO OPEN NEGOTIATIONS WITH TOKYO, ET CETERA ET CETERA.
SHALL I ORDER A KILL-TEAM ENABLED, SIR?
NO. THE BASTARD WOULD CUT THE BEST WE'VE GOT TO RIBBONS.
IT'LL HAVE TO BE THE VATMAN.

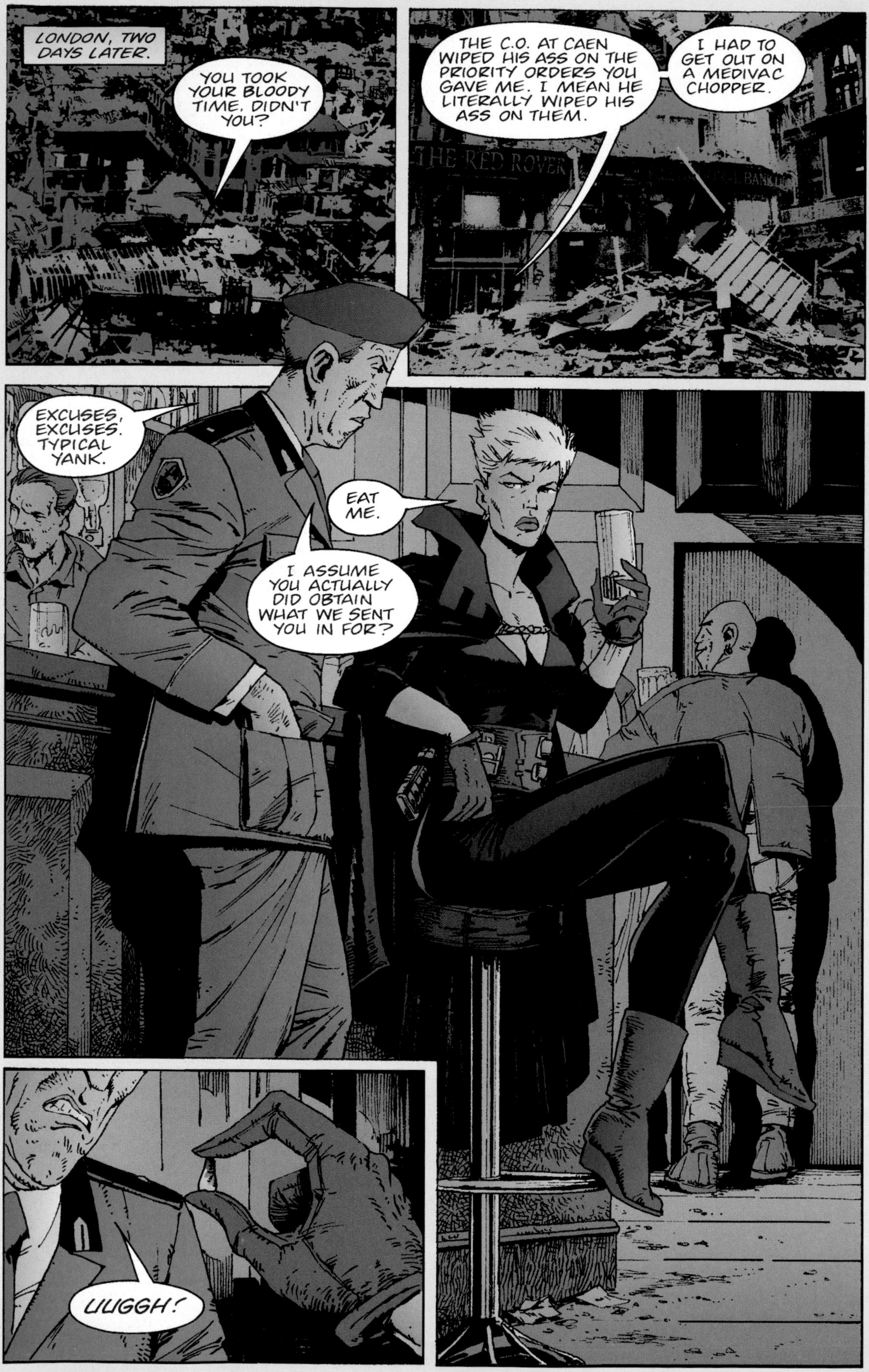
LONDON, TWO DAYS LATER.
YOU TOOK YOUR BLOODY TIME, DIDN'T YOU?
THE C.O. AT CAEN WIPED HIS ASS ON THE PRIORITY ORDERS YOU GAVE ME. I MEAN HE LITERALLY WIPED HIS ASS ON THEM.
I HAD TO GET OUT ON A MEDIVAC CHOPPER.
THE RED ROVER
EXCUSES, EXCUSES. TYPICAL YANK.
EAT ME.
I ASSUME YOU ACTUALLY DID OBTAIN WHAT WE SENT YOU IN FOR?
UUGGH!

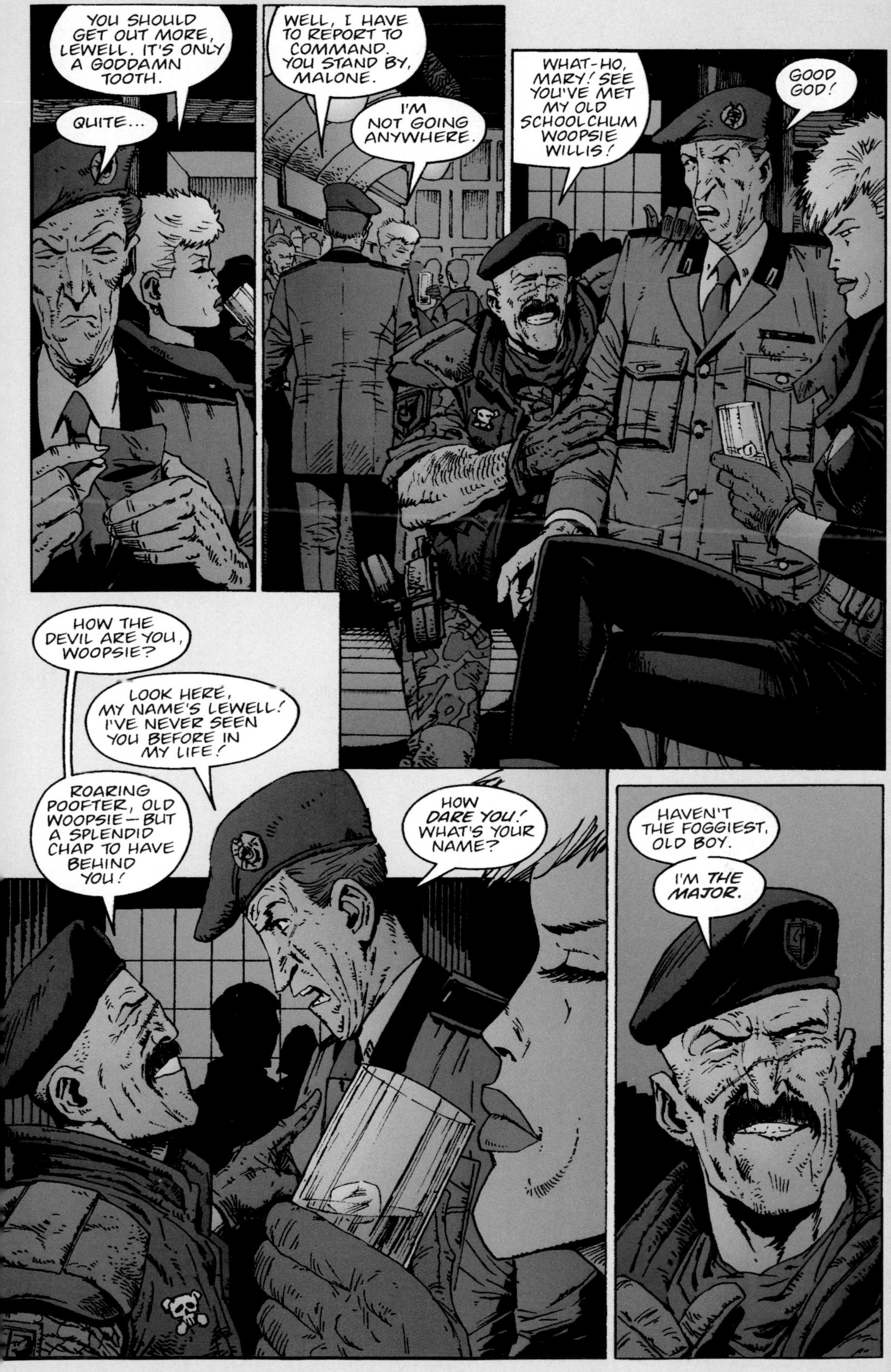

YOU SHOULD GET OUT MORE, LEWELL. IT'S ONLY A GODDAMN TOOTH.
QUITE...
WELL, I HAVE TO REPORT TO COMMAND. YOU STAND BY, MALONE.
I'M NOT GOING ANYWHERE.
WHAT-HO, MARY! SEE YOU'VE MET MY OLD SCHOOLCHUM WOOPSIE WILLIS!
GOOD GOD!
HOW THE DEVIL ARE YOU, WOOPSIE?
LOOK HERE, MY NAME'S LEWELL! I'VE NEVER SEEN YOU BEFORE IN MY LIFE!
ROARING POOFTER, OLD WOOPSIE—BUT A SPLENDID CHAP TO HAVE BEHIND YOU!
HOW DARE YOU! WHAT'S YOUR NAME?
HAVEN'T THE FOGGIEST, OLD BOY.
I'M THE MAJOR.

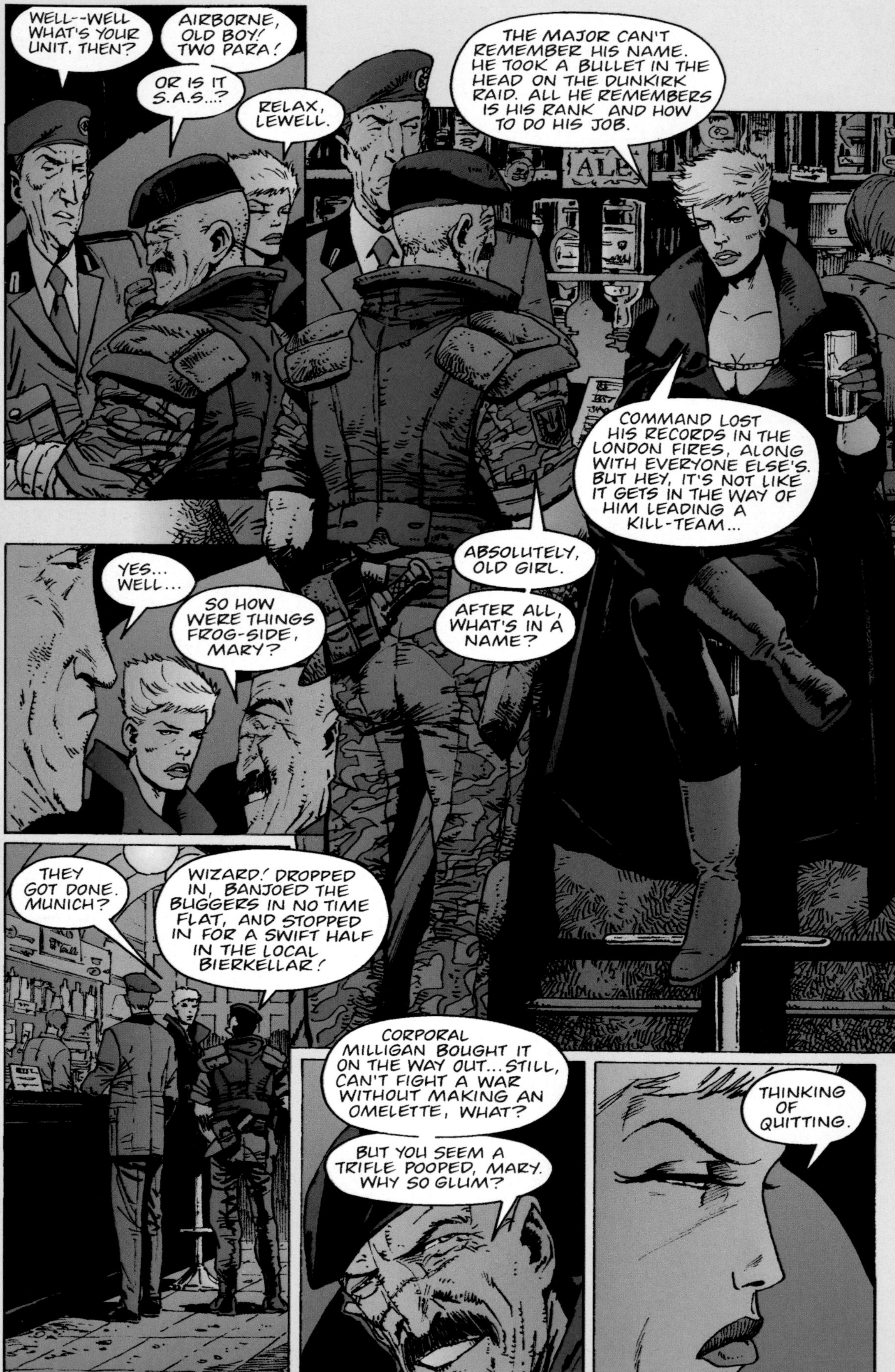
WELL--WELL WHAT'S YOUR UNIT, THEN?
AIRBORNE, OLD BOY! TWO PARA!
OR IS IT S.A.S...?
RELAX, LEWELL.
THE MAJOR CAN'T REMEMBER HIS NAME. HE TOOK A BULLET IN THE HEAD ON THE DUNKIRK RAID. ALL HE REMEMBERS IS HIS RANK AND HOW TO DO HIS JOB.
COMMAND LOST HIS RECORDS IN THE LONDON FIRES, ALONG WITH EVERYONE ELSE'S. BUT HEY, IT'S NOT LIKE IT GETS IN THE WAY OF HIM LEADING A KILL-TEAM...
ABSOLUTELY, OLD GIRL.
AFTER ALL, WHAT'S IN A NAME?
YES... WELL...
SO HOW WERE THINGS FROG-SIDE, MARY?
THEY GOT DONE. MUNICH?
WIZARD! DROPPED IN, BANJOED THE BUGGERS IN NO TIME FLAT, AND STOPPED IN FOR A SWIFT HALF IN THE LOCAL BIERKELLAR!
CORPORAL MILLIGAN BOUGHT IT ON THE WAY OUT... STILL, CAN'T FIGHT A WAR WITHOUT MAKING AN OMELETTE, WHAT?
BUT YOU SEEM A TRIFLE POOPED, MARY. WHY SO GLUM?
THINKING OF QUITTING.

OH, I SAY! POOR SHOW!

WHAT CAN I SAY, MAJOR. I'M TIRED.

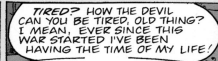

TIRED? HOW THE DEVIL CAN YOU BE TIRED, OLD THING? I MEAN, EVER SINCE THIS WAR STARTED I'VE BEEN HAVING THE TIME OF MY LIFE!

DROPPING DEEP BEHIND ENEMY LINES, BLOWING EVERYTHING IN SIGHT TO BUGGERY, MACHINE-GUNNING A COUPLE OF DOZEN EUROS WITH THEIR NOSES STILL STUCK IN THEIR GARLIC SAUSAGE AND HOME IN TIME FOR AFTERNOON TEA!

WHY, I COULD SIMPLY GO ON AND ON...!

MM. BUT BACK ON EARTH WITH THE REST OF US, MAJOR, I'M STILL TIRED.

I'M TIRED OF FIGHTING A WAR THAT'S NEVER GOING TO END. TIRED OF HOPING THAT SON OF A BITCH'LL SHOW UP AGAIN SO I CAN EVEN THE SCORE. TIRED OF KILLING EVERYONE I MEET, EVERYWHERE I GO...

BUT MOSTLY JUST TIRED.

AND HEY, YOU KNOW WHAT ELSE?

WHAT'S THAT?

I WAS THIRTY-NINE LAST WEEK.

I SAY! BIT OF A BLOW FOR A LADY, WHAT?

WELL, OKAY.

FORTY.

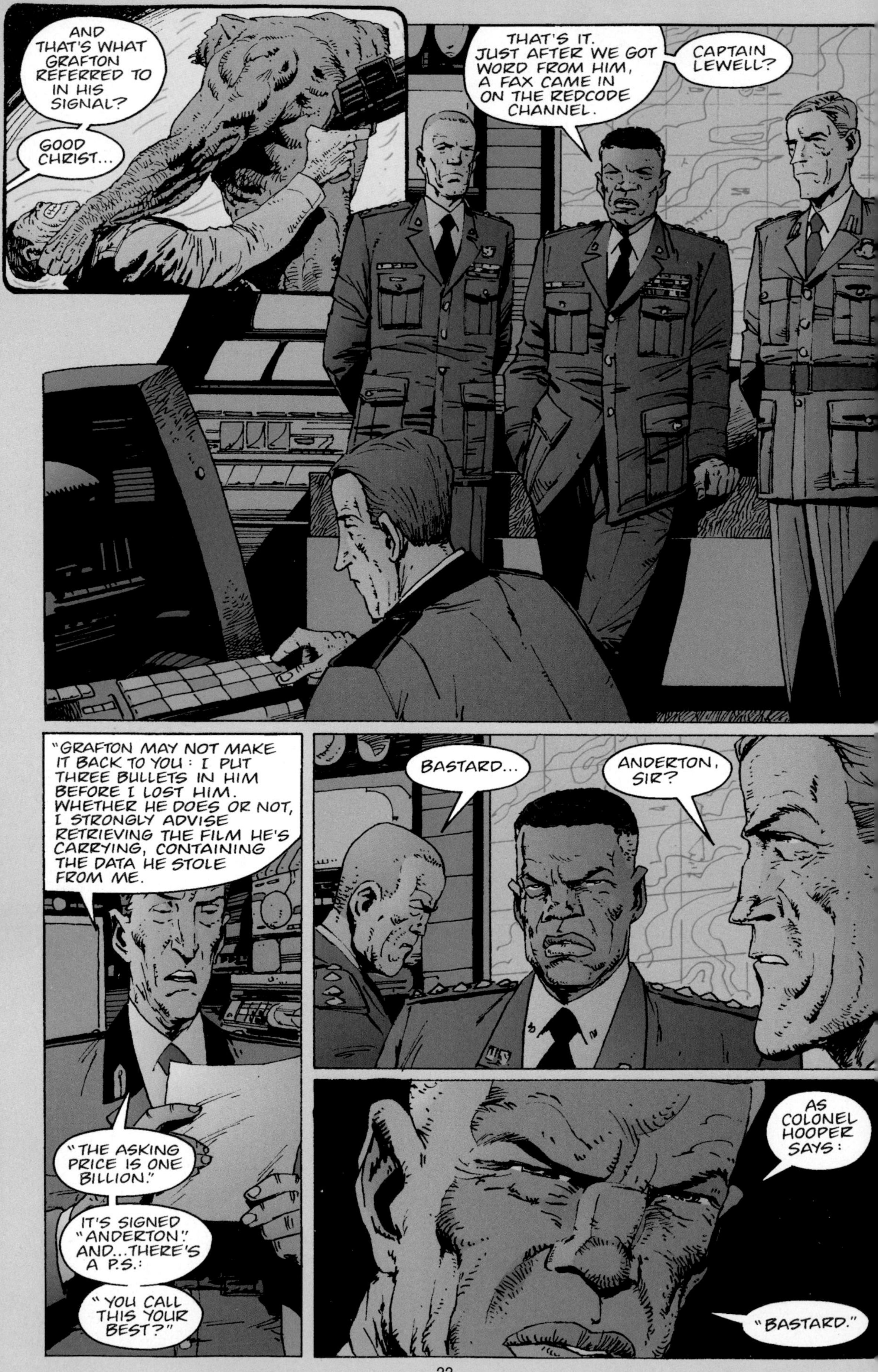

AND THAT'S WHAT GRAFTON REFERRED TO IN HIS SIGNAL?
GOOD CHRIST...
THAT'S IT. JUST AFTER WE GOT WORD FROM HIM, A FAX CAME IN ON THE REDCODE CHANNEL.
CAPTAIN LEWELL?
"GRAFTON MAY NOT MAKE IT BACK TO YOU: I PUT THREE BULLETS IN HIM BEFORE I LOST HIM. WHETHER HE DOES OR NOT, I STRONGLY ADVISE RETRIEVING THE FILM HE'S CARRYING, CONTAINING THE DATA HE STOLE FROM ME.
"THE ASKING PRICE IS ONE BILLION."
IT'S SIGNED "ANDERTON." AND...THERE'S A P.S.:
"YOU CALL THIS YOUR BEST?"
BASTARD...
ANDERTON, SIR?
AS COLONEL HOOPER SAYS:
"BASTARD."

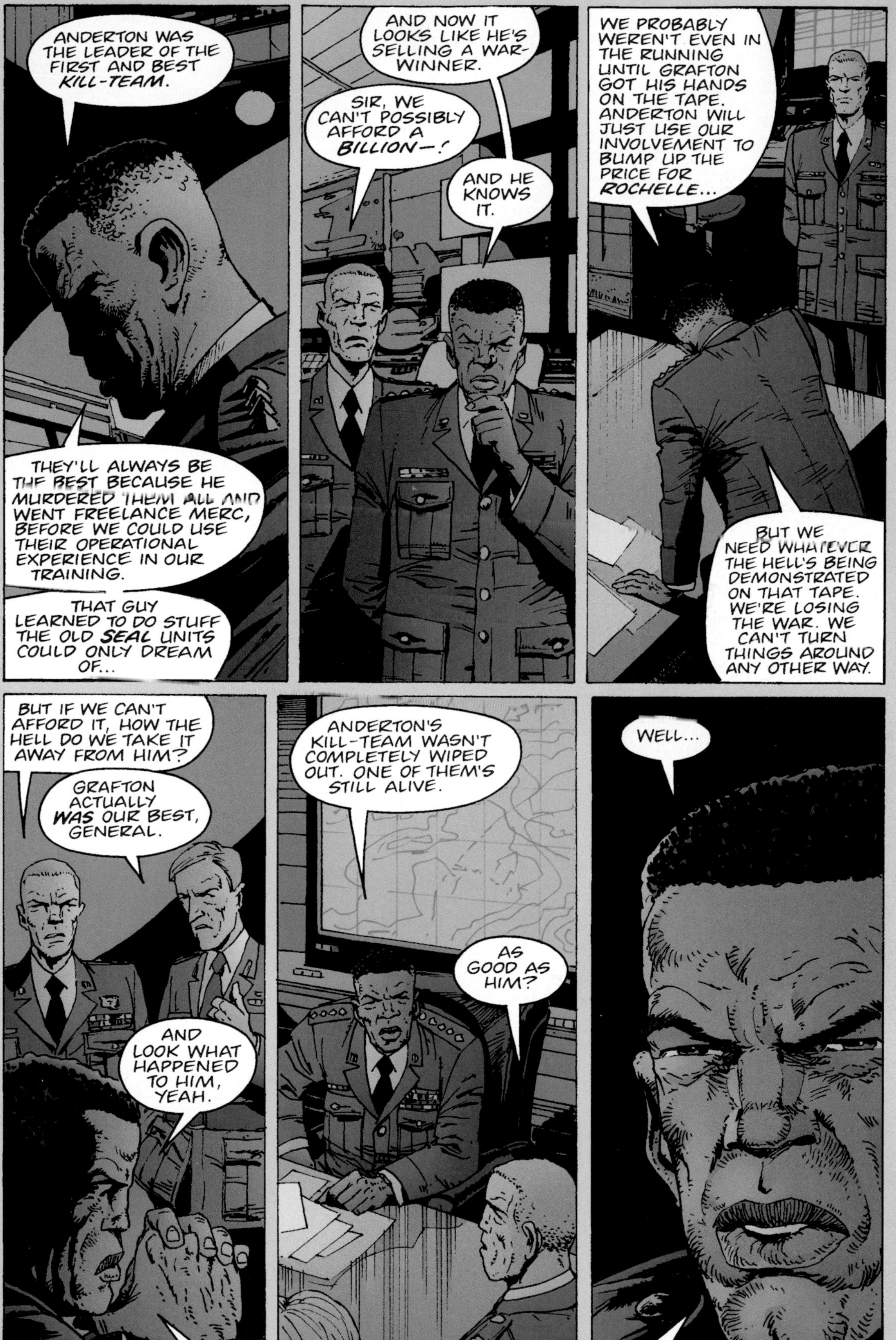
ANDERTON WAS THE LEADER OF THE FIRST AND BEST KILL-TEAM.
THEY'LL ALWAYS BE THE BEST BECAUSE HE MURDERED THEM ALL AND WENT FREELANCE MERC, BEFORE WE COULD USE THEIR OPERATIONAL EXPERIENCE IN OUR TRAINING.
THAT GUY LEARNED TO DO STUFF THE OLD SEAL UNITS COULD ONLY DREAM OF...
AND NOW IT LOOKS LIKE HE'S SELLING A WAR-WINNER.
SIR, WE CAN'T POSSIBLY AFFORD A BILLION—!
AND HE KNOWS IT.
WE PROBABLY WEREN'T EVEN IN THE RUNNING UNTIL GRAFTON GOT HIS HANDS ON THE TAPE. ANDERTON WILL JUST USE OUR INVOLVEMENT TO BUMP UP THE PRICE FOR ROCHELLE...
BUT WE NEED WHATEVER THE HELL'S BEING DEMONSTRATED ON THAT TAPE. WE'RE LOSING THE WAR. WE CAN'T TURN THINGS AROUND ANY OTHER WAY.
BUT IF WE CAN'T AFFORD IT, HOW THE HELL DO WE TAKE IT AWAY FROM HIM?
GRAFTON ACTUALLY WAS OUR BEST, GENERAL.
AND LOOK WHAT HAPPENED TO HIM, YEAH.
BUT...
ANDERTON'S KILL-TEAM WASN'T COMPLETELY WIPED OUT. ONE OF THEM'S STILL ALIVE.
AS GOOD AS HIM?
WELL...
STILL ALIVE.

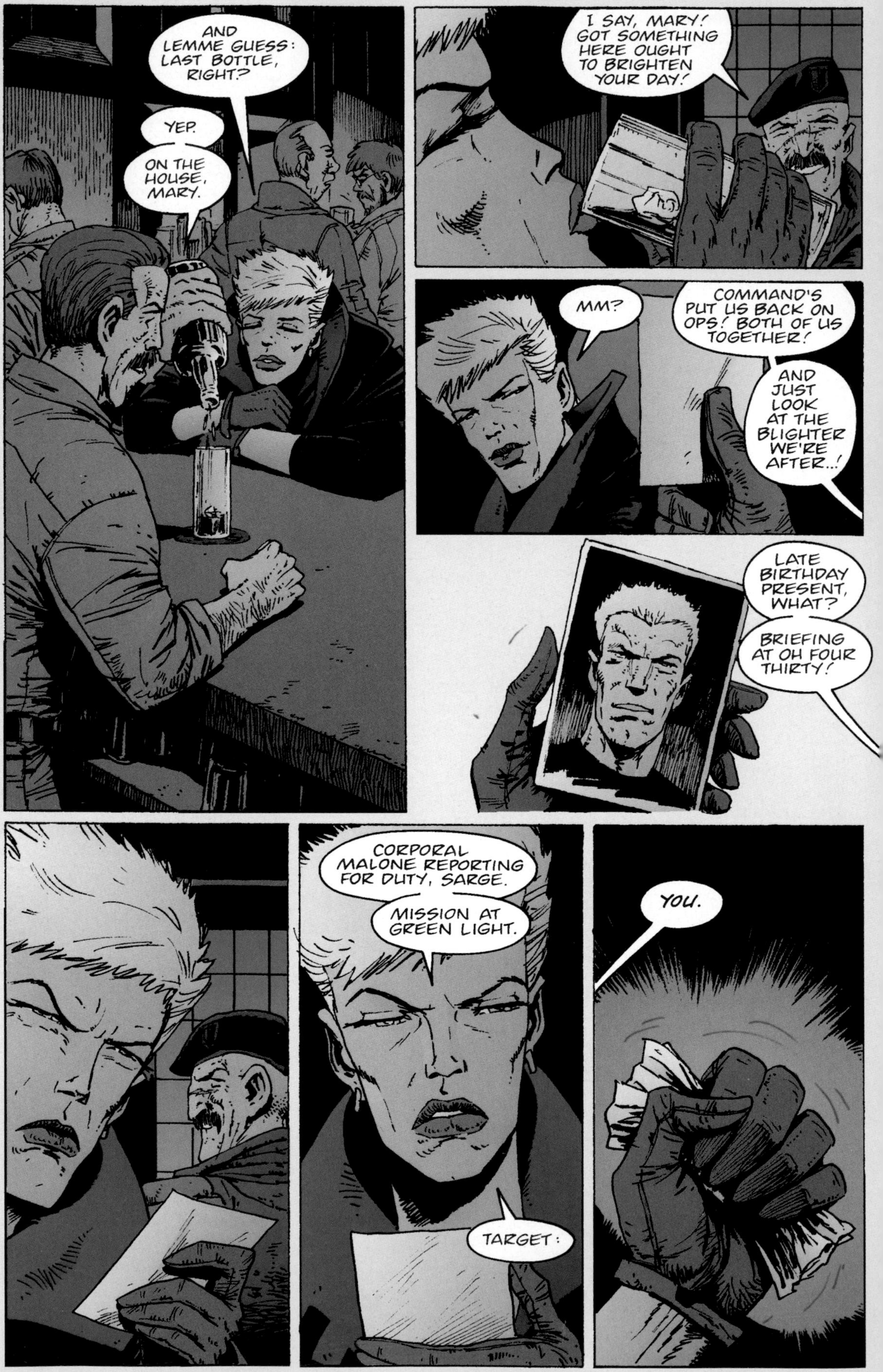
AND LEMME GUESS: LAST BOTTLE, RIGHT?
YEP.
ON THE HOUSE, MARY.
I SAY, MARY! GOT SOMETHING HERE OUGHT TO BRIGHTEN YOUR DAY!
MM?
COMMAND'S PUT US BACK ON OPS! BOTH OF US TOGETHER!
AND JUST LOOK AT THE BLIGHTER WE'RE AFTER...!
LATE BIRTHDAY PRESENT, WHAT?
BRIEFING AT OH FOUR THIRTY!
CORPORAL MALONE REPORTING FOR DUTY, SARGE.
MISSION AT GREEN LIGHT.
TARGET:
YOU.

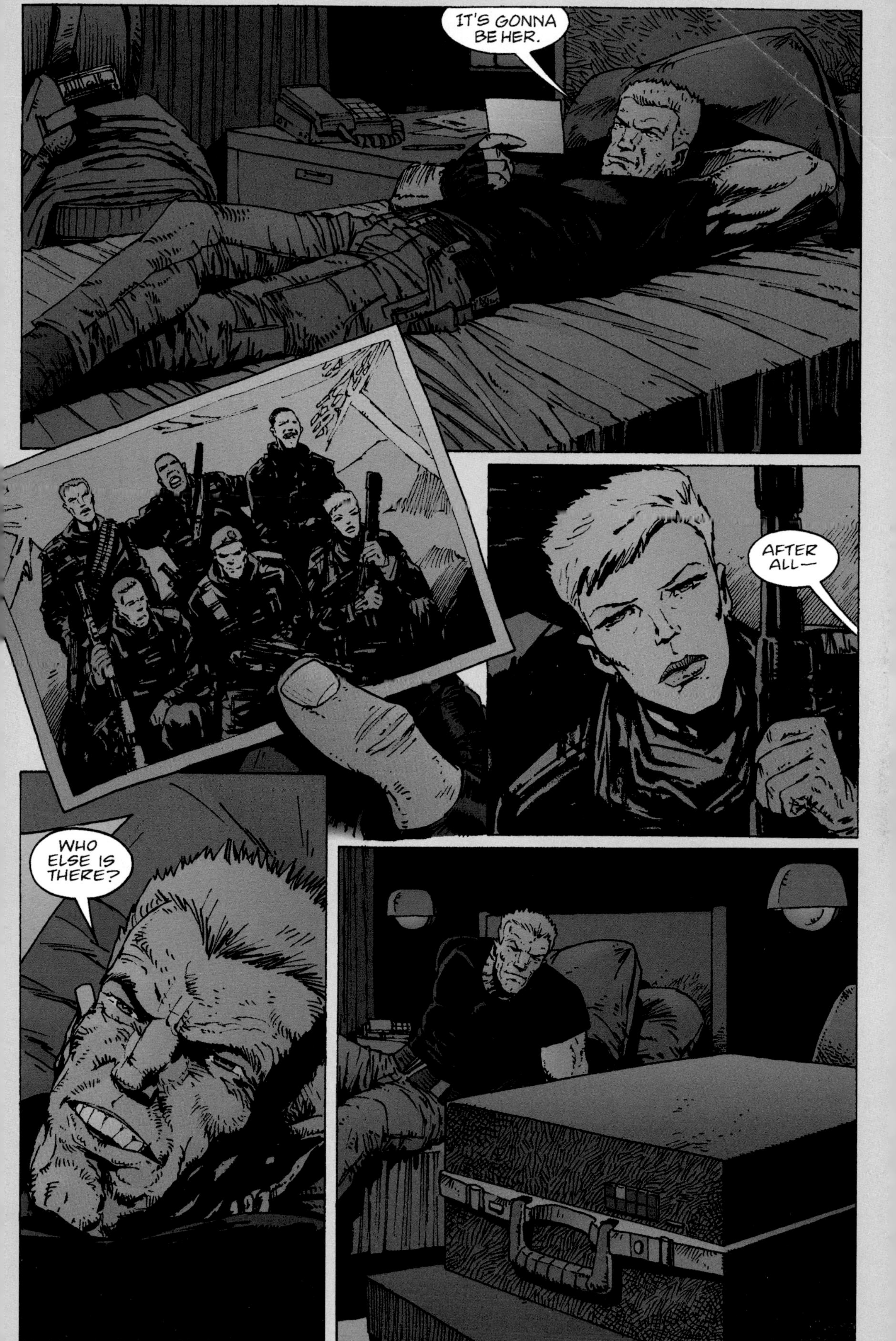
IT'S GONNA BE HER.
AFTER ALL—
WHO ELSE IS THERE?

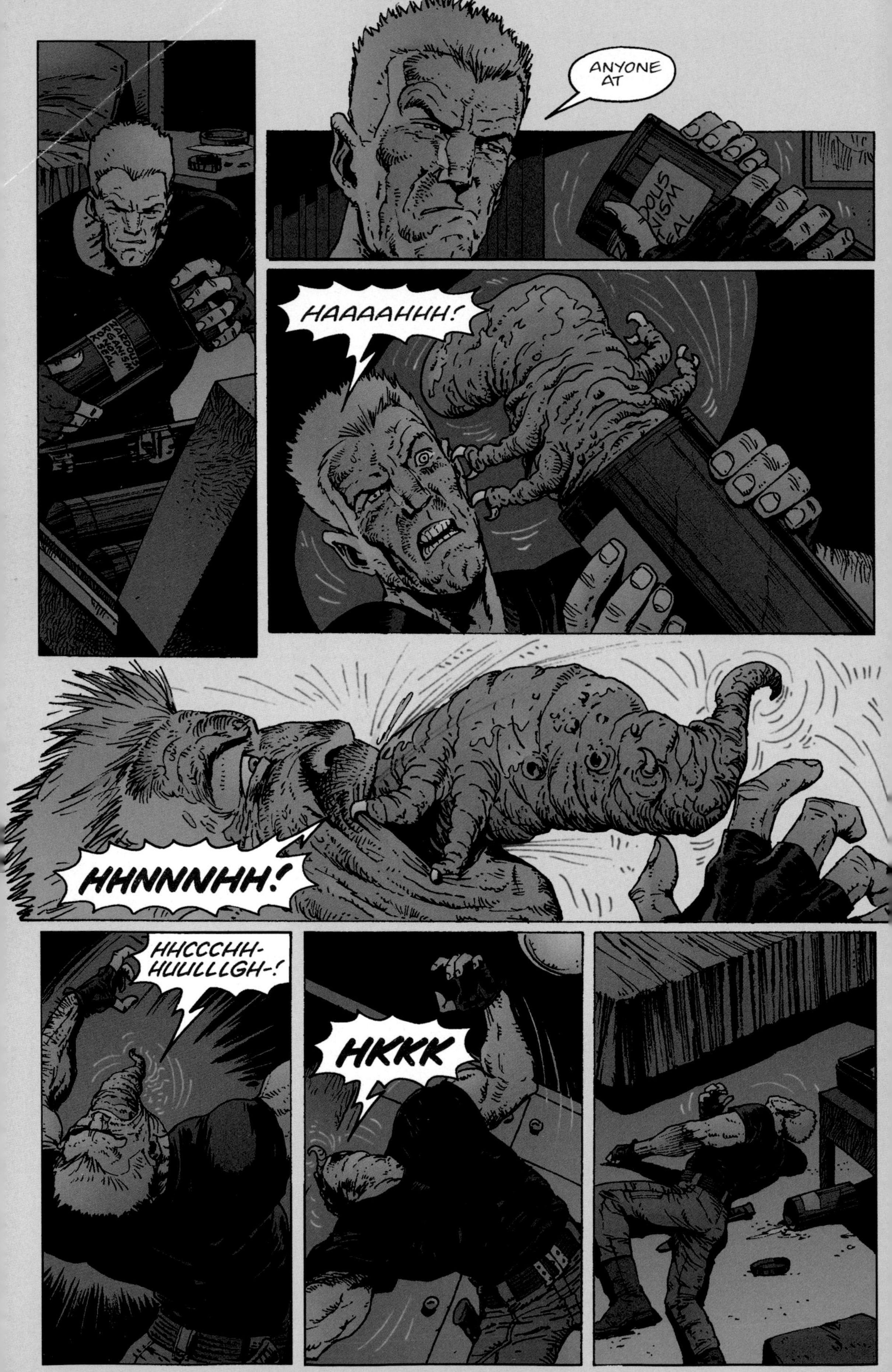

ANYONE AT
HAAAAHHH!
HHNNNHH!
HHCCCHH-
HUULLLGH-!
HKKK

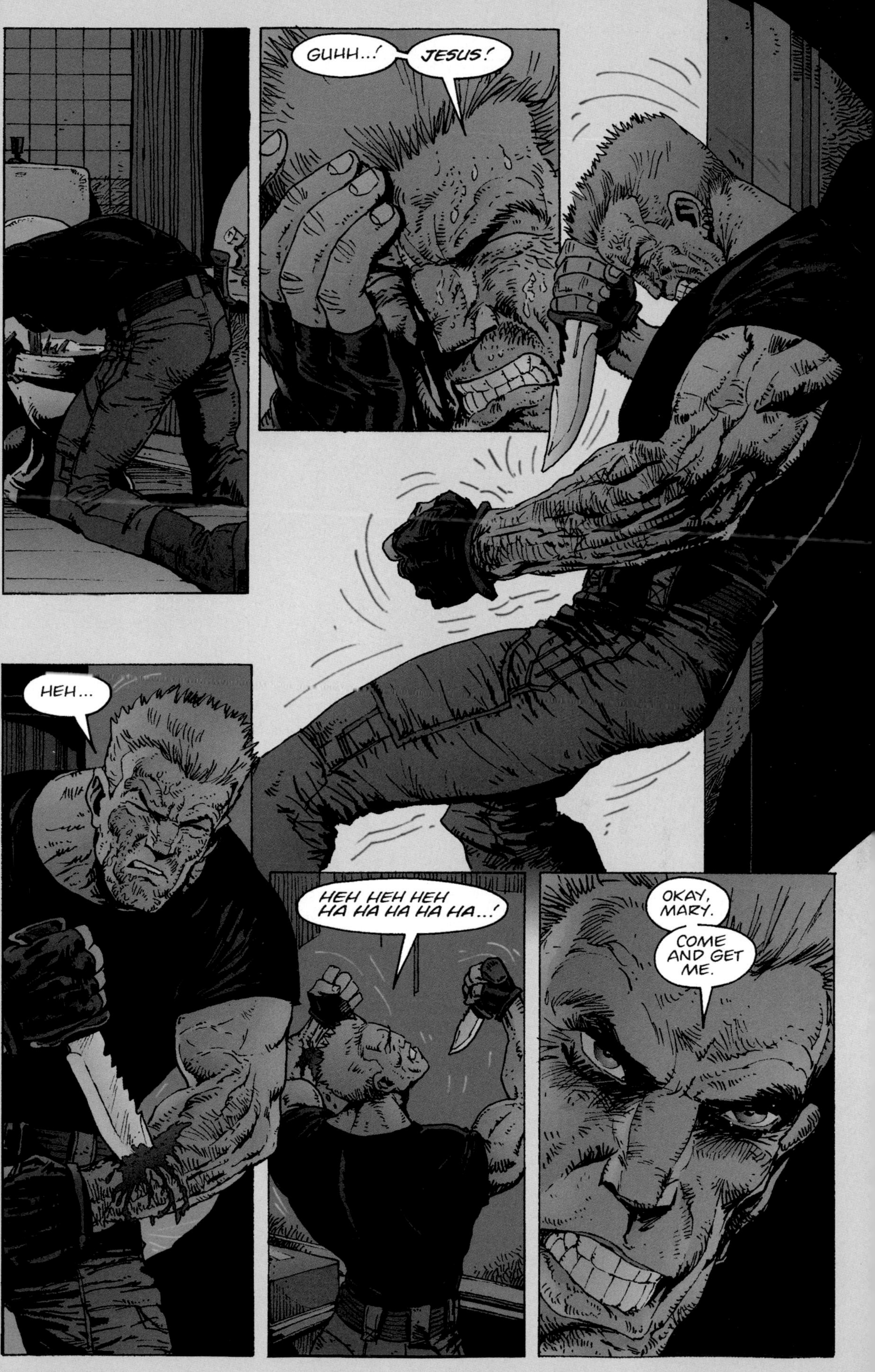
GUHH...!
JESUS!
HEH...
HEH HEH HEH
HA HA HA HA HA...!
OKAY, MARY.
COME AND GET ME.

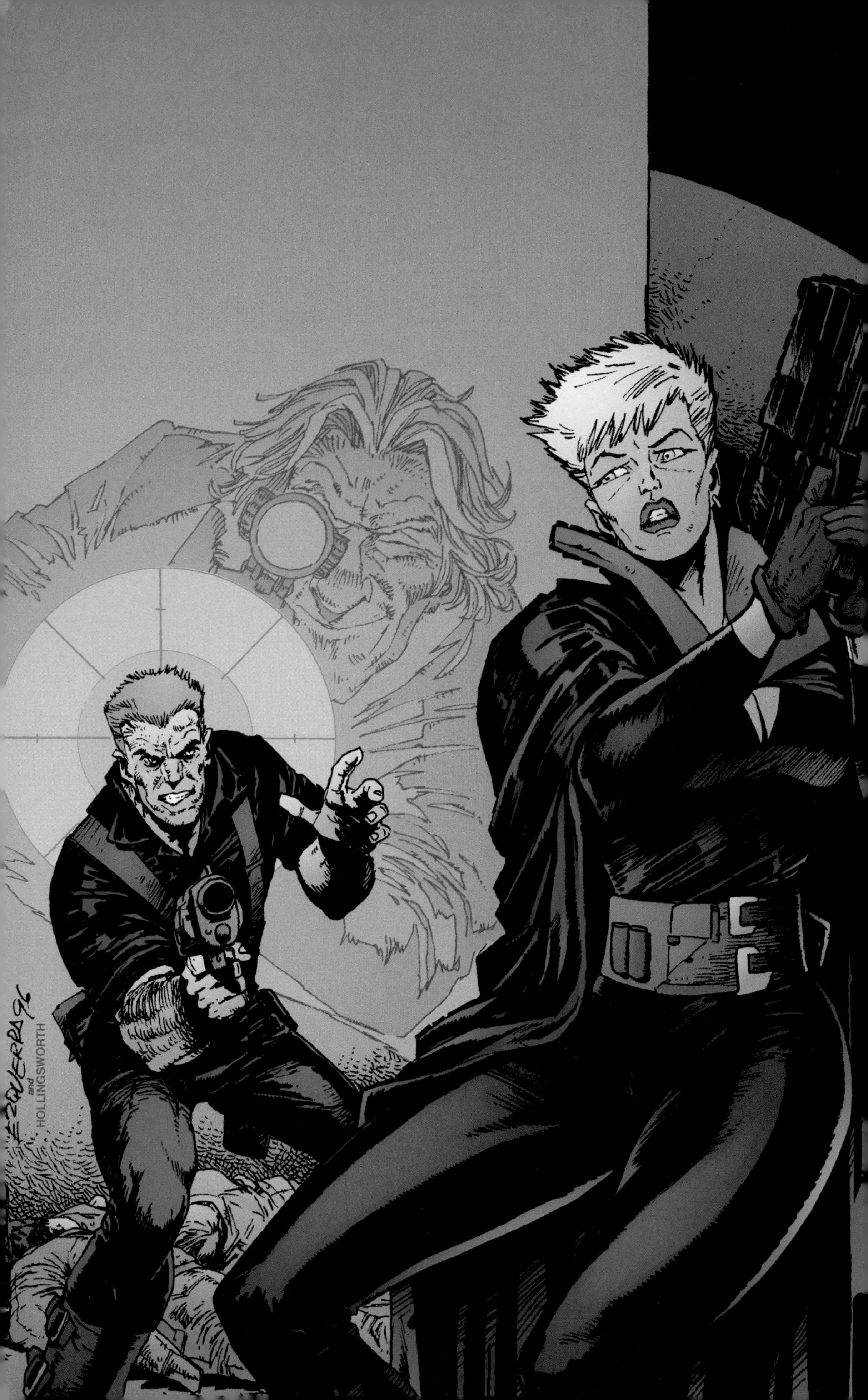

EZQUERRA 96
and
HOLLINGSWORTH

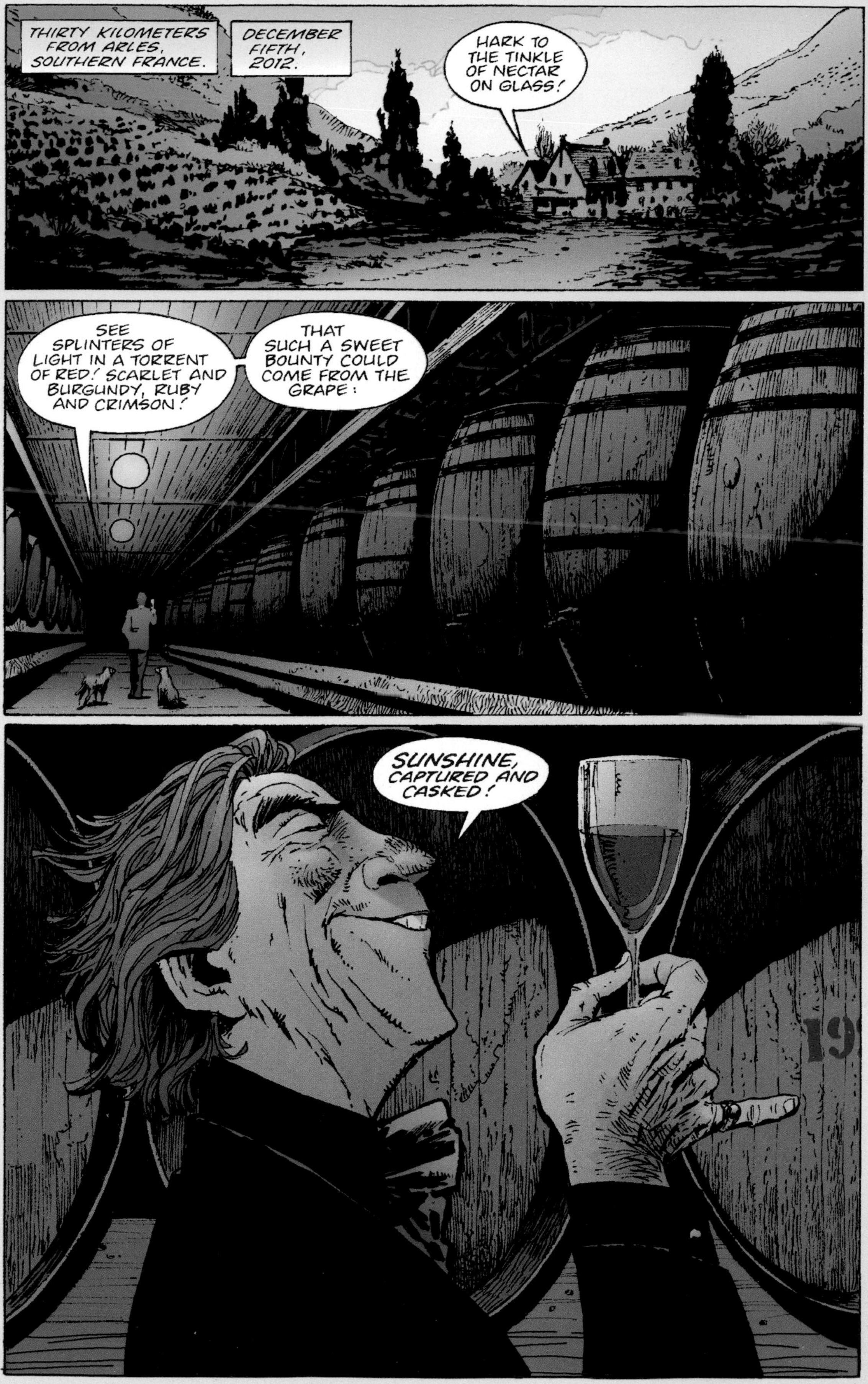
THIRTY KILOMETERS FROM ARLES, SOUTHERN FRANCE.
DECEMBER FIFTH, 2012.
HARK TO THE TINKLE OF NECTAR ON GLASS!
SEE SPLINTERS OF LIGHT IN A TORRENT OF RED! SCARLET AND BURGUNDY, RUBY AND CRIMSON!
THAT SUCH A SWEET BOUNTY COULD COME FROM THE GRAPE:
SUNSHINE, CAPTURED AND CASKED!

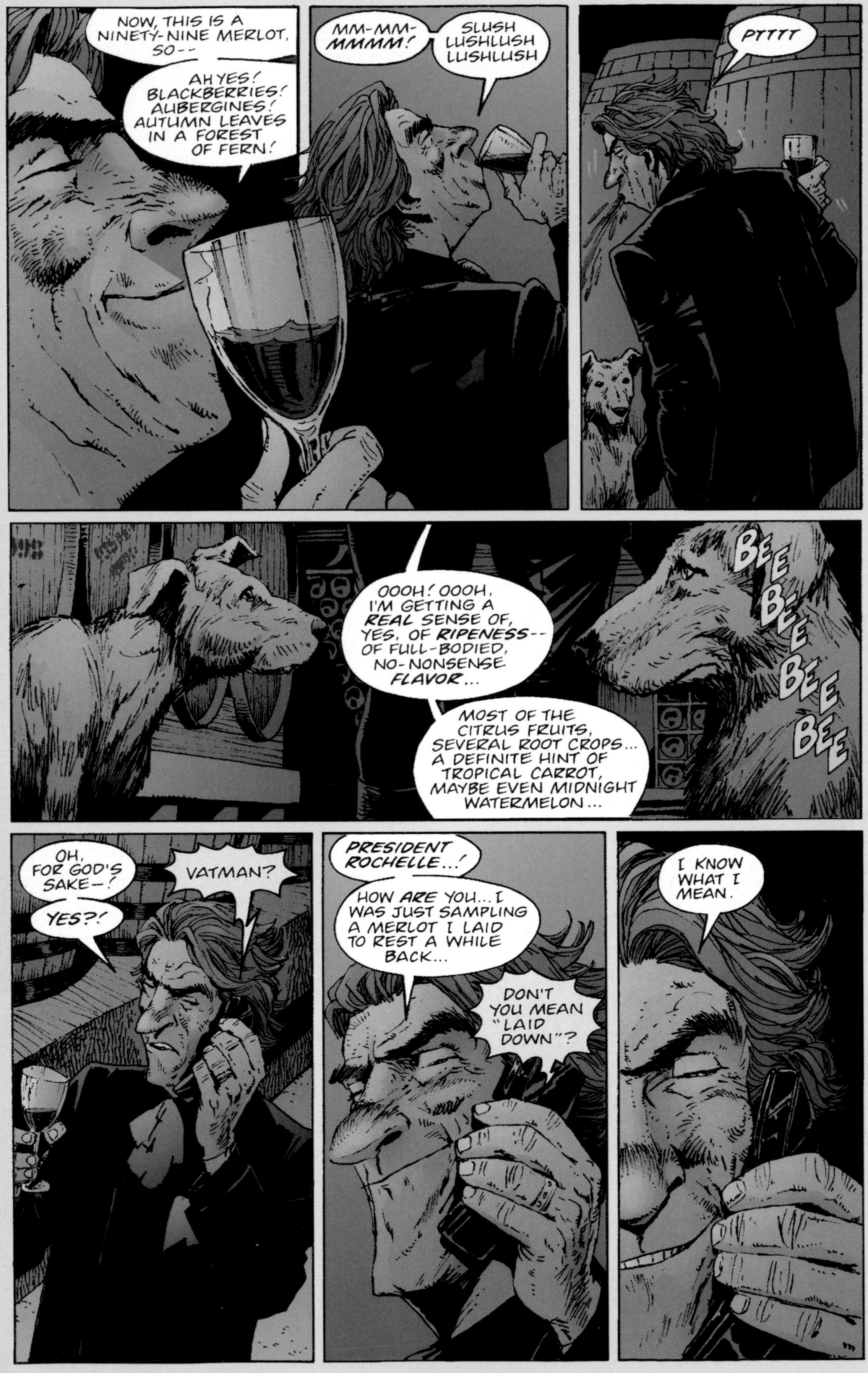
NOW, THIS IS A NINETY-NINE MERLOT, SO--
AH YES! BLACKBERRIES! AUBERGINES! AUTUMN LEAVES IN A FOREST OF FERN!
MM-MM-MMMMM!
SLUSH LUSHLUSH LUSHLUSH
PTTTT
OOOH! OOOH, I'M GETTING A REAL SENSE OF, YES, OF RIPENESS--OF FULL-BODIED, NO-NONSENSE FLAVOR...
MOST OF THE CITRUS FRUITS, SEVERAL ROOT CROPS... A DEFINITE HINT OF TROPICAL CARROT, MAYBE EVEN MIDNIGHT WATERMELON...
BEEBEEBEEBEE
OH, FOR GOD'S SAKE--!
VATMAN?
YES?!
PRESIDENT ROCHELLE...!
HOW ARE YOU... I WAS JUST SAMPLING A MERLOT I LAID TO REST A WHILE BACK...
DON'T YOU MEAN "LAID DOWN"?
I KNOW WHAT I MEAN.

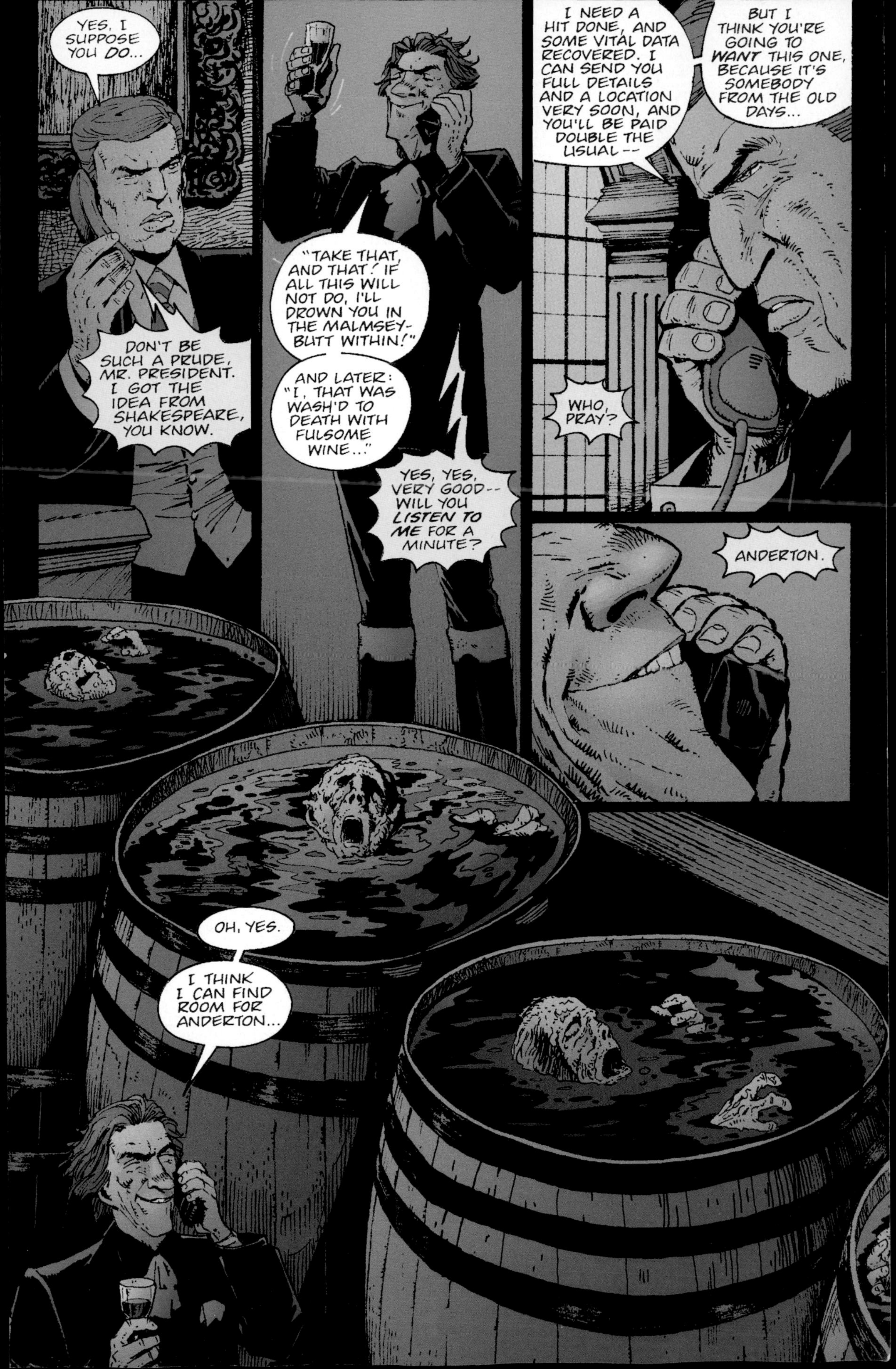
YES, I SUPPOSE YOU DO...
DON'T BE SUCH A PRUDE, MR. PRESIDENT. I GOT THE IDEA FROM SHAKESPEARE, YOU KNOW.
"TAKE THAT, AND THAT! IF ALL THIS WILL NOT DO, I'LL DROWN YOU IN THE MALMSEY-BUTT WITHIN!"
AND LATER: "I, THAT WAS WASH'D TO DEATH WITH FULSOME WINE..."
YES, YES, VERY GOOD-- WILL YOU LISTEN TO ME FOR A MINUTE?
I NEED A HIT DONE, AND SOME VITAL DATA RECOVERED. I CAN SEND YOU FULL DETAILS AND A LOCATION VERY SOON, AND YOU'LL BE PAID DOUBLE THE USUAL --
BUT I THINK YOU'RE GOING TO WANT THIS ONE, BECAUSE IT'S SOMEBODY FROM THE OLD DAYS...
WHO, PRAY?
ANDERTON.
OH, YES.
I THINK I CAN FIND ROOM FOR ANDERTON...

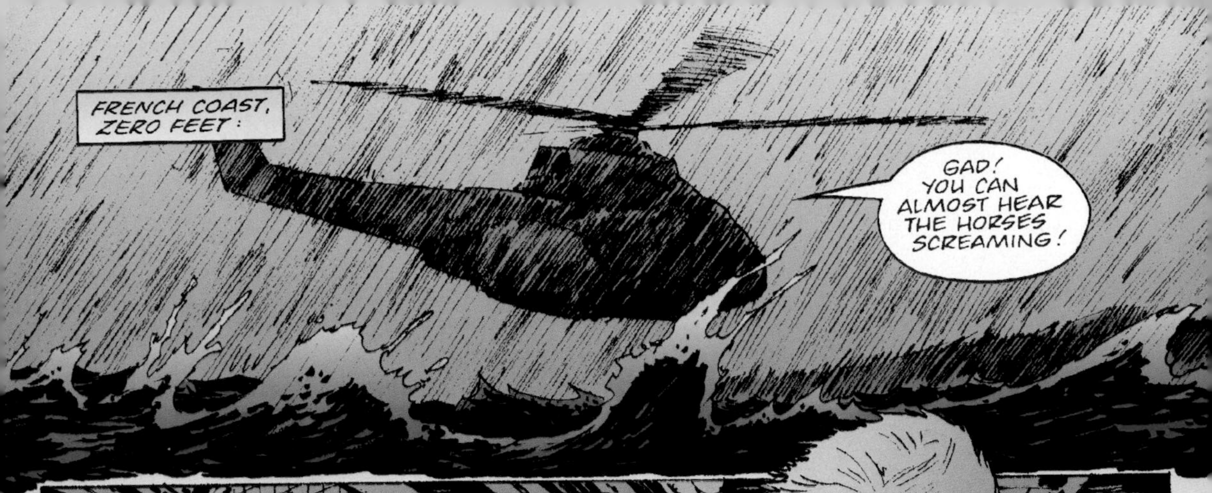
FRENCH COAST, ZERO FEET:
GAD! YOU CAN ALMOST HEAR THE HORSES SCREAMING!

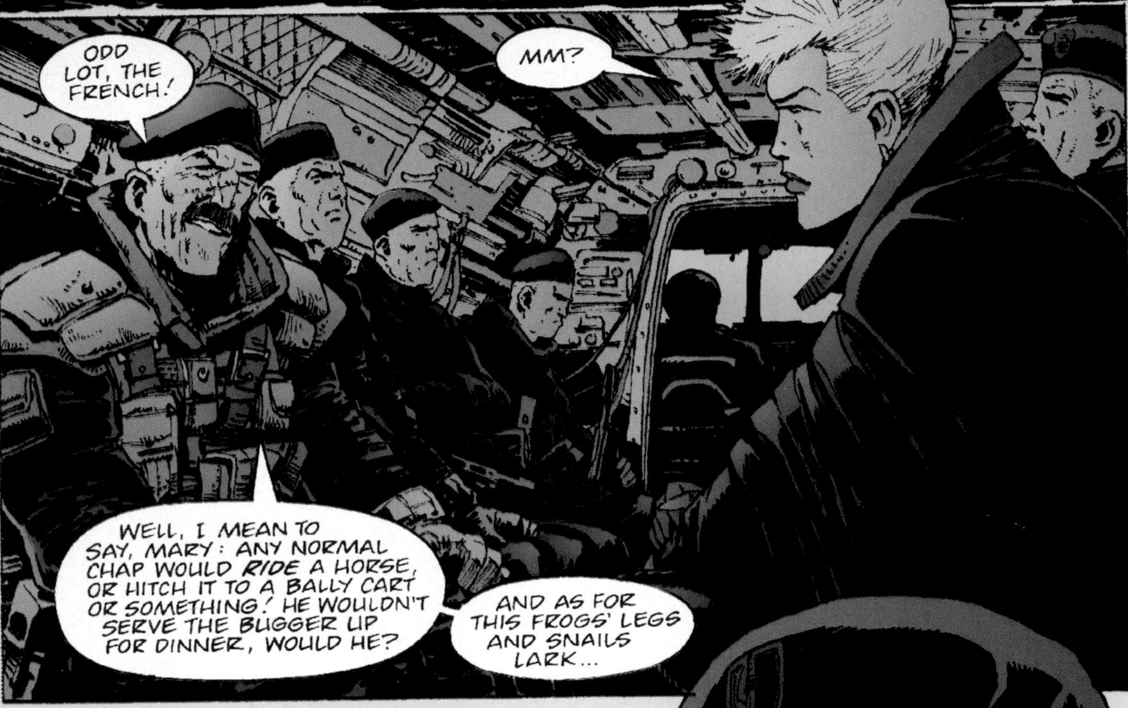
ODD LOT, THE FRENCH!
MM?
WELL, I MEAN TO SAY, MARY: ANY NORMAL CHAP WOULD RIDE A HORSE, OR HITCH IT TO A BALLY CART OR SOMETHING! HE WOULDN'T SERVE THE BUGGER UP FOR DINNER, WOULD HE?
AND AS FOR THIS FROGS' LEGS AND SNAILS LARK...

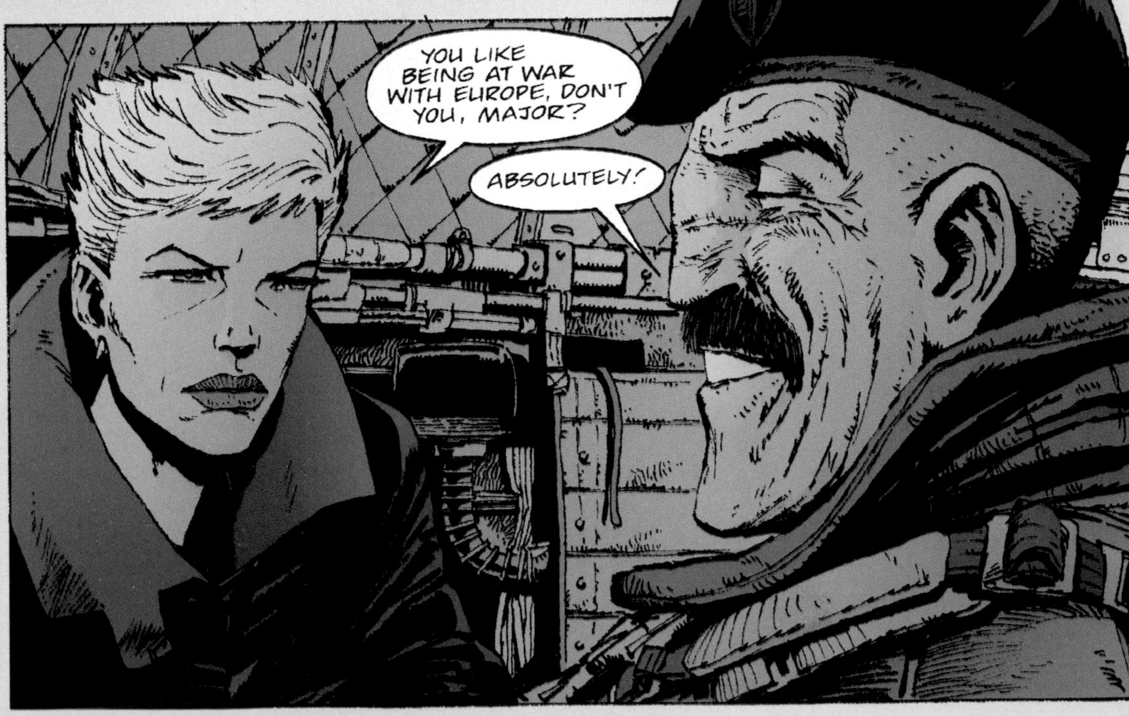
YOU LIKE BEING AT WAR WITH EUROPE, DON'T YOU, MAJOR?
ABSOLUTELY!

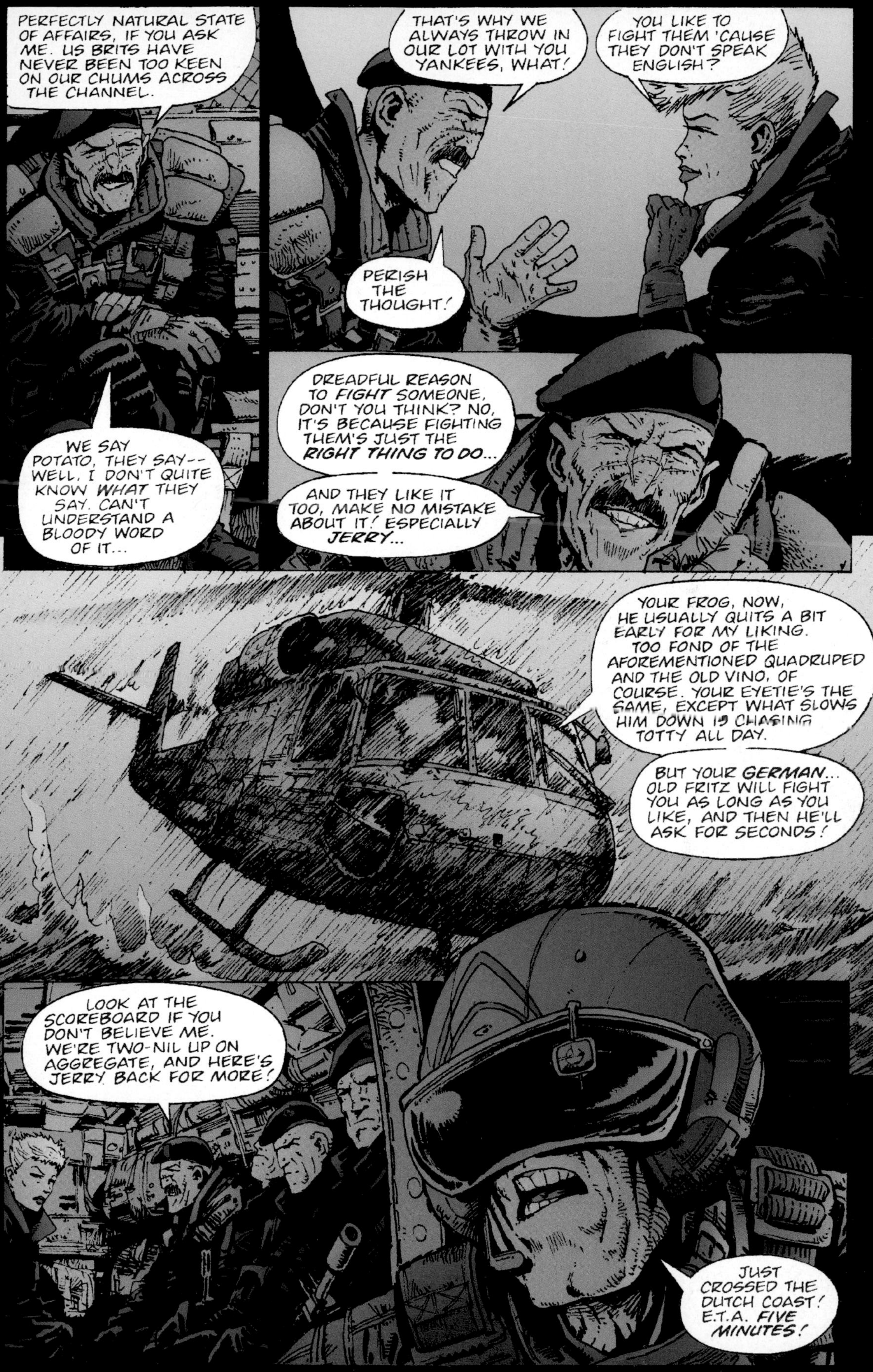
PERFECTLY NATURAL STATE OF AFFAIRS, IF YOU ASK ME. US BRITS HAVE NEVER BEEN TOO KEEN ON OUR CHUMS ACROSS THE CHANNEL.
THAT'S WHY WE ALWAYS THROW IN OUR LOT WITH YOU YANKEES, WHAT!
YOU LIKE TO FIGHT THEM 'CAUSE THEY DON'T SPEAK ENGLISH?
PERISH THE THOUGHT!
WE SAY POTATO, THEY SAY-- WELL, I DON'T QUITE KNOW WHAT THEY SAY. CAN'T UNDERSTAND A BLOODY WORD OF IT...
DREADFUL REASON TO FIGHT SOMEONE, DON'T YOU THINK? NO, IT'S BECAUSE FIGHTING THEM'S JUST THE RIGHT THING TO DO...
AND THEY LIKE IT TOO, MAKE NO MISTAKE ABOUT IT! ESPECIALLY JERRY...
YOUR FROG, NOW, HE USUALLY QUITS A BIT EARLY FOR MY LIKING. TOO FOND OF THE AFOREMENTIONED QUADRUPED AND THE OLD VINO, OF COURSE. YOUR EYETIE'S THE SAME, EXCEPT WHAT SLOWS HIM DOWN IS CHASING TOTTY ALL DAY.
BUT YOUR GERMAN... OLD FRITZ WILL FIGHT YOU AS LONG AS YOU LIKE, AND THEN HE'LL ASK FOR SECONDS!
LOOK AT THE SCOREBOARD IF YOU DON'T BELIEVE ME. WE'RE TWO-NIL UP ON AGGREGATE, AND HERE'S JERRY BACK FOR MORE!
JUST CROSSED THE DUTCH COAST! E.T.A. FIVE MINUTES!

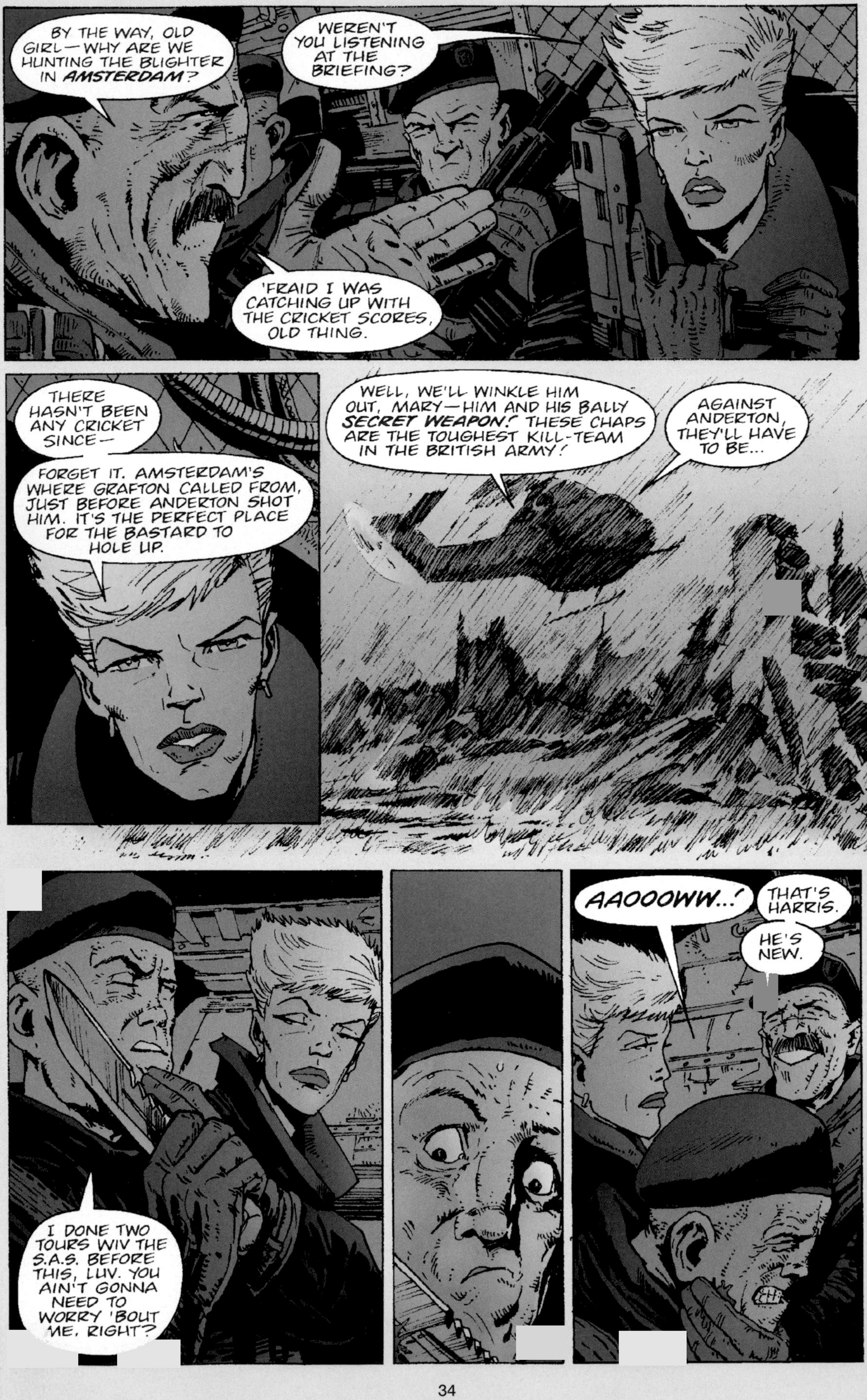
BY THE WAY, OLD GIRL—WHY ARE WE HUNTING THE BLIGHTER IN AMSTERDAM?
WEREN'T YOU LISTENING AT THE BRIEFING?
'FRAID I WAS CATCHING UP WITH THE CRICKET SCORES, OLD THING.
THERE HASN'T BEEN ANY CRICKET SINCE—
FORGET IT. AMSTERDAM'S WHERE GRAFTON CALLED FROM, JUST BEFORE ANDERTON SHOT HIM. IT'S THE PERFECT PLACE FOR THE BASTARD TO HOLE UP.
WELL, WE'LL WINKLE HIM OUT, MARY—HIM AND HIS BALLY SECRET WEAPON! THESE CHAPS ARE THE TOUGHEST KILL-TEAM IN THE BRITISH ARMY!
AGAINST ANDERTON, THEY'LL HAVE TO BE...
I DONE TWO TOURS WIV THE S.A.S. BEFORE THIS, LUV. YOU AIN'T GONNA NEED TO WORRY 'BOUT ME, RIGHT?
AAOOOWW...!
THAT'S HARRIS.
HE'S NEW.

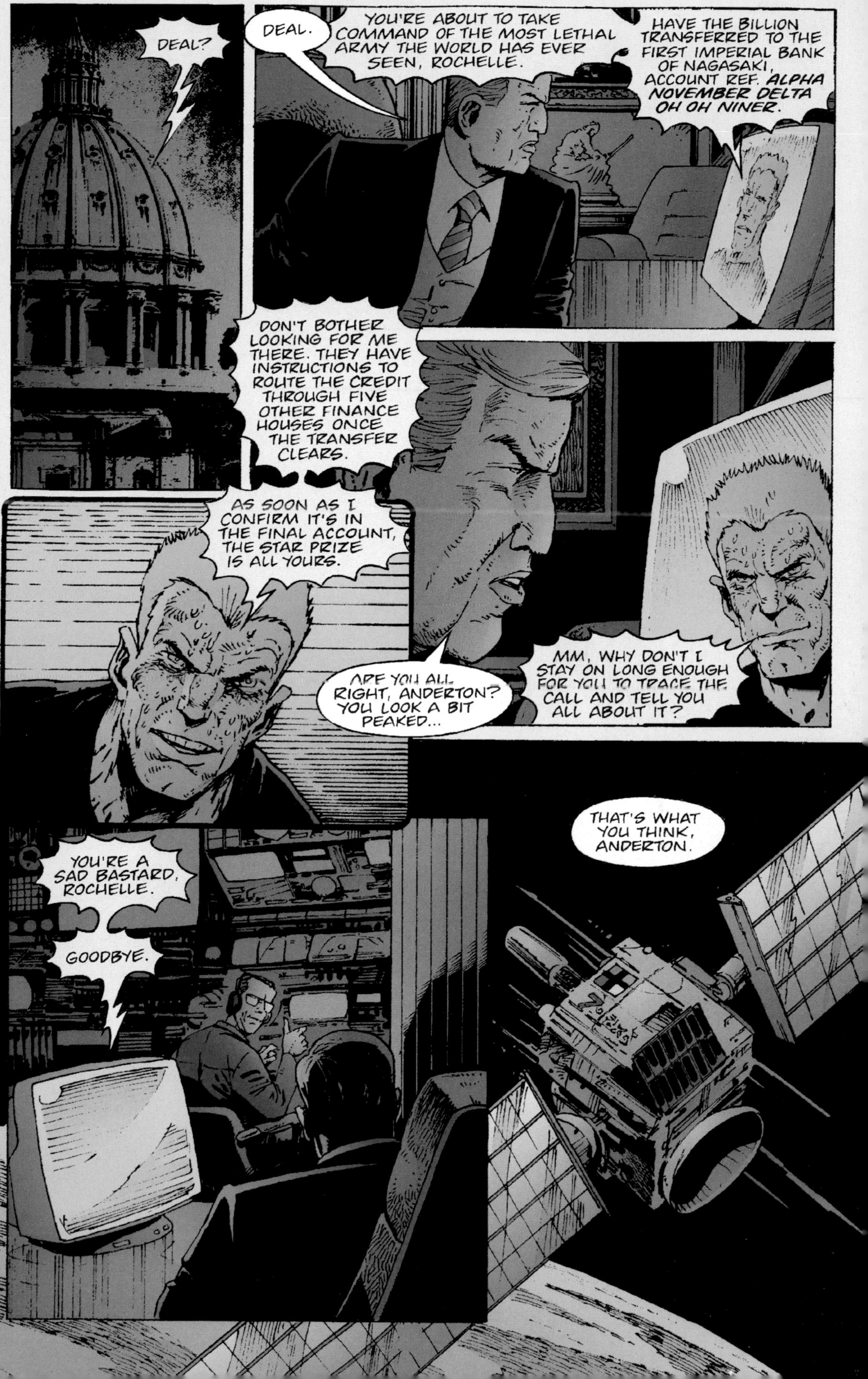
DEAL?
DEAL.
YOU'RE ABOUT TO TAKE COMMAND OF THE MOST LETHAL ARMY THE WORLD HAS EVER SEEN, ROCHELLE.
HAVE THE BILLION TRANSFERRED TO THE FIRST IMPERIAL BANK OF NAGASAKI, ACCOUNT REF. ALPHA NOVEMBER DELTA OH OH NINER.
DON'T BOTHER LOOKING FOR ME THERE. THEY HAVE INSTRUCTIONS TO ROUTE THE CREDIT THROUGH FIVE OTHER FINANCE HOUSES ONCE THE TRANSFER CLEARS.
AS SOON AS I CONFIRM IT'S IN THE FINAL ACCOUNT, THE STAR PRIZE IS ALL YOURS.
ARE YOU ALL RIGHT, ANDERTON? YOU LOOK A BIT PEAKED...
MM, WHY DON'T I STAY ON LONG ENOUGH FOR YOU TO TRACE THE CALL AND TELL YOU ALL ABOUT IT?
YOU'RE A SAD BASTARD, ROCHELLE.
GOODBYE.
THAT'S WHAT YOU THINK, ANDERTON.

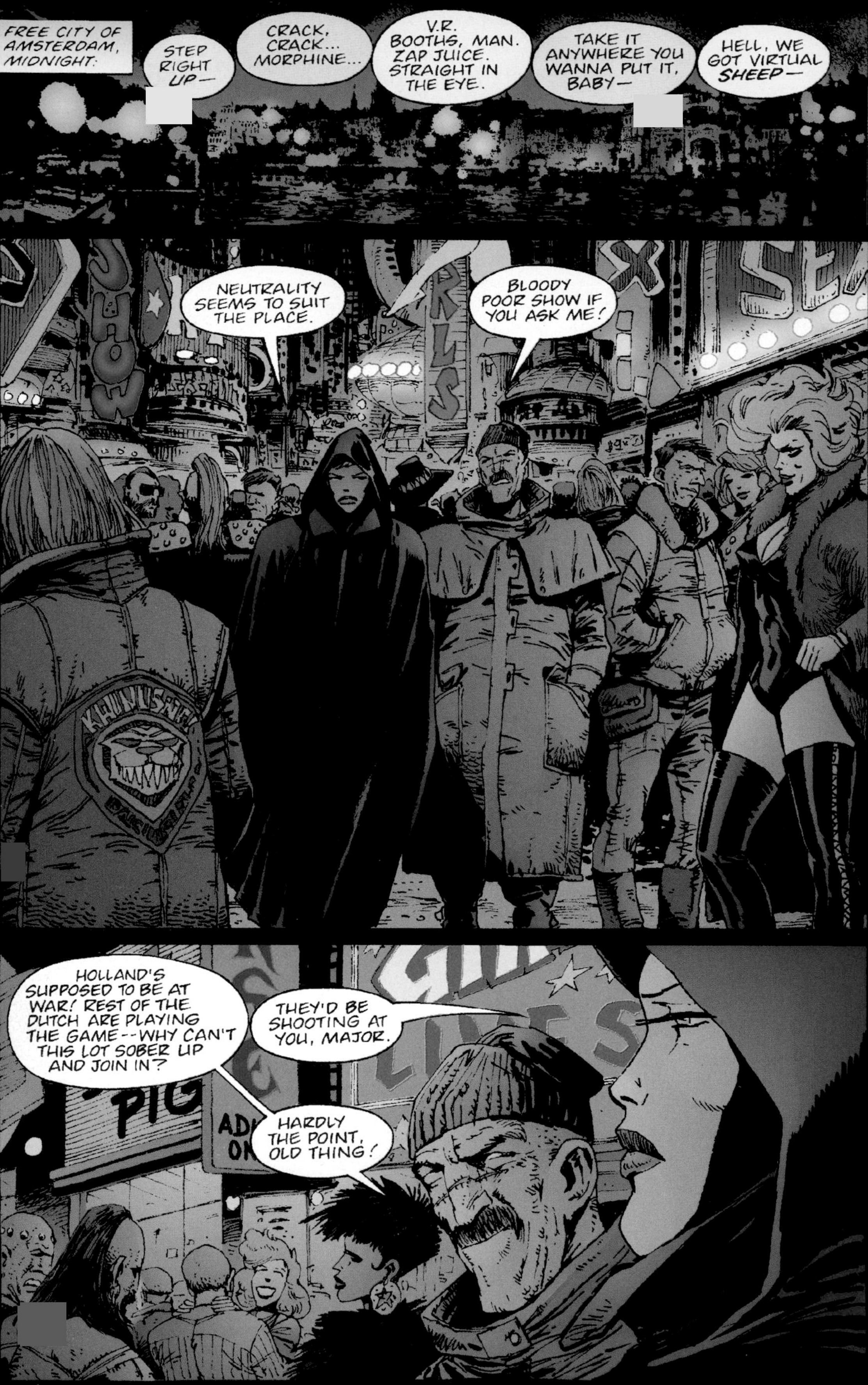
FREE CITY OF AMSTERDAM, MIDNIGHT:
STEP RIGHT UP—
CRACK, CRACK... MORPHINE...
V.R. BOOTHS, MAN. ZAP JUICE. STRAIGHT IN THE EYE.
TAKE IT ANYWHERE YOU WANNA PUT IT, BABY—
HELL, WE GOT VIRTUAL SHEEP—
NEUTRALITY SEEMS TO SUIT THE PLACE.
BLOODY POOR SHOW IF YOU ASK ME!
HOLLAND'S SUPPOSED TO BE AT WAR! REST OF THE DUTCH ARE PLAYING THE GAME--WHY CAN'T THIS LOT SOBER UP AND JOIN IN?
THEY'D BE SHOOTING AT YOU, MAJOR.
HARDLY THE POINT, OLD THING!

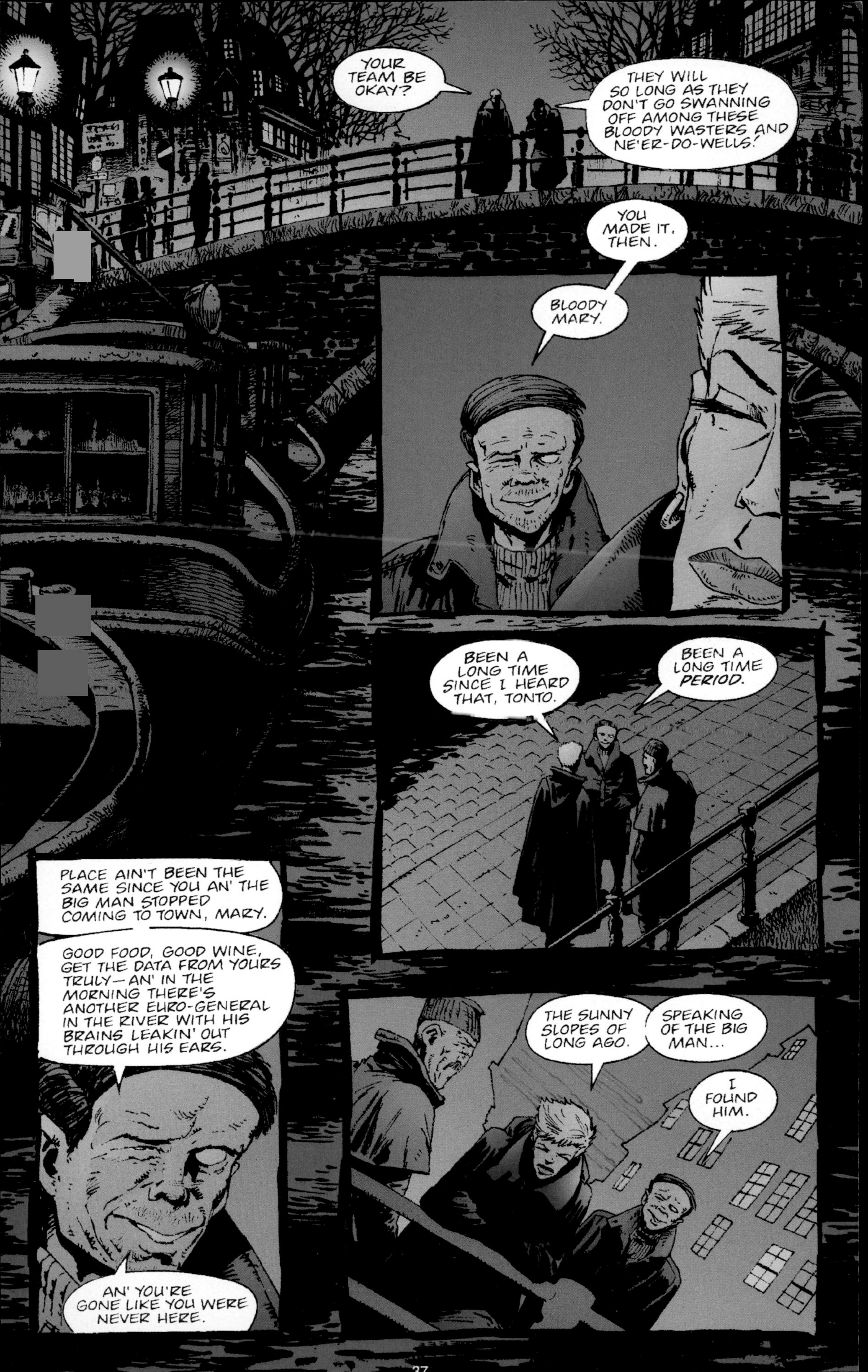
YOUR TEAM BE OKAY?
THEY WILL SO LONG AS THEY DON'T GO SWANNING OFF AMONG THESE BLOODY WASTERS AND NE'ER-DO-WELLS!
YOU MADE IT, THEN.
BLOODY MARY.
BEEN A LONG TIME SINCE I HEARD THAT, TONTO.
BEEN A LONG TIME *PERIOD*.
PLACE AIN'T BEEN THE SAME SINCE YOU AN' THE BIG MAN STOPPED COMING TO TOWN, MARY.
GOOD FOOD, GOOD WINE, GET THE DATA FROM YOURS TRULY— AN' IN THE MORNING THERE'S ANOTHER EURO-GENERAL IN THE RIVER WITH HIS BRAINS LEAKIN' OUT THROUGH HIS EARS.
AN' YOU'RE GONE LIKE YOU WERE NEVER HERE.
THE SUNNY SLOPES OF LONG AGO.
SPEAKING OF THE BIG MAN...
I FOUND HIM.

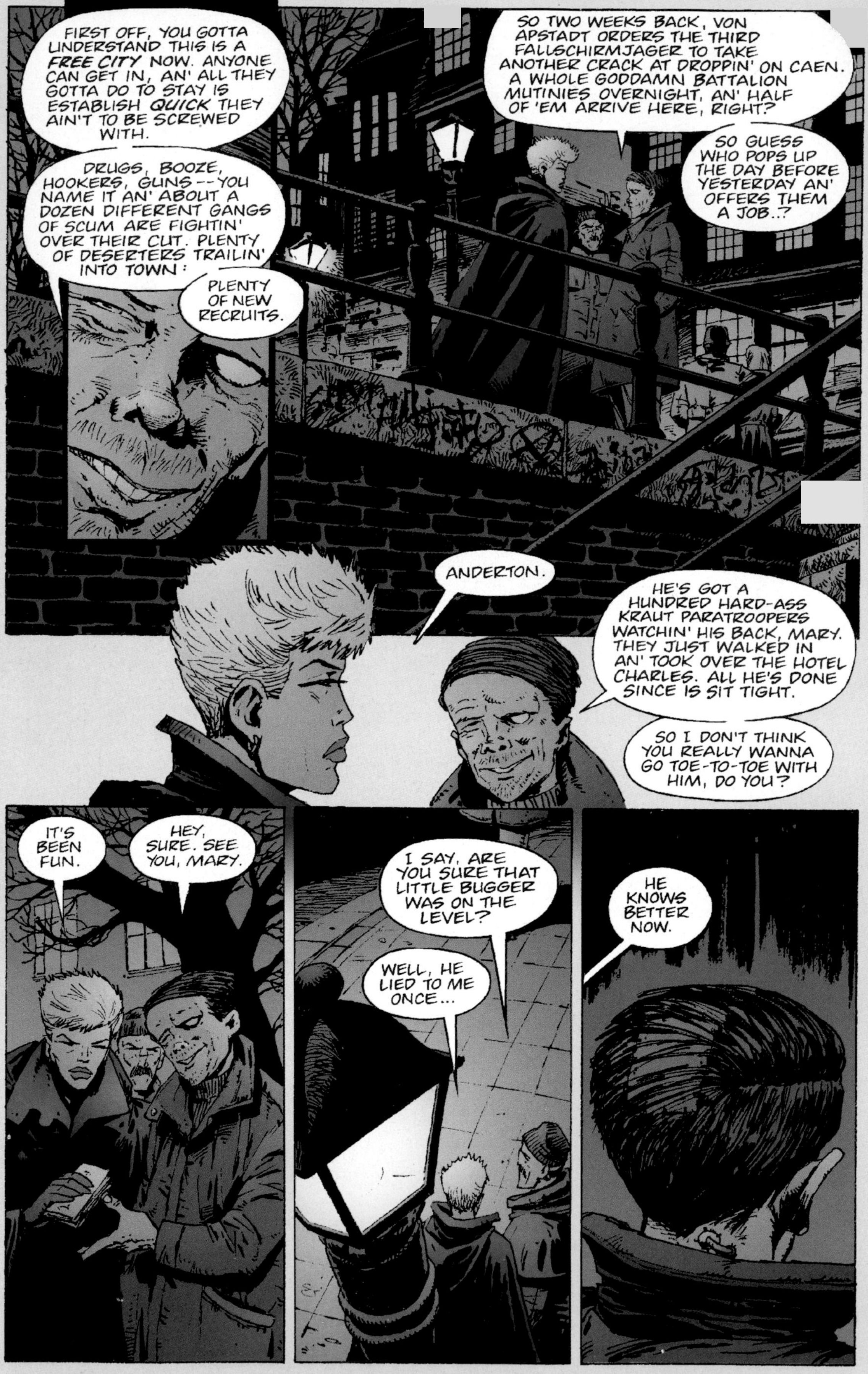
FIRST OFF, YOU GOTTA UNDERSTAND THIS IS A FREE CITY NOW. ANYONE CAN GET IN, AN' ALL THEY GOTTA DO TO STAY IS ESTABLISH QUICK THEY AIN'T TO BE SCREWED WITH.
DRUGS, BOOZE, HOOKERS, GUNS--YOU NAME IT AN' ABOUT A DOZEN DIFFERENT GANGS OF SCUM ARE FIGHTIN' OVER THEIR CUT. PLENTY OF DESERTERS TRAILIN' INTO TOWN:
PLENTY OF NEW RECRUITS.
SO TWO WEEKS BACK, VON APSTADT ORDERS THE THIRD FALLSCHIRMJAGER TO TAKE ANOTHER CRACK AT DROPPIN' ON CAEN. A WHOLE GODDAMN BATTALION MUTINIES OVERNIGHT, AN' HALF OF 'EM ARRIVE HERE, RIGHT?
SO GUESS WHO POPS UP THE DAY BEFORE YESTERDAY AN' OFFERS THEM A JOB..?
ANDERTON.
HE'S GOT A HUNDRED HARD-ASS KRAUT PARATROOPERS WATCHIN' HIS BACK, MARY. THEY JUST WALKED IN AN' TOOK OVER THE HOTEL CHARLES. ALL HE'S DONE SINCE IS SIT TIGHT.
SO I DON'T THINK YOU REALLY WANNA GO TOE-TO-TOE WITH HIM, DO YOU?
IT'S BEEN FUN.
HEY, SURE. SEE YOU, MARY.
I SAY, ARE YOU SURE THAT LITTLE BUGGER WAS ON THE LEVEL?
WELL, HE LIED TO ME ONCE...
HE KNOWS BETTER NOW.

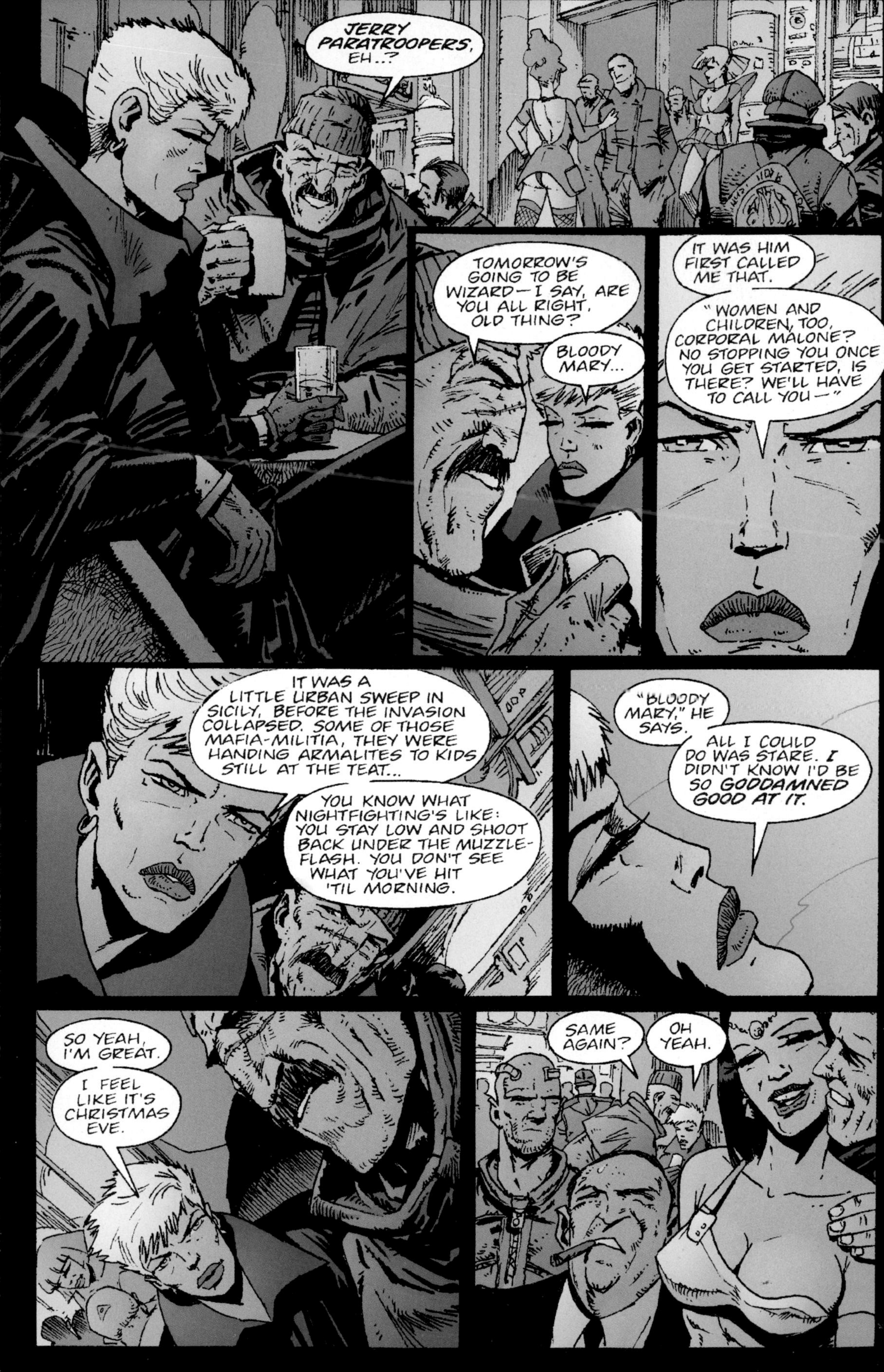

JERRY PARATROOPERS, EH..?
TOMORROW'S GOING TO BE WIZARD—I SAY, ARE YOU ALL RIGHT, OLD THING?
BLOODY MARY...
IT WAS HIM FIRST CALLED ME THAT.
"WOMEN AND CHILDREN, TOO, CORPORAL MALONE? NO STOPPING YOU ONCE YOU GET STARTED, IS THERE? WE'LL HAVE TO CALL YOU—"
IT WAS A LITTLE URBAN SWEEP IN SICILY, BEFORE THE INVASION COLLAPSED. SOME OF THOSE MAFIA-MILITIA, THEY WERE HANDING ARMALITES TO KIDS STILL AT THE TEAT...
YOU KNOW WHAT NIGHTFIGHTING'S LIKE: YOU STAY LOW AND SHOOT BACK UNDER THE MUZZLE-FLASH. YOU DON'T SEE WHAT YOU'VE HIT 'TIL MORNING.
"BLOODY MARY," HE SAYS.
ALL I COULD DO WAS STARE. *I* DIDN'T KNOW I'D BE SO ***GODDAMNED GOOD AT IT.***
SO YEAH, I'M GREAT.
I FEEL LIKE IT'S CHRISTMAS EVE.
SAME AGAIN?
OH YEAH.

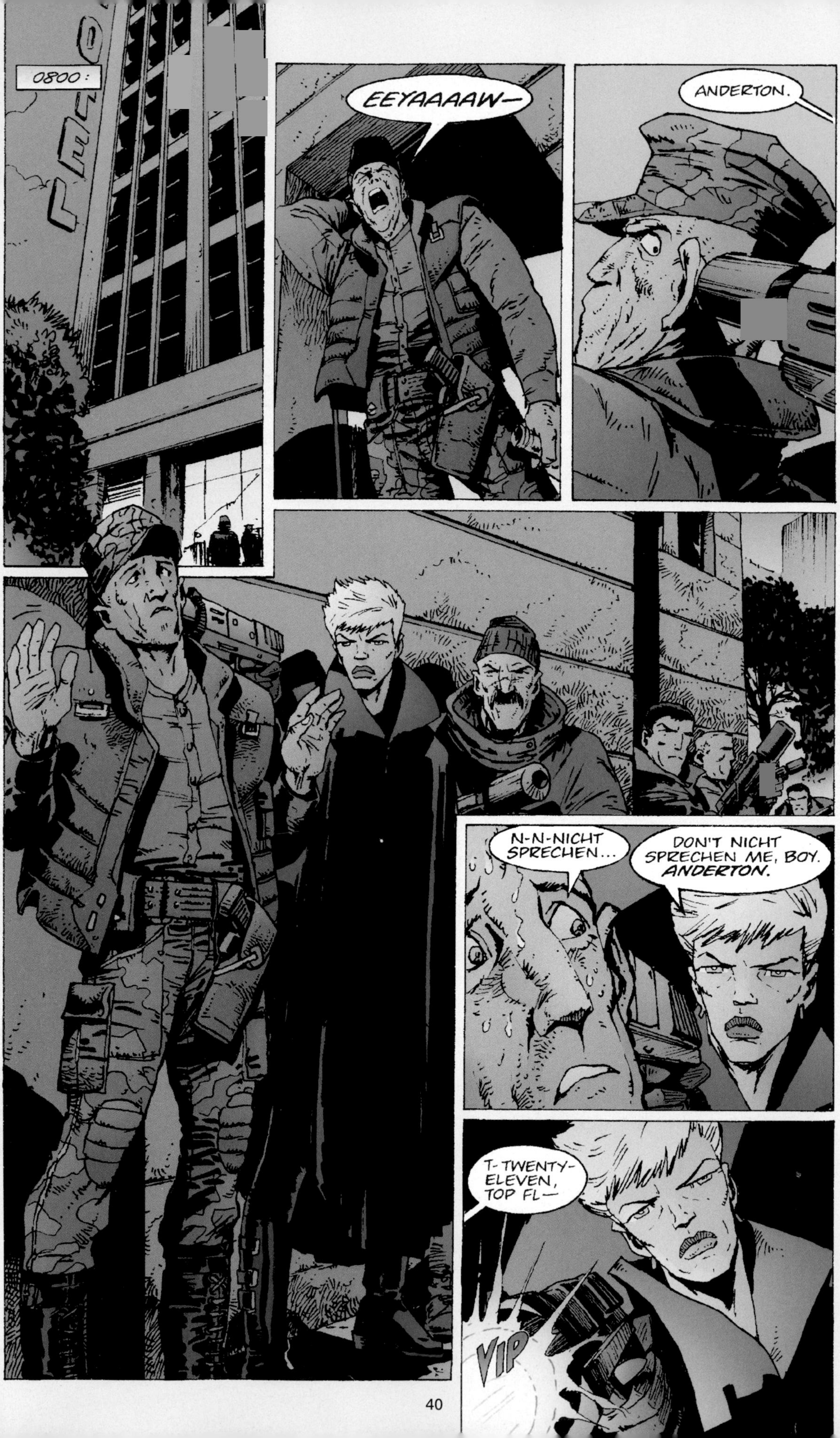
0800:
EEYAAAAW—
ANDERTON.
N-N-NICHT SPRECHEN...
DON'T NICHT SPRECHEN ME, BOY. ANDERTON.
T-TWENTY-ELEVEN, TOP FL—
VIP

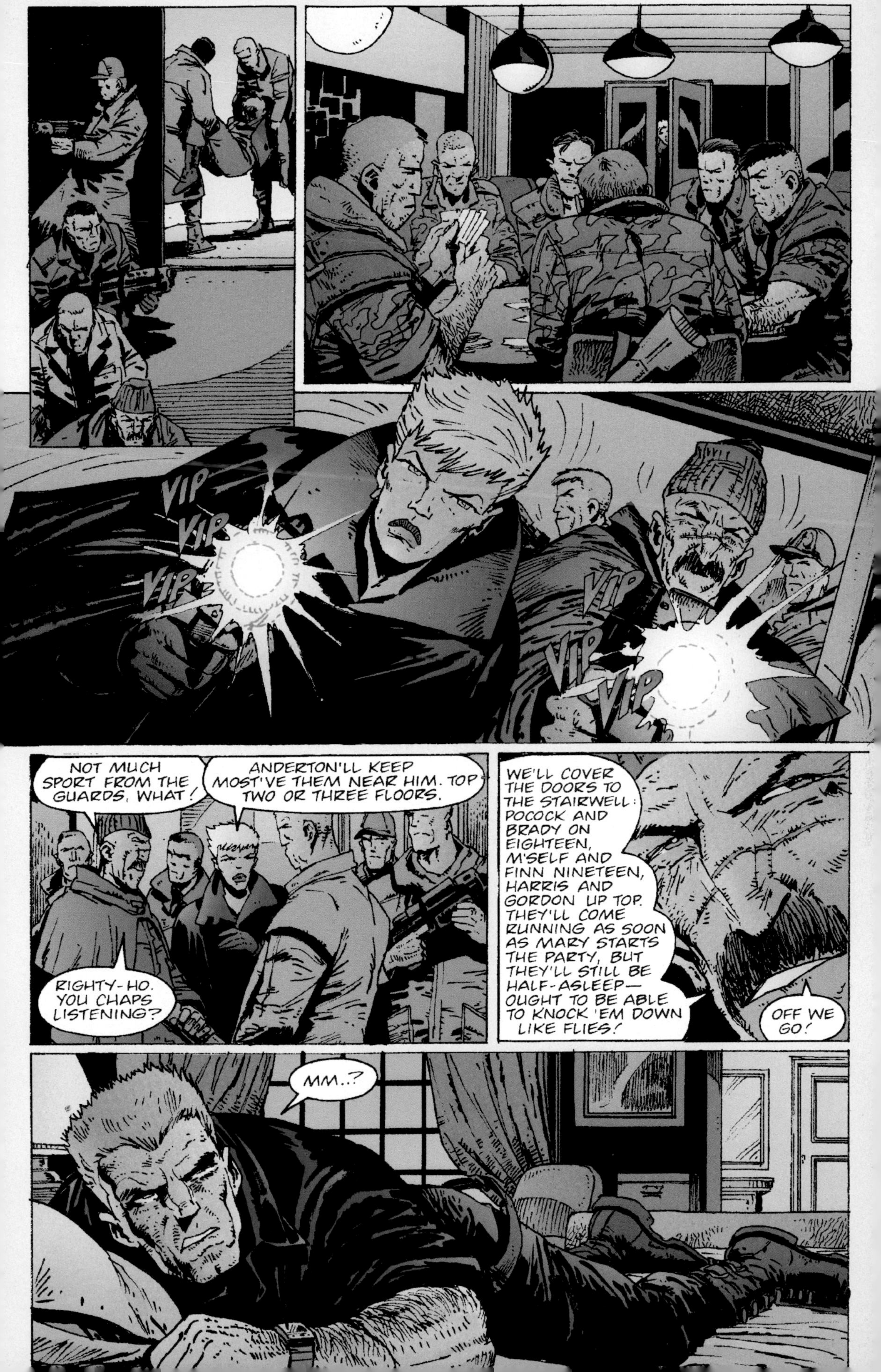
VIP
VIP
VIP
VIP
VIP
VIP
NOT MUCH SPORT FROM THE GUARDS, WHAT!
ANDERTON'LL KEEP MOST'VE THEM NEAR HIM. TOP TWO OR THREE FLOORS.
RIGHTY-HO. YOU CHAPS LISTENING?
WE'LL COVER THE DOORS TO THE STAIRWELL: POCOCK AND BRADY ON EIGHTEEN, M'SELF AND FINN NINETEEN, HARRIS AND GORDON UP TOP. THEY'LL COME RUNNING AS SOON AS MARY STARTS THE PARTY, BUT THEY'LL STILL BE HALF-ASLEEP— OUGHT TO BE ABLE TO KNOCK 'EM DOWN LIKE FLIES!
OFF WE GO!
MM..?

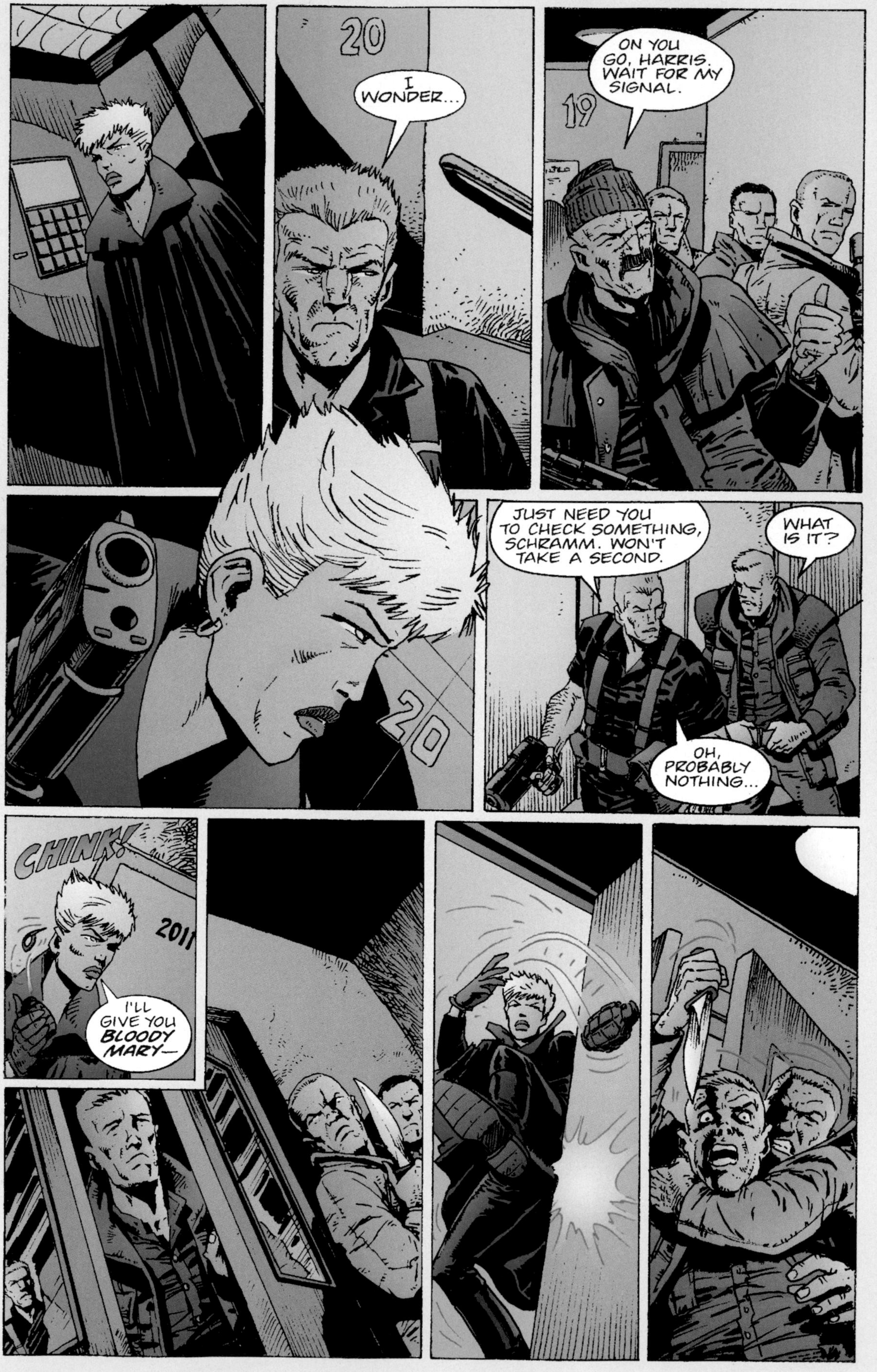
I WONDER...
ON YOU GO, HARRIS. WAIT FOR MY SIGNAL.
JUST NEED YOU TO CHECK SOMETHING, SCHRAMM. WON'T TAKE A SECOND.
WHAT IS IT?
OH, PROBABLY NOTHING...
CHINK!
I'LL GIVE YOU *BLOODY MARY*—

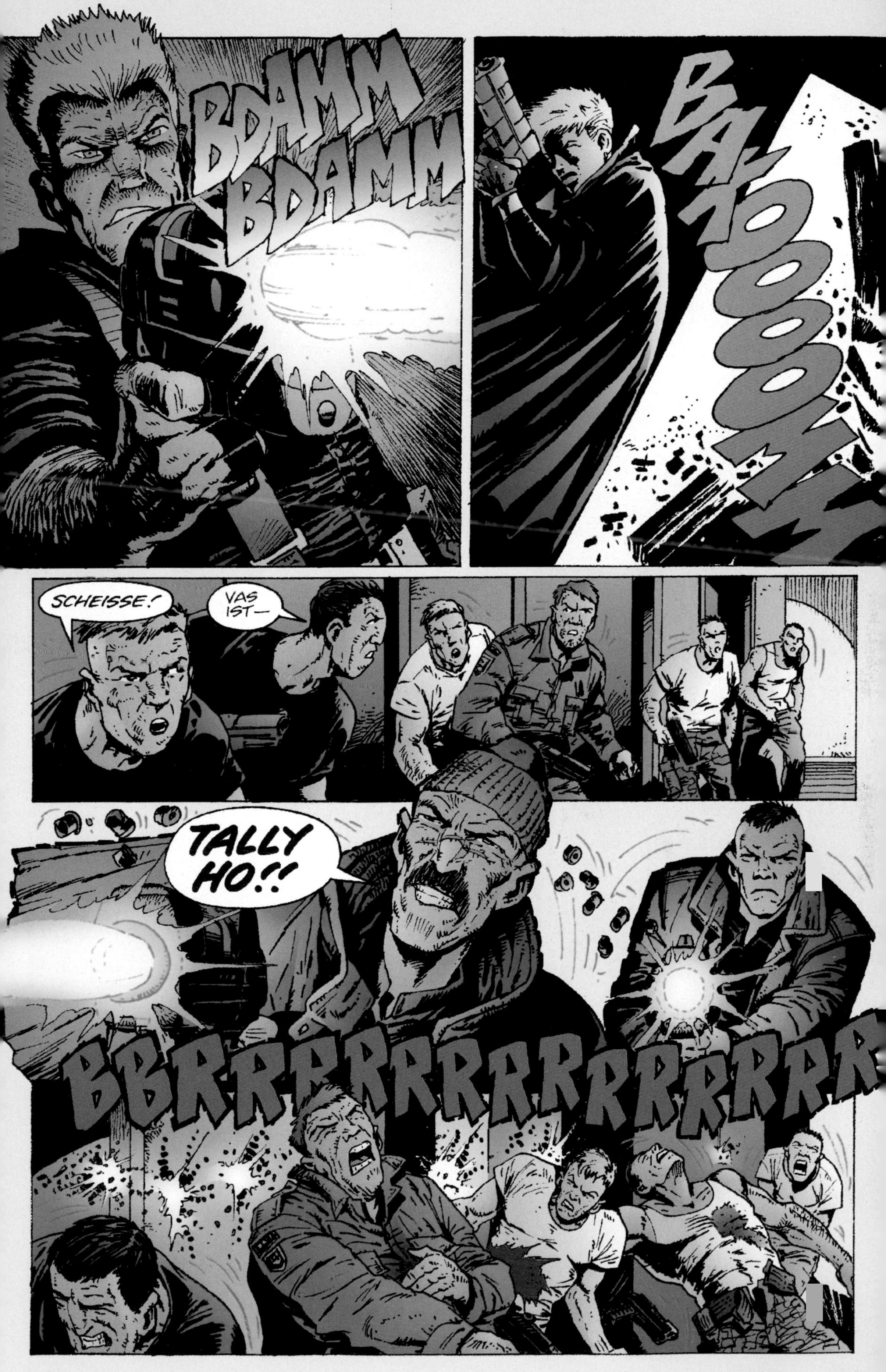
BDAMM
BDAMM
BAROOOOOM
SCHEISSE!
VAS IST—
TALLY HO?!
BBRRRRRRRRRRRRRRRR

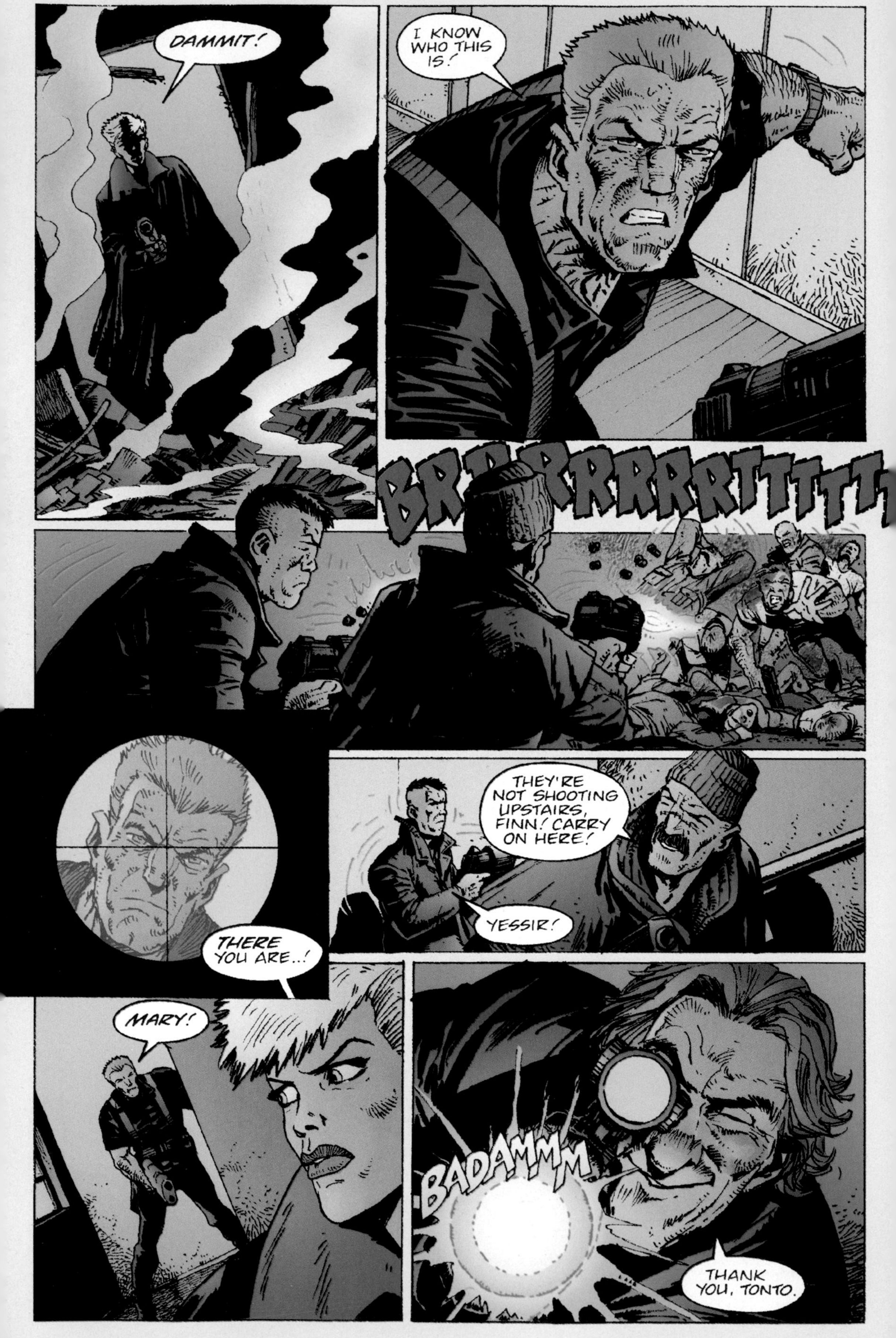
DAMMIT!
I KNOW WHO THIS IS!
BRRRRRRRRTTTTT
THEY'RE NOT SHOOTING UPSTAIRS, FINN! CARRY ON HERE!
YESSIR!
THERE YOU ARE...!
MARY!
BADAMMM
THANK YOU, TONTO.

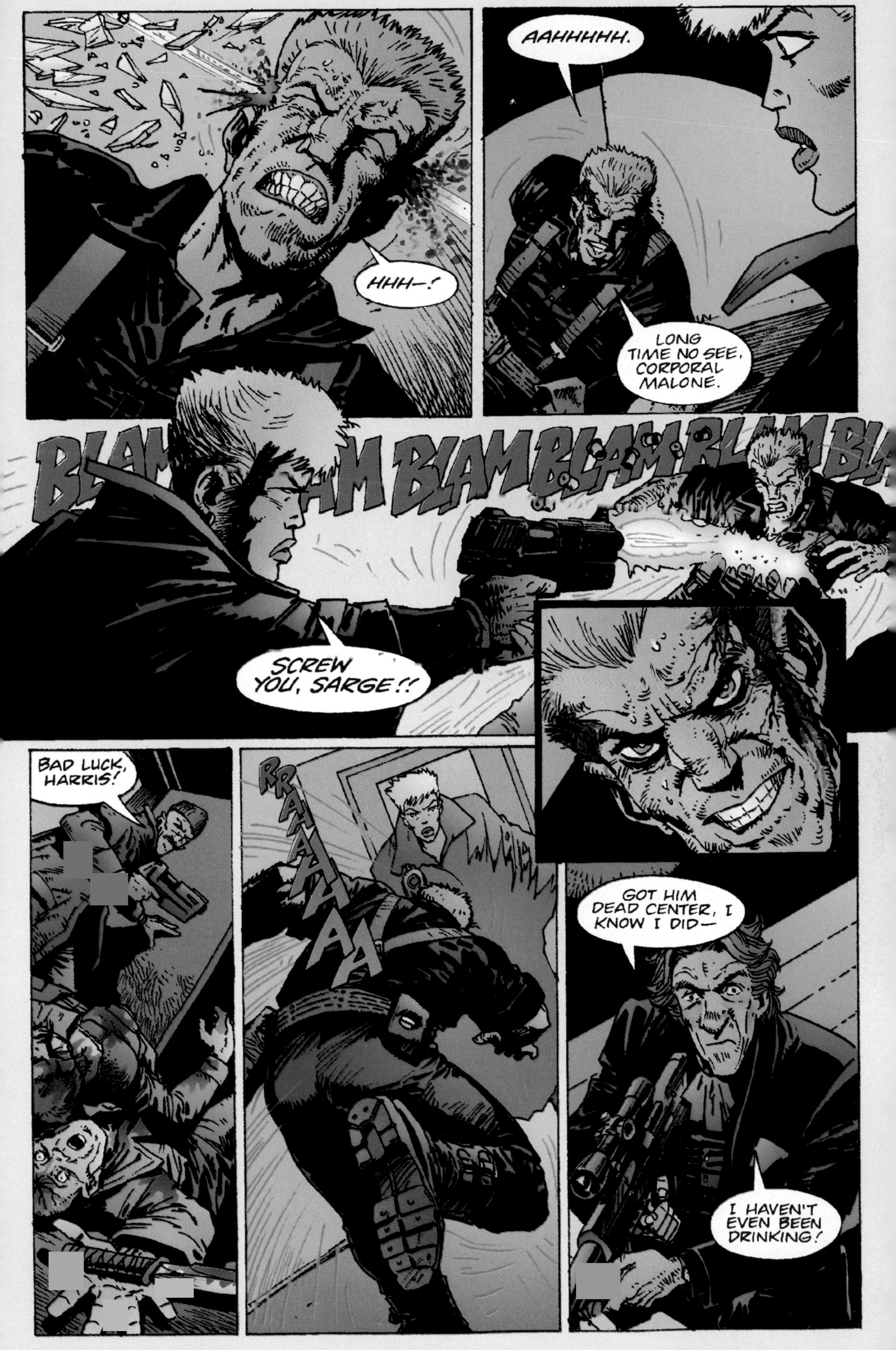
HHH--!
AAHHHHH.
LONG TIME NO SEE, CORPORAL MALONE.
BLAM BLAM BLAM BLAM BLAM BLA
SCREW YOU, SARGE!!
BAD LUCK, HARRIS!
RRAAAAAAAA
GOT HIM DEAD CENTER, I KNOW I DID--
I HAVEN'T EVEN BEEN DRINKING!

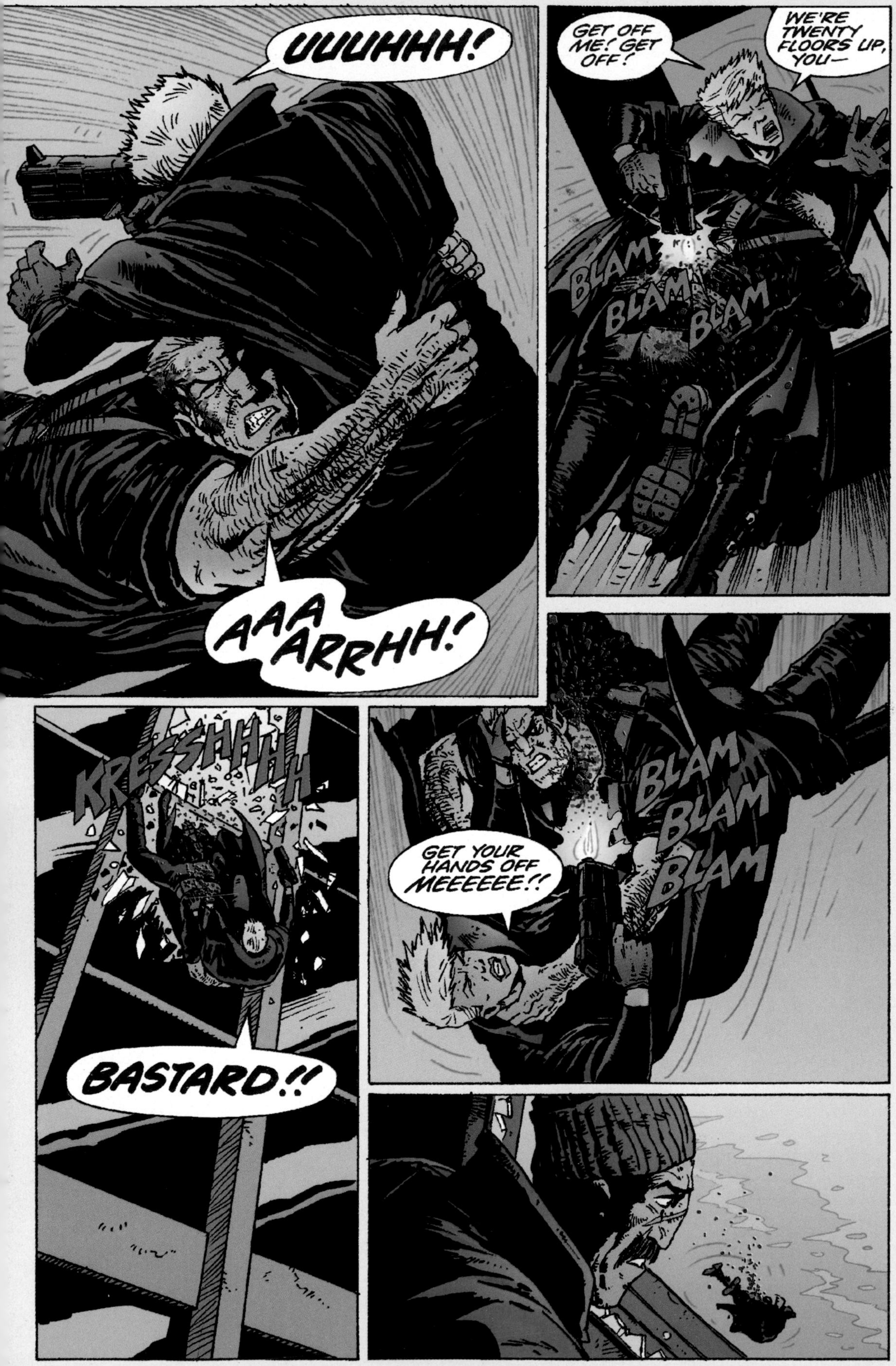
UUUHHH!
AAA ARRHH!
GET OFF ME! GET OFF!
WE'RE TWENTY FLOORS UP, YOU—
BLAM BLAM BLAM
GET YOUR HANDS OFF MEEEEEE!!
BLAM BLAM BLAM
KRESSHHHH
BASTARD!!

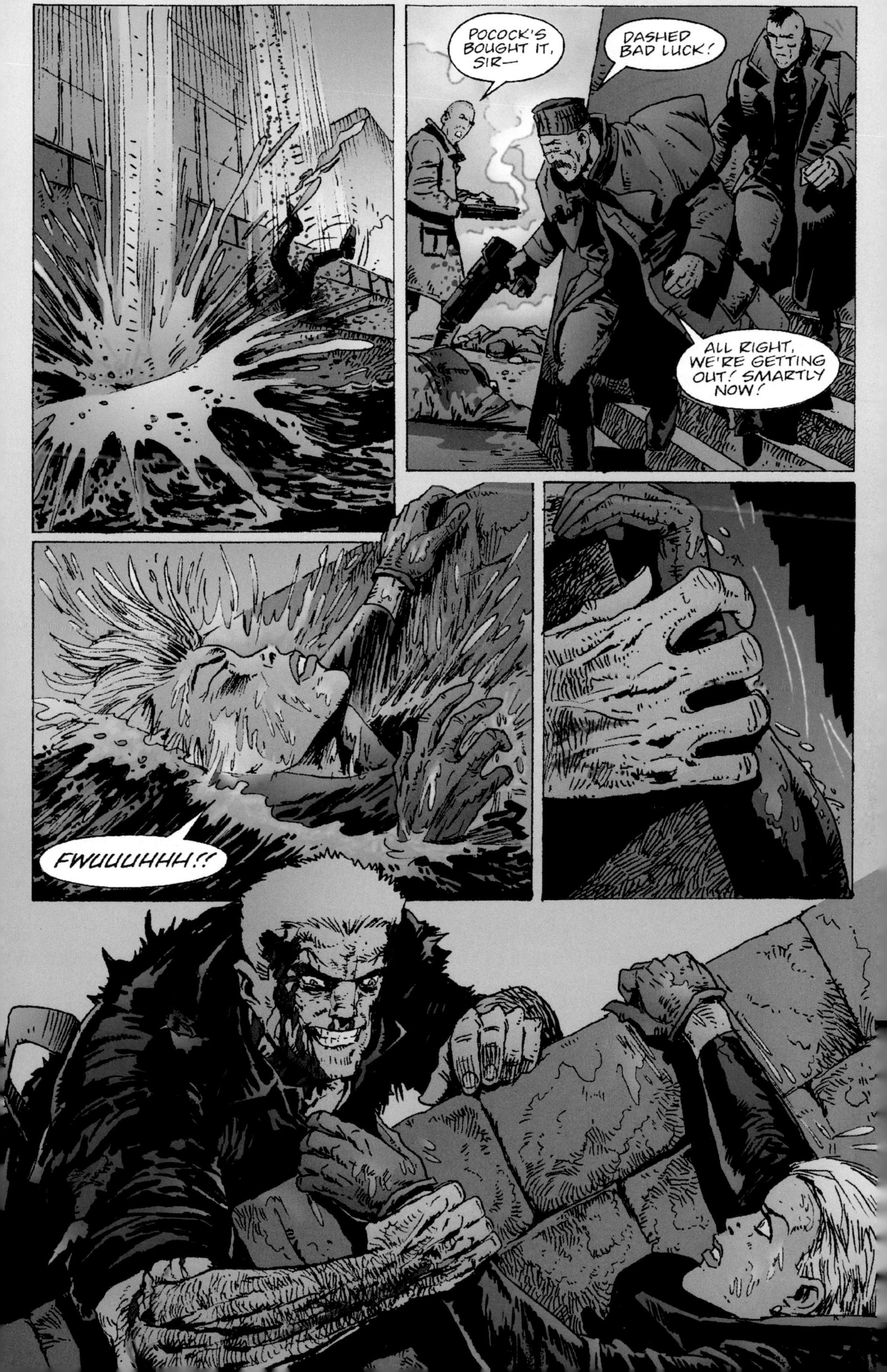
POCOCK'S BOUGHT IT, SIR—
DASHED BAD LUCK!
ALL RIGHT, WE'RE GETTING OUT! SMARTLY NOW!
FWUUUHHH?!

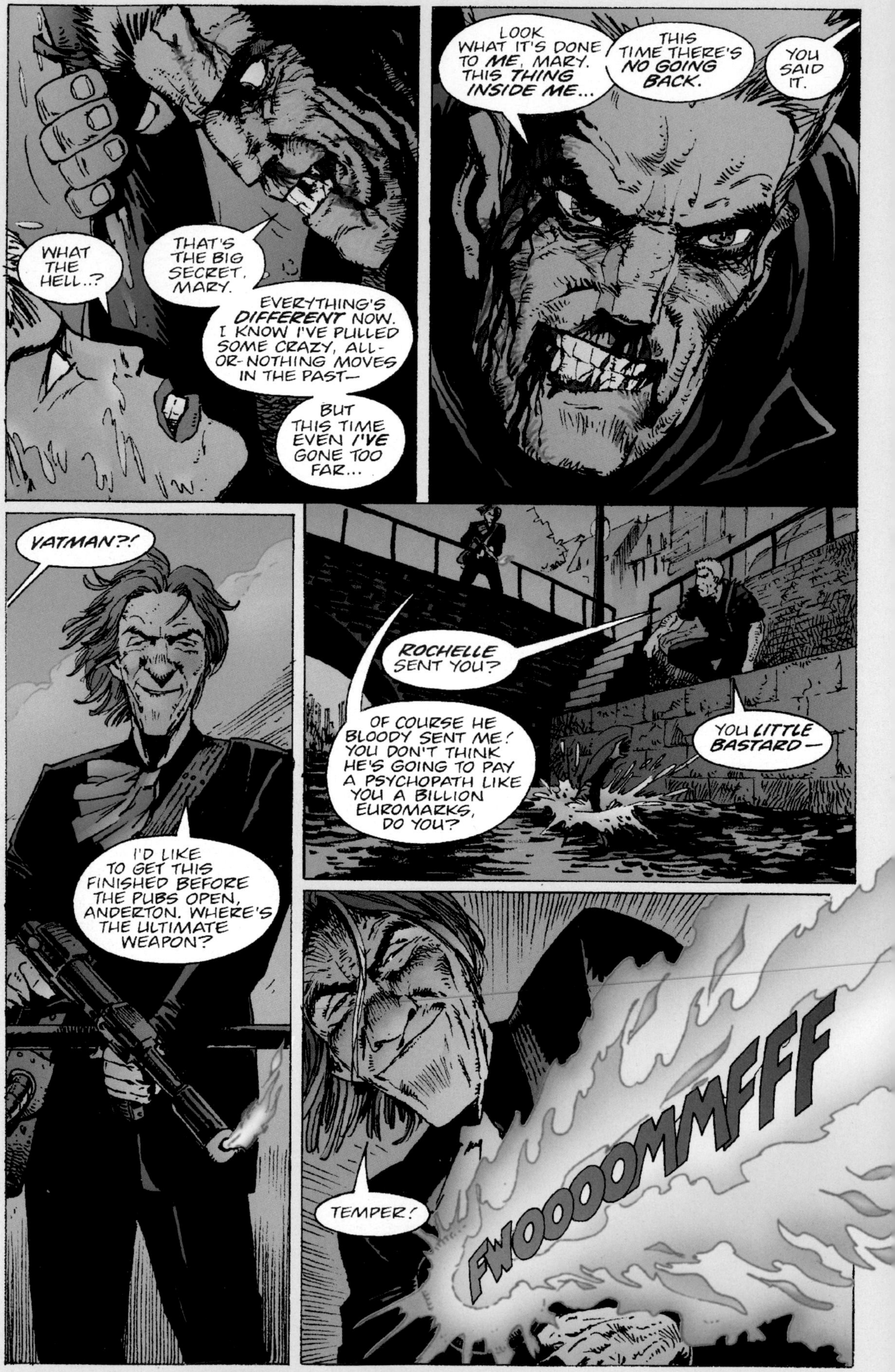
WHAT THE HELL..?
THAT'S THE BIG SECRET, MARY.
EVERYTHING'S DIFFERENT NOW. I KNOW I'VE PULLED SOME CRAZY, ALL-OR-NOTHING MOVES IN THE PAST—
BUT THIS TIME EVEN I'VE GONE TOO FAR...
LOOK WHAT IT'S DONE TO ME, MARY. THIS THING INSIDE ME...
THIS TIME THERE'S NO GOING BACK.
YOU SAID IT.
VATMAN?!
I'D LIKE TO GET THIS FINISHED BEFORE THE PUBS OPEN, ANDERTON. WHERE'S THE ULTIMATE WEAPON?
ROCHELLE SENT YOU?
OF COURSE HE BLOODY SENT ME! YOU DON'T THINK HE'S GOING TO PAY A PSYCHOPATH LIKE YOU A BILLION EUROMARKS, DO YOU?
YOU LITTLE BASTARD—
TEMPER!
FWOOOOMMFFF

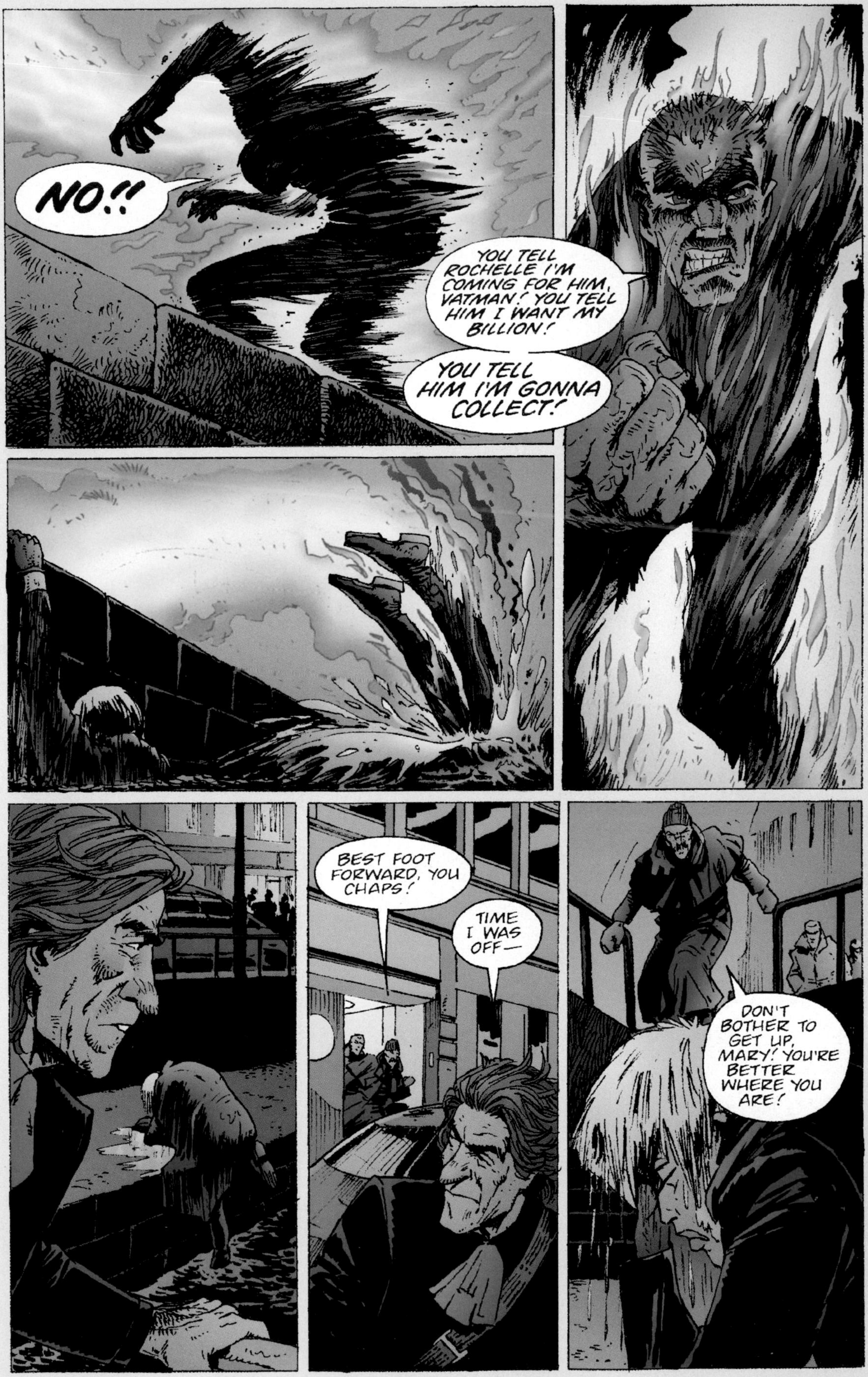
NO.!!
YOU TELL ROCHELLE I'M COMING FOR HIM, VATMAN! YOU TELL HIM I WANT MY BILLION!
YOU TELL HIM I'M GONNA COLLECT!
BEST FOOT FORWARD, YOU CHAPS!
TIME I WAS OFF—
DON'T BOTHER TO GET UP, MARY! YOU'RE BETTER WHERE YOU ARE!

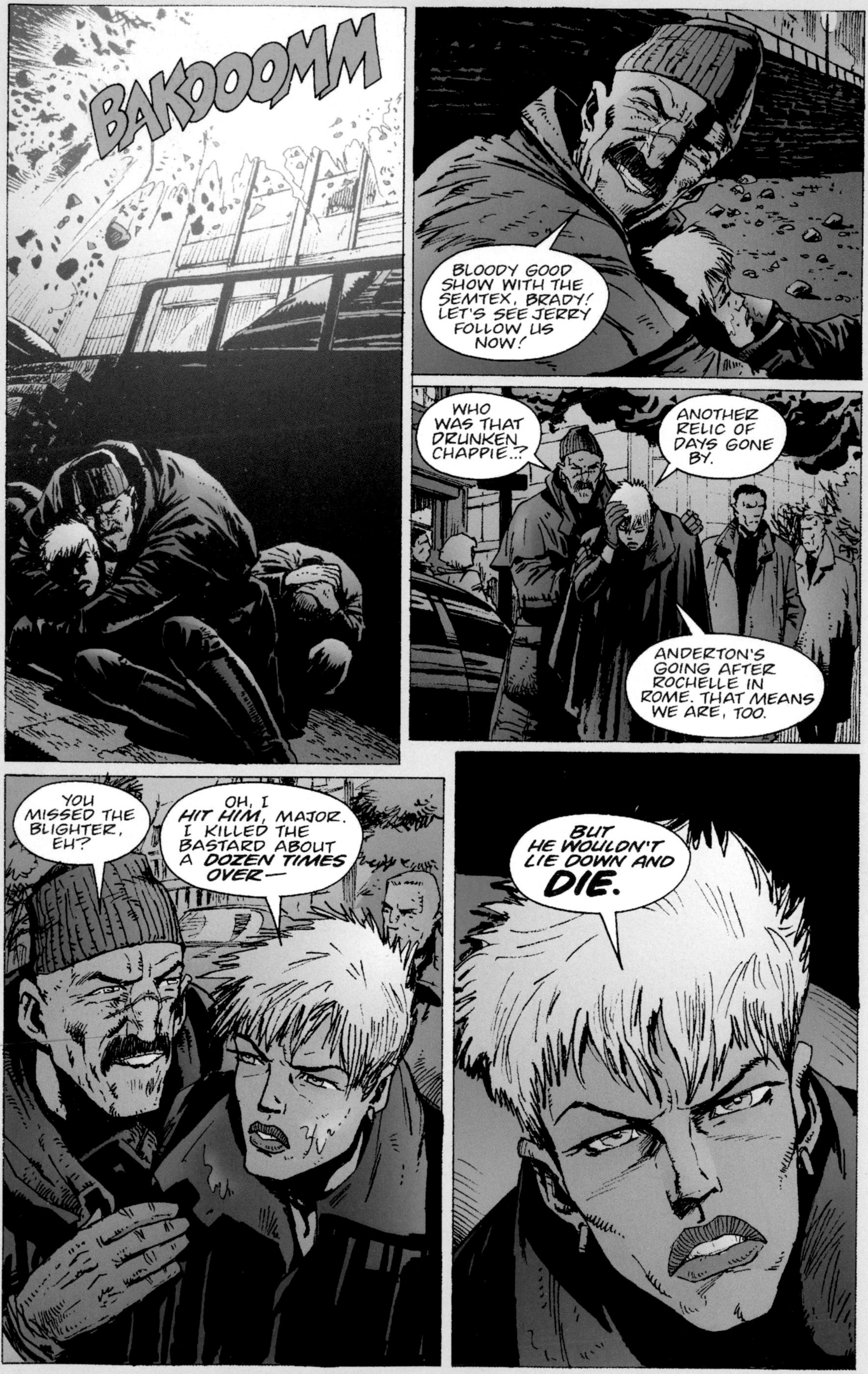
BAKOOOMM
BLOODY GOOD SHOW WITH THE SEMTEX, BRADY! LET'S SEE JERRY FOLLOW US NOW!
WHO WAS THAT DRUNKEN CHAPPIE..?
ANOTHER RELIC OF DAYS GONE BY.
ANDERTON'S GOING AFTER ROCHELLE IN ROME. THAT MEANS WE ARE, TOO.
YOU MISSED THE BLIGHTER, EH?
OH, I HIT HIM, MAJOR. I KILLED THE BASTARD ABOUT A DOZEN TIMES OVER—
BUT HE WOULDN'T LIE DOWN AND DIE.

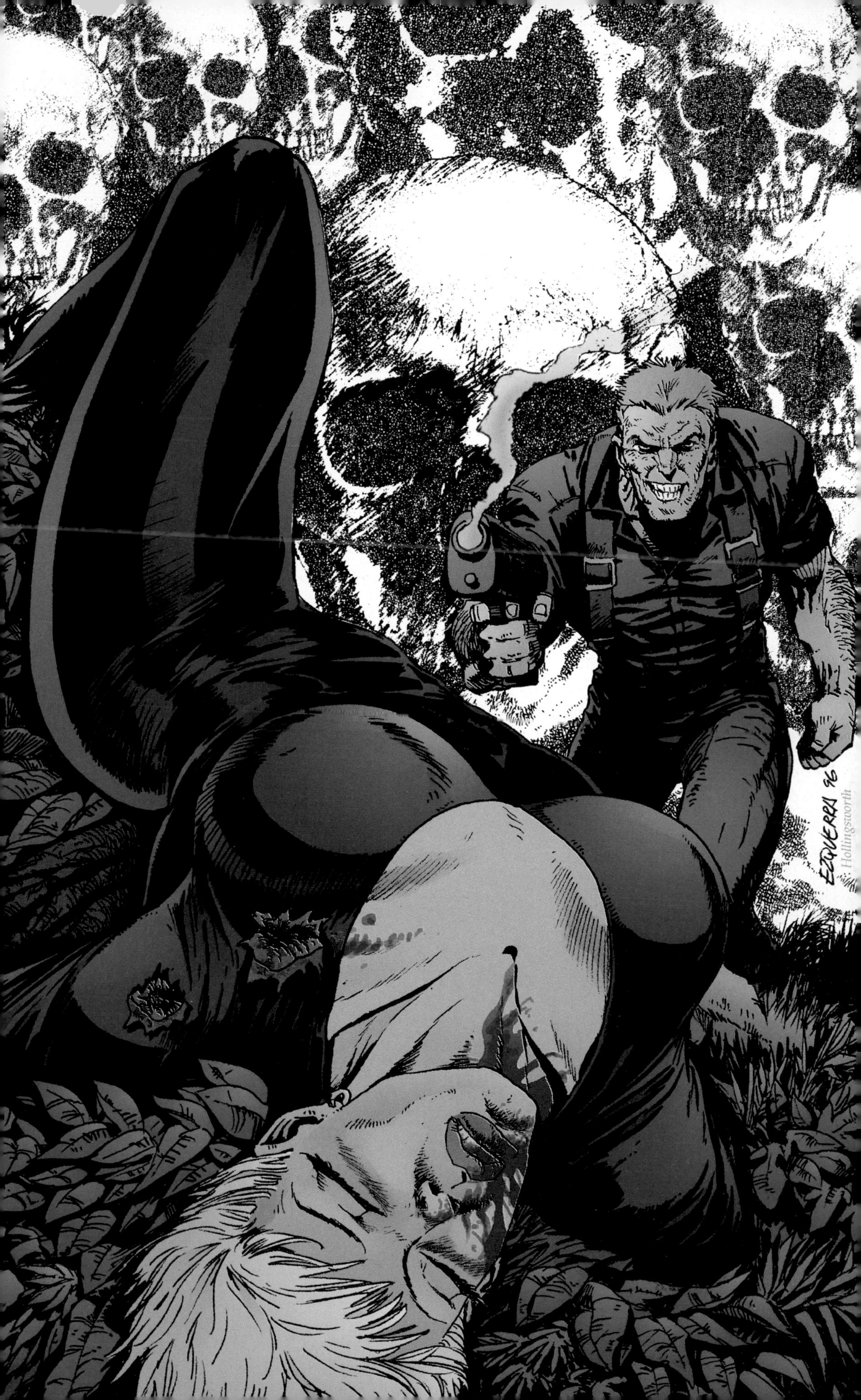
EZQUERRA '96
Hollingsworth

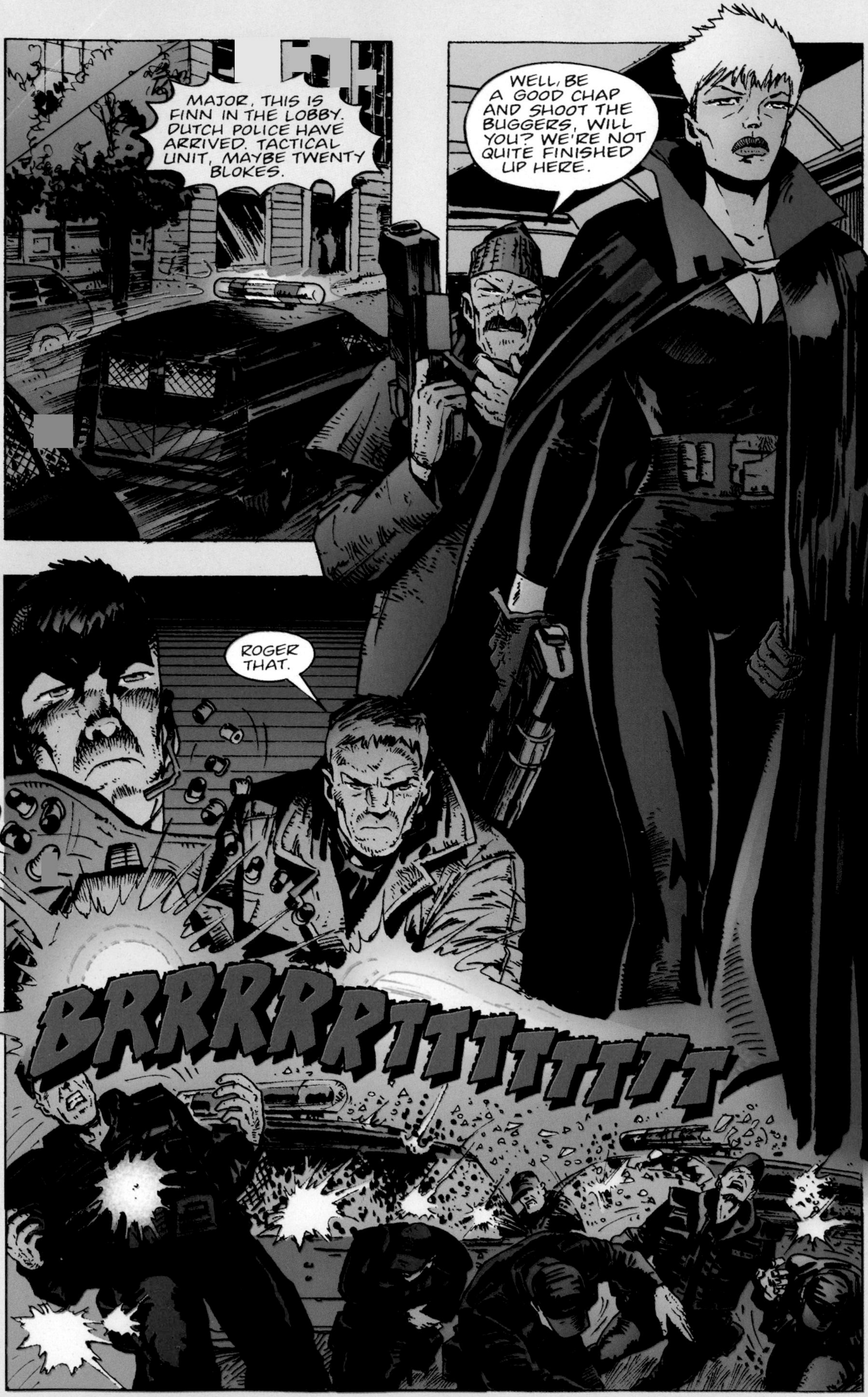
MAJOR, THIS IS FINN IN THE LOBBY. DUTCH POLICE HAVE ARRIVED. TACTICAL UNIT, MAYBE TWENTY BLOKES.
WELL, BE A GOOD CHAP AND SHOOT THE BUGGERS, WILL YOU? WE'RE NOT QUITE FINISHED UP HERE.
ROGER THAT.
BRRRRRTTTTTTTTTT

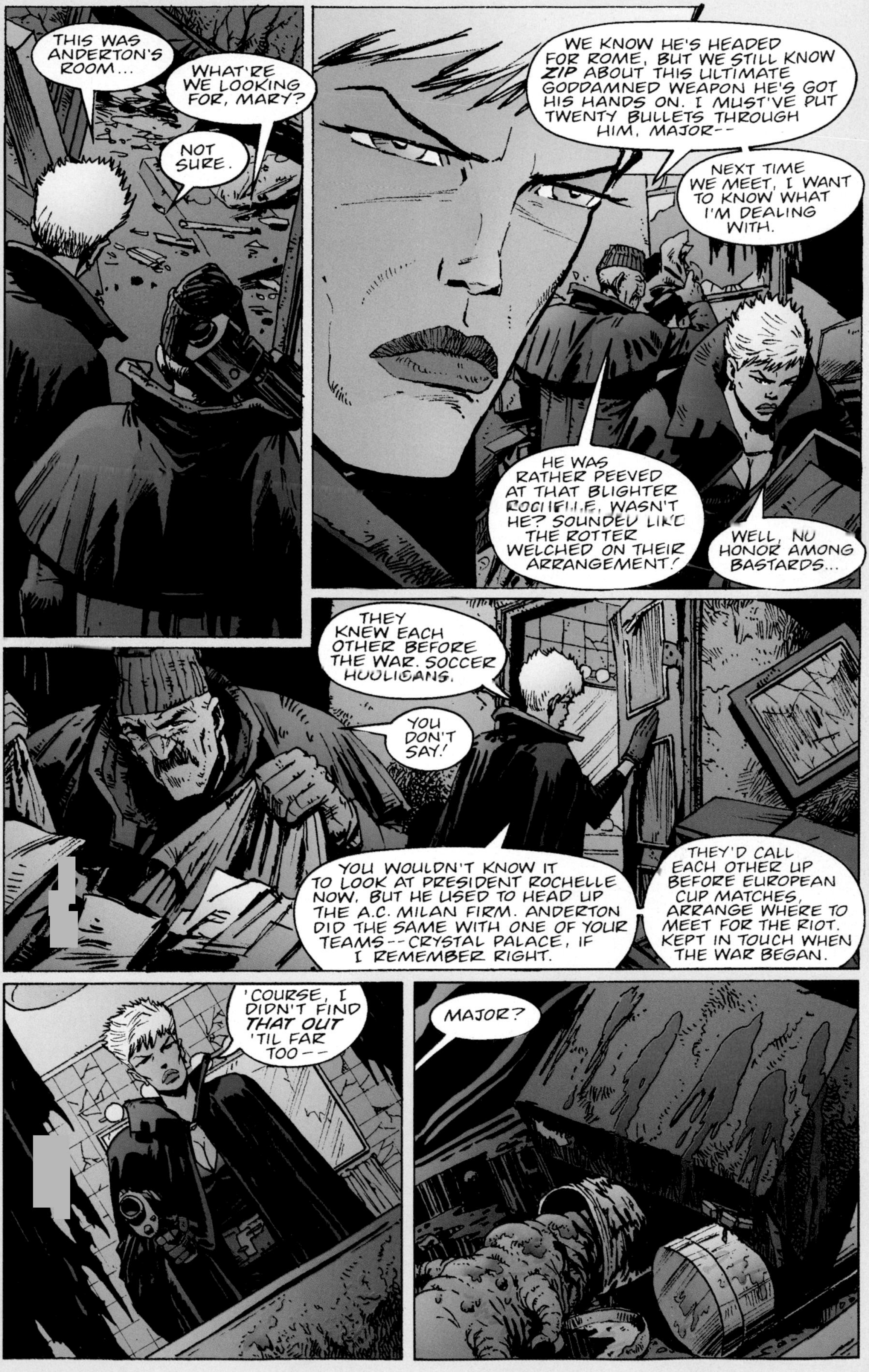

THIS WAS ANDERTON'S ROOM...
WHAT'RE WE LOOKING FOR, MARY?
NOT SURE.
WE KNOW HE'S HEADED FOR ROME, BUT WE STILL KNOW **ZIP** ABOUT THIS ULTIMATE GODDAMNED WEAPON HE'S GOT HIS HANDS ON. I MUST'VE PUT TWENTY BULLETS THROUGH HIM, MAJOR--
NEXT TIME WE MEET, I WANT TO KNOW WHAT I'M DEALING WITH.
HE WAS RATHER PEEVED AT THAT BLIGHTER ROCHELLE, WASN'T HE? SOUNDED LIKE THE ROTTER WELCHED ON THEIR ARRANGEMENT!
WELL, NO HONOR AMONG BASTARDS...
THEY KNEW EACH OTHER BEFORE THE WAR. SOCCER HOOLIGANS.
YOU DON'T SAY!
YOU WOULDN'T KNOW IT TO LOOK AT PRESIDENT ROCHELLE NOW, BUT HE USED TO HEAD UP THE A.C. MILAN FIRM. ANDERTON DID THE SAME WITH ONE OF YOUR TEAMS--CRYSTAL PALACE, IF I REMEMBER RIGHT.
THEY'D CALL EACH OTHER UP BEFORE EUROPEAN CUP MATCHES, ARRANGE WHERE TO MEET FOR THE RIOT. KEPT IN TOUCH WHEN THE WAR BEGAN.
'COURSE, I DIDN'T FIND **THAT OUT** 'TIL FAR TOO--
MAJOR?

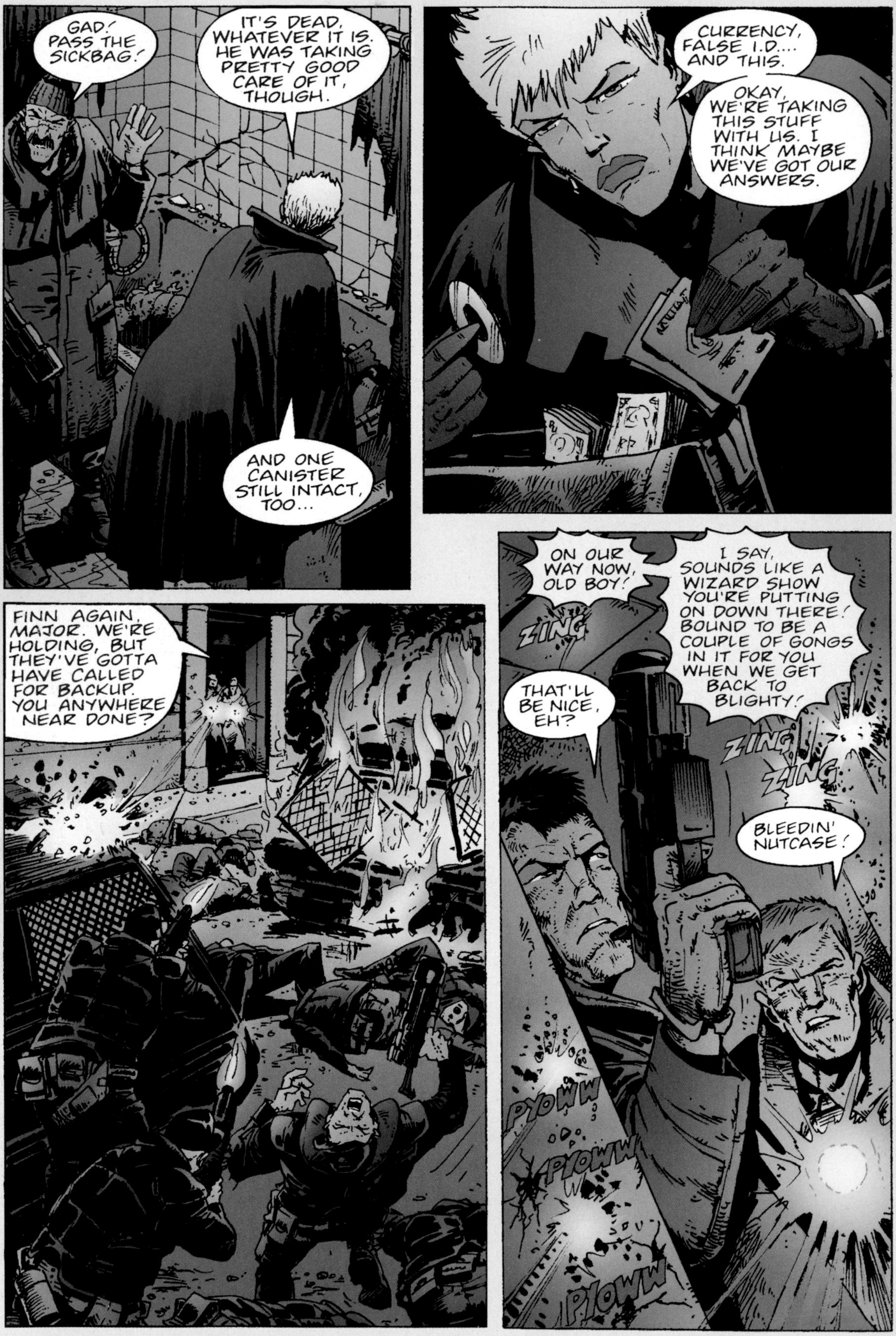
GAD! PASS THE SICKBAG!
IT'S DEAD, WHATEVER IT IS. HE WAS TAKING PRETTY GOOD CARE OF IT, THOUGH.
AND ONE CANISTER STILL INTACT, TOO...
CURRENCY, FALSE I.D.... AND THIS.
OKAY, WE'RE TAKING THIS STUFF WITH US. I THINK MAYBE WE'VE GOT OUR ANSWERS.
FINN AGAIN, MAJOR. WE'RE HOLDING, BUT THEY'VE GOTTA HAVE CALLED FOR BACKUP. YOU ANYWHERE NEAR DONE?
ON OUR WAY NOW, OLD BOY!
I SAY, SOUNDS LIKE A WIZARD SHOW YOU'RE PUTTING ON DOWN THERE! BOUND TO BE A COUPLE OF GONGS IN IT FOR YOU WHEN WE GET BACK TO BLIGHTY!
ZING
THAT'LL BE NICE, EH?
ZING
ZING
BLEEDIN' NUTCASE!
PYOWW
PYOWW
PYOWW

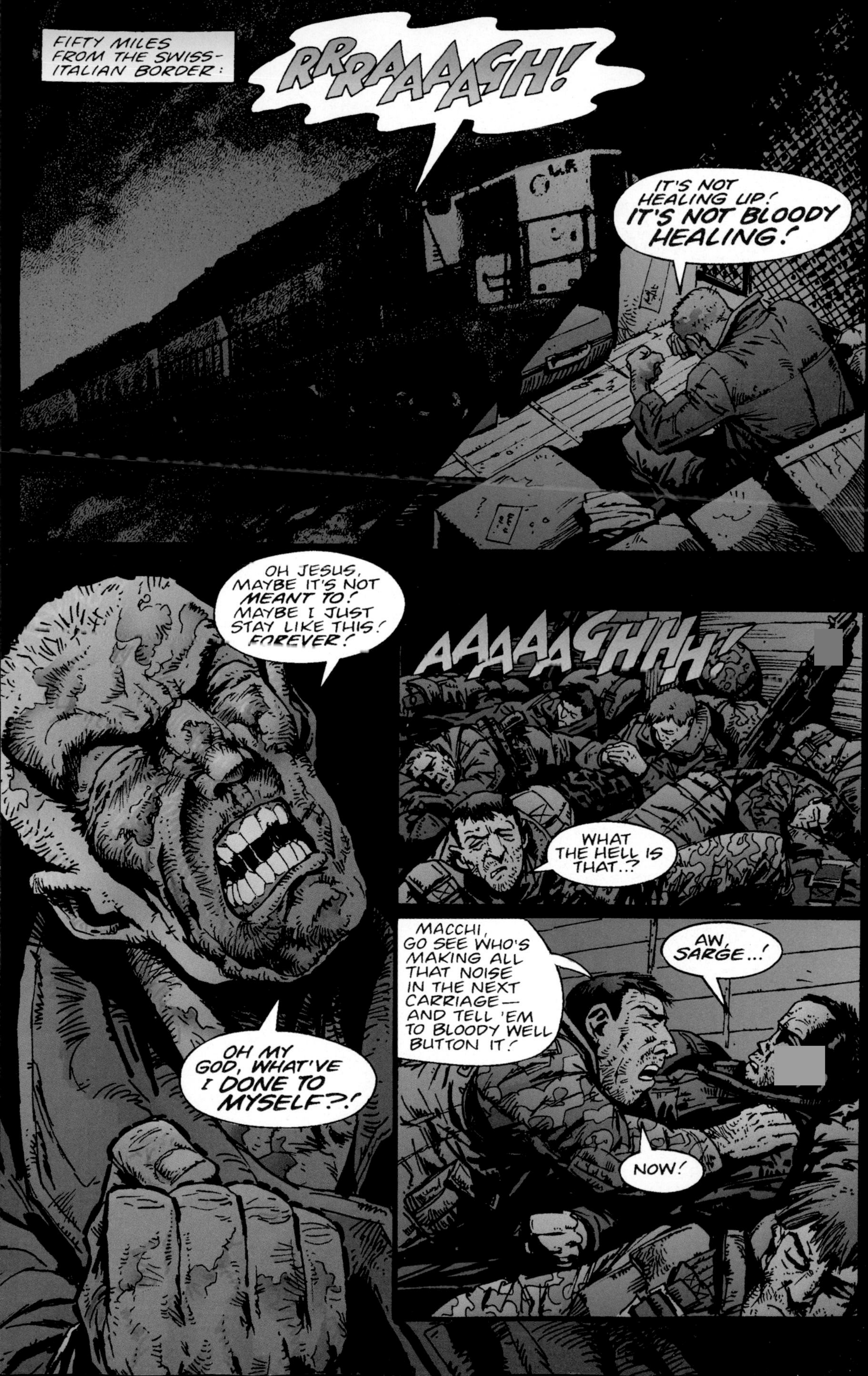
FIFTY MILES FROM THE SWISS-ITALIAN BORDER:
RRRAAAAGH!
IT'S NOT HEALING UP! IT'S NOT BLOODY HEALING!
OH JESUS, MAYBE IT'S NOT MEANT TO! MAYBE I JUST STAY LIKE THIS! FOREVER!
OH MY GOD, WHAT'VE I DONE TO MYSELF?!
AAAAAGHHH!
WHAT THE HELL IS THAT..?
MACCHI, GO SEE WHO'S MAKING ALL THAT NOISE IN THE NEXT CARRIAGE— AND TELL 'EM TO BLOODY WELL BUTTON IT!
AW, SARGE...!
NOW!

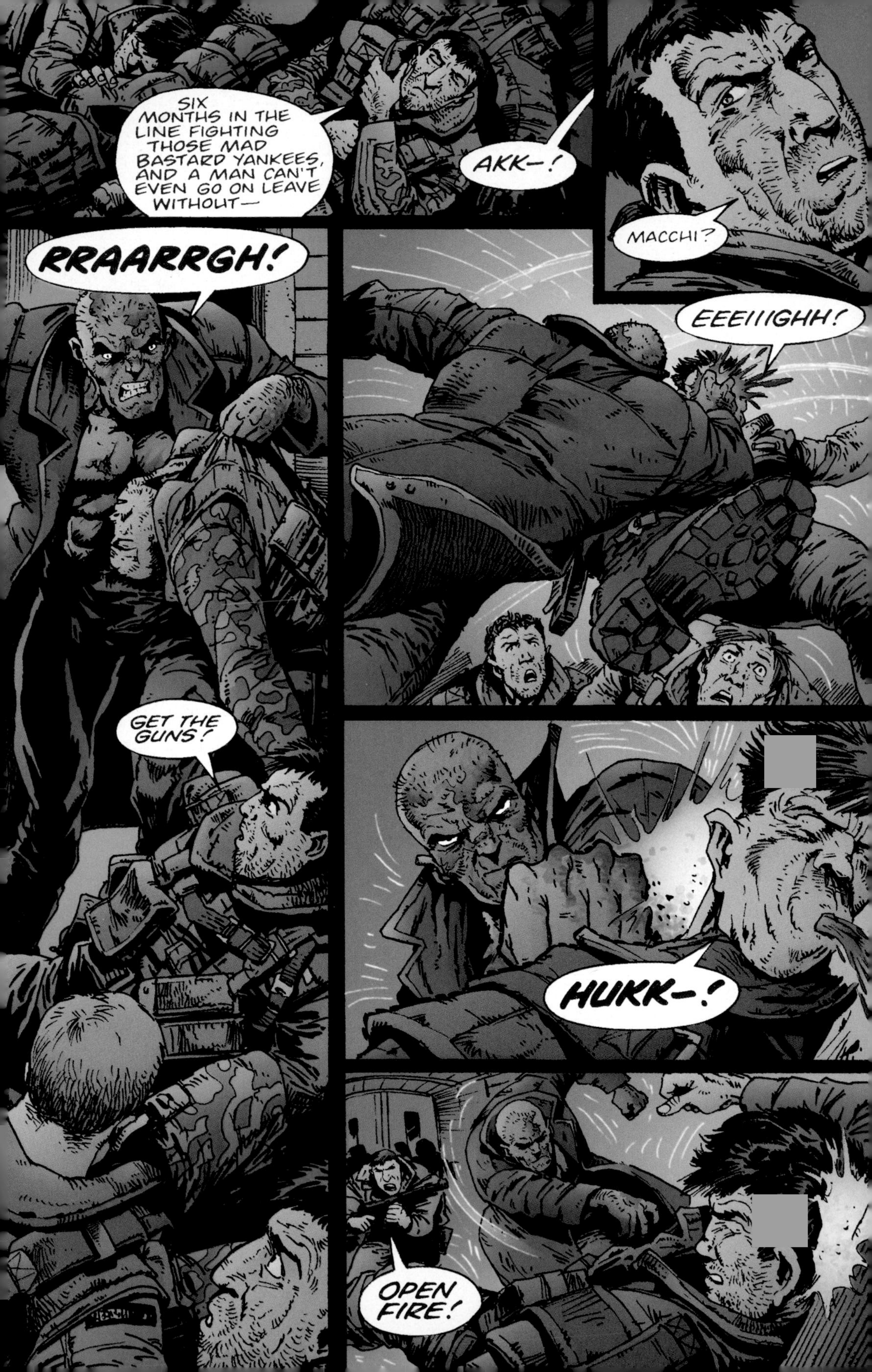
SIX MONTHS IN THE LINE FIGHTING THOSE MAD BASTARD YANKEES, AND A MAN CAN'T EVEN GO ON LEAVE WITHOUT—
AKK—!
MACCHI?
RRAARRGH!
GET THE GUNS!
EEEIIIGHH!
HUKK—!
OPEN FIRE!

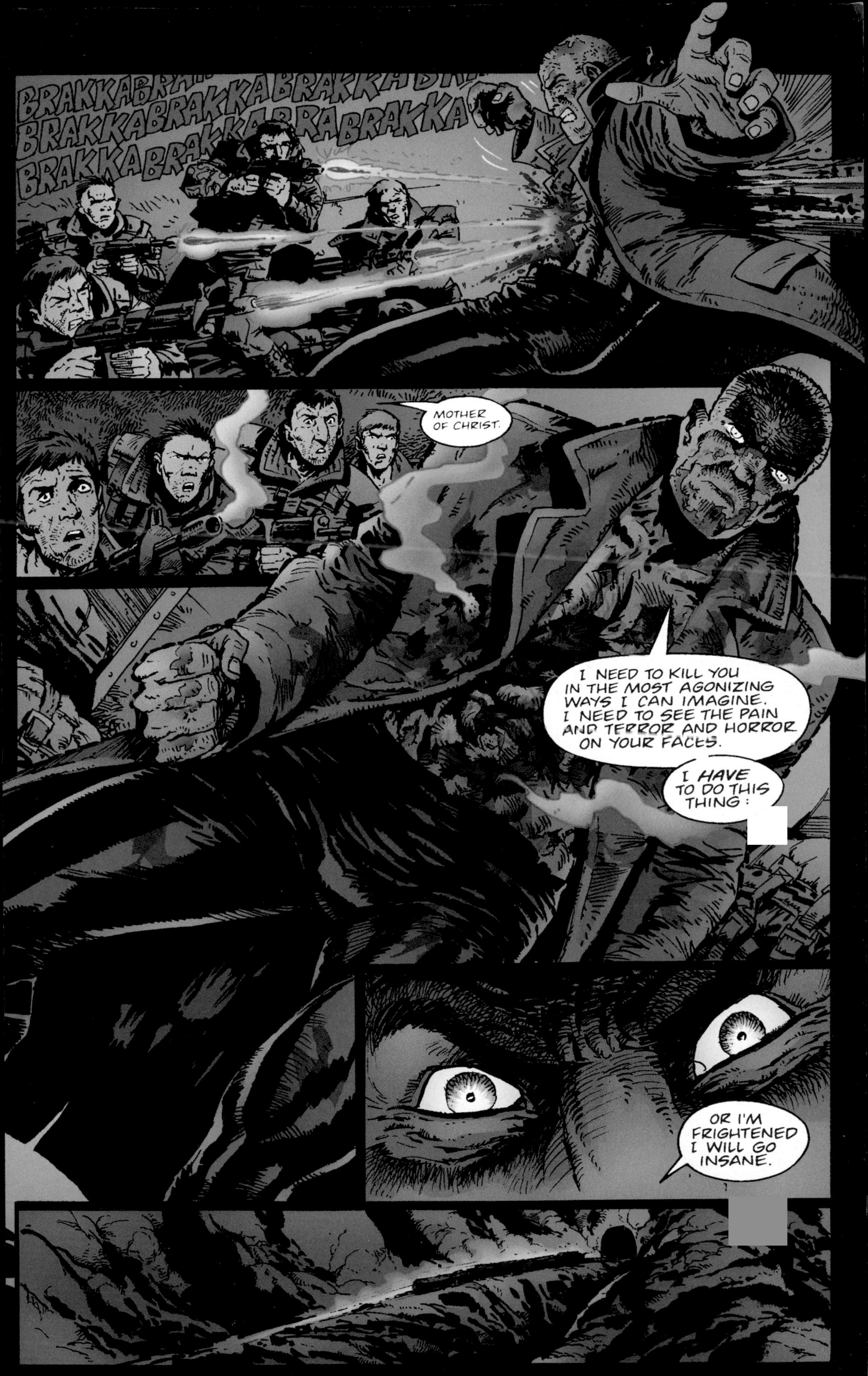
BRAKKABRAKKABRAKKA
BRAKKABRAKKABRAKKA
MOTHER OF CHRIST.
I NEED TO KILL YOU IN THE MOST AGONIZING WAYS I CAN IMAGINE. I NEED TO SEE THE PAIN AND TERROR AND HORROR ON YOUR FACES.
I *HAVE* TO DO THIS THING:
OR I'M FRIGHTENED I WILL GO INSANE.

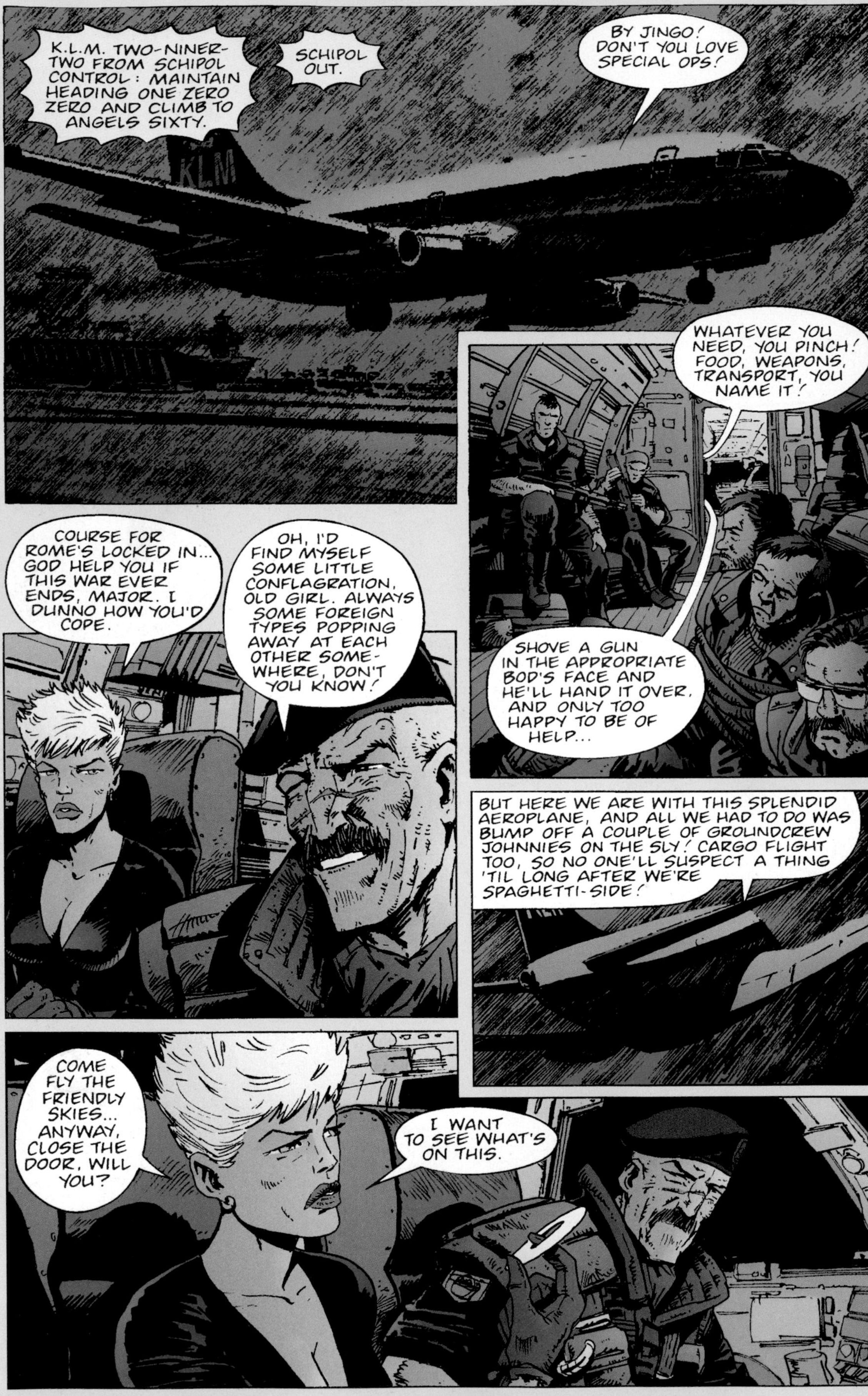
K.L.M. TWO-NINER-TWO FROM SCHIPOL CONTROL: MAINTAIN HEADING ONE ZERO ZERO AND CLIMB TO ANGELS SIXTY.
SCHIPOL OUT.
BY JINGO! DON'T YOU LOVE SPECIAL OPS!
WHATEVER YOU NEED, YOU PINCH! FOOD, WEAPONS, TRANSPORT, YOU NAME IT!
SHOVE A GUN IN THE APPROPRIATE BOD'S FACE AND HE'LL HAND IT OVER, AND ONLY TOO HAPPY TO BE OF HELP...
COURSE FOR ROME'S LOCKED IN... GOD HELP YOU IF THIS WAR EVER ENDS, MAJOR. I DUNNO HOW YOU'D COPE.
OH, I'D FIND MYSELF SOME LITTLE CONFLAGRATION, OLD GIRL. ALWAYS SOME FOREIGN TYPES POPPING AWAY AT EACH OTHER SOMEWHERE, DON'T YOU KNOW!
BUT HERE WE ARE WITH THIS SPLENDID AEROPLANE, AND ALL WE HAD TO DO WAS BUMP OFF A COUPLE OF GROUNDCREW JOHNNIES ON THE SLY! CARGO FLIGHT TOO, SO NO ONE'LL SUSPECT A THING 'TIL LONG AFTER WE'RE SPAGHETTI-SIDE!
COME FLY THE FRIENDLY SKIES... ANYWAY, CLOSE THE DOOR, WILL YOU?
I WANT TO SEE WHAT'S ON THIS.

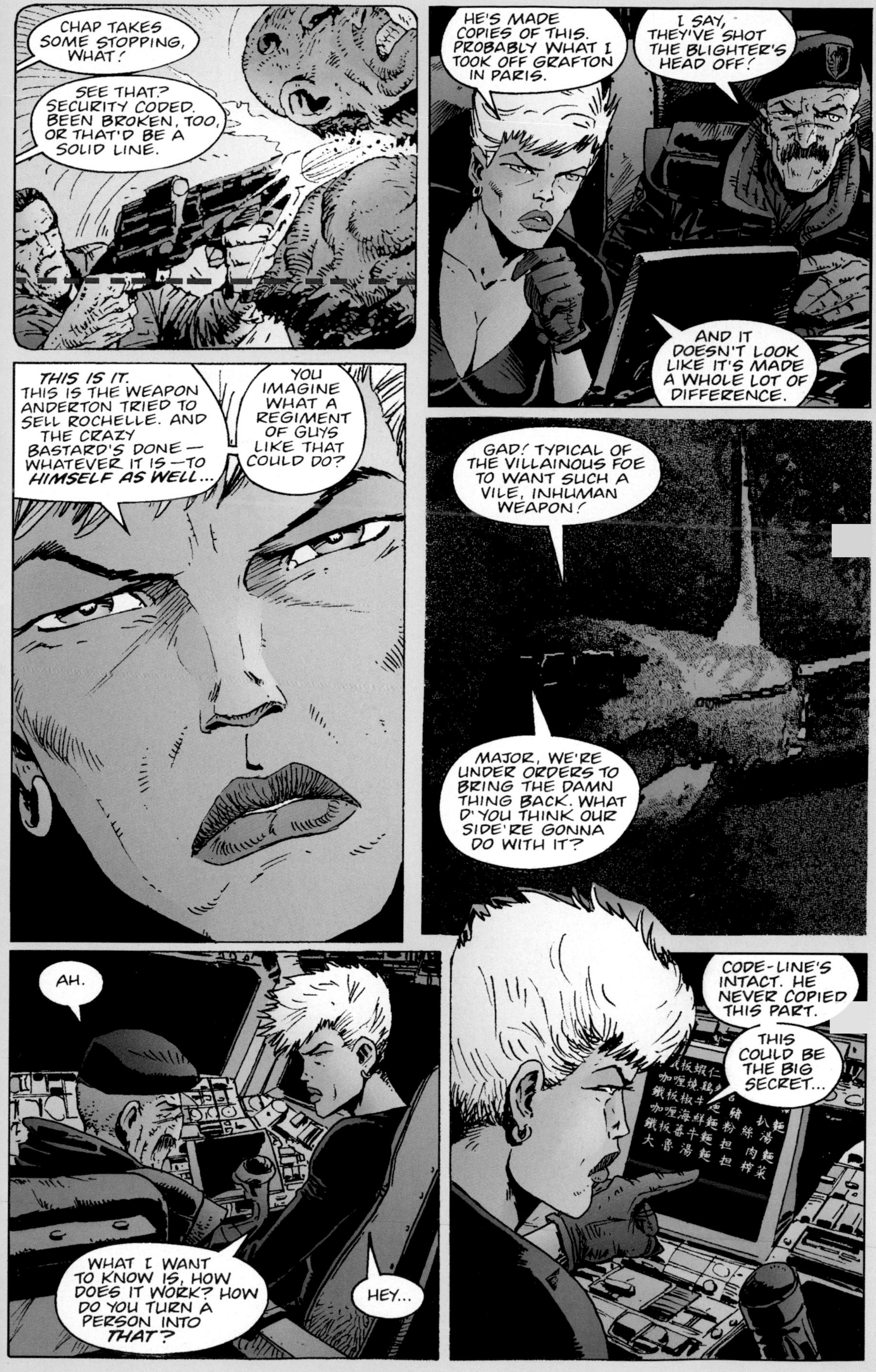
CHAP TAKES SOME STOPPING, WHAT!
SEE THAT? SECURITY CODED. BEEN BROKEN, TOO, OR THAT'D BE A SOLID LINE.
HE'S MADE COPIES OF THIS. PROBABLY WHAT I TOOK OFF GRAFTON IN PARIS.
I SAY, THEY'VE SHOT THE BLIGHTER'S HEAD OFF!
AND IT DOESN'T LOOK LIKE IT'S MADE A WHOLE LOT OF DIFFERENCE.
THIS IS IT. THIS IS THE WEAPON ANDERTON TRIED TO SELL ROCHELLE. AND THE CRAZY BASTARD'S DONE — WHATEVER IT IS — TO HIMSELF AS WELL...
YOU IMAGINE WHAT A REGIMENT OF GUYS LIKE THAT COULD DO?
GAD! TYPICAL OF THE VILLAINOUS FOE TO WANT SUCH A VILE, INHUMAN WEAPON!
MAJOR, WE'RE UNDER ORDERS TO BRING THE DAMN THING BACK. WHAT D'YOU THINK OUR SIDE'RE GONNA DO WITH IT?
AH.
WHAT I WANT TO KNOW IS, HOW DOES IT WORK? HOW DO YOU TURN A PERSON INTO THAT?
HEY...
CODE-LINE'S INTACT. HE NEVER COPIED THIS PART.
THIS COULD BE THE BIG SECRET...

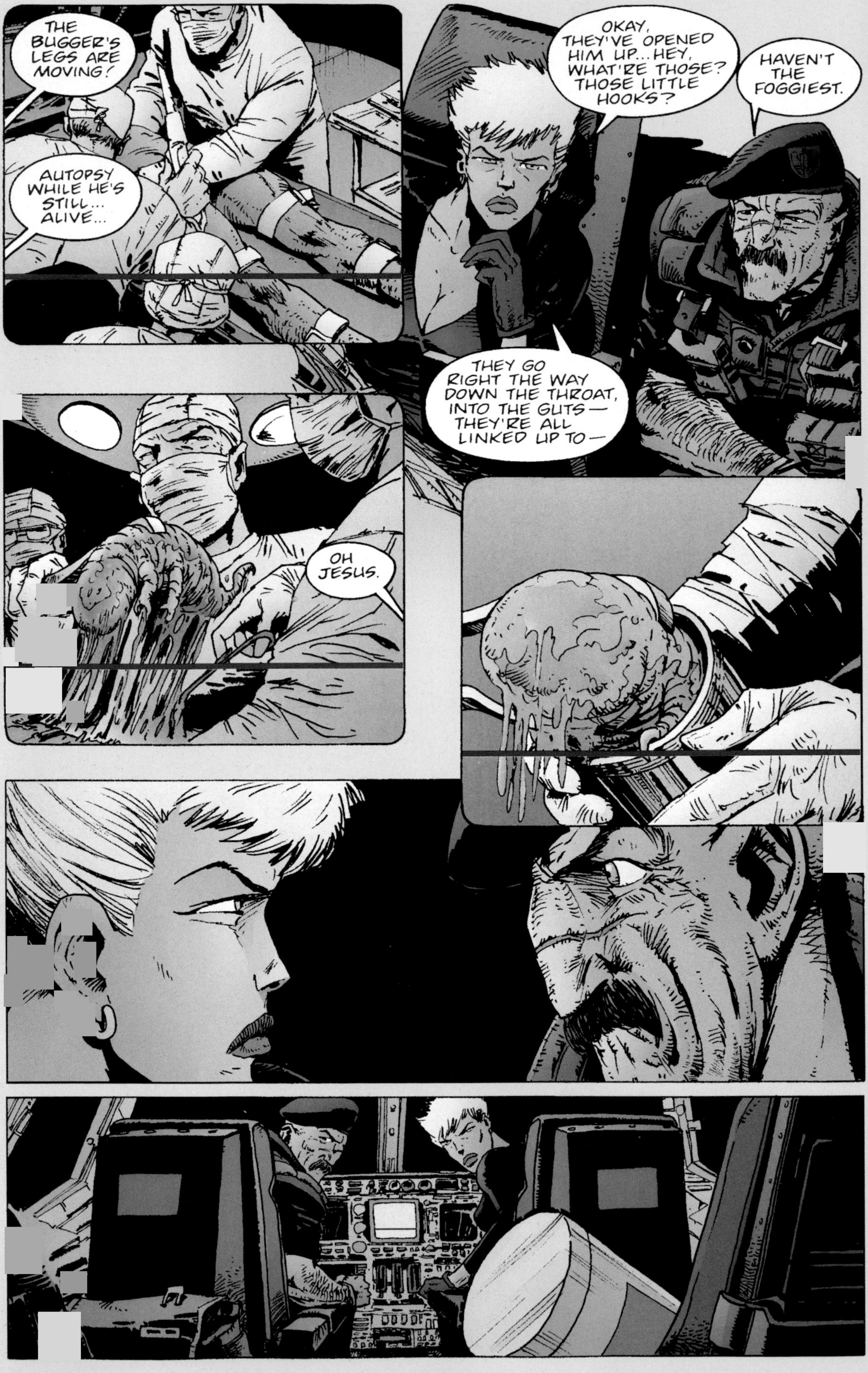
THE BUGGER'S LEGS ARE MOVING!
AUTOPSY WHILE HE'S STILL... ALIVE...
OKAY, THEY'VE OPENED HIM UP...HEY, WHAT'RE THOSE? THOSE LITTLE HOOKS?
HAVEN'T THE FOGGIEST.
THEY GO RIGHT THE WAY DOWN THE THROAT, INTO THE GUTS— THEY'RE ALL LINKED UP TO—
OH JESUS.

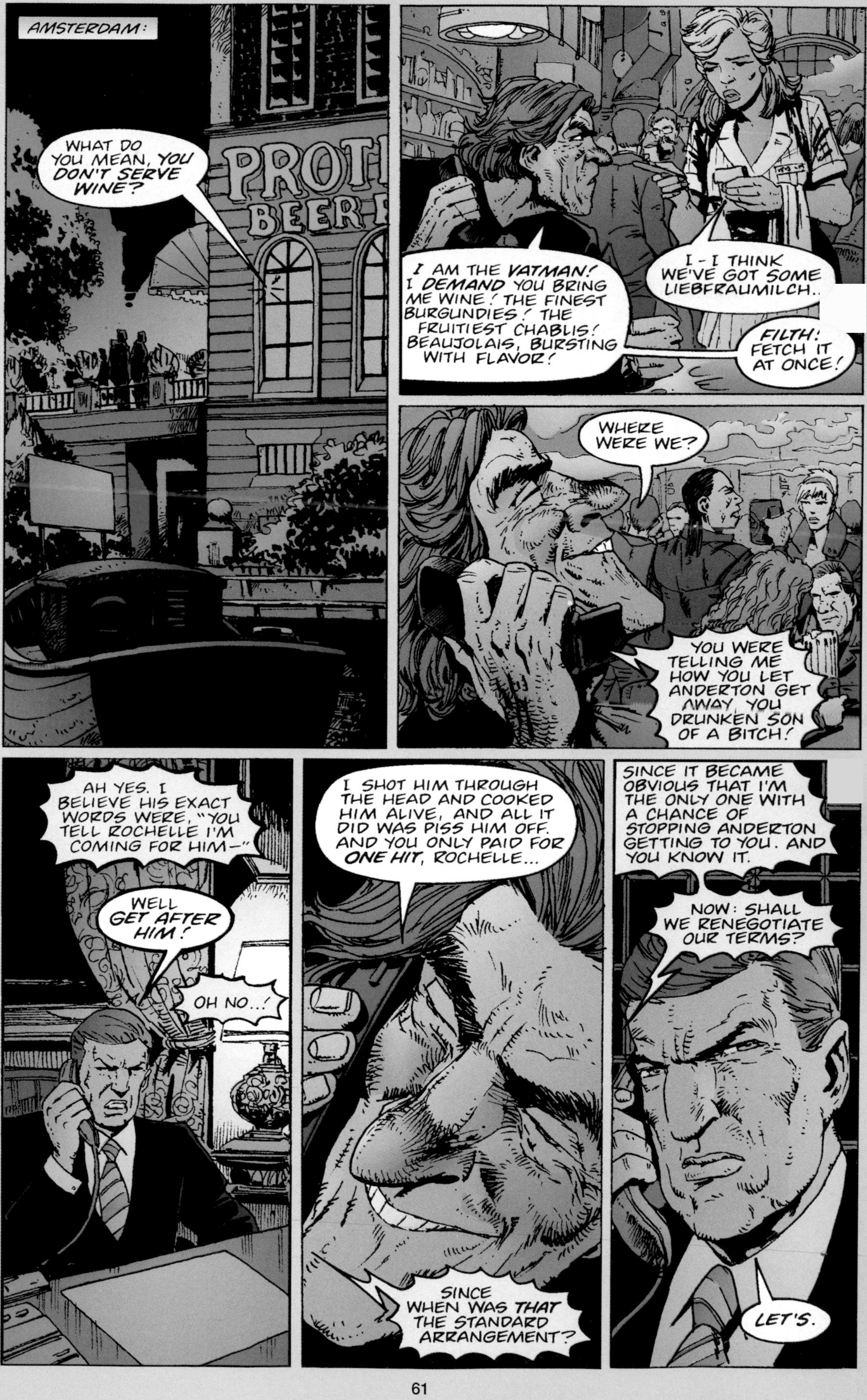
AMSTERDAM:
WHAT DO YOU MEAN, YOU DON'T SERVE WINE?
I AM THE VATMAN! I DEMAND YOU BRING ME WINE! THE FINEST BURGUNDIES! THE FRUITIEST CHABLIS! BEAUJOLAIS, BURSTING WITH FLAVOR!
I - I THINK WE'VE GOT SOME LIEBFRAUMILCH..
FILTH! FETCH IT AT ONCE!
WHERE WERE WE?
YOU WERE TELLING ME HOW YOU LET ANDERTON GET AWAY, YOU DRUNKEN SON OF A BITCH!
AH YES. I BELIEVE HIS EXACT WORDS WERE, "YOU TELL ROCHELLE I'M COMING FOR HIM—"
WELL GET AFTER HIM!
"YOU
OH NO...!
I SHOT HIM THROUGH THE HEAD AND COOKED HIM ALIVE, AND ALL IT DID WAS PISS HIM OFF. AND YOU ONLY PAID FOR ONE HIT, ROCHELLE...
SINCE WHEN WAS THAT THE STANDARD ARRANGEMENT?
SINCE IT BECAME OBVIOUS THAT I'M THE ONLY ONE WITH A CHANCE OF STOPPING ANDERTON GETTING TO YOU. AND YOU KNOW IT.
NOW: SHALL WE RENEGOTIATE OUR TERMS?
LET'S.

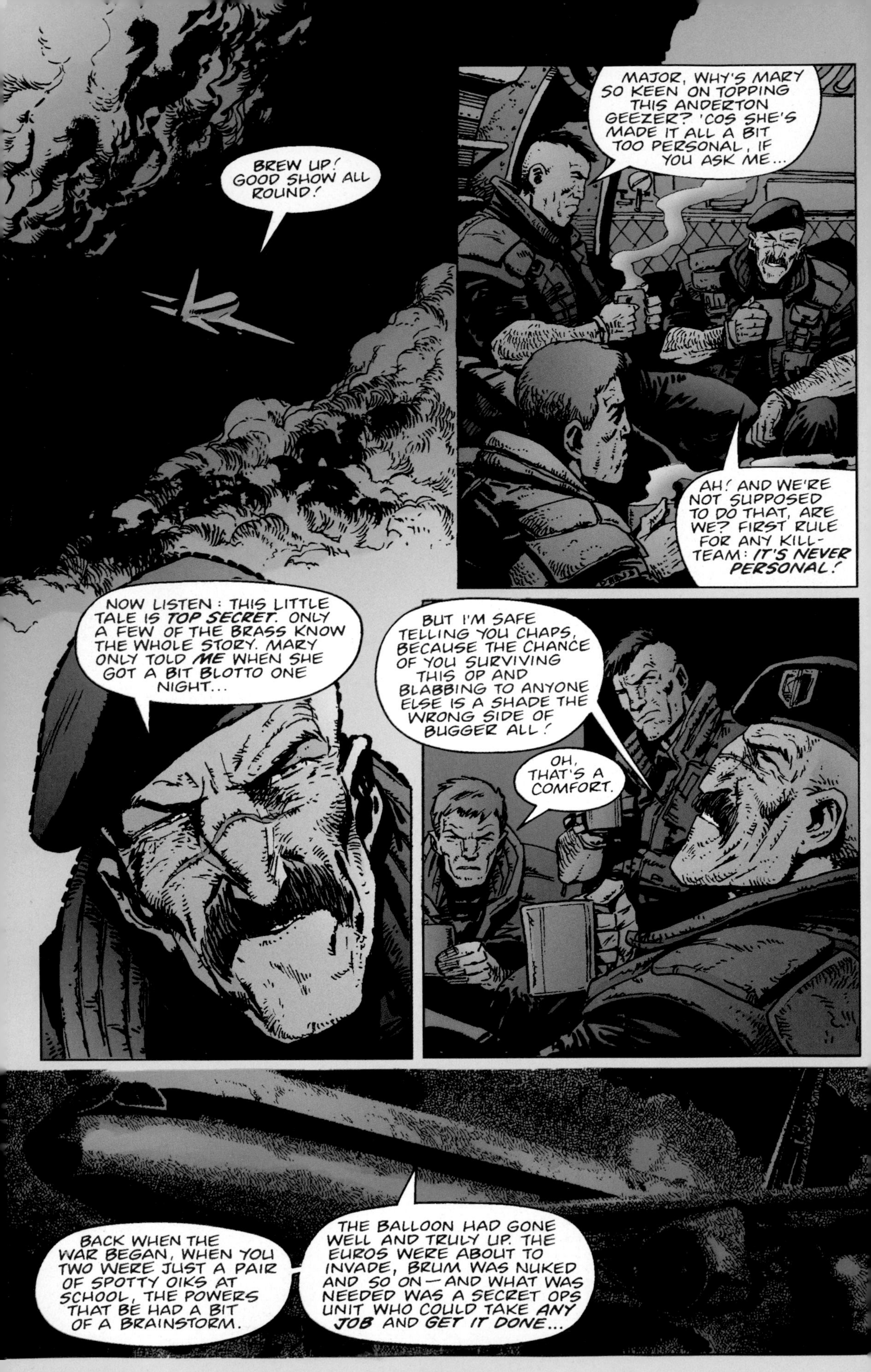
BREW UP! GOOD SHOW ALL ROUND!
MAJOR, WHY'S MARY SO KEEN ON TOPPING THIS ANDERTON GEEZER? 'COS SHE'S MADE IT ALL A BIT TOO PERSONAL, IF YOU ASK ME...
AH! AND WE'RE NOT SUPPOSED TO DO THAT, ARE WE? FIRST RULE FOR ANY KILL-TEAM: IT'S NEVER PERSONAL!
NOW LISTEN: THIS LITTLE TALE IS TOP SECRET. ONLY A FEW OF THE BRASS KNOW THE WHOLE STORY. MARY ONLY TOLD ME WHEN SHE GOT A BIT BLOTTO ONE NIGHT...
BUT I'M SAFE TELLING YOU CHAPS, BECAUSE THE CHANCE OF YOU SURVIVING THIS OP AND BLABBING TO ANYONE ELSE IS A SHADE THE WRONG SIDE OF BUGGER ALL!
OH, THAT'S A COMFORT.
BACK WHEN THE WAR BEGAN, WHEN YOU TWO WERE JUST A PAIR OF SPOTTY OIKS AT SCHOOL, THE POWERS THAT BE HAD A BIT OF A BRAINSTORM.
THE BALLOON HAD GONE WELL AND TRULY UP. THE EUROS WERE ABOUT TO INVADE, BRUM WAS NUKED AND SO ON—AND WHAT WAS NEEDED WAS A SECRET OPS UNIT WHO COULD TAKE ANY JOB AND GET IT DONE...

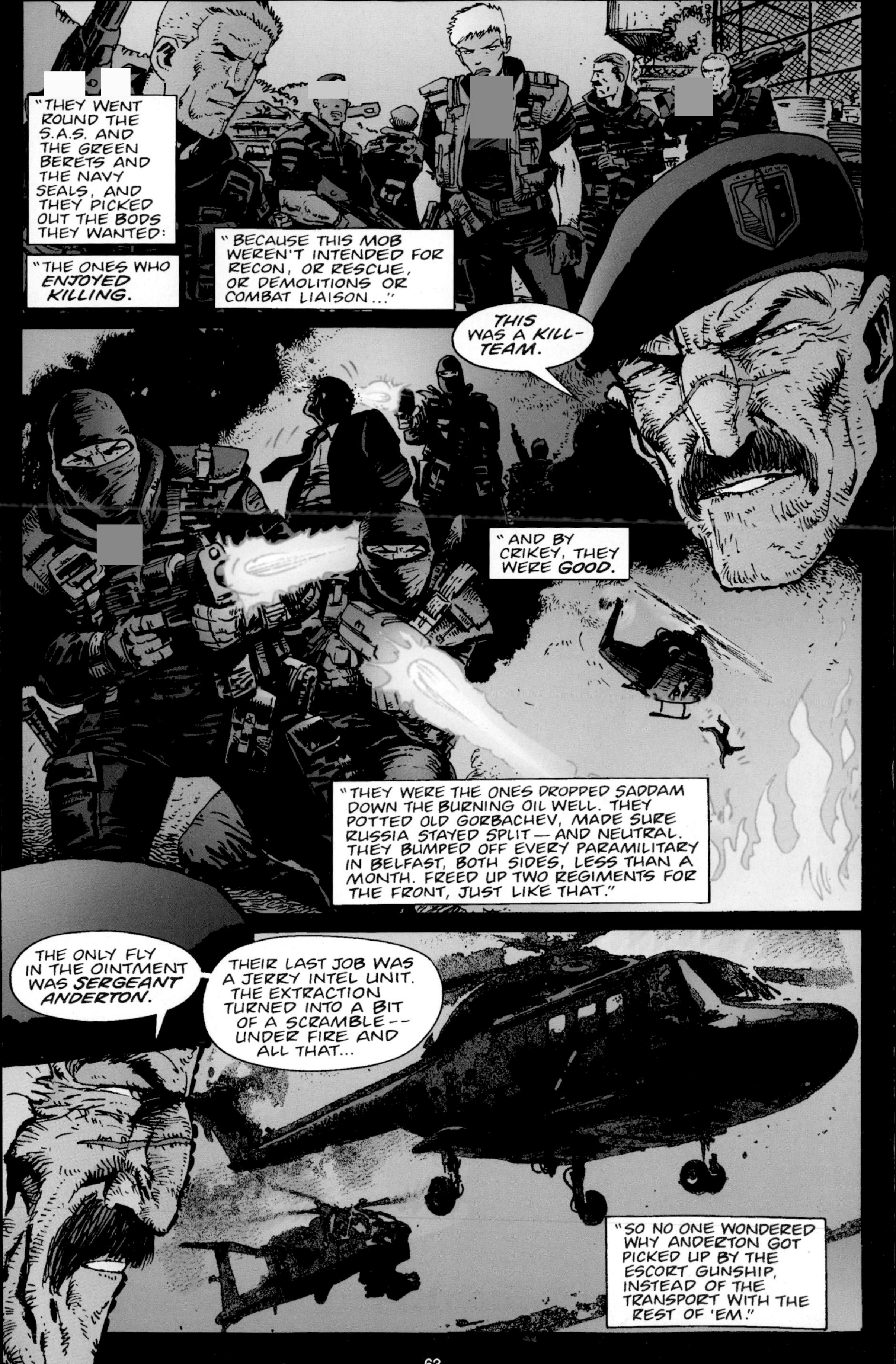
"THEY WENT ROUND THE S.A.S. AND THE GREEN BERETS AND THE NAVY SEALS, AND THEY PICKED OUT THE BODS THEY WANTED:
"THE ONES WHO ENJOYED KILLING.
"BECAUSE THIS MOB WEREN'T INTENDED FOR RECON, OR RESCUE, OR DEMOLITIONS OR COMBAT LIAISON..."
THIS WAS A KILL-TEAM.
"AND BY CRIKEY, THEY WERE GOOD.
"THEY WERE THE ONES DROPPED SADDAM DOWN THE BURNING OIL WELL. THEY POTTED OLD GORBACHEV, MADE SURE RUSSIA STAYED SPLIT—AND NEUTRAL. THEY BUMPED OFF EVERY PARAMILITARY IN BELFAST, BOTH SIDES, LESS THAN A MONTH. FREED UP TWO REGIMENTS FOR THE FRONT, JUST LIKE THAT."
THE ONLY FLY IN THE OINTMENT WAS SERGEANT ANDERTON.
THEIR LAST JOB WAS A JERRY INTEL UNIT. THE EXTRACTION TURNED INTO A BIT OF A SCRAMBLE-- UNDER FIRE AND ALL THAT...
"SO NO ONE WONDERED WHY ANDERTON GOT PICKED UP BY THE ESCORT GUNSHIP, INSTEAD OF THE TRANSPORT WITH THE REST OF 'EM."

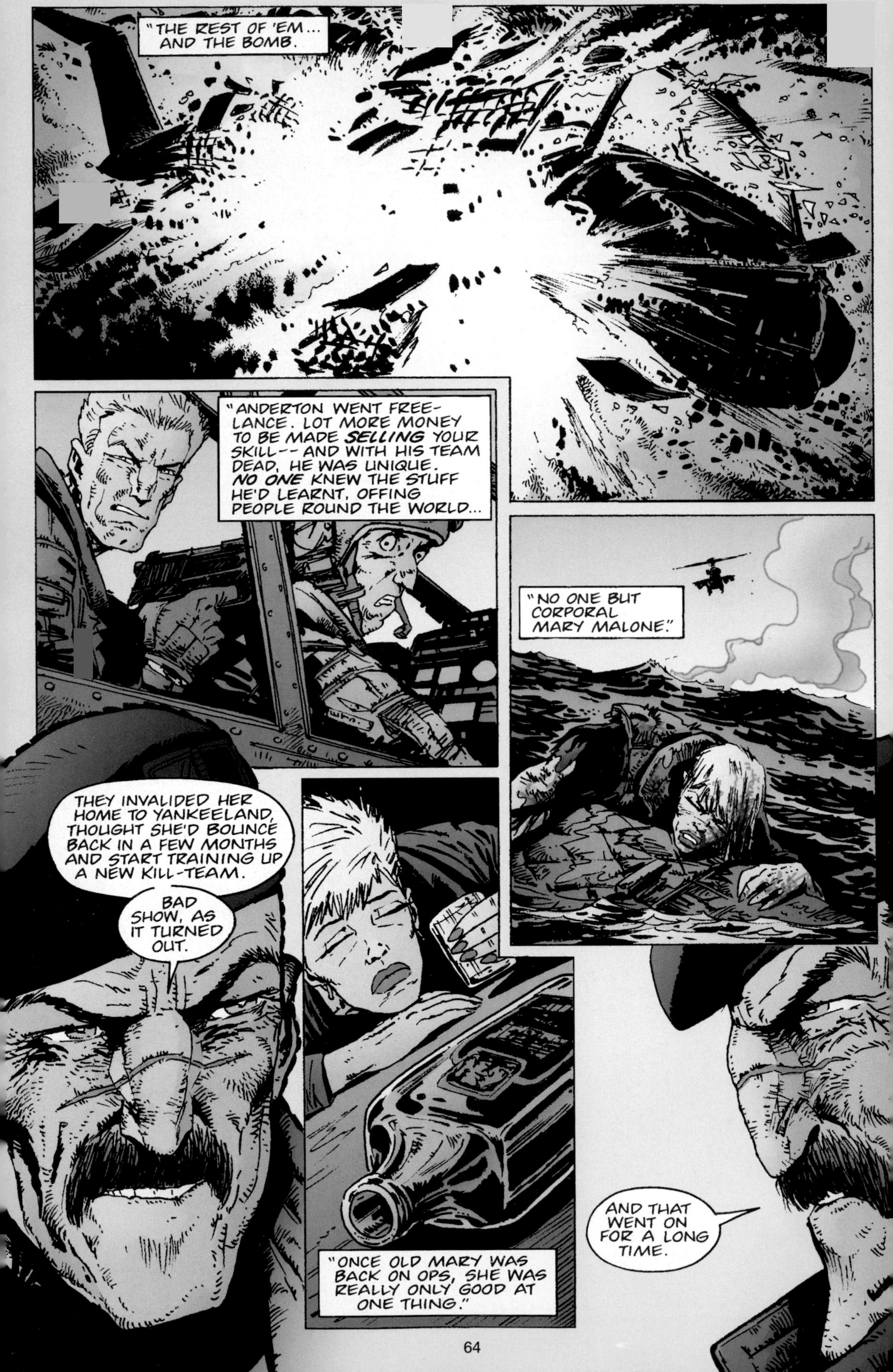

"THE REST OF 'EM... AND THE BOMB.
"ANDERTON WENT FREE-LANCE. LOT MORE MONEY TO BE MADE SELLING YOUR SKILL-- AND WITH HIS TEAM DEAD, HE WAS UNIQUE. NO ONE KNEW THE STUFF HE'D LEARNT, OFFING PEOPLE ROUND THE WORLD...
"NO ONE BUT CORPORAL MARY MALONE."
THEY INVALIDED HER HOME TO YANKEELAND, THOUGHT SHE'D BOUNCE BACK IN A FEW MONTHS AND START TRAINING UP A NEW KILL-TEAM.
BAD SHOW, AS IT TURNED OUT.
"ONCE OLD MARY WAS BACK ON OPS, SHE WAS REALLY ONLY GOOD AT ONE THING."
AND THAT WENT ON FOR A LONG TIME.

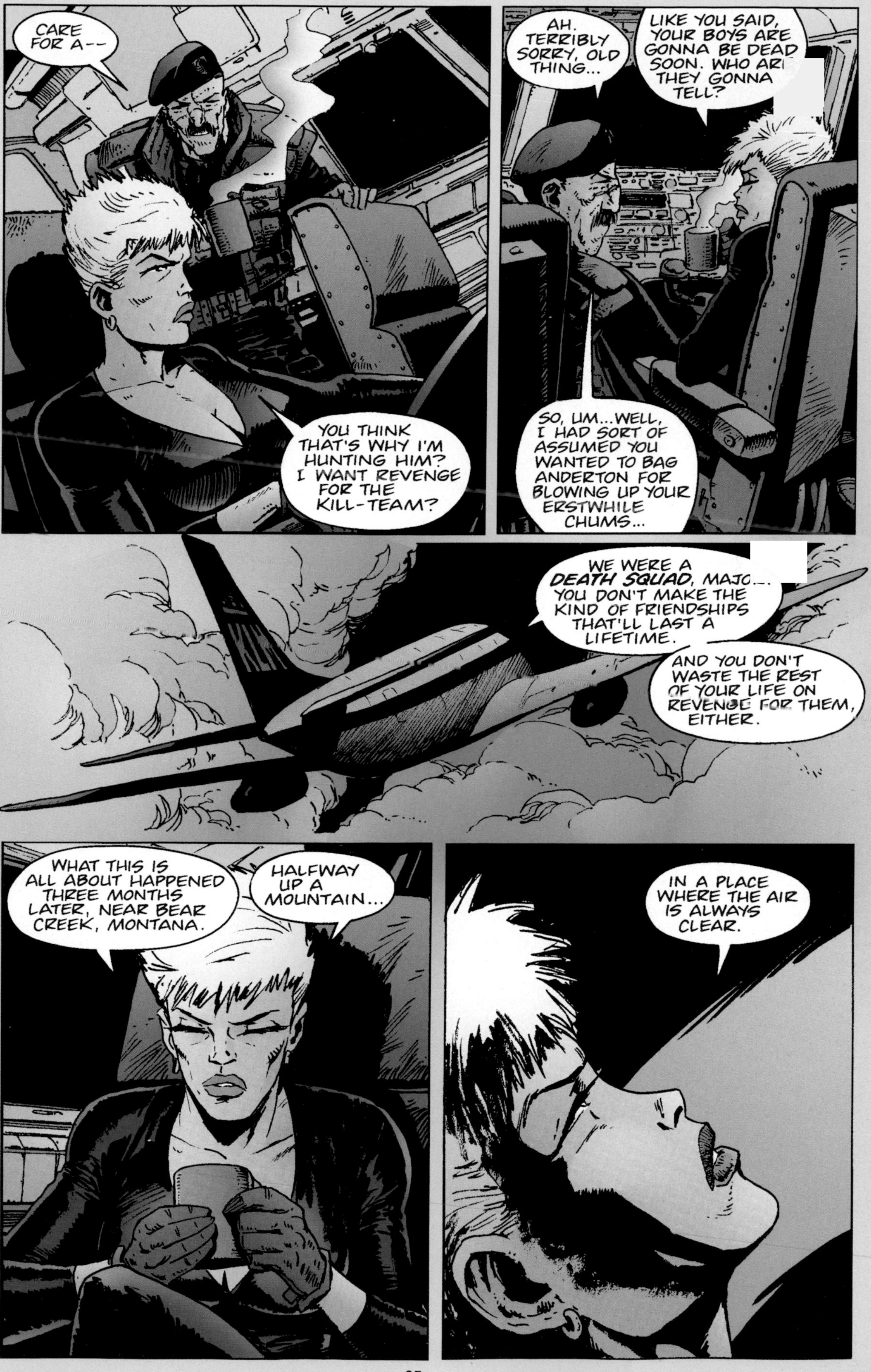
CARE FOR A--
AH. TERRIBLY SORRY, OLD THING...
LIKE YOU SAID, YOUR BOYS ARE GONNA BE DEAD SOON. WHO AR
THEY GONNA TELL?
SO, UM...WELL, I HAD SORT OF ASSUMED YOU WANTED TO BAG ANDERTON FOR BLOWING UP YOUR ERSTWHILE CHUMS...
YOU THINK THAT'S WHY I'M HUNTING HIM? I WANT REVENGE FOR THE KILL-TEAM?
WE WERE A DEATH SQUAD, MAJO
YOU DON'T MAKE THE KIND OF FRIENDSHIPS THAT'LL LAST A LIFETIME.
AND YOU DON'T WASTE THE REST OF YOUR LIFE ON REVENGE FOR THEM, EITHER.
WHAT THIS IS ALL ABOUT HAPPENED THREE MONTHS LATER, NEAR BEAR CREEK, MONTANA.
HALFWAY UP A MOUNTAIN...
IN A PLACE WHERE THE AIR IS ALWAYS CLEAR.

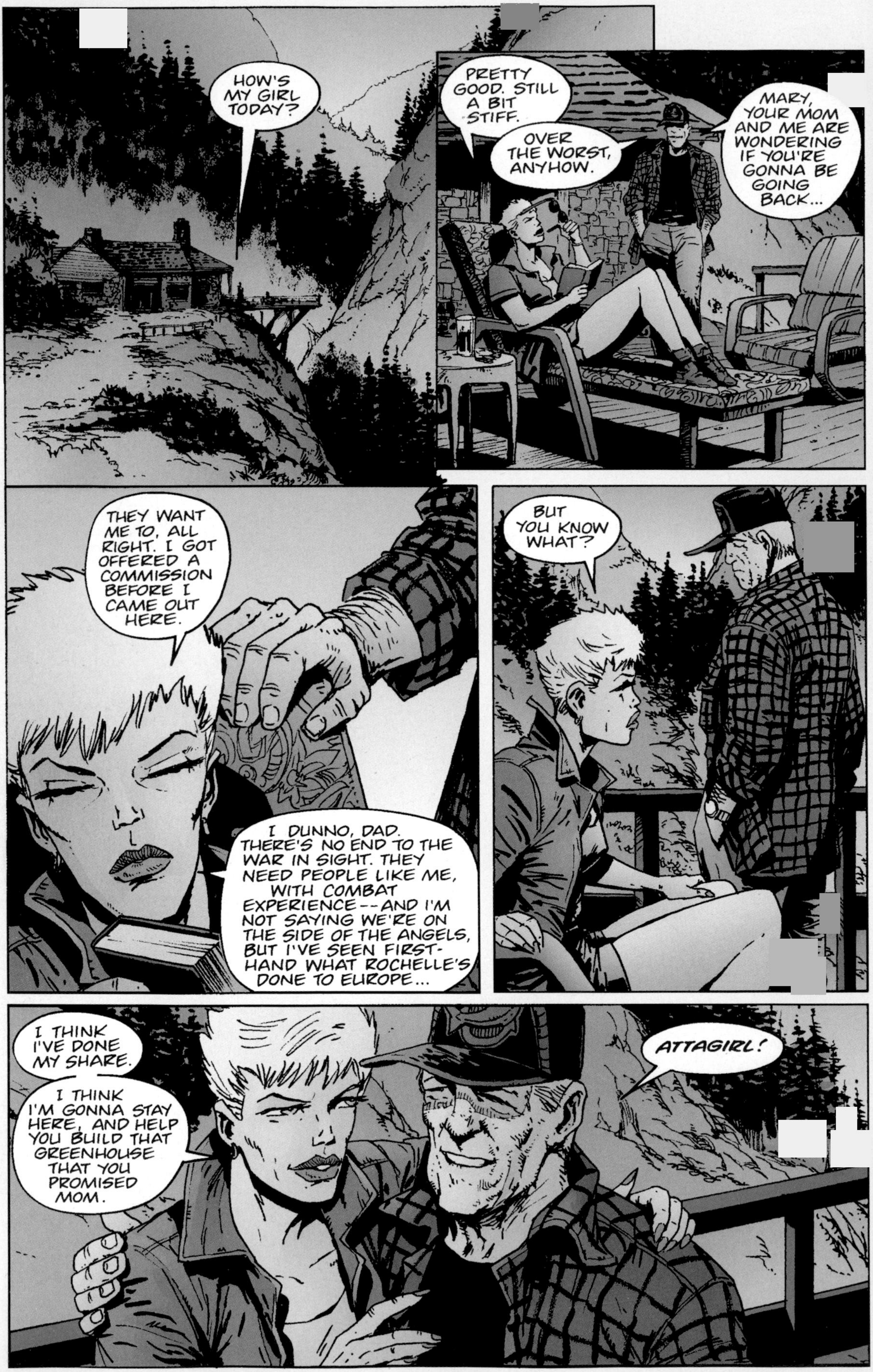
HOW'S MY GIRL TODAY?
PRETTY GOOD. STILL A BIT STIFF.
OVER THE WORST, ANYHOW.
MARY, YOUR MOM AND ME ARE WONDERING IF YOU'RE GONNA BE GOING BACK...
THEY WANT ME TO, ALL RIGHT. I GOT OFFERED A COMMISSION BEFORE I CAME OUT HERE.
I DUNNO, DAD. THERE'S NO END TO THE WAR IN SIGHT. THEY NEED PEOPLE LIKE ME, WITH COMBAT EXPERIENCE--AND I'M NOT SAYING WE'RE ON THE SIDE OF THE ANGELS, BUT I'VE SEEN FIRST-HAND WHAT ROCHELLE'S DONE TO EUROPE...
BUT YOU KNOW WHAT?
I THINK I'VE DONE MY SHARE.
I THINK I'M GONNA STAY HERE, AND HELP YOU BUILD THAT GREENHOUSE THAT YOU PROMISED MOM.
ATTAGIRL!

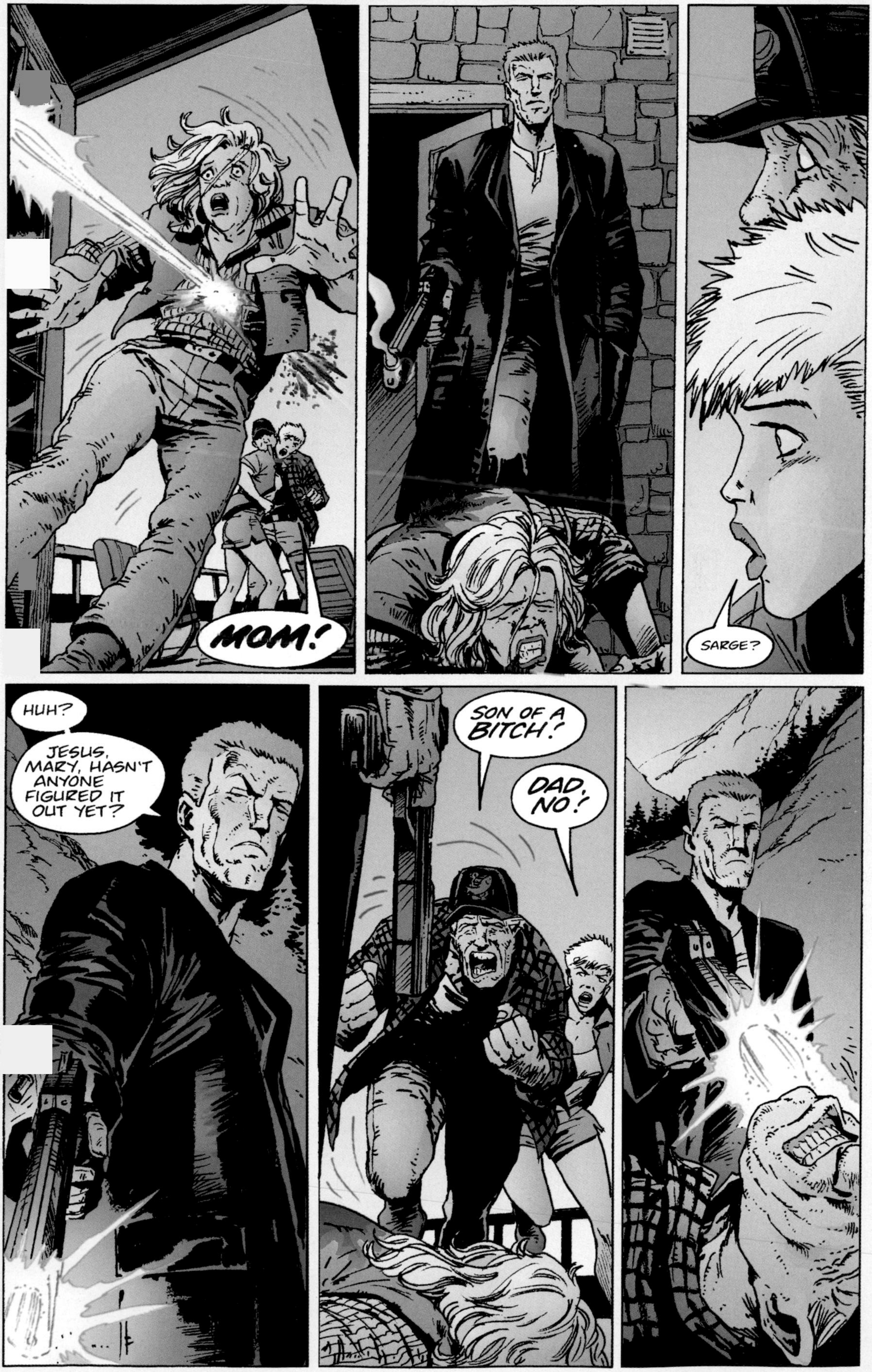
MOM!
SARGE?
HUH?
JESUS, MARY, HASN'T ANYONE FIGURED IT OUT YET?
SON OF A BITCH!
DAD, NO!

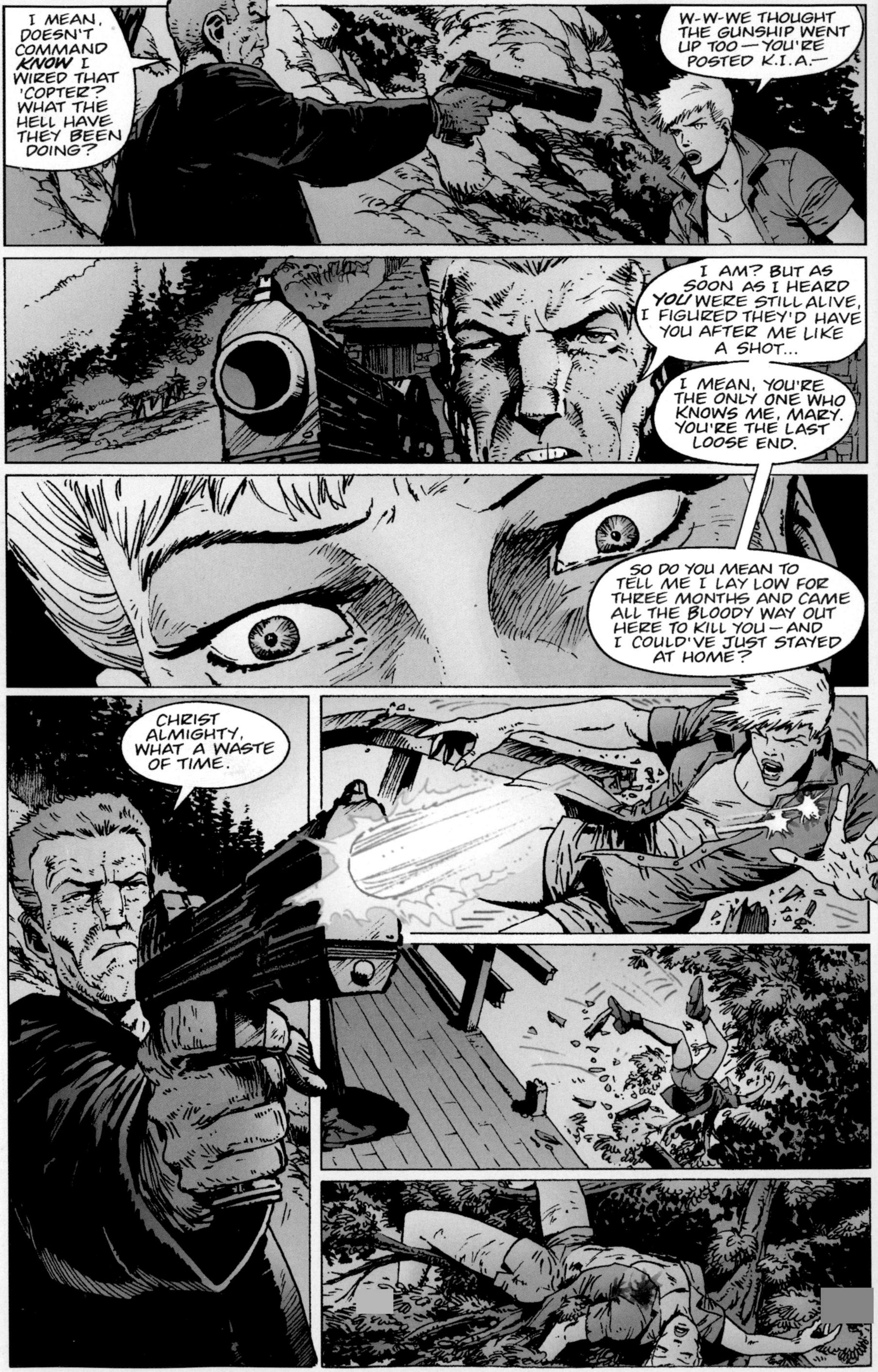
I MEAN, DOESN'T COMMAND KNOW I WIRED THAT 'COPTER? WHAT THE HELL HAVE THEY BEEN DOING?
W-W-WE THOUGHT THE GUNSHIP WENT UP TOO — YOU'RE POSTED K.I.A.—
I AM? BUT AS SOON AS I HEARD YOU WERE STILL ALIVE, I FIGURED THEY'D HAVE YOU AFTER ME LIKE A SHOT...
I MEAN, YOU'RE THE ONLY ONE WHO KNOWS ME, MARY. YOU'RE THE LAST LOOSE END.
SO DO YOU MEAN TO TELL ME I LAY LOW FOR THREE MONTHS AND CAME ALL THE BLOODY WAY OUT HERE TO KILL YOU — AND I COULD'VE JUST STAYED AT HOME?
CHRIST ALMIGHTY, WHAT A WASTE OF TIME.

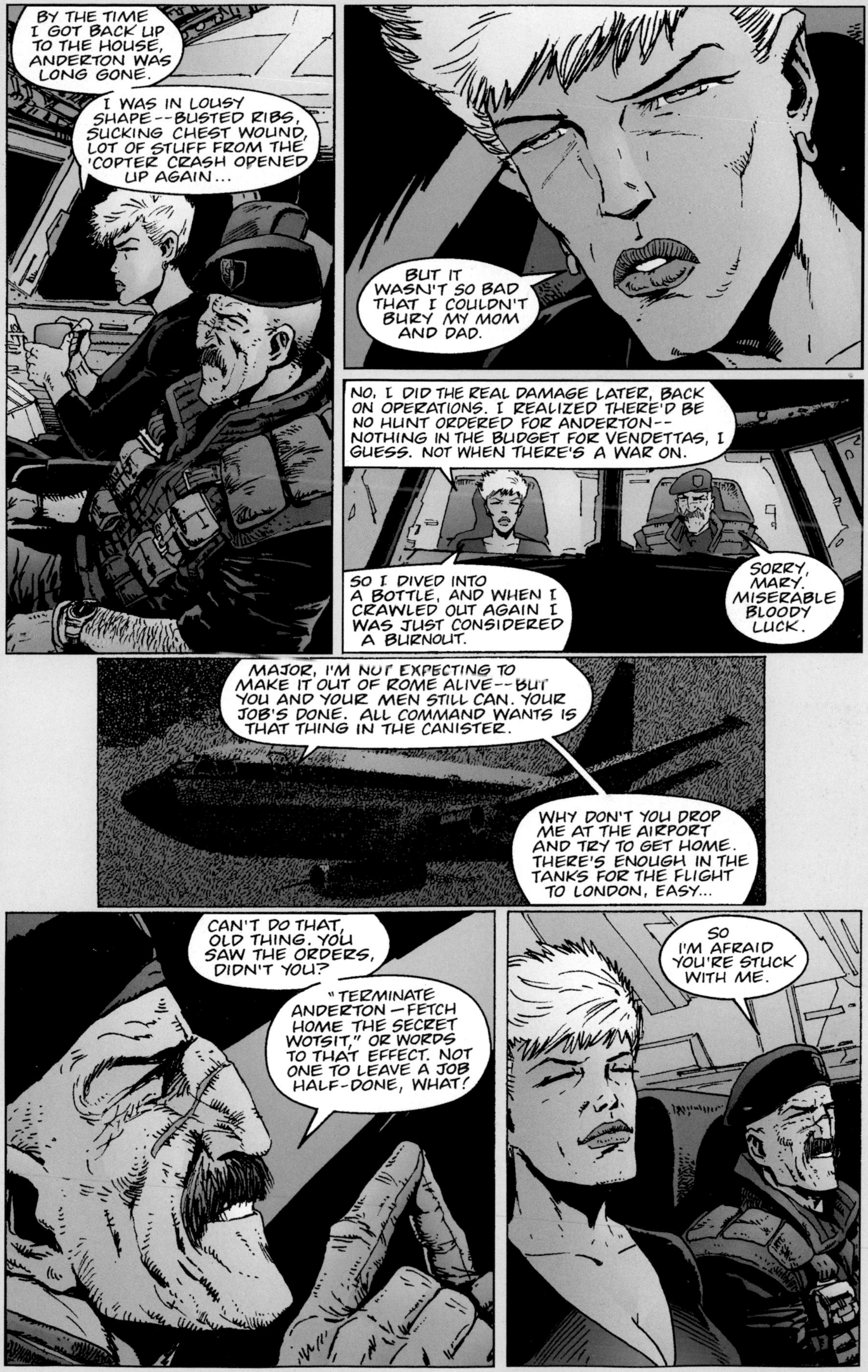
BY THE TIME I GOT BACK UP TO THE HOUSE, ANDERTON WAS LONG GONE.
I WAS IN LOUSY SHAPE--BUSTED RIBS, SUCKING CHEST WOUND, LOT OF STUFF FROM THE 'COPTER CRASH OPENED UP AGAIN...
BUT IT WASN'T SO BAD THAT I COULDN'T BURY MY MOM AND DAD.
NO, I DID THE REAL DAMAGE LATER, BACK ON OPERATIONS. I REALIZED THERE'D BE NO HUNT ORDERED FOR ANDERTON--NOTHING IN THE BUDGET FOR VENDETTAS, I GUESS. NOT WHEN THERE'S A WAR ON.
SO I DIVED INTO A BOTTLE, AND WHEN I CRAWLED OUT AGAIN I WAS JUST CONSIDERED A BURNOUT.
SORRY, MARY. MISERABLE BLOODY LUCK.
MAJOR, I'M NOT EXPECTING TO MAKE IT OUT OF ROME ALIVE--BUT YOU AND YOUR MEN STILL CAN. YOUR JOB'S DONE. ALL COMMAND WANTS IS THAT THING IN THE CANISTER.
WHY DON'T YOU DROP ME AT THE AIRPORT AND TRY TO GET HOME. THERE'S ENOUGH IN THE TANKS FOR THE FLIGHT TO LONDON, EASY...
CAN'T DO THAT, OLD THING. YOU SAW THE ORDERS, DIDN'T YOU?
"TERMINATE ANDERTON—FETCH HOME THE SECRET WOTSIT," OR WORDS TO THAT EFFECT. NOT ONE TO LEAVE A JOB HALF-DONE, WHAT!
SO I'M AFRAID YOU'RE STUCK WITH ME.

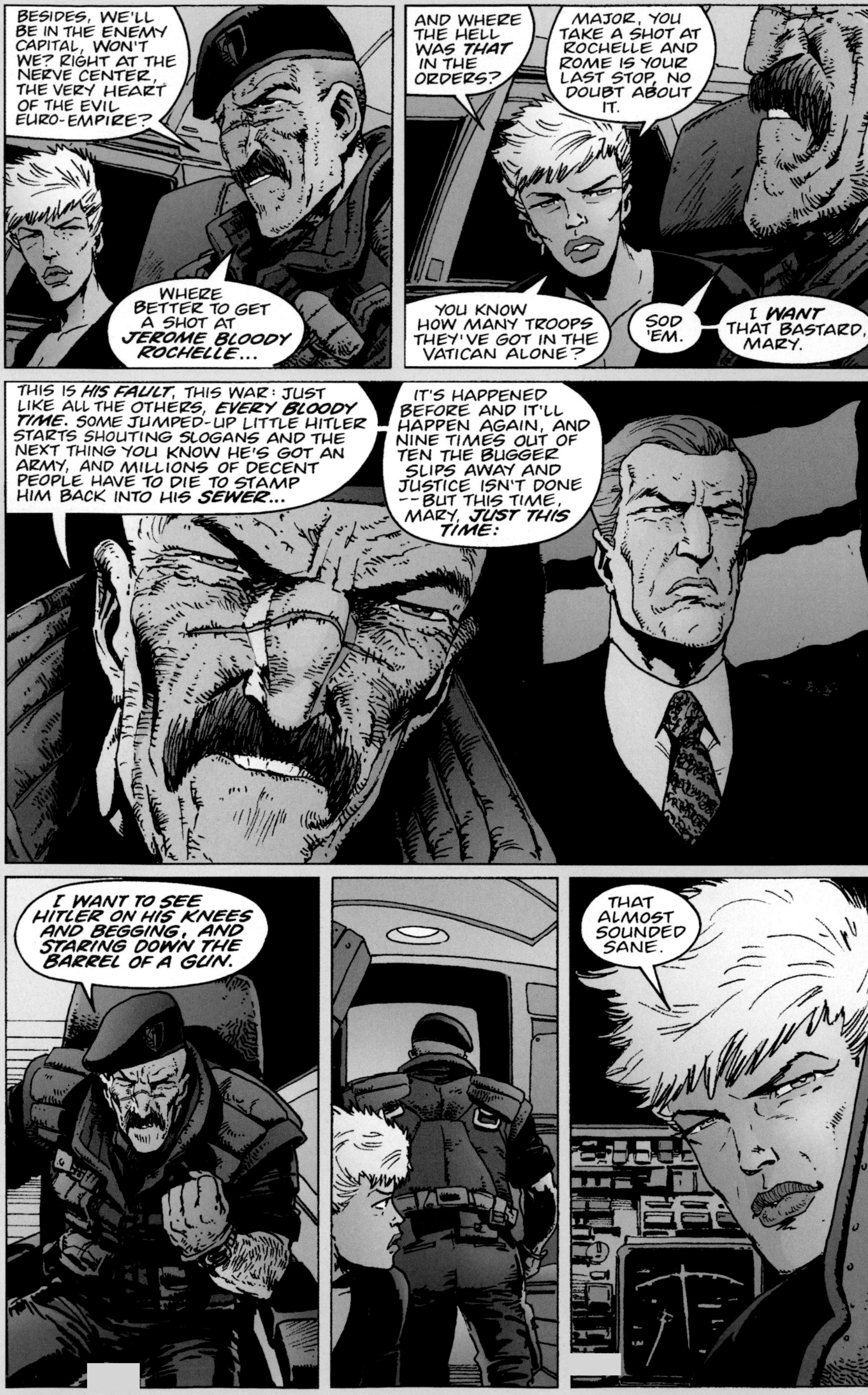
BESIDES, WE'LL BE IN THE ENEMY CAPITAL, WON'T WE? RIGHT AT THE NERVE CENTER, THE VERY HEART OF THE EVIL EURO-EMPIRE?
WHERE BETTER TO GET A SHOT AT JEROME BLOODY ROCHELLE...
AND WHERE THE HELL WAS THAT IN THE ORDERS?
MAJOR, YOU TAKE A SHOT AT ROCHELLE AND ROME IS YOUR LAST STOP, NO DOUBT ABOUT IT.
YOU KNOW HOW MANY TROOPS THEY'VE GOT IN THE VATICAN ALONE?
SOD 'EM.
I WANT THAT BASTARD, MARY.
THIS IS HIS FAULT, THIS WAR: JUST LIKE ALL THE OTHERS, EVERY BLOODY TIME. SOME JUMPED-UP LITTLE HITLER STARTS SHOUTING SLOGANS AND THE NEXT THING YOU KNOW HE'S GOT AN ARMY, AND MILLIONS OF DECENT PEOPLE HAVE TO DIE TO STAMP HIM BACK INTO HIS SEWER...
IT'S HAPPENED BEFORE AND IT'LL HAPPEN AGAIN, AND NINE TIMES OUT OF TEN THE BUGGER SLIPS AWAY AND JUSTICE ISN'T DONE --BUT THIS TIME, MARY, JUST THIS TIME:
I WANT TO SEE HITLER ON HIS KNEES AND BEGGING, AND STARING DOWN THE BARREL OF A GUN.
THAT ALMOST SOUNDED SANE.

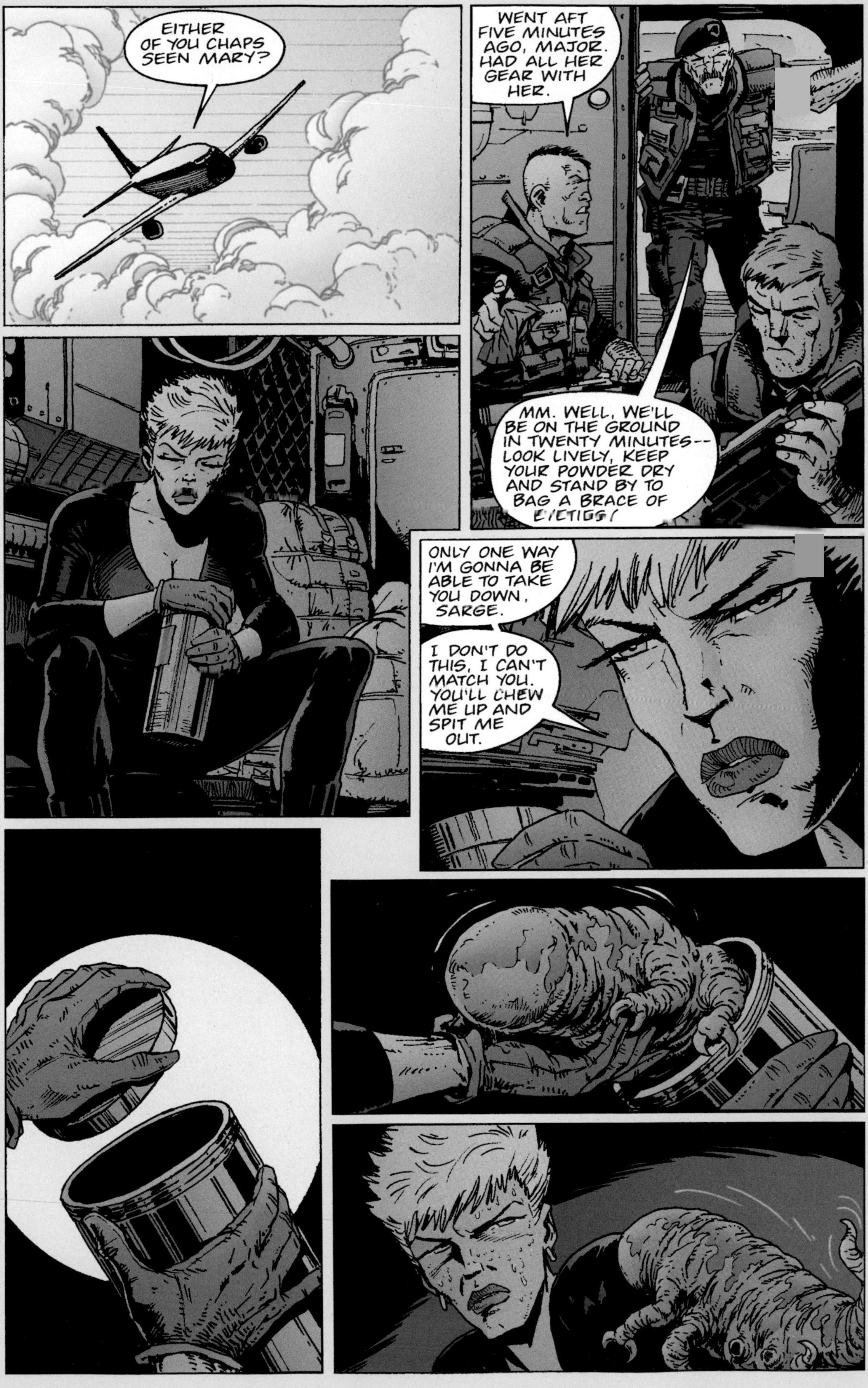
EITHER OF YOU CHAPS SEEN MARY?
WENT AFT FIVE MINUTES AGO, MAJOR. HAD ALL HER GEAR WITH HER.
MM. WELL, WE'LL BE ON THE GROUND IN TWENTY MINUTES-- LOOK LIVELY, KEEP YOUR POWDER DRY AND STAND BY TO BAG A BRACE OF
ONLY ONE WAY I'M GONNA BE ABLE TO TAKE YOU DOWN, SARGE.
I DON'T DO THIS, I CAN'T MATCH YOU. YOU'LL CHEW ME UP AND SPIT ME OUT.

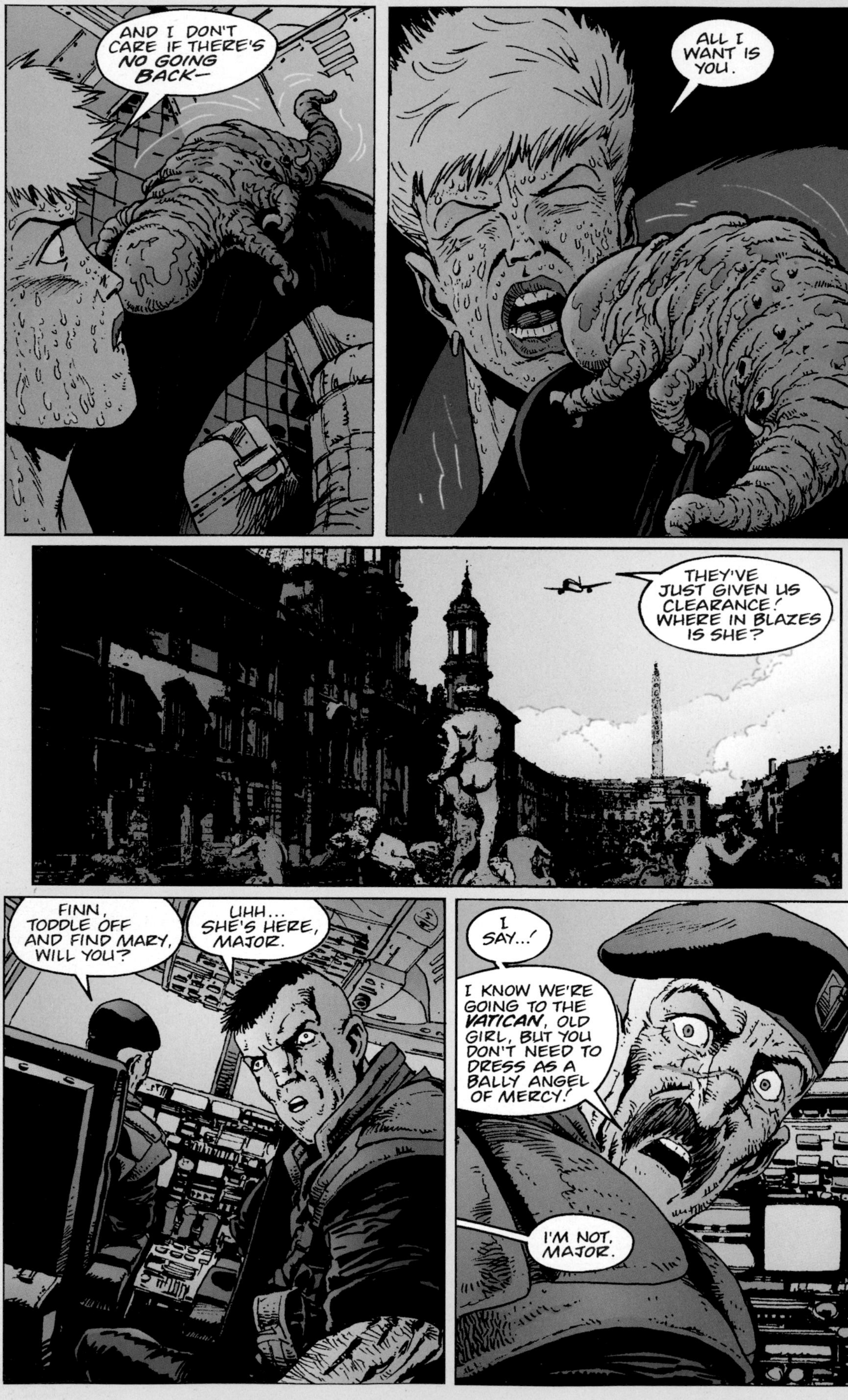
AND I DON'T CARE IF THERE'S NO GOING BACK—
ALL I WANT IS YOU.
THEY'VE JUST GIVEN US CLEARANCE! WHERE IN BLAZES IS SHE?
FINN, TODDLE OFF AND FIND MARY, WILL YOU?
UHH... SHE'S HERE, MAJOR.
I SAY...!
I KNOW WE'RE GOING TO THE VATICAN, OLD GIRL, BUT YOU DON'T NEED TO DRESS AS A BALLY ANGEL OF MERCY!
I'M NOT, MAJOR.

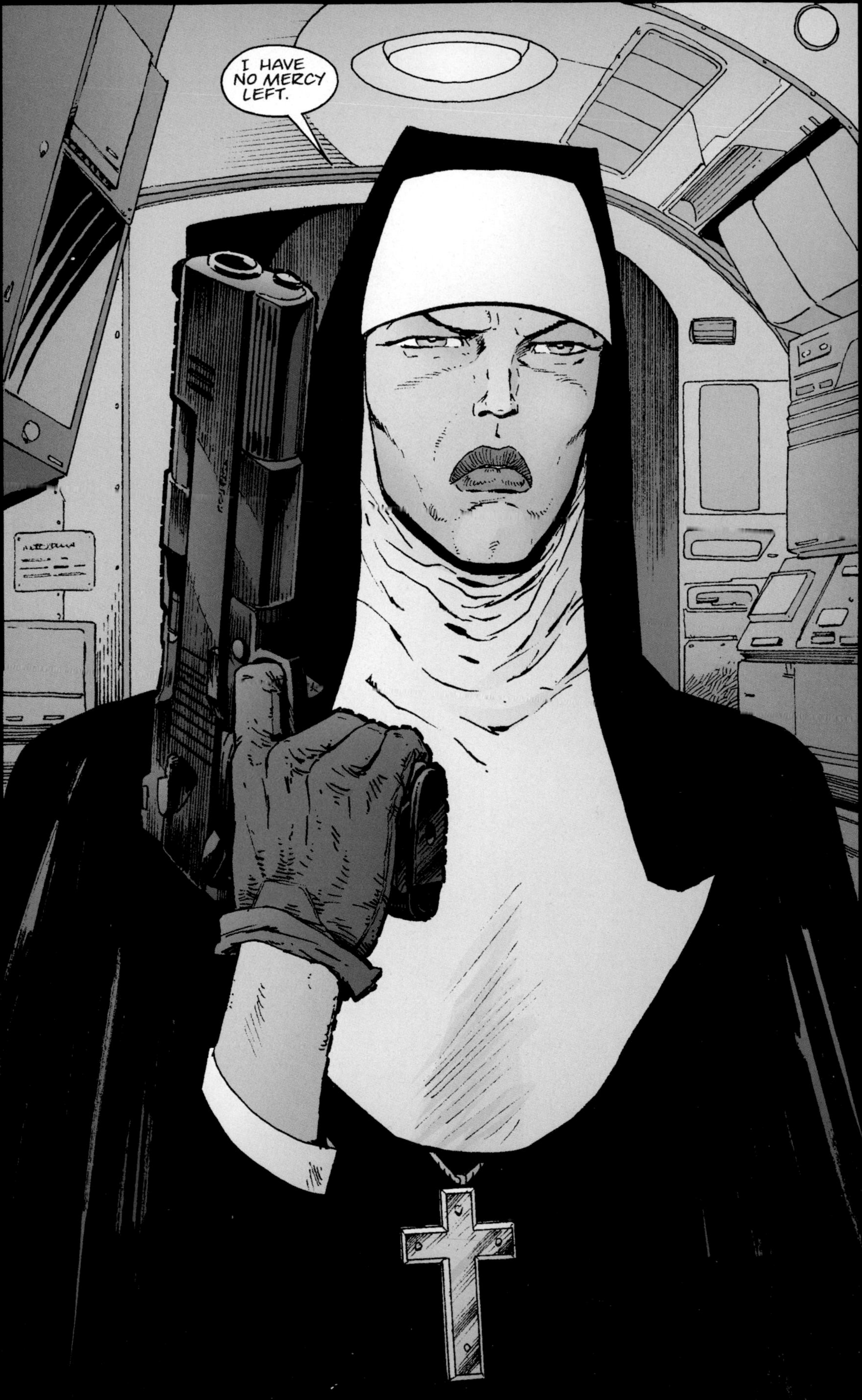
I HAVE NO MERCY LEFT.

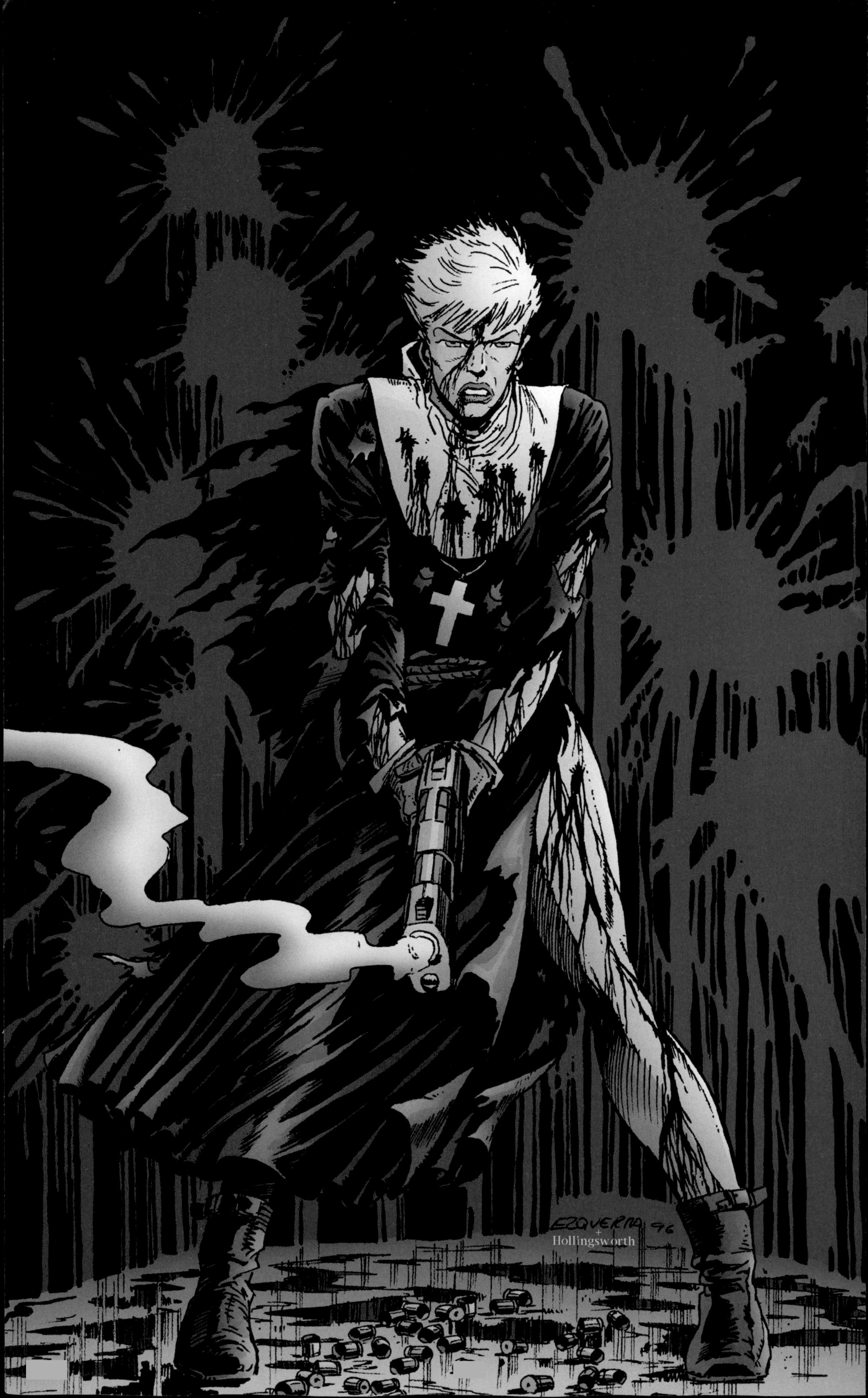
EZQUERRA '96
+
Hollingsworth

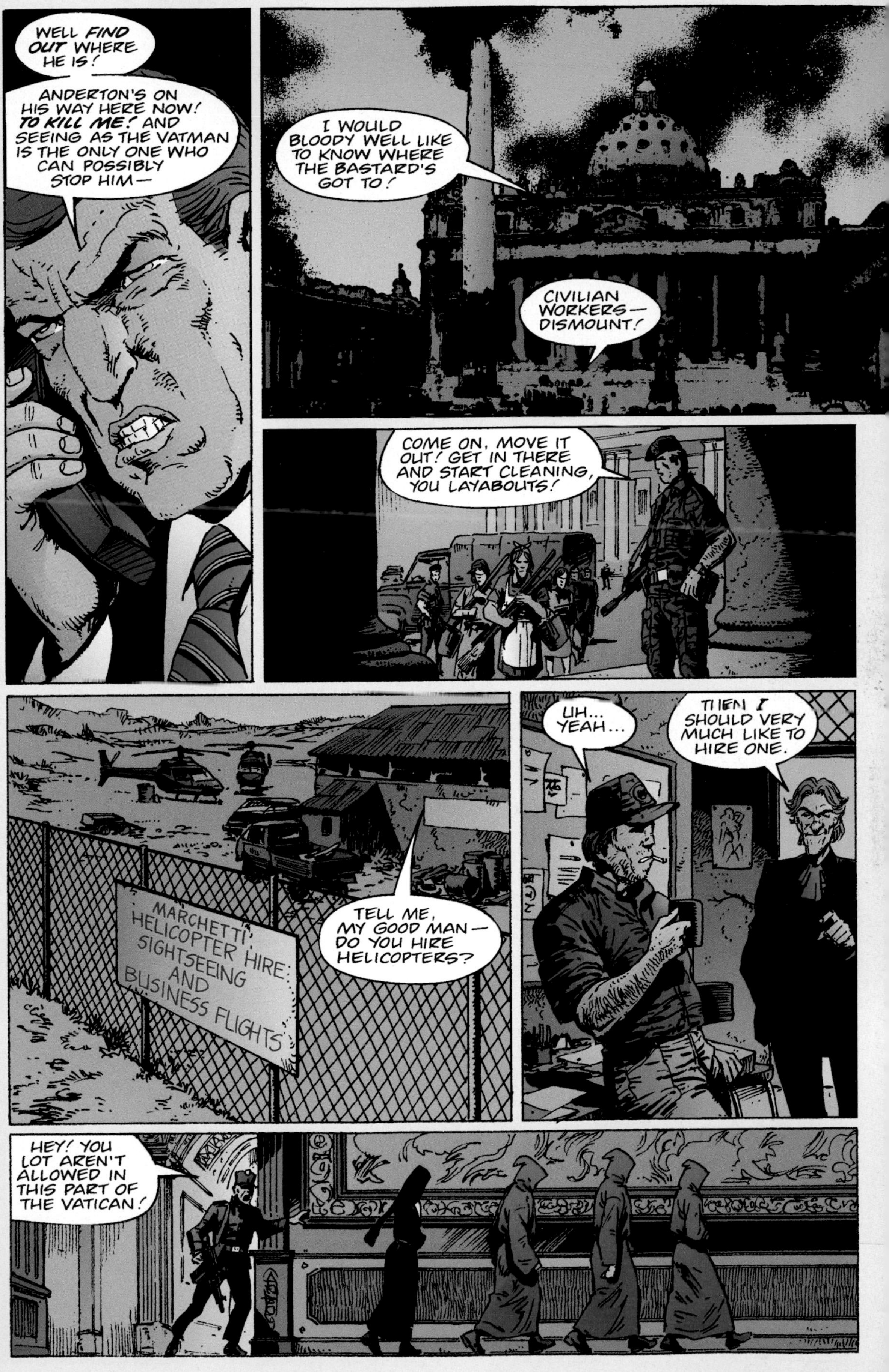
WELL FIND OUT WHERE HE IS!
ANDERTON'S ON HIS WAY HERE NOW! TO KILL ME! AND SEEING AS THE VATMAN IS THE ONLY ONE WHO CAN POSSIBLY STOP HIM—
I WOULD BLOODY WELL LIKE TO KNOW WHERE THE BASTARD'S GOT TO!
CIVILIAN WORKERS— DISMOUNT!
COME ON, MOVE IT OUT! GET IN THERE AND START CLEANING, YOU LAYABOUTS!
MARCHETTI HELICOPTER HIRE: SIGHTSEEING AND BUSINESS FLIGHTS
TELL ME, MY GOOD MAN— DO YOU HIRE HELICOPTERS?
UH... YEAH...
THEN I SHOULD VERY MUCH LIKE TO HIRE ONE.
HEY! YOU LOT AREN'T ALLOWED IN THIS PART OF THE VATICAN!

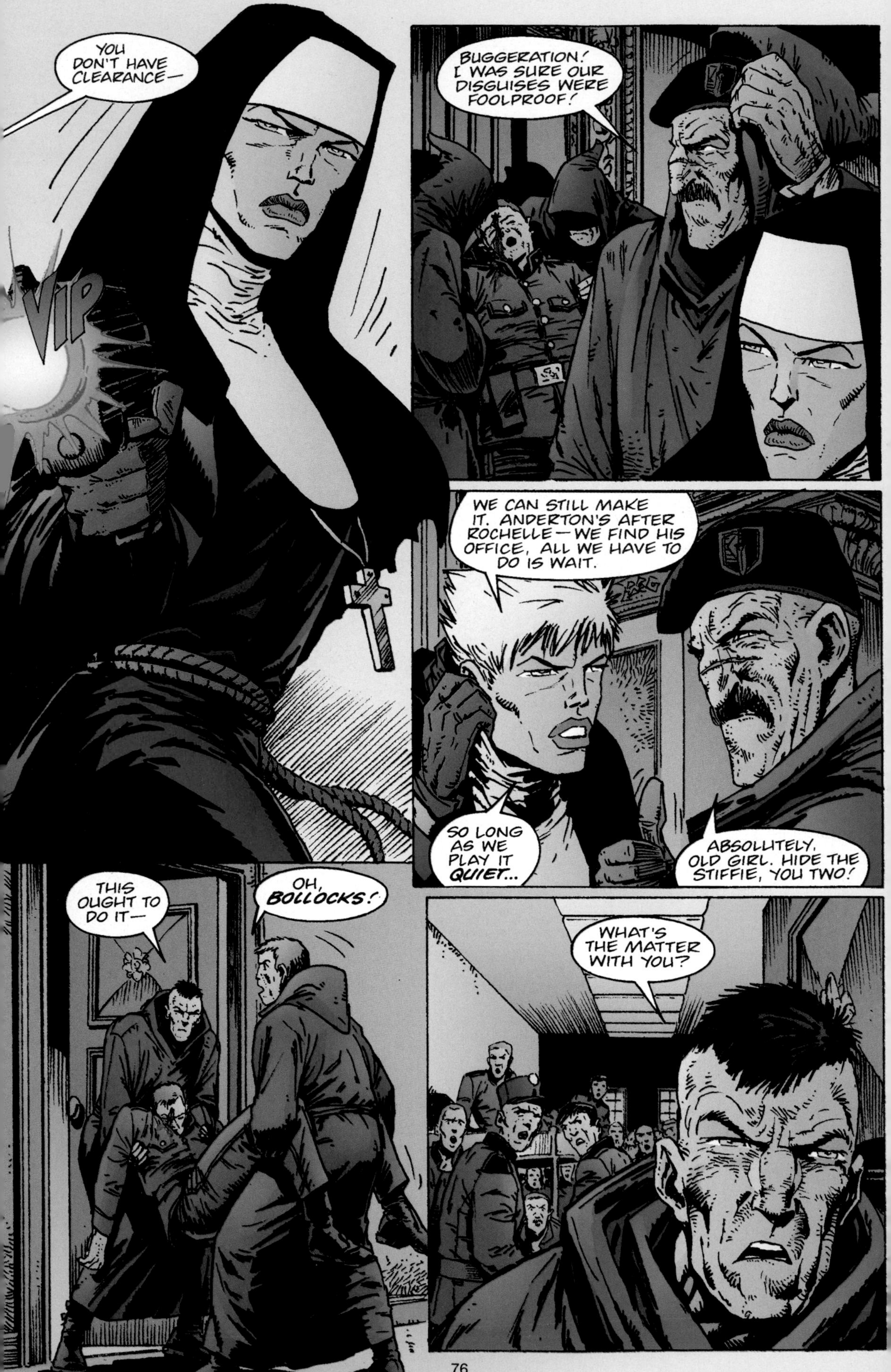

YOU DON'T HAVE CLEARANCE—
VIP
BUGGERATION! I WAS SURE OUR DISGUISES WERE FOOLPROOF!
WE CAN STILL MAKE IT. ANDERTON'S AFTER ROCHELLE—WE FIND HIS OFFICE, ALL WE HAVE TO DO IS WAIT.
SO LONG AS WE PLAY IT QUIET...
ABSOLUTELY, OLD GIRL. HIDE THE STIFFIE, YOU TWO!
THIS OUGHT TO DO IT—
OH, BOLLOCKS!
WHAT'S THE MATTER WITH YOU?

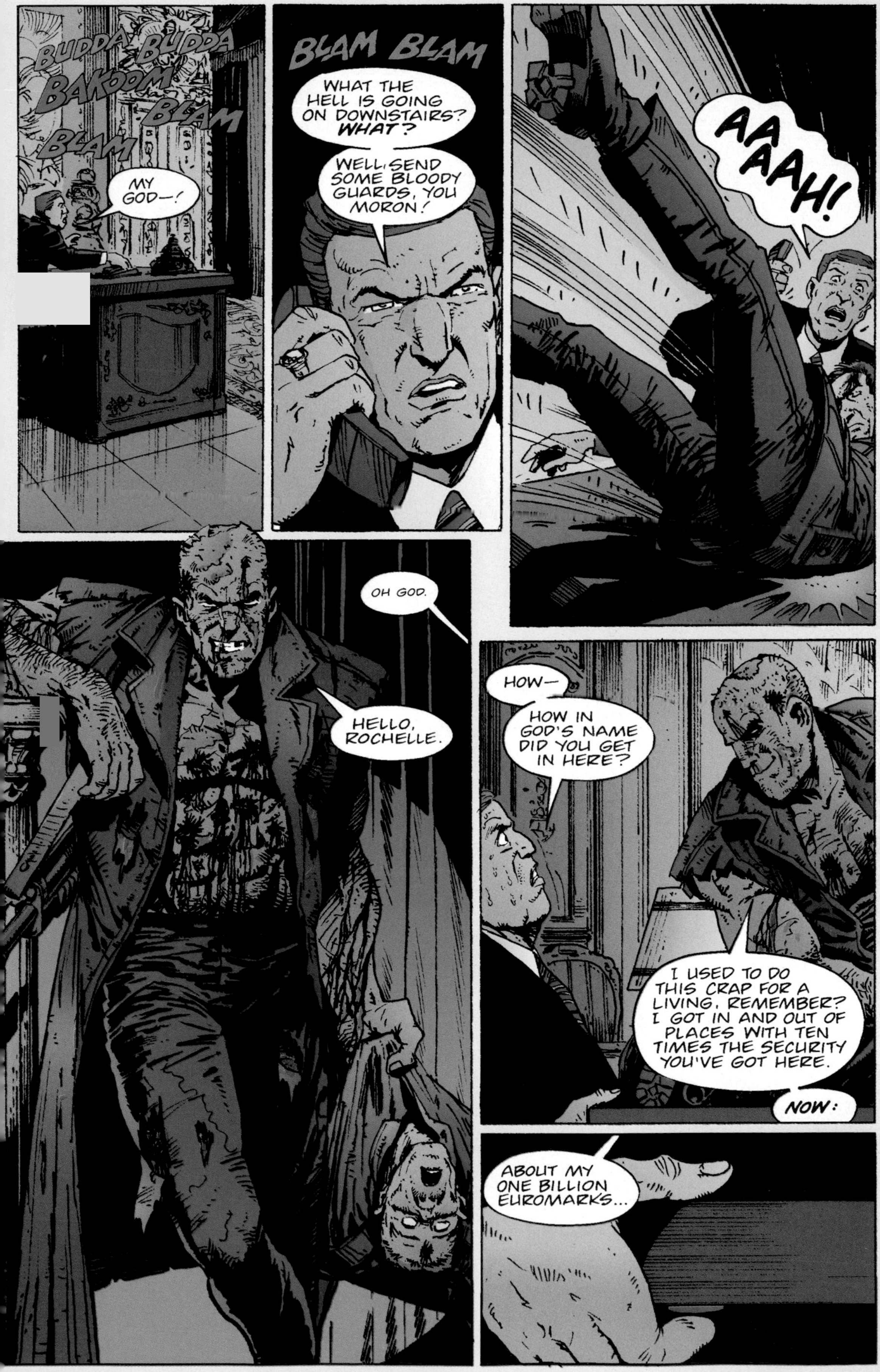
BUDDA BUDDA
BAKOOM
BLAM
BLAM
MY GOD—!
BLAM BLAM
WHAT THE HELL IS GOING ON DOWNSTAIRS? WHAT?
WELL, SEND SOME BLOODY GUARDS, YOU MORON!
AAAAAH!
OH GOD.
HELLO, ROCHELLE.
HOW—
HOW IN GOD'S NAME DID YOU GET IN HERE?
I USED TO DO THIS CRAP FOR A LIVING, REMEMBER? I GOT IN AND OUT OF PLACES WITH TEN TIMES THE SECURITY YOU'VE GOT HERE.
NOW:
ABOUT MY ONE BILLION EUROMARKS...

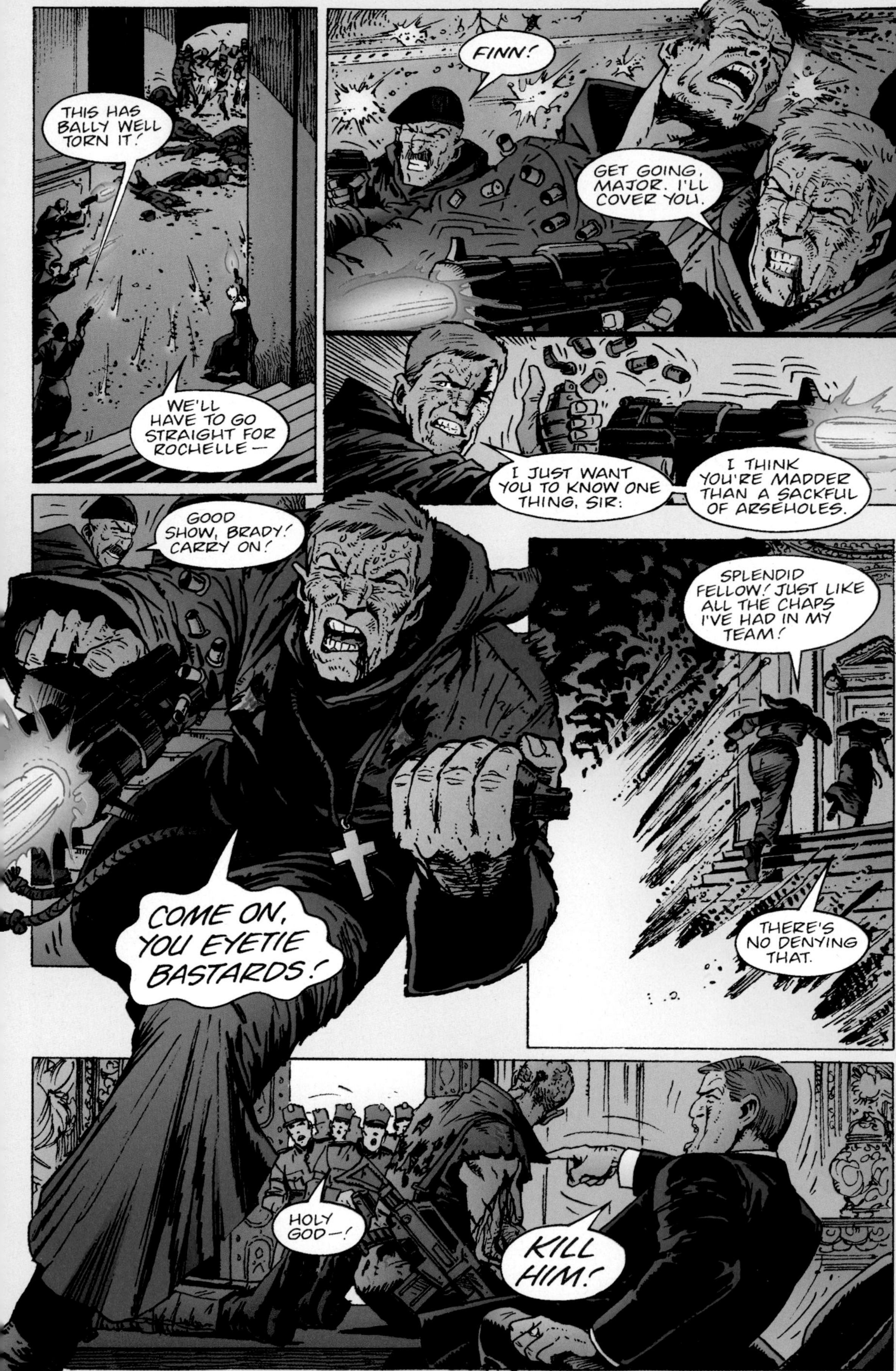
THIS HAS BALLY WELL TORN IT!
WE'LL HAVE TO GO STRAIGHT FOR ROCHELLE—
FINN!
GET GOING, MAJOR. I'LL COVER YOU.
I JUST WANT YOU TO KNOW ONE THING, SIR:
I THINK YOU'RE MADDER THAN A SACKFUL OF ARSEHOLES.
GOOD SHOW, BRADY! CARRY ON!
SPLENDID FELLOW! JUST LIKE ALL THE CHAPS I'VE HAD IN MY TEAM!
THERE'S NO DENYING THAT.
COME ON, YOU EYETIE BASTARDS!
HOLY GOD—!
KILL HIM!

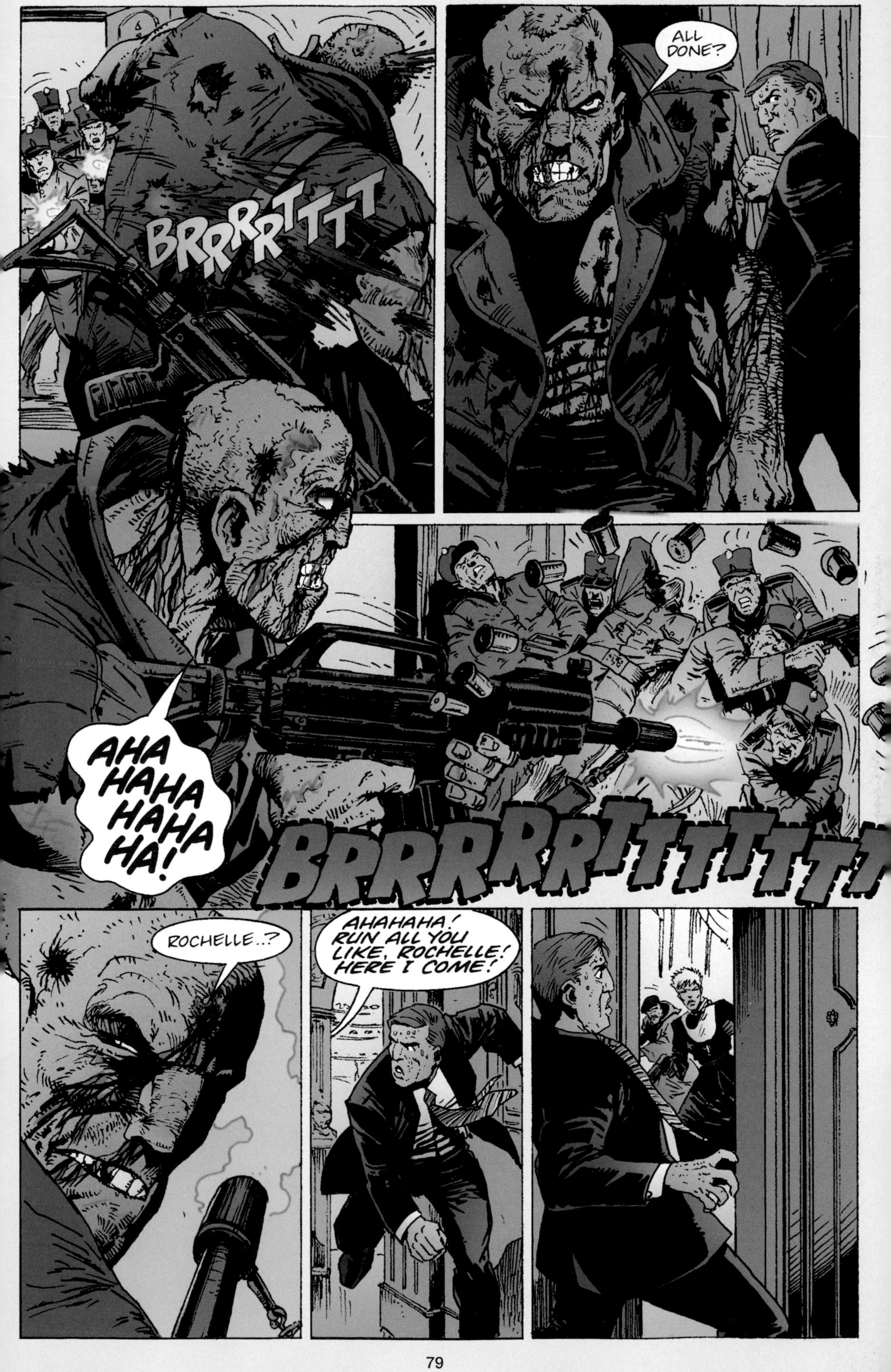
BRRRRTTTT
ALL DONE?
AHA HAHA HAHA HA!
BRRRRRRTTTTTTTT
ROCHELLE..?
AHAHAHA! RUN ALL YOU LIKE, ROCHELLE! HERE I COME!

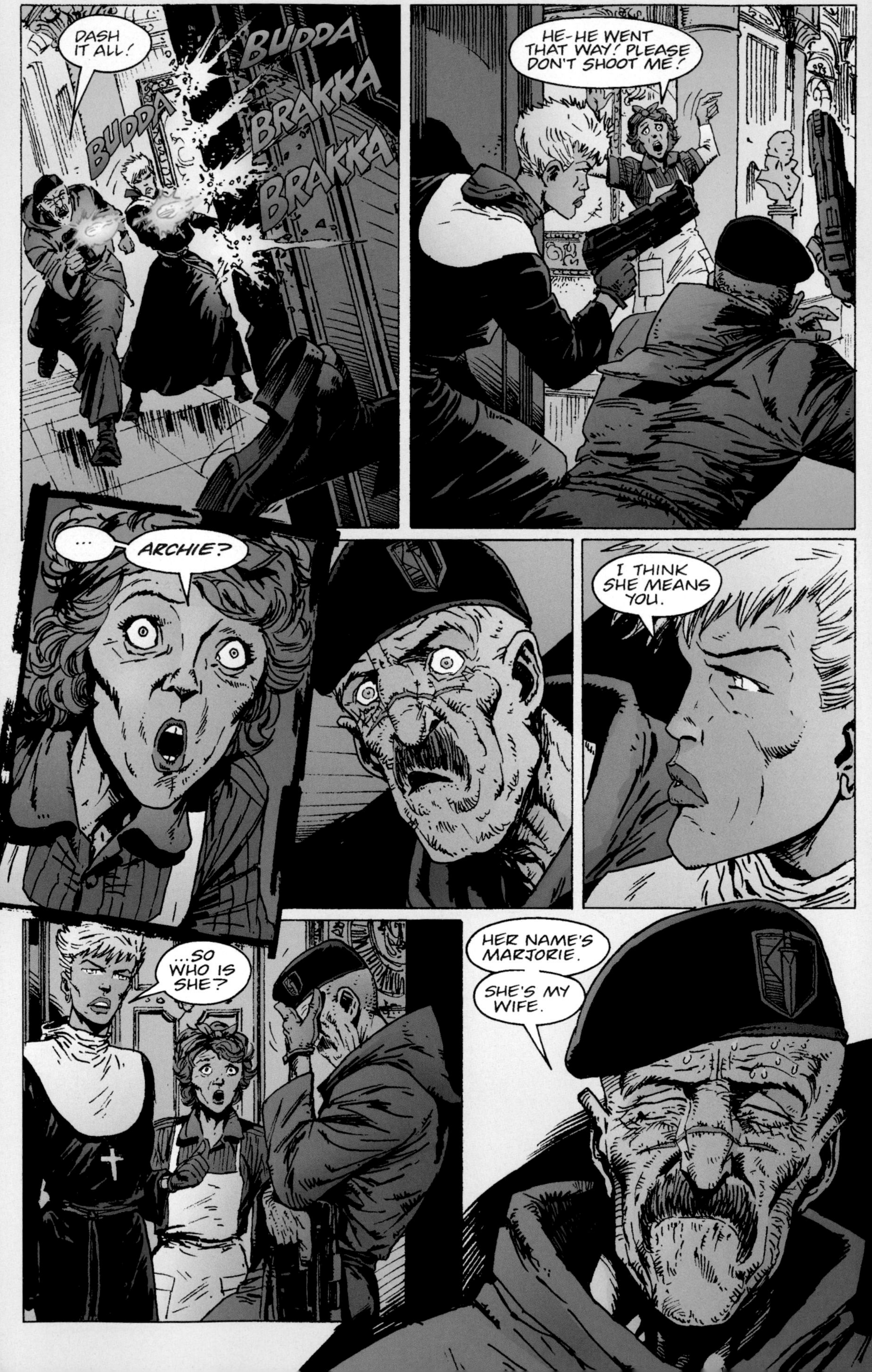
DASH IT ALL!
BUDDA
BUDDA
BRAKKA
BRAKKA
HE-HE WENT THAT WAY! PLEASE DON'T SHOOT ME!
... ARCHIE?
I THINK SHE MEANS YOU.
...SO WHO IS SHE?
HER NAME'S MARJORIE.
SHE'S MY WIFE.

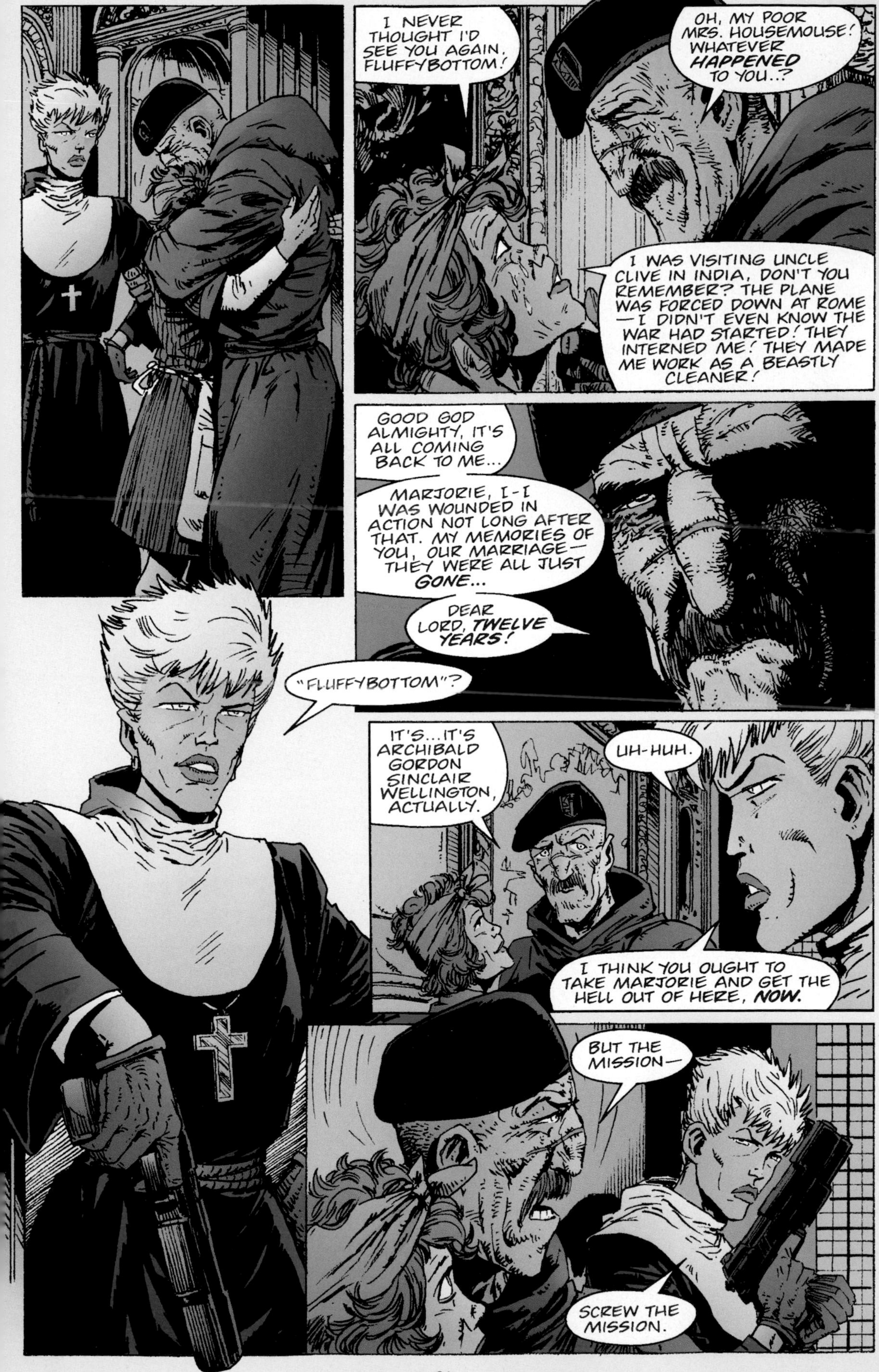

I NEVER THOUGHT I'D SEE YOU AGAIN, FLUFFYBOTTOM!
OH, MY POOR MRS. HOUSEMOUSE! WHATEVER **HAPPENED** TO YOU..?
I WAS VISITING UNCLE CLIVE IN INDIA, DON'T YOU REMEMBER? THE PLANE WAS FORCED DOWN AT ROME —I DIDN'T EVEN KNOW THE WAR HAD STARTED! THEY INTERNED ME! THEY MADE ME WORK AS A BEASTLY CLEANER!
GOOD GOD ALMIGHTY, IT'S ALL COMING BACK TO ME...
MARJORIE, I-I WAS WOUNDED IN ACTION NOT LONG AFTER THAT. MY MEMORIES OF YOU, OUR MARRIAGE— THEY WERE ALL JUST **GONE...**
DEAR LORD, **TWELVE YEARS!**
"FLUFFYBOTTOM"?
IT'S...IT'S ARCHIBALD GORDON SINCLAIR WELLINGTON, ACTUALLY.
UH-HUH.
I THINK YOU OUGHT TO TAKE MARJORIE AND GET THE HELL OUT OF HERE, **NOW.**
BUT THE MISSION—
SCREW THE MISSION.

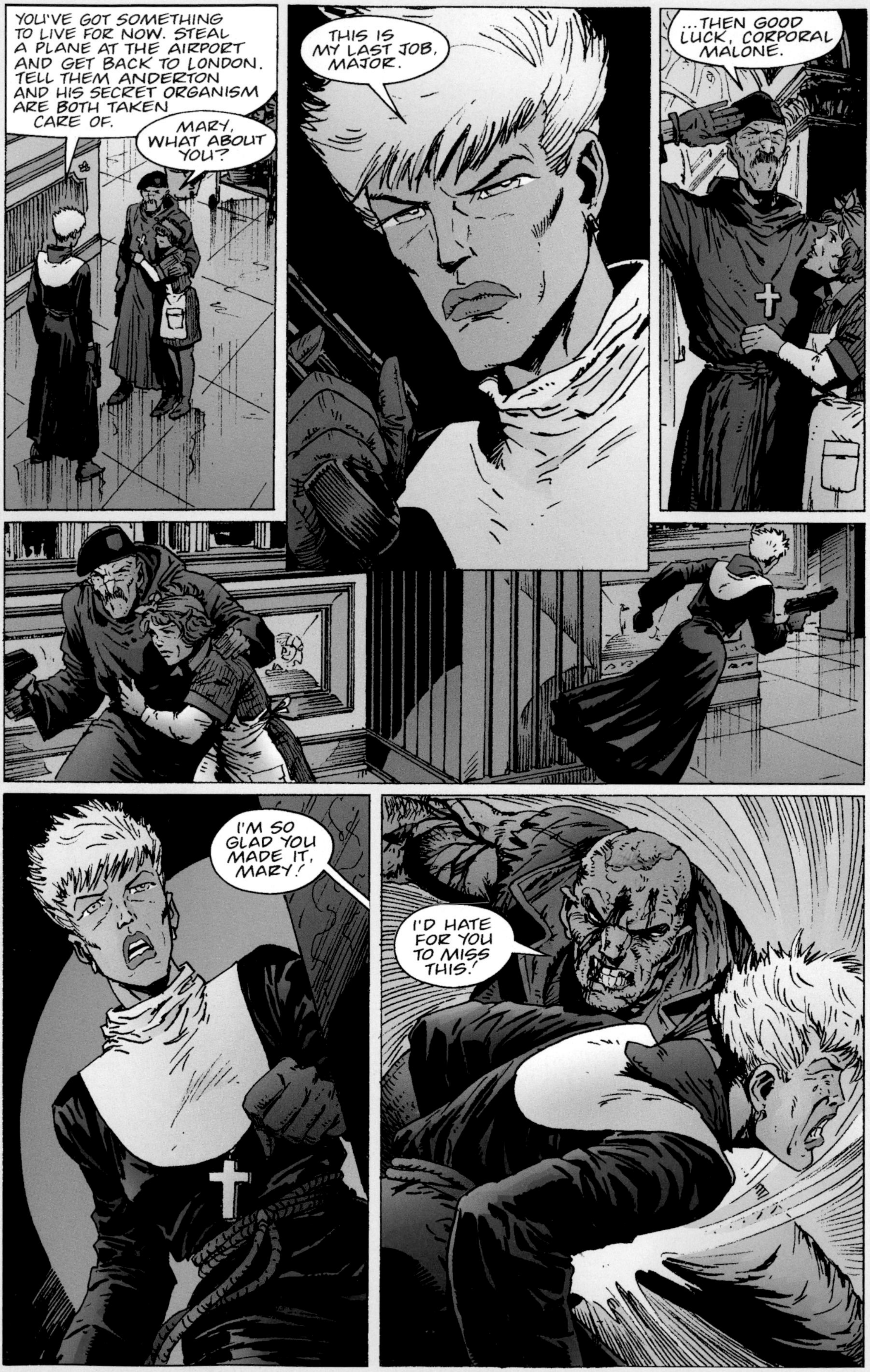
YOU'VE GOT SOMETHING TO LIVE FOR NOW. STEAL A PLANE AT THE AIRPORT AND GET BACK TO LONDON. TELL THEM ANDERTON AND HIS SECRET ORGANISM ARE BOTH TAKEN CARE OF.
MARY, WHAT ABOUT YOU?
THIS IS MY LAST JOB, MAJOR.
...THEN GOOD LUCK, CORPORAL MALONE.
I'M SO GLAD YOU MADE IT, MARY!
I'D HATE FOR YOU TO MISS THIS!

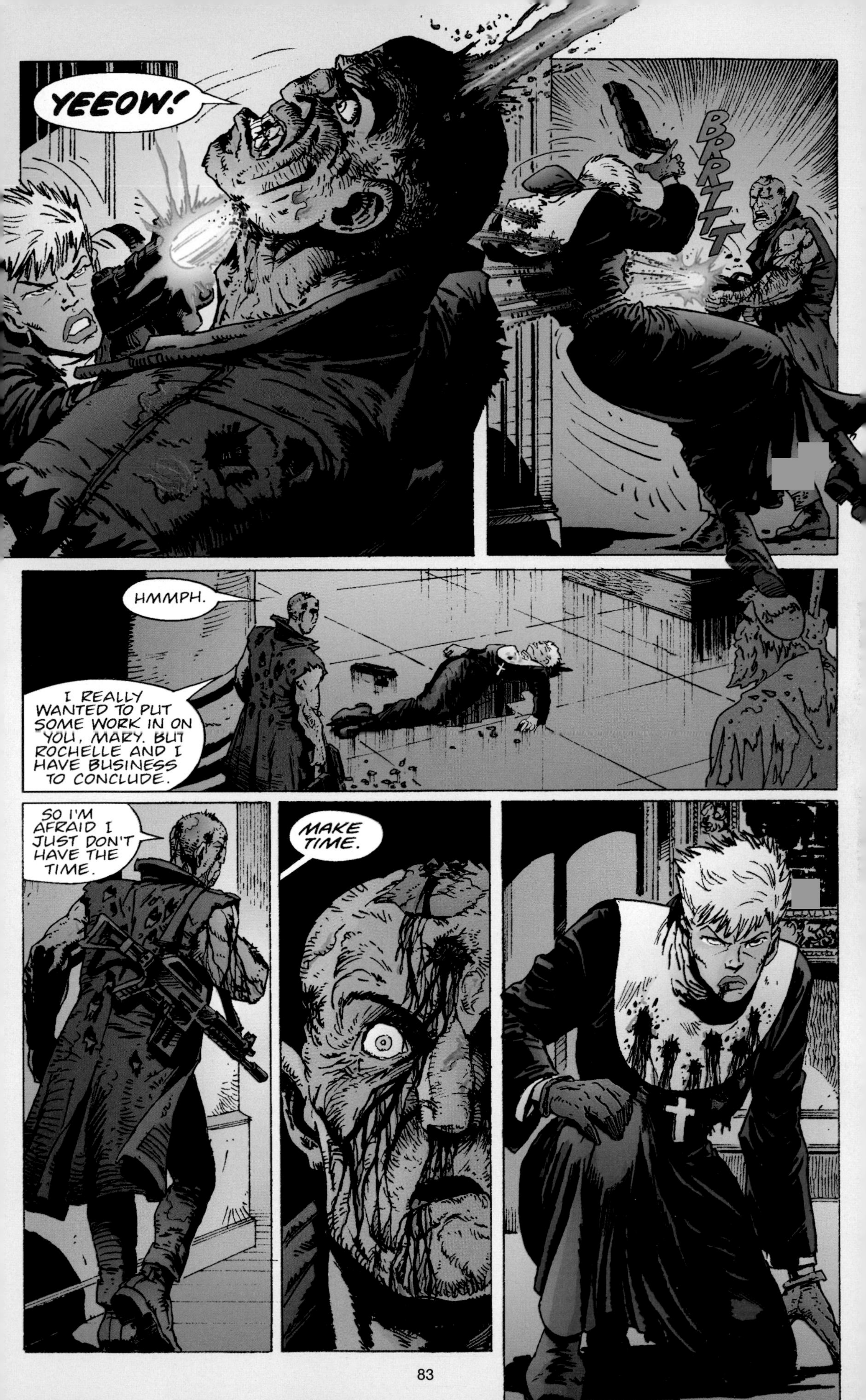
YEEOW!
BRRTTT
HMMPH.
I REALLY WANTED TO PUT SOME WORK IN ON YOU, MARY. BUT ROCHELLE AND I HAVE BUSINESS TO CONCLUDE.
SO I'M AFRAID I JUST DON'T HAVE THE TIME.
MAKE TIME.

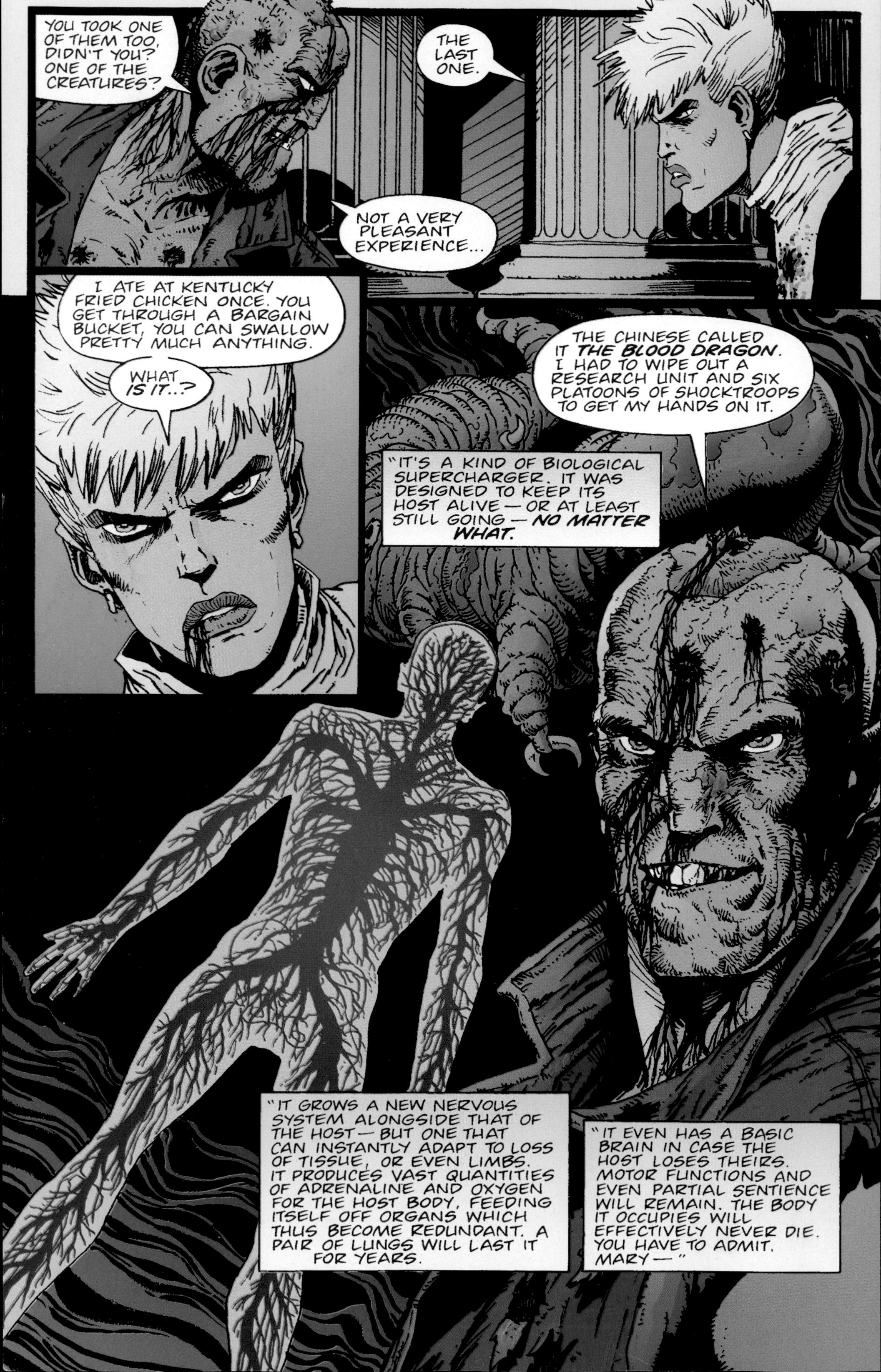
YOU TOOK ONE OF THEM TOO, DIDN'T YOU? ONE OF THE CREATURES?
THE LAST ONE.
NOT A VERY PLEASANT EXPERIENCE...
I ATE AT KENTUCKY FRIED CHICKEN ONCE. YOU GET THROUGH A BARGAIN BUCKET, YOU CAN SWALLOW PRETTY MUCH ANYTHING.
WHAT *IS IT*..?
THE CHINESE CALLED IT *THE BLOOD DRAGON*. I HAD TO WIPE OUT A RESEARCH UNIT AND SIX PLATOONS OF SHOCKTROOPS TO GET MY HANDS ON IT.
"IT'S A KIND OF BIOLOGICAL SUPERCHARGER. IT WAS DESIGNED TO KEEP ITS HOST ALIVE — OR AT LEAST STILL GOING — *NO MATTER WHAT*.
"IT GROWS A NEW NERVOUS SYSTEM ALONGSIDE THAT OF THE HOST — BUT ONE THAT CAN INSTANTLY ADAPT TO LOSS OF TISSUE, OR EVEN LIMBS. IT PRODUCES VAST QUANTITIES OF ADRENALINE AND OXYGEN FOR THE HOST BODY, FEEDING ITSELF OFF ORGANS WHICH THUS BECOME REDUNDANT. A PAIR OF LUNGS WILL LAST IT FOR YEARS.
"IT EVEN HAS A BASIC BRAIN IN CASE THE HOST LOSES THEIRS. MOTOR FUNCTIONS AND EVEN PARTIAL SENTIENCE WILL REMAIN. THE BODY IT OCCUPIES WILL EFFECTIVELY NEVER DIE. YOU HAVE TO ADMIT, MARY — "

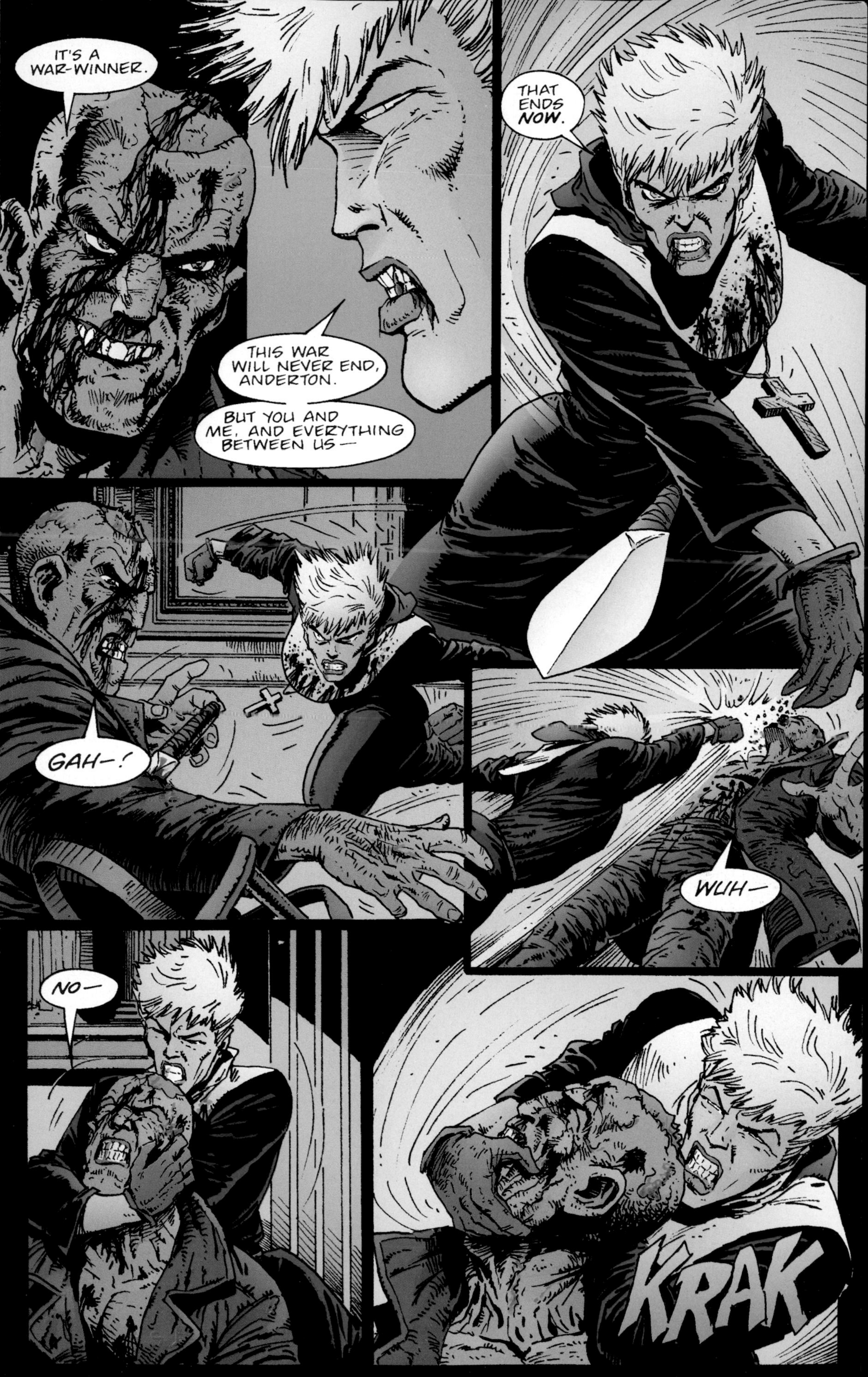
IT'S A WAR-WINNER.
THIS WAR WILL NEVER END, ANDERTON.
BUT YOU AND ME, AND EVERYTHING BETWEEN US—
THAT ENDS NOW.
GAH—!
WUH—
NO—
KRAK

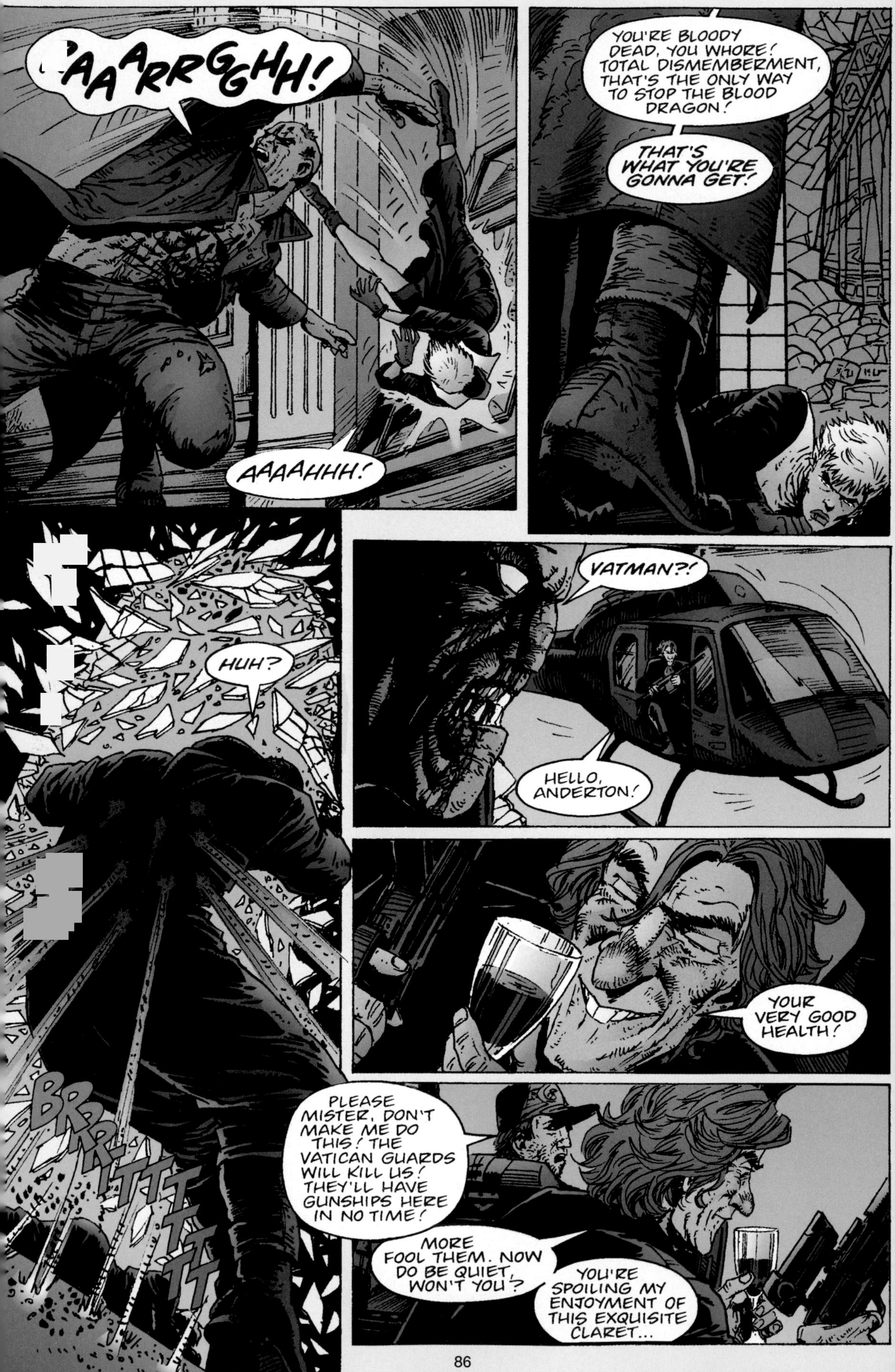
AAARRGGHH!
AAAAHHH!
YOU'RE BLOODY DEAD, YOU WHORE! TOTAL DISMEMBERMENT, THAT'S THE ONLY WAY TO STOP THE BLOOD DRAGON!
THAT'S WHAT YOU'RE GONNA GET!
HUH?
BRRRTTTTTTT
VATMAN?!
HELLO, ANDERTON!
YOUR VERY GOOD HEALTH!
PLEASE MISTER, DON'T MAKE ME DO THIS! THE VATICAN GUARDS WILL KILL US! THEY'LL HAVE GUNSHIPS HERE IN NO TIME!
MORE FOOL THEM. NOW DO BE QUIET, WON'T YOU?
YOU'RE SPOILING MY ENJOYMENT OF THIS EXQUISITE CLARET...

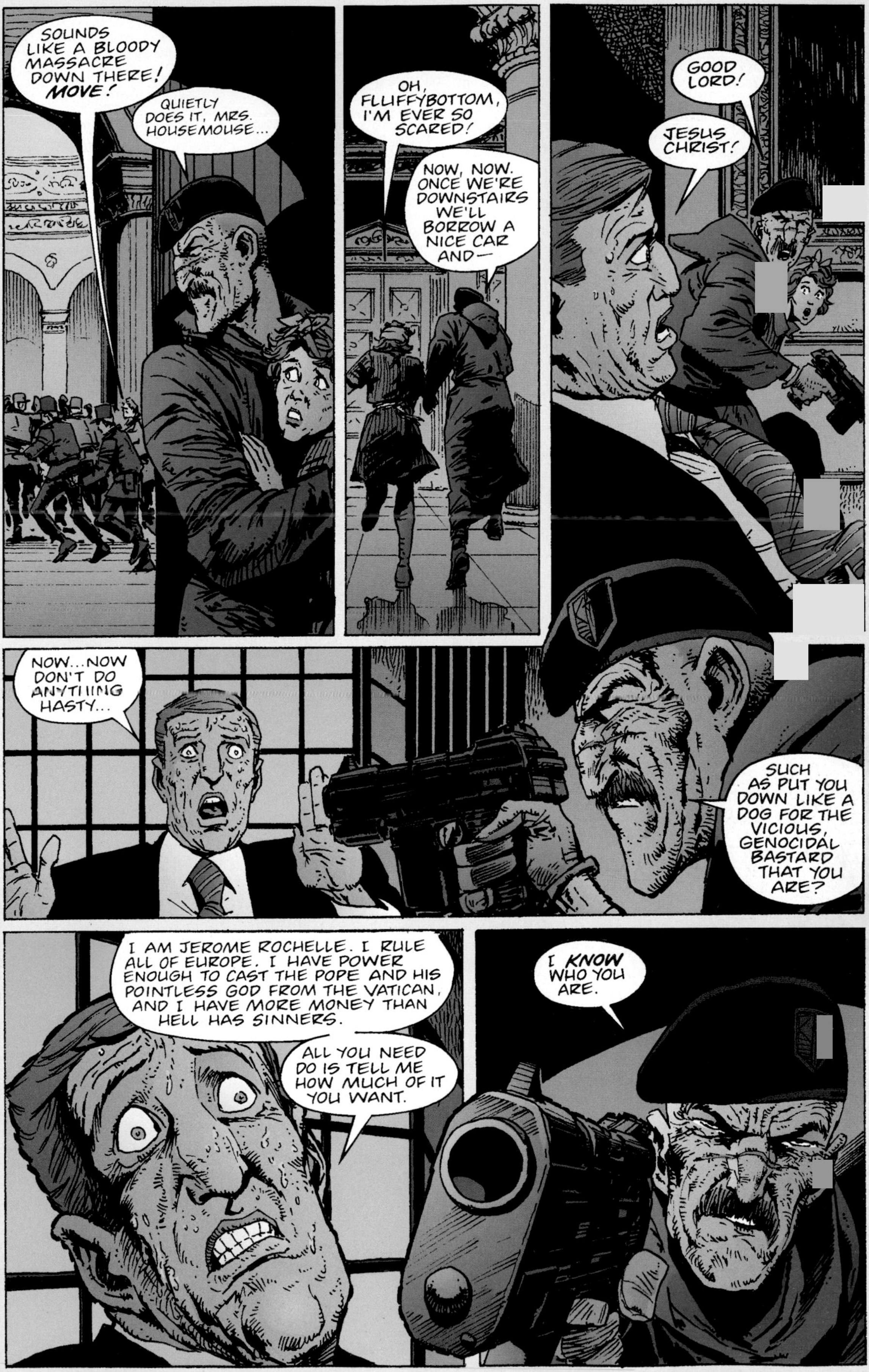
SOUNDS LIKE A BLOODY MASSACRE DOWN THERE! MOVE!
QUIETLY DOES IT, MRS. HOUSEMOUSE...
OH, FLUFFYBOTTOM, I'M EVER SO SCARED!
NOW, NOW. ONCE WE'RE DOWNSTAIRS WE'LL BORROW A NICE CAR AND—
GOOD LORD!
JESUS CHRIST!
NOW...NOW DON'T DO ANYTHING HASTY...
SUCH AS PUT YOU DOWN LIKE A DOG FOR THE VICIOUS, GENOCIDAL BASTARD THAT YOU ARE?
I AM JEROME ROCHELLE. I RULE ALL OF EUROPE. I HAVE POWER ENOUGH TO CAST THE POPE AND HIS POINTLESS GOD FROM THE VATICAN, AND I HAVE MORE MONEY THAN HELL HAS SINNERS.
ALL YOU NEED DO IS TELL ME HOW MUCH OF IT YOU WANT.
I KNOW WHO YOU ARE.

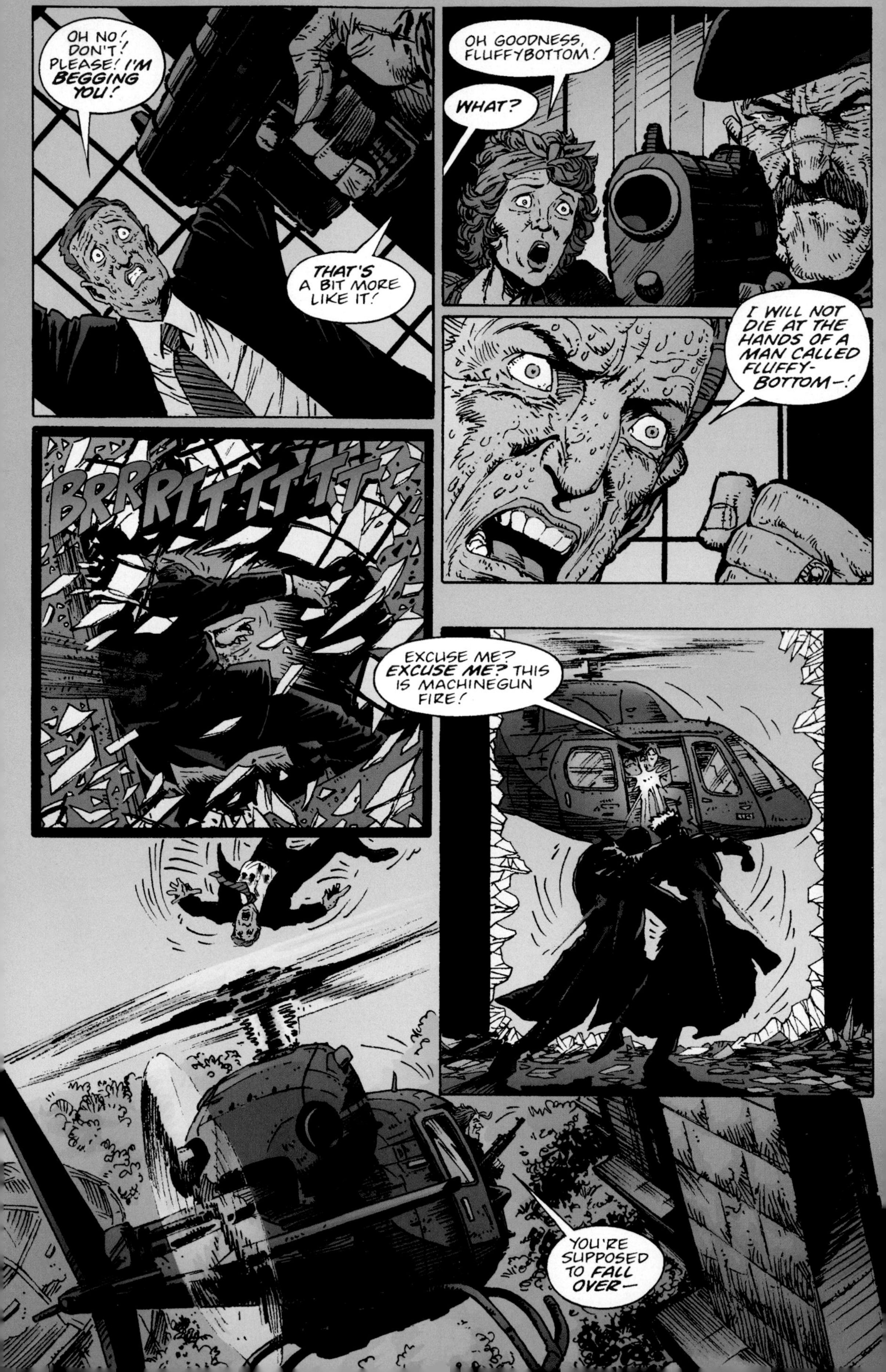
OH NO! DON'T! PLEASE! I'M BEGGING YOU!
THAT'S A BIT MORE LIKE IT!
OH GOODNESS, FLUFFYBOTTOM!
WHAT?
I WILL NOT DIE AT THE HANDS OF A MAN CALLED FLUFFY-BOTTOM-!
BRRRTTTTTT
EXCUSE ME? EXCUSE ME? THIS IS MACHINEGUN FIRE!
YOU'RE SUPPOSED TO FALL OVER—

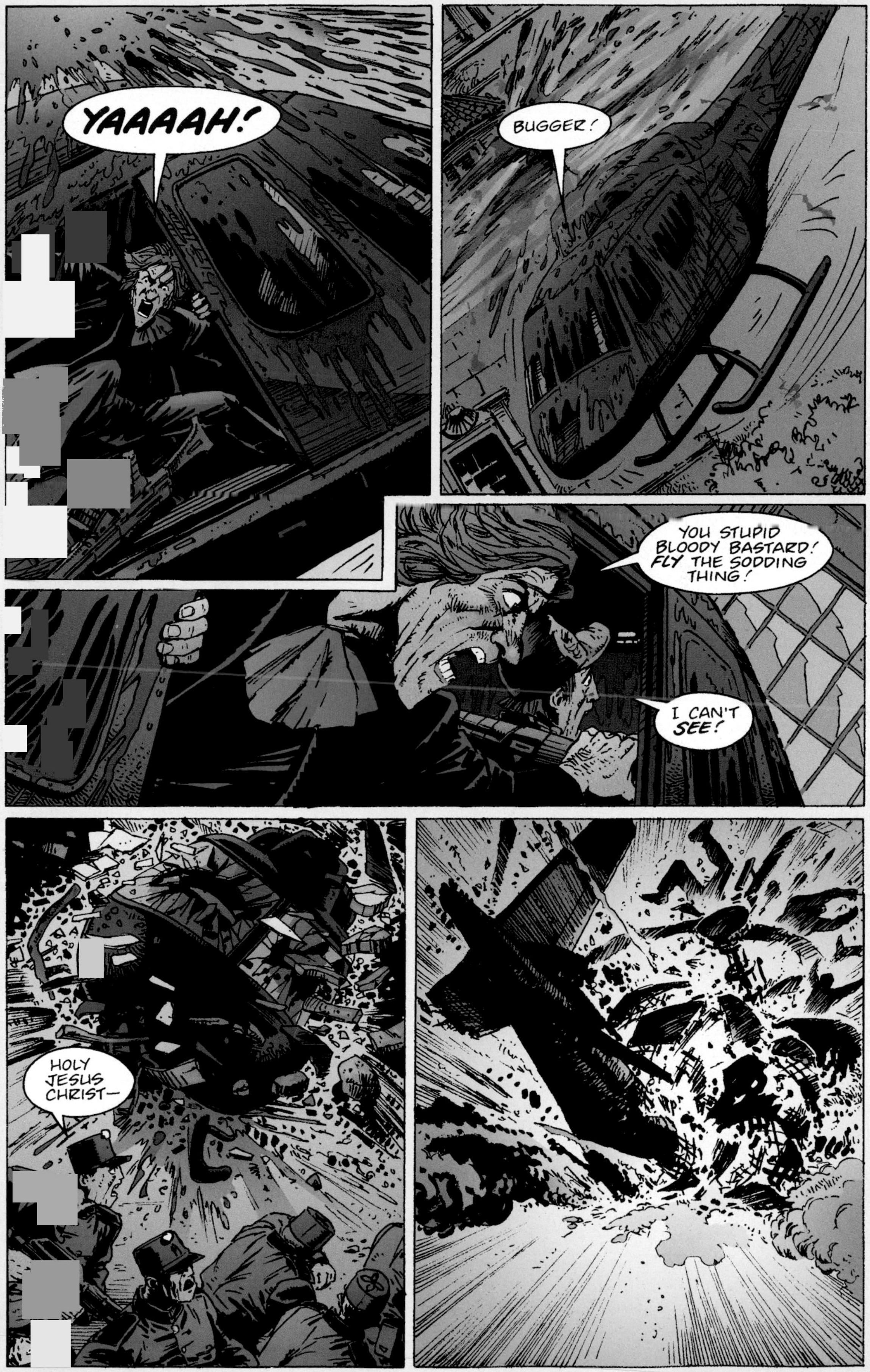

YAAAAH!
BUGGER!
YOU STUPID BLOODY BASTARD! FLY THE SODDING THING!
I CAN'T SEE!
HOLY JESUS CHRIST—

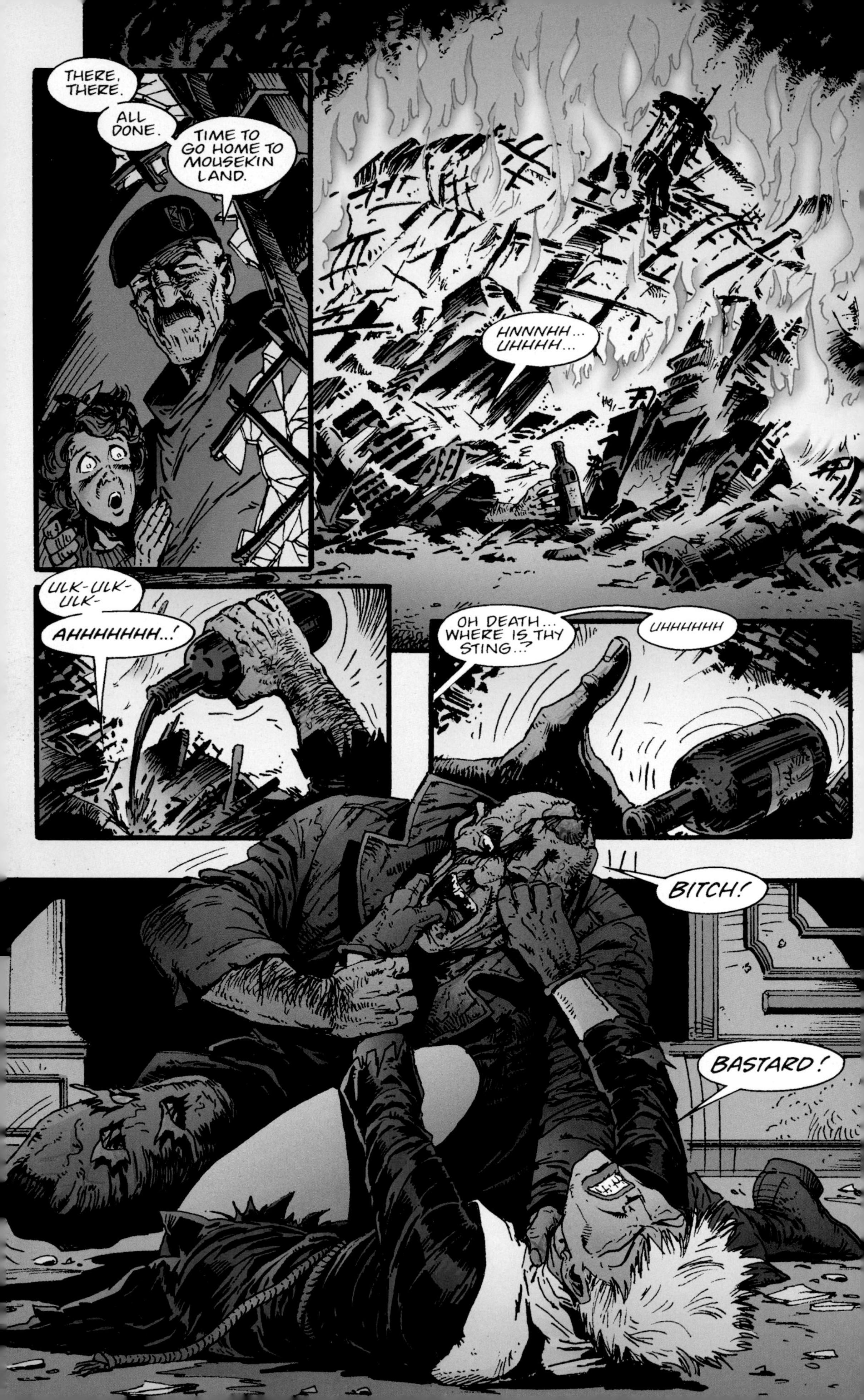
THERE, THERE.
ALL DONE.
TIME TO GO HOME TO MOUSEKIN LAND.
HNNNHH... UHHHH...
ULK-ULK-ULK-
AHHHHHHH...!
OH DEATH... WHERE IS THY STING..?
UHHHHHH
BITCH!
BASTARD!

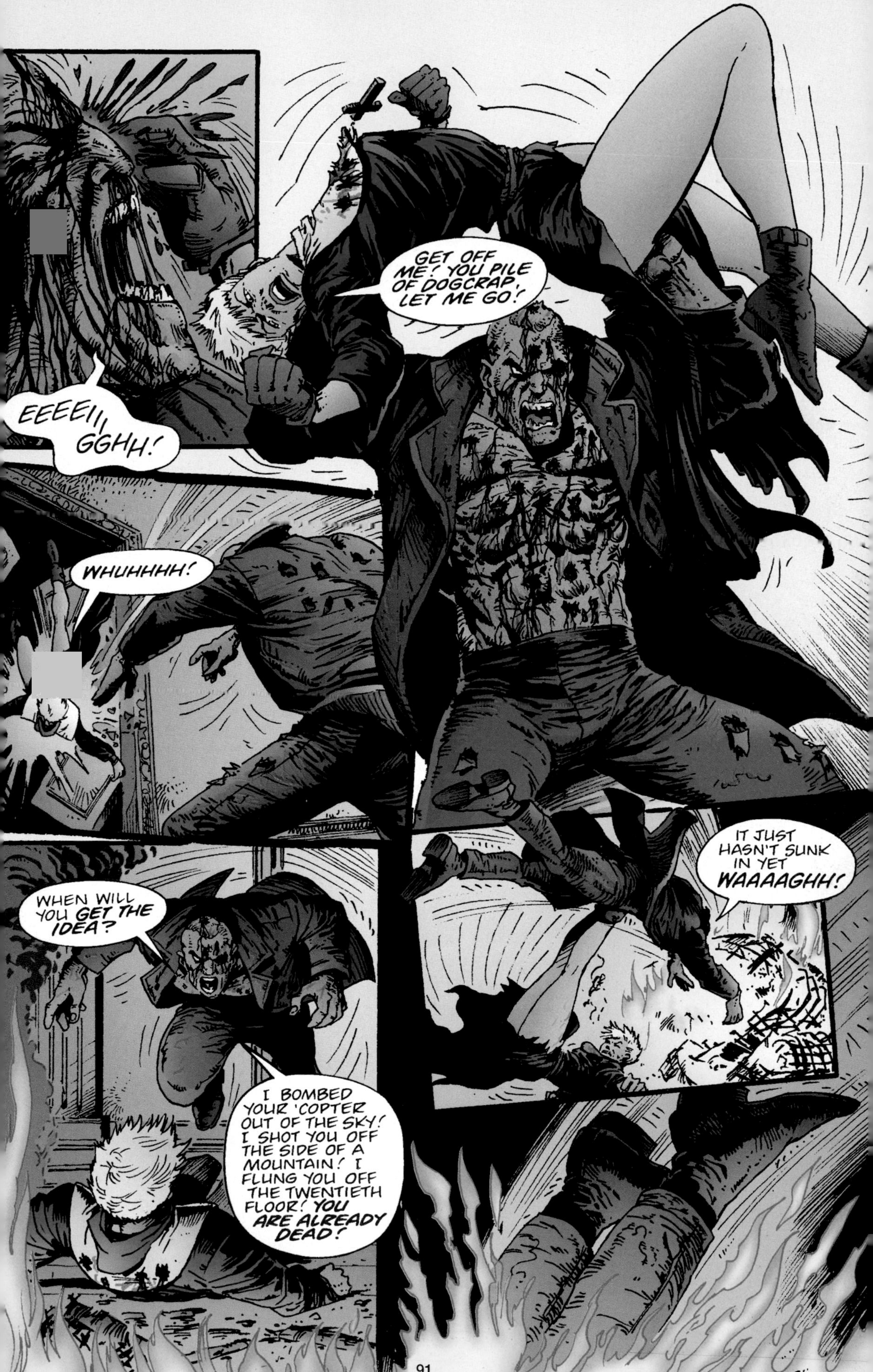
GET OFF ME! YOU PILE OF DOGCRAP! LET ME GO!
EEEEI,, GGHH!
WHUHHHH!
WHEN WILL YOU GET THE IDEA?
I BOMBED YOUR 'COPTER OUT OF THE SKY! I SHOT YOU OFF THE SIDE OF A MOUNTAIN! I FLUNG YOU OFF THE TWENTIETH FLOOR! YOU ARE ALREADY DEAD!
IT JUST HASN'T SUNK IN YET
WAAAAGHH!

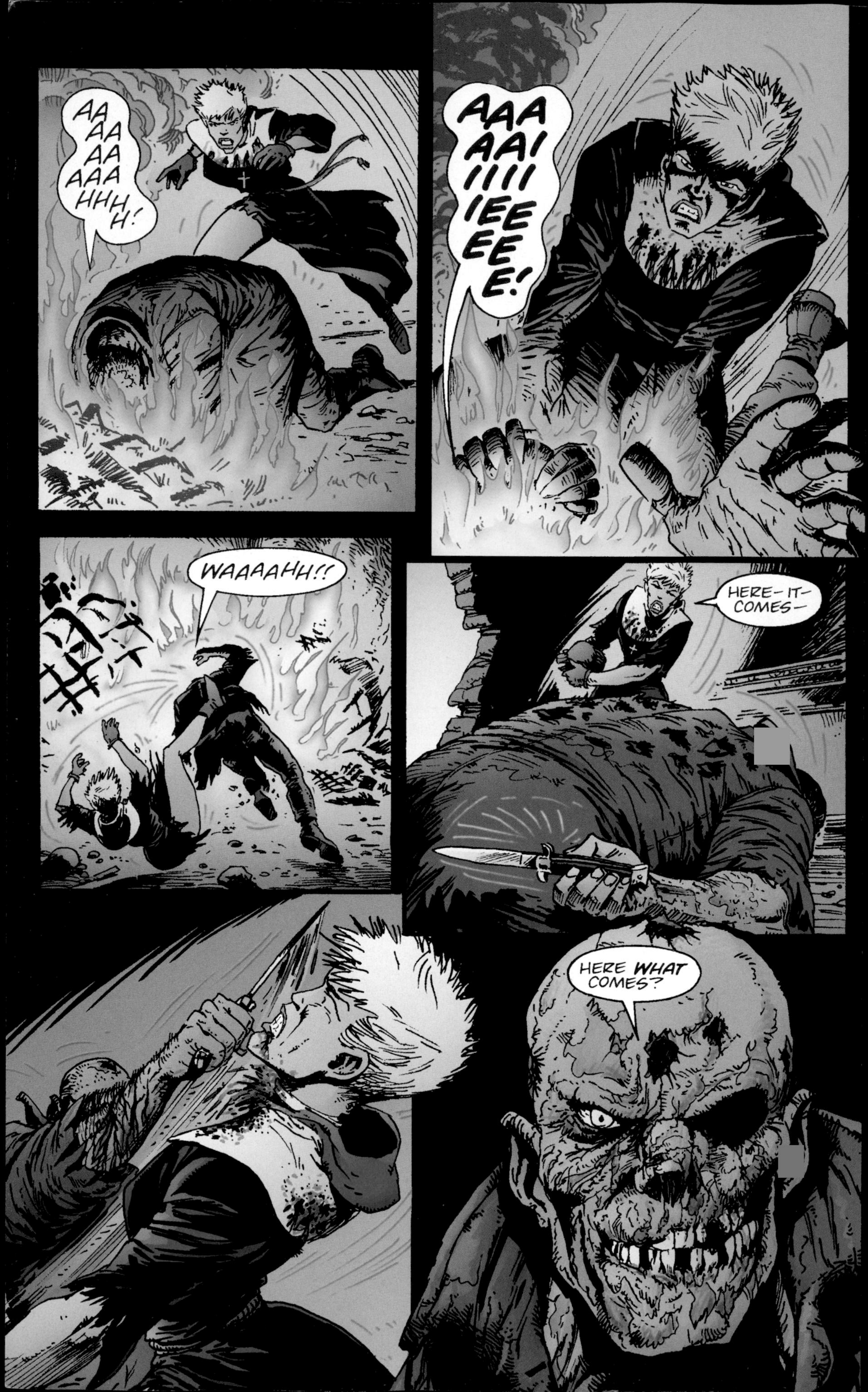
AA AA AA AAA HHH H!
AAA AAI IIII IEE EEE E!
WAAAAHH!!
HERE-IT-COMES-
HERE WHAT COMES?

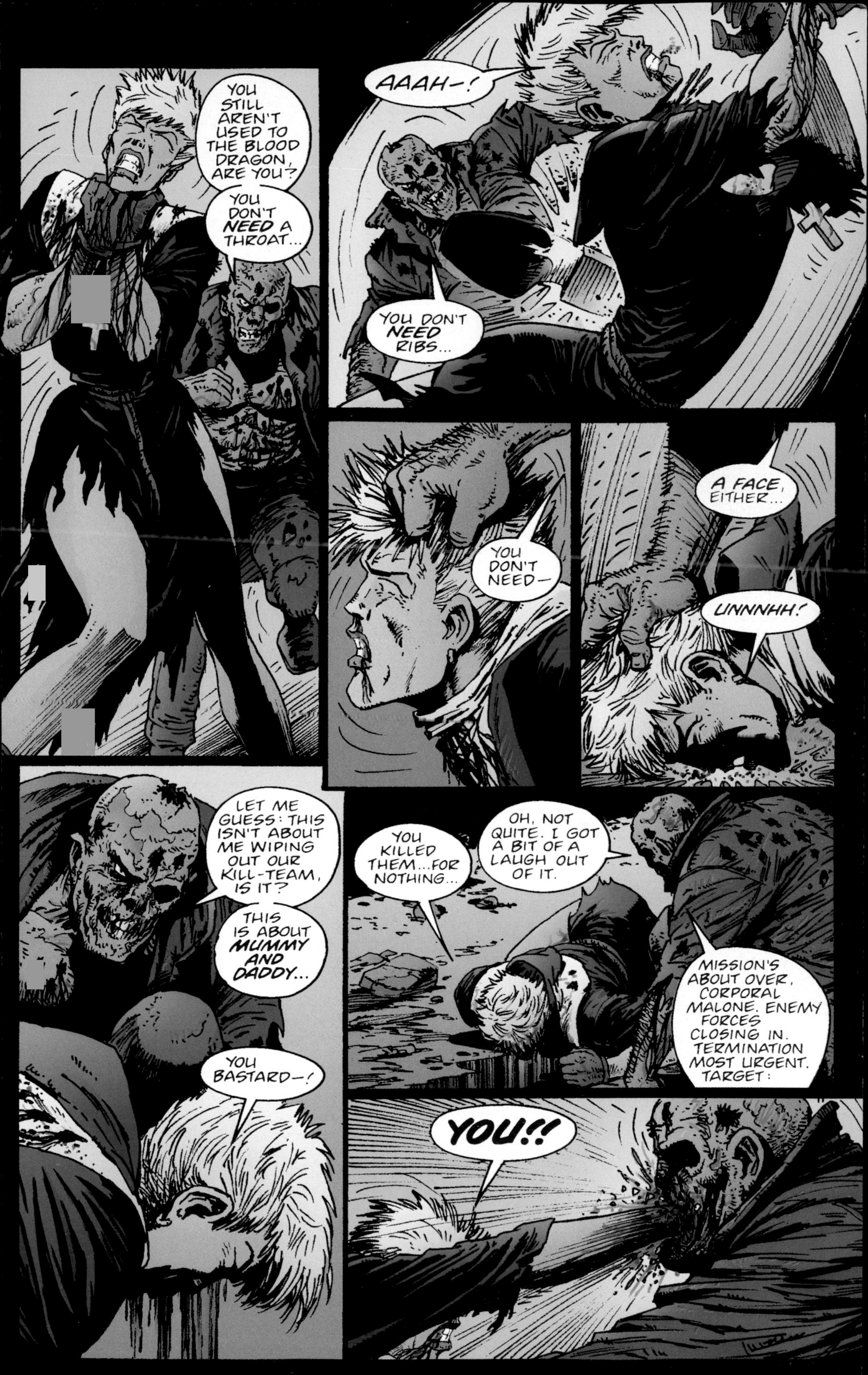
YOU STILL AREN'T USED TO THE BLOOD DRAGON, ARE YOU?
YOU DON'T NEED A THROAT...
AAAH-!
YOU DON'T NEED RIBS...
YOU DON'T NEED—
A FACE, EITHER...
UNNNHH!
LET ME GUESS: THIS ISN'T ABOUT ME WIPING OUT OUR KILL-TEAM, IS IT?
THIS IS ABOUT MUMMY AND DADDY...
YOU BASTARD-!
YOU KILLED THEM...FOR NOTHING...
OH, NOT QUITE. I GOT A BIT OF A LAUGH OUT OF IT.
MISSION'S ABOUT OVER, CORPORAL MALONE. ENEMY FORCES CLOSING IN. TERMINATION MOST URGENT. TARGET:
YOU?!

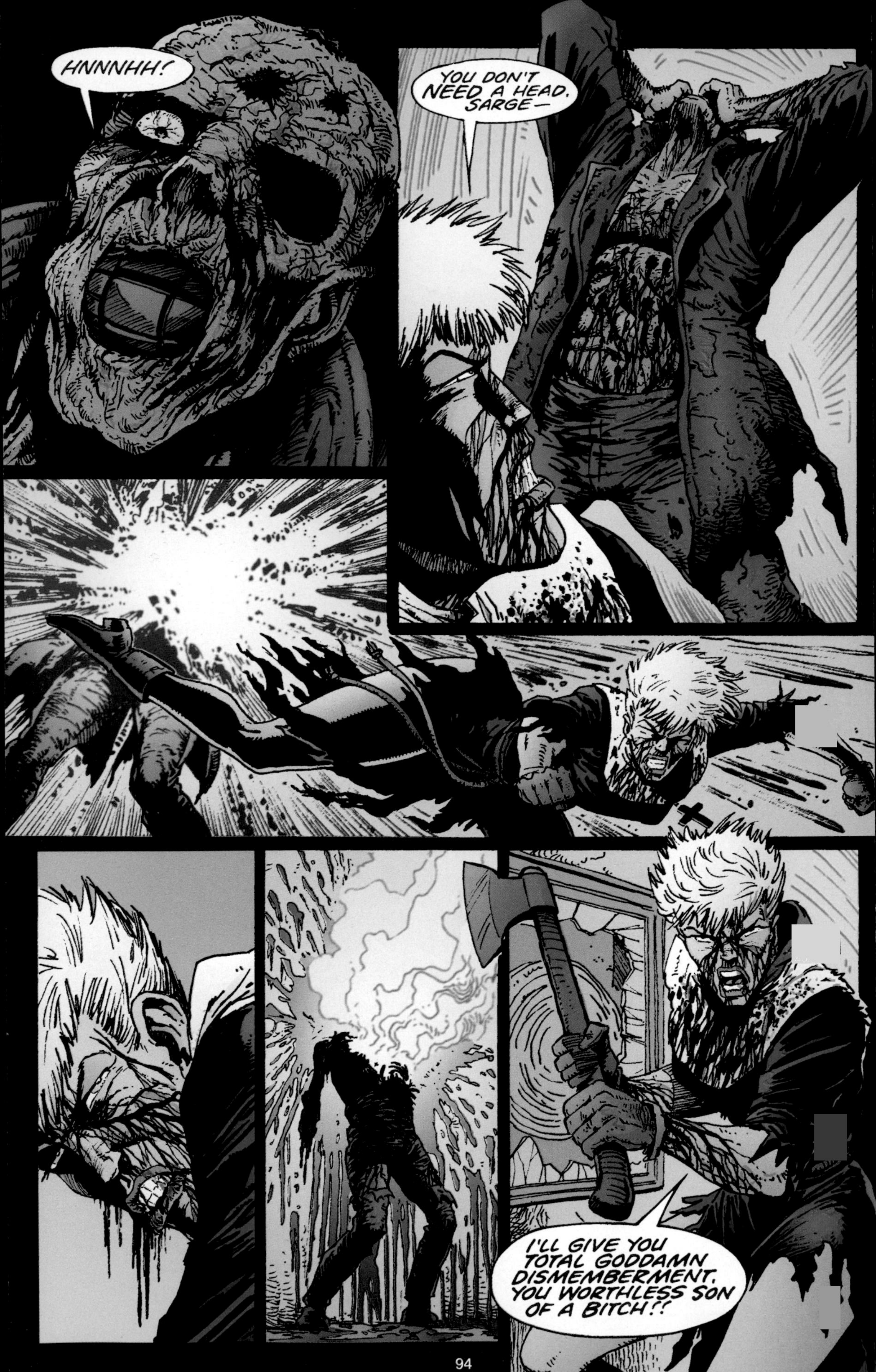
HNNNHH!
YOU DON'T NEED A HEAD, SARGE—
I'LL GIVE YOU TOTAL GODDAMN DISMEMBERMENT, YOU WORTHLESS SON OF A BITCH!?

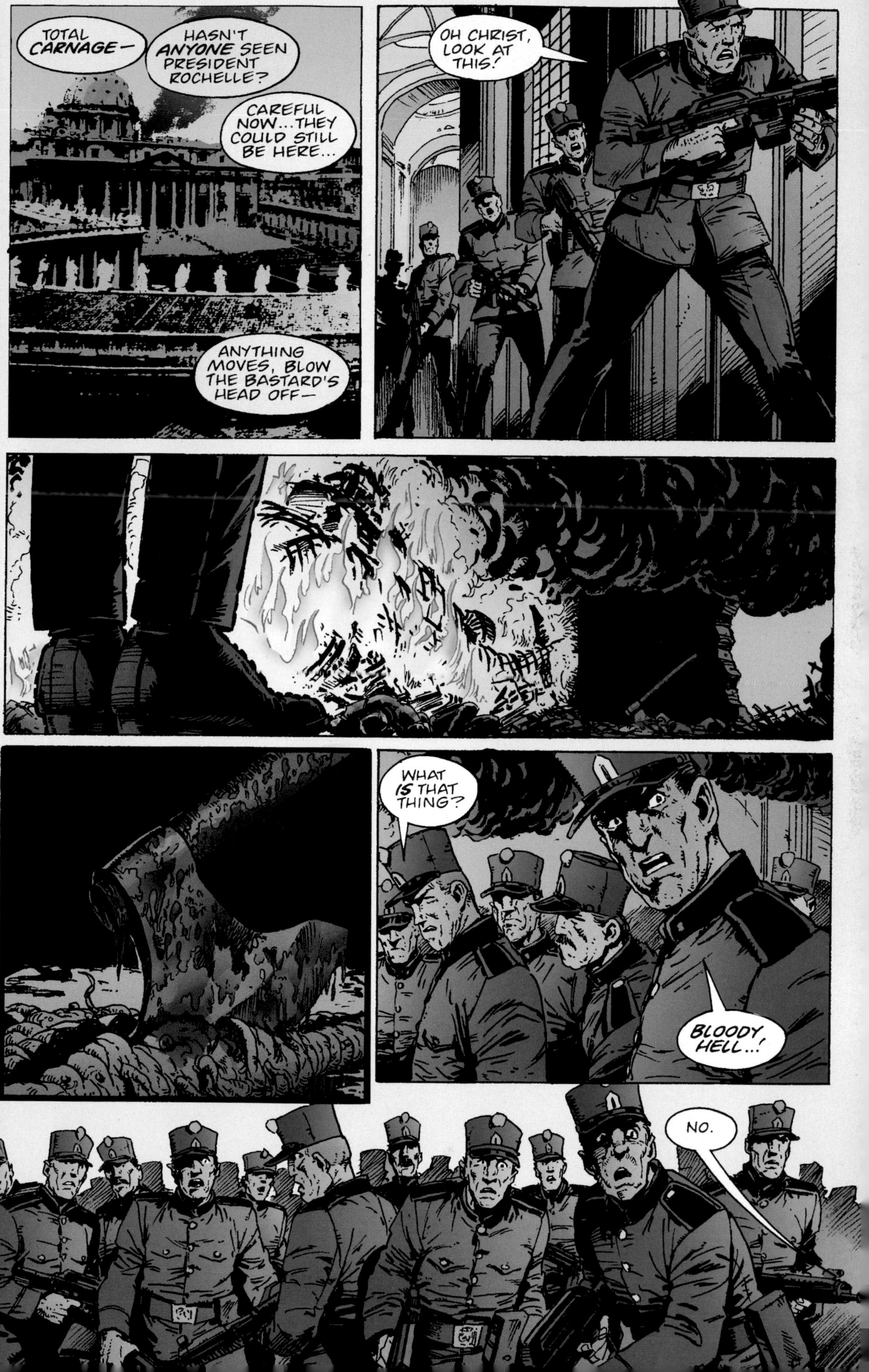
TOTAL CARNAGE—
HASN'T ANYONE SEEN PRESIDENT ROCHELLE?
CAREFUL NOW... THEY COULD STILL BE HERE...
ANYTHING MOVES, BLOW THE BASTARD'S HEAD OFF—
OH CHRIST, LOOK AT THIS!
WHAT IS THAT THING?
BLOODY HELL...!
NO.

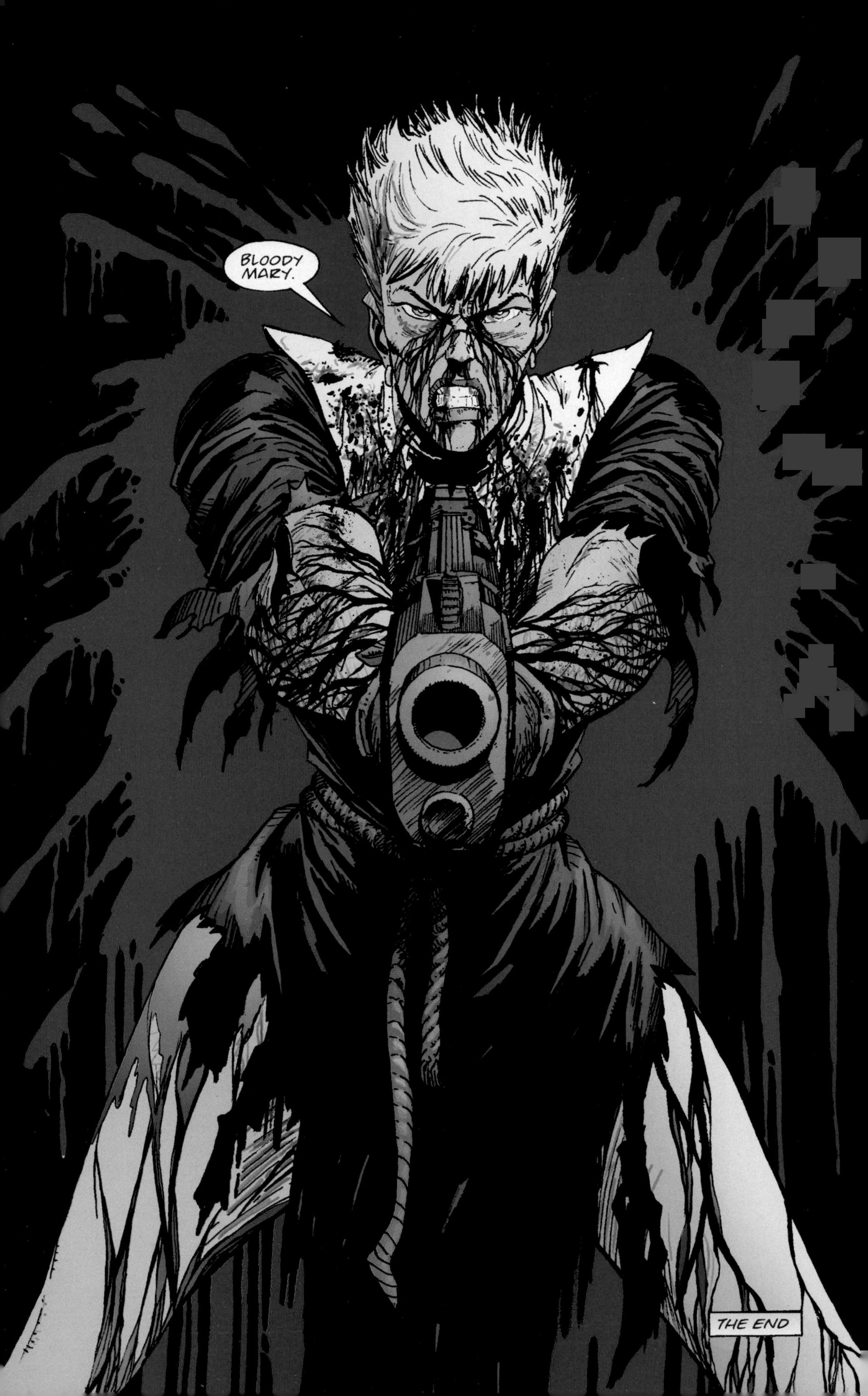
BLOODY MARY.
THE END

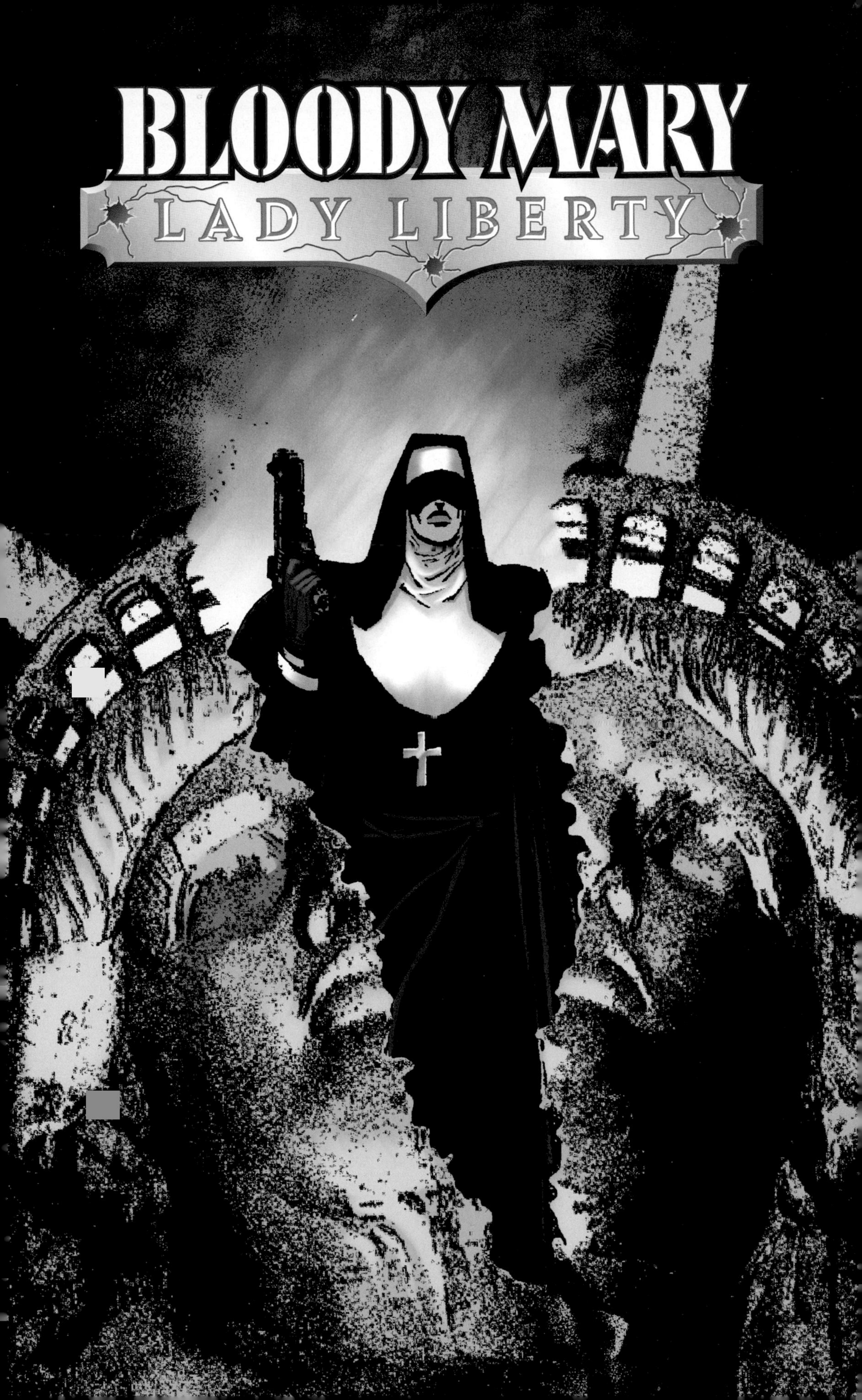
BLOODY MARY
LADY LIBERTY

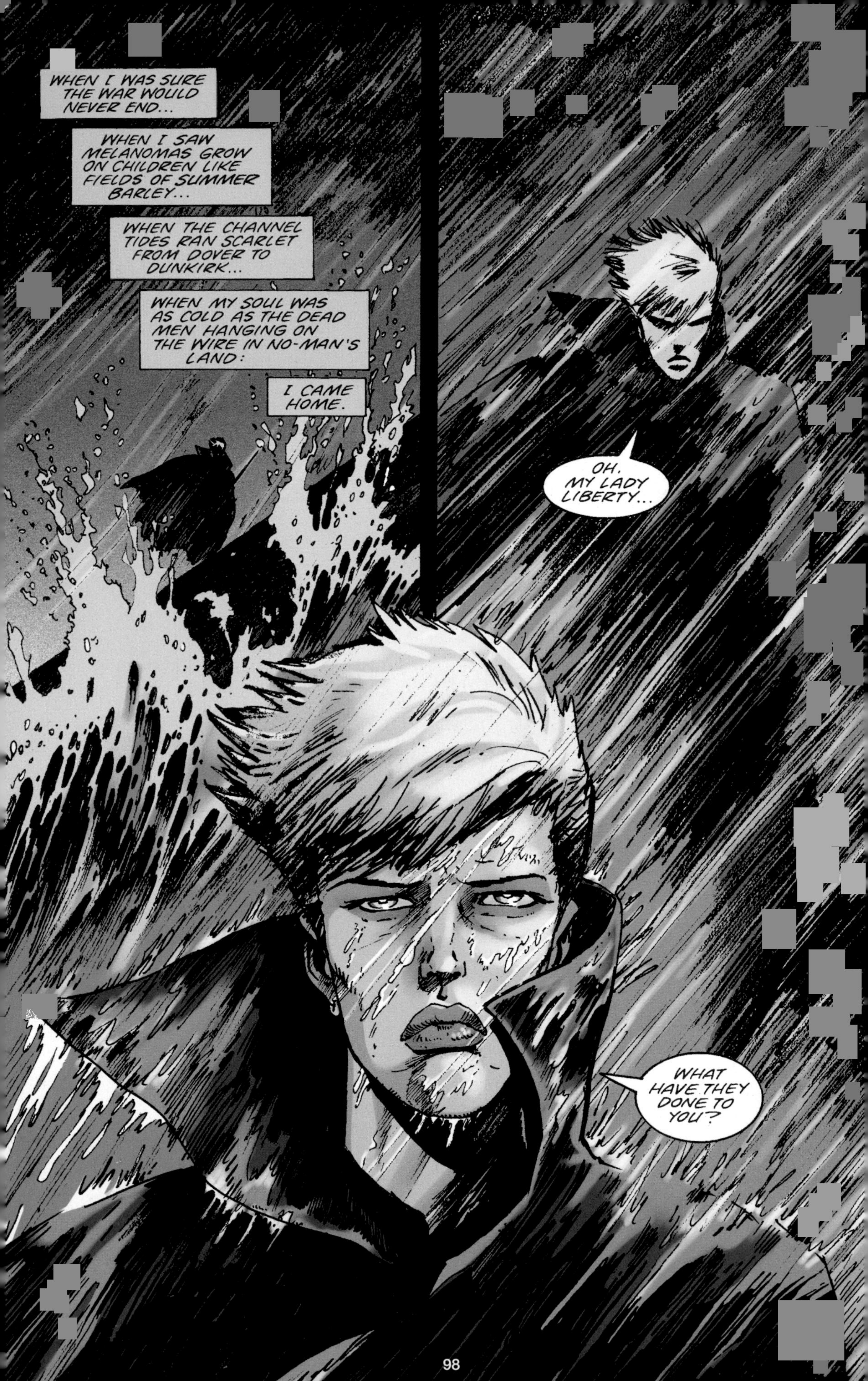
WHEN I WAS SURE THE WAR WOULD NEVER END...
WHEN I SAW MELANOMAS GROW ON CHILDREN LIKE FIELDS OF SUMMER BARLEY...
WHEN THE CHANNEL TIDES RAN SCARLET FROM DOVER TO DUNKIRK...
WHEN MY SOUL WAS AS COLD AS THE DEAD MEN HANGING ON THE WIRE IN NO-MAN'S LAND:
I CAME HOME.
OH. MY LADY LIBERTY...
WHAT HAVE THEY DONE TO YOU?

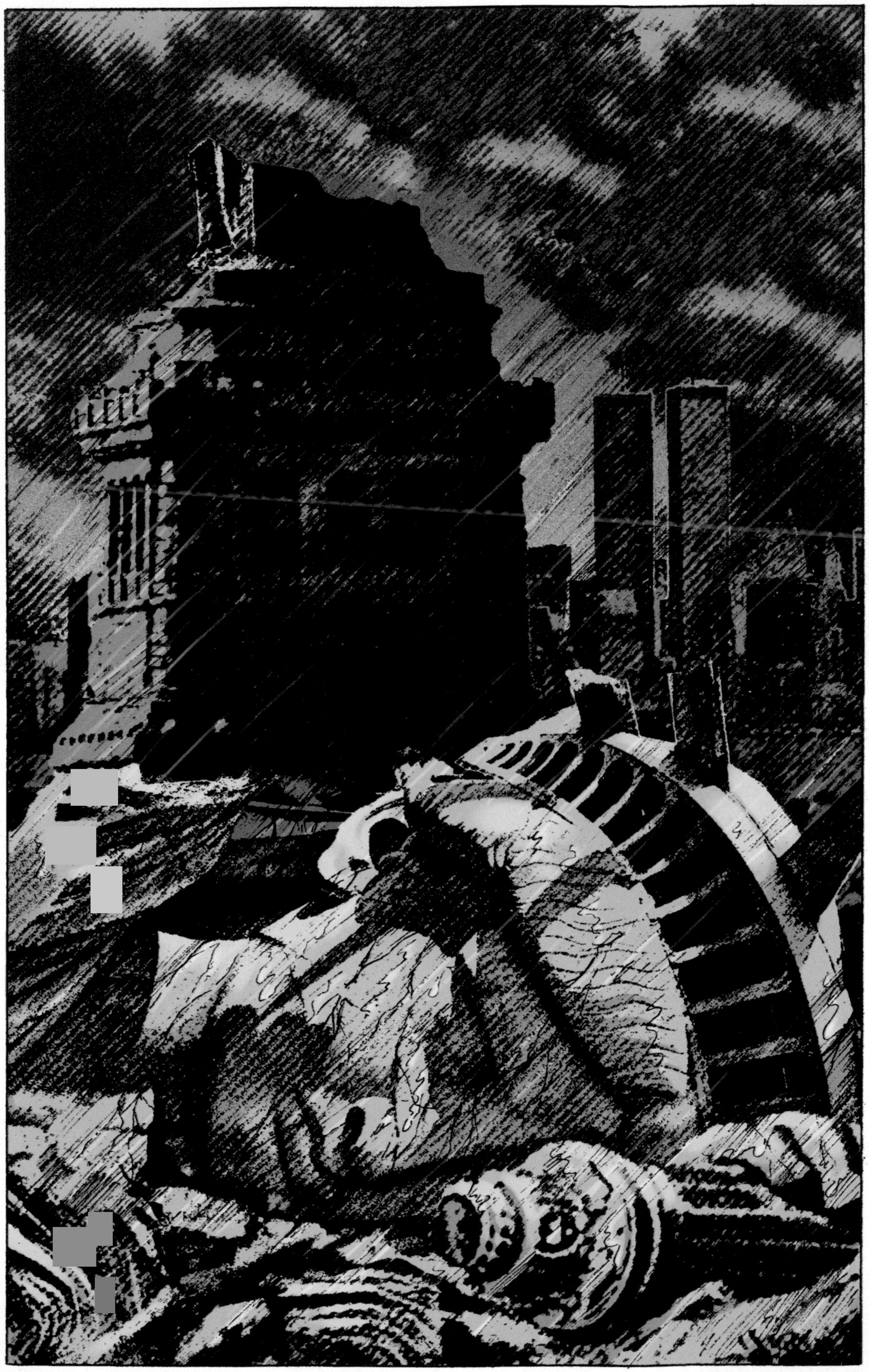

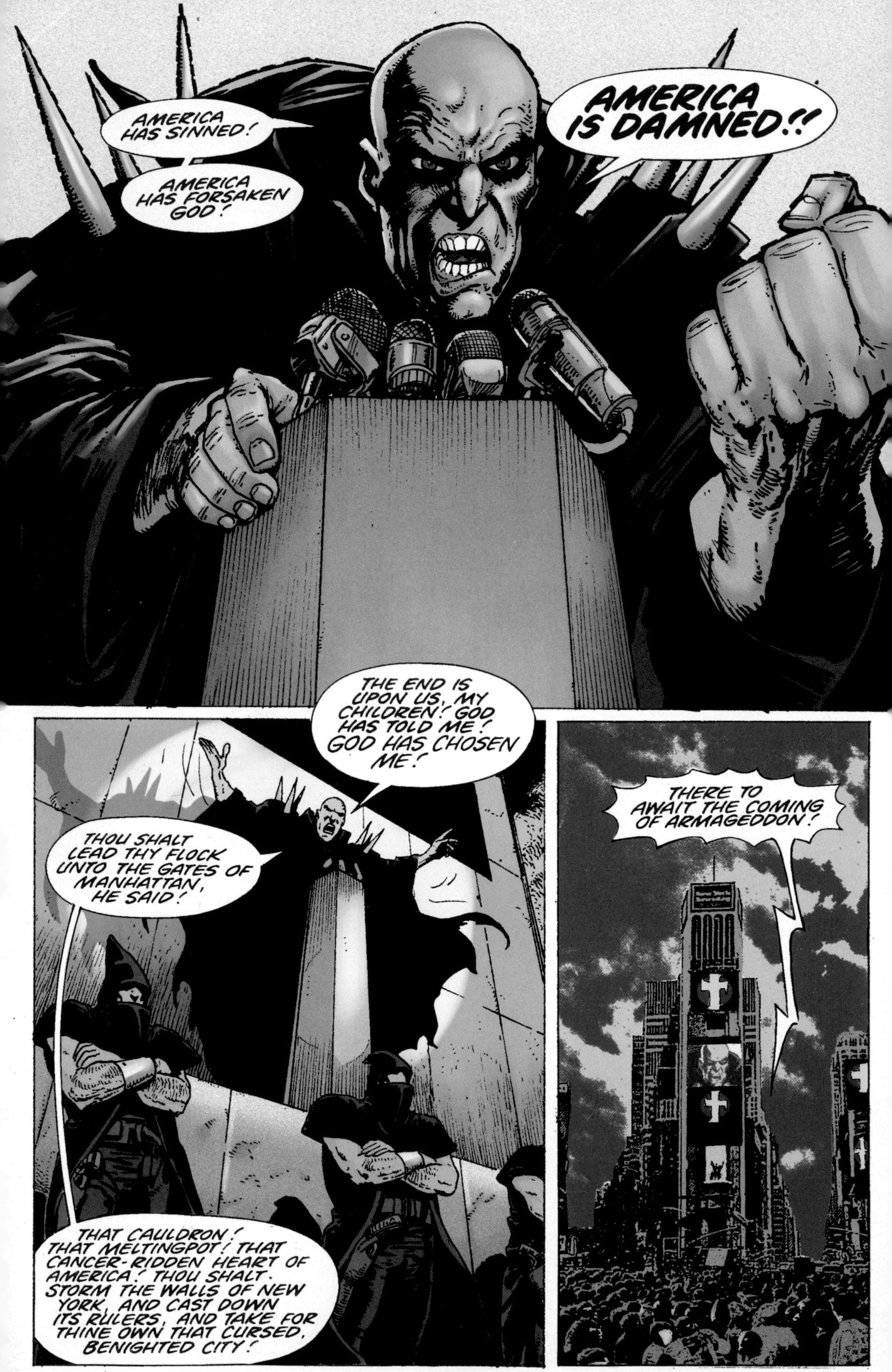
AMERICA HAS SINNED!
AMERICA HAS FORSAKEN GOD!
AMERICA IS DAMNED!!
THE END IS UPON US, MY CHILDREN! GOD HAS TOLD ME! GOD HAS CHOSEN ME!
THOU SHALT LEAD THY FLOCK UNTO THE GATES OF MANHATTAN, HE SAID!
THAT CAULDRON! THAT MELTINGPOT! THAT CANCER-RIDDEN HEART OF AMERICA! THOU SHALT STORM THE WALLS OF NEW YORK, AND CAST DOWN ITS RULERS, AND TAKE FOR THINE OWN THAT CURSED, BENIGHTED CITY!
THERE TO AWAIT THE COMING OF ARMAGEDDON!

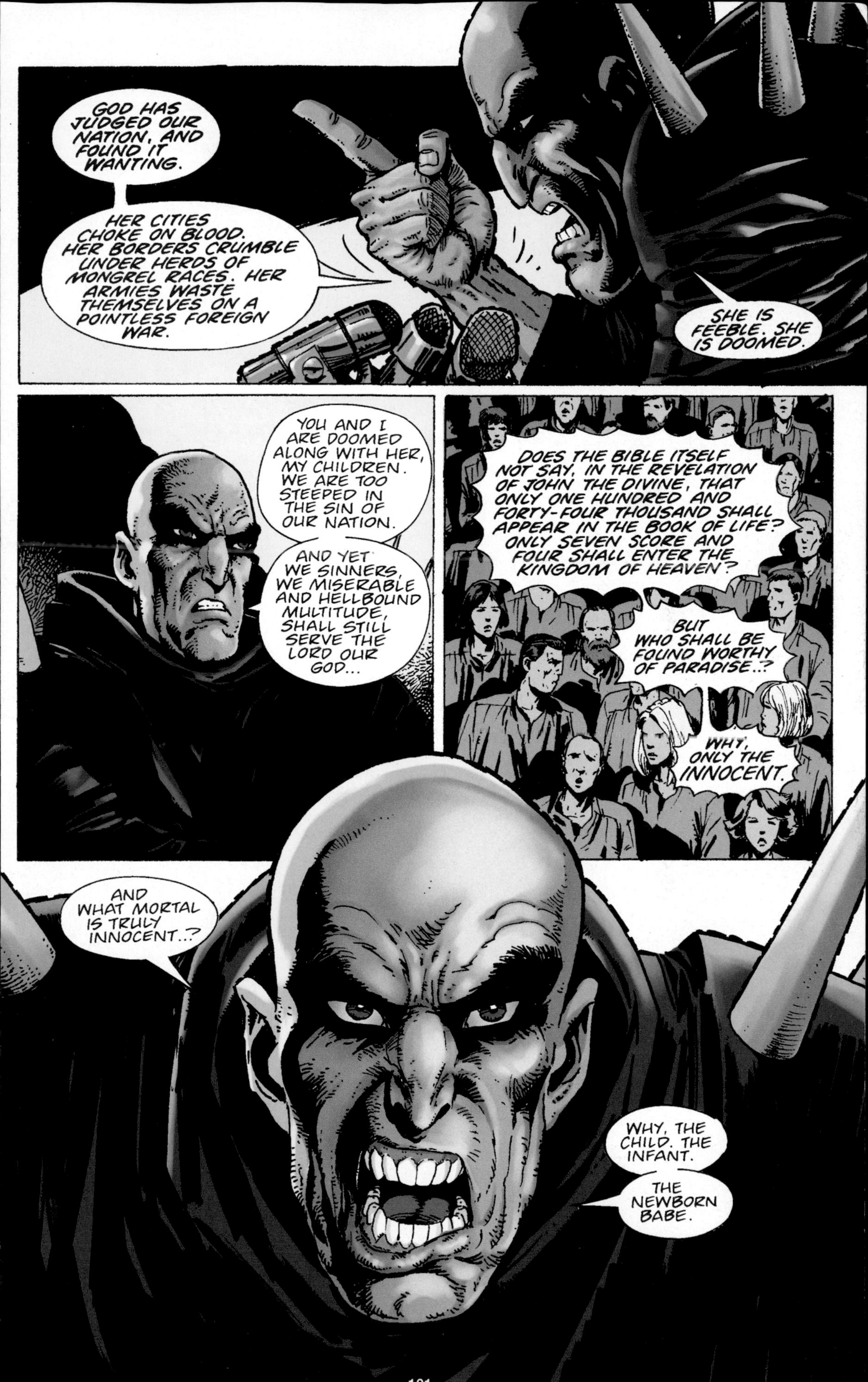
GOD HAS JUDGED OUR NATION, AND FOUND IT WANTING.
HER CITIES CHOKE ON BLOOD. HER BORDERS CRUMBLE UNDER HERDS OF MONGREL RACES. HER ARMIES WASTE THEMSELVES ON A POINTLESS FOREIGN WAR.
SHE IS FEEBLE. SHE IS DOOMED.
YOU AND I ARE DOOMED ALONG WITH HER, MY CHILDREN. WE ARE TOO STEEPED IN THE SIN OF OUR NATION.
AND YET WE SINNERS, WE MISERABLE AND HELLBOUND MULTITUDE, SHALL STILL SERVE THE LORD OUR GOD...
DOES THE BIBLE ITSELF NOT SAY, IN THE REVELATION OF JOHN THE DIVINE, THAT ONLY ONE HUNDRED AND FORTY-FOUR THOUSAND SHALL APPEAR IN THE BOOK OF LIFE? ONLY SEVEN SCORE AND FOUR SHALL ENTER THE KINGDOM OF HEAVEN?
BUT WHO SHALL BE FOUND WORTHY OF PARADISE..?
WHY, ONLY THE INNOCENT.
AND WHAT MORTAL IS TRULY INNOCENT..?
WHY, THE CHILD. THE INFANT.
THE NEWBORN BABE.

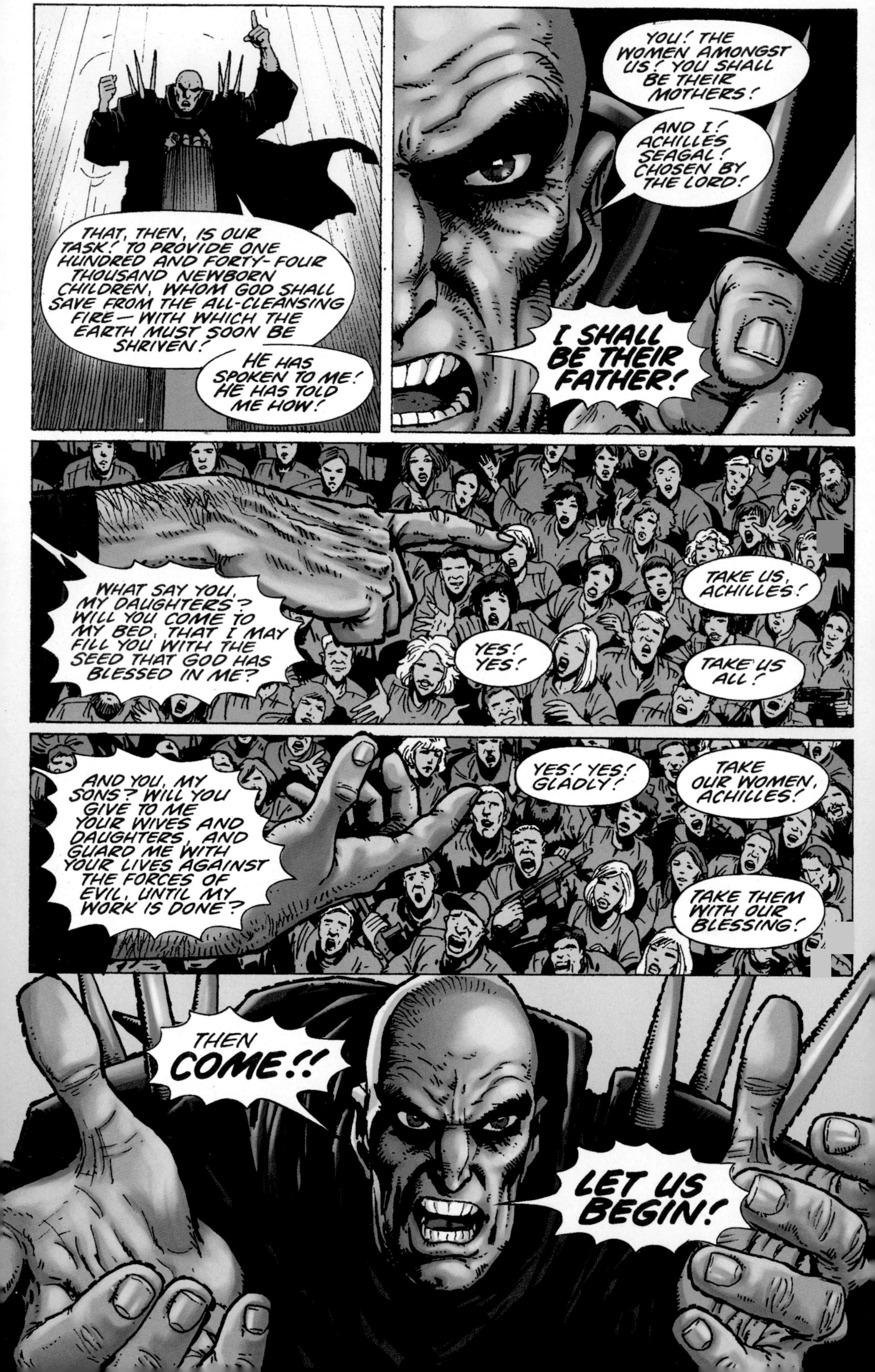
THAT, THEN, IS OUR TASK! TO PROVIDE ONE HUNDRED AND FORTY-FOUR THOUSAND NEWBORN CHILDREN, WHOM GOD SHALL SAVE FROM THE ALL-CLEANSING FIRE—WITH WHICH THE EARTH MUST SOON BE SHRIVEN!
HE HAS SPOKEN TO ME! HE HAS TOLD ME HOW!
YOU! THE WOMEN AMONGST US! YOU SHALL BE THEIR MOTHERS!
AND I! ACHILLES SEAGAL! CHOSEN BY THE LORD!
I SHALL BE THEIR FATHER!
WHAT SAY YOU, MY DAUGHTERS? WILL YOU COME TO MY BED, THAT I MAY FILL YOU WITH THE SEED THAT GOD HAS BLESSED IN ME?
YES! YES!
TAKE US, ACHILLES!
TAKE US ALL!
AND YOU, MY SONS? WILL YOU GIVE TO ME YOUR WIVES AND DAUGHTERS, AND GUARD ME WITH YOUR LIVES AGAINST THE FORCES OF EVIL, UNTIL MY WORK IS DONE?
YES! YES! GLADLY!
TAKE OUR WOMEN, ACHILLES!
TAKE THEM WITH OUR BLESSING!
THEN COME!!
LET US BEGIN!

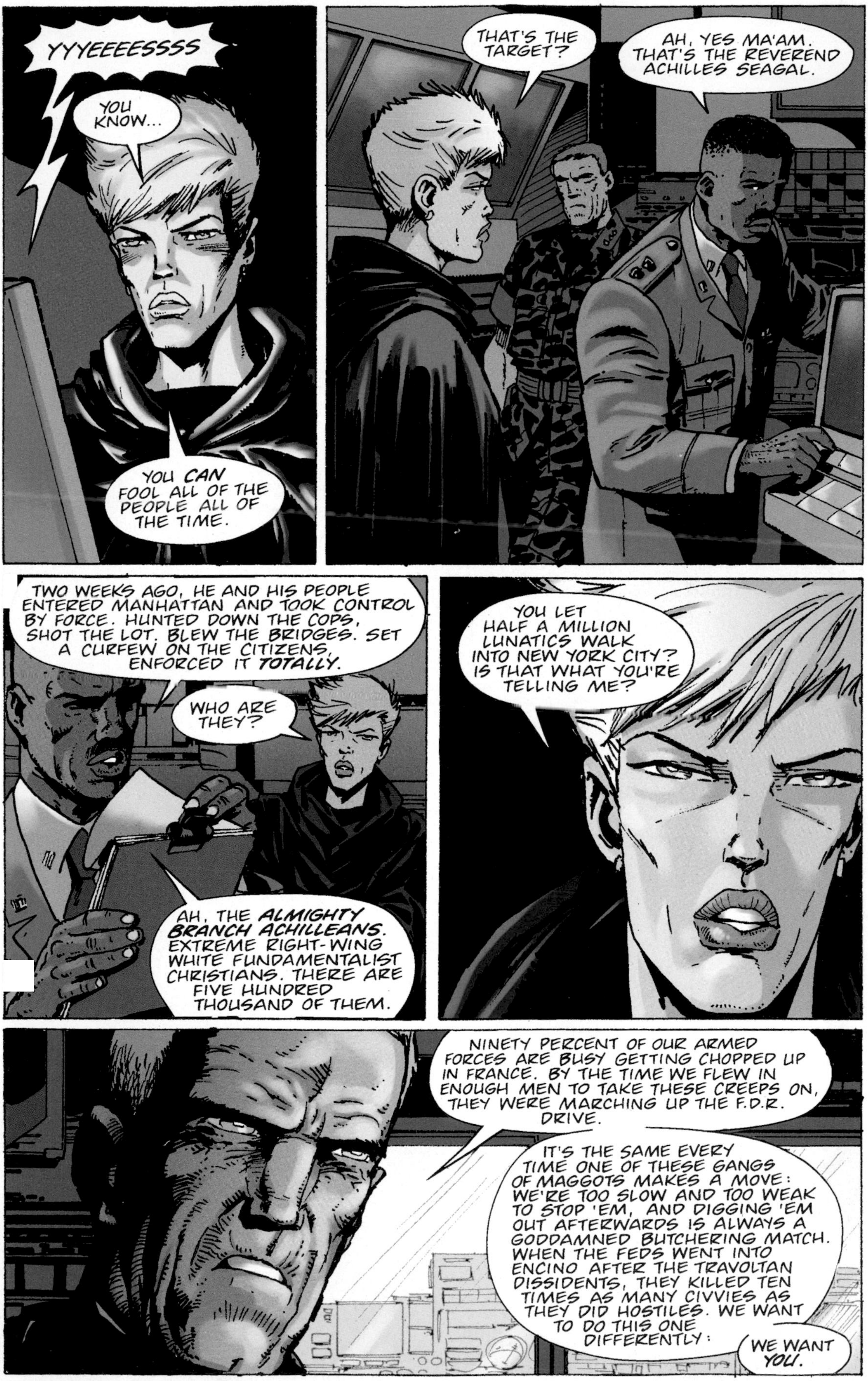

YYYEEEEESSSS
YOU KNOW...
YOU CAN FOOL ALL OF THE PEOPLE ALL OF THE TIME.
THAT'S THE TARGET?
AH, YES MA'AM. THAT'S THE REVEREND ACHILLES SEAGAL.
TWO WEEKS AGO, HE AND HIS PEOPLE ENTERED MANHATTAN AND TOOK CONTROL BY FORCE. HUNTED DOWN THE COPS, SHOT THE LOT. BLEW THE BRIDGES. SET A CURFEW ON THE CITIZENS, ENFORCED IT TOTALLY.
WHO ARE THEY?
AH, THE ALMIGHTY BRANCH ACHILLEANS. EXTREME RIGHT-WING WHITE FUNDAMENTALIST CHRISTIANS. THERE ARE FIVE HUNDRED THOUSAND OF THEM.
YOU LET HALF A MILLION LUNATICS WALK INTO NEW YORK CITY? IS THAT WHAT YOU'RE TELLING ME?
NINETY PERCENT OF OUR ARMED FORCES ARE BUSY GETTING CHOPPED UP IN FRANCE. BY THE TIME WE FLEW IN ENOUGH MEN TO TAKE THESE CREEPS ON, THEY WERE MARCHING UP THE F.D.R. DRIVE.
IT'S THE SAME EVERY TIME ONE OF THESE GANGS OF MAGGOTS MAKES A MOVE: WE'RE TOO SLOW AND TOO WEAK TO STOP 'EM, AND DIGGING 'EM OUT AFTERWARDS IS ALWAYS A GODDAMNED BUTCHERING MATCH. WHEN THE FEDS WENT INTO ENCINO AFTER THE TRAVOLTAN DISSIDENTS, THEY KILLED TEN TIMES AS MANY CIVVIES AS THEY DID HOSTILES. WE WANT TO DO THIS ONE DIFFERENTLY:
WE WANT YOU.

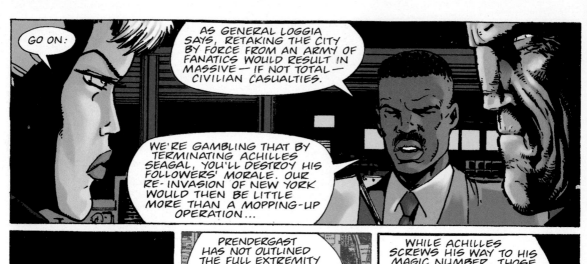

GO ON:

AS GENERAL LOGGIA SAYS, RETAKING THE CITY BY FORCE FROM AN ARMY OF FANATICS WOULD RESULT IN MASSIVE — IF NOT TOTAL — CIVILIAN CASUALTIES.

WE'RE GAMBLING THAT BY TERMINATING ACHILLES SEAGAL, YOU'LL DESTROY HIS FOLLOWERS' MORALE. OUR RE-INVASION OF NEW YORK WOULD THEN BE LITTLE MORE THAN A MOPPING-UP OPERATION...

WHY ME?

QUITE SIMPLY BECAUSE THERE'S NO ONE ELSE AS GOOD AS YOU. YOU'RE THE LAST SURVIVING KILL-TEAM COMMANDO ON RECORD. YOUR SKILLS, AND THE LEVEL YOU OPERATE ON, MAKE YOU UNIQUE.

PRENDERGAST HAS NOT OUTLINED THE FULL EXTREMITY OF THE SITUATION. THE BRANCH ACHILLEANS HAVE ALREADY BEGUN CLEANSING THE POPULATION OF THE CITY, ACCORDING TO THEIR OWN CRITERIA.

ACCORDING TO THE HiSAT PICTURES WE'VE BEEN GETTING, CHINA-TOWN AND GREENWICH VILLAGE HAVE BEEN RAZED. HARLEM IS THE ONE PART OF TOWN STILL IN THE HANDS OF ITS CITIZENS, BUT IT IS VERY OBVIOUSLY GOING TO BE NEXT.

WHILE ACHILLES SCREWS HIS WAY TO HIS MAGIC NUMBER, THOSE BASTARDS OF HIS ARE COMMITTING GENOCIDE IN THE GREATEST CITY ON EARTH — AND BY GOD, CORPORAL MALONE, IT IS YOUR DUTY AS AN AMERICAN SOLDIER TO GO IN THERE AND TERMINATE HIS WORTHLESS ASS WITH ULTIMATE PREJUDICE: NOW.

WHAT HAPPENED TO THE STATUE?

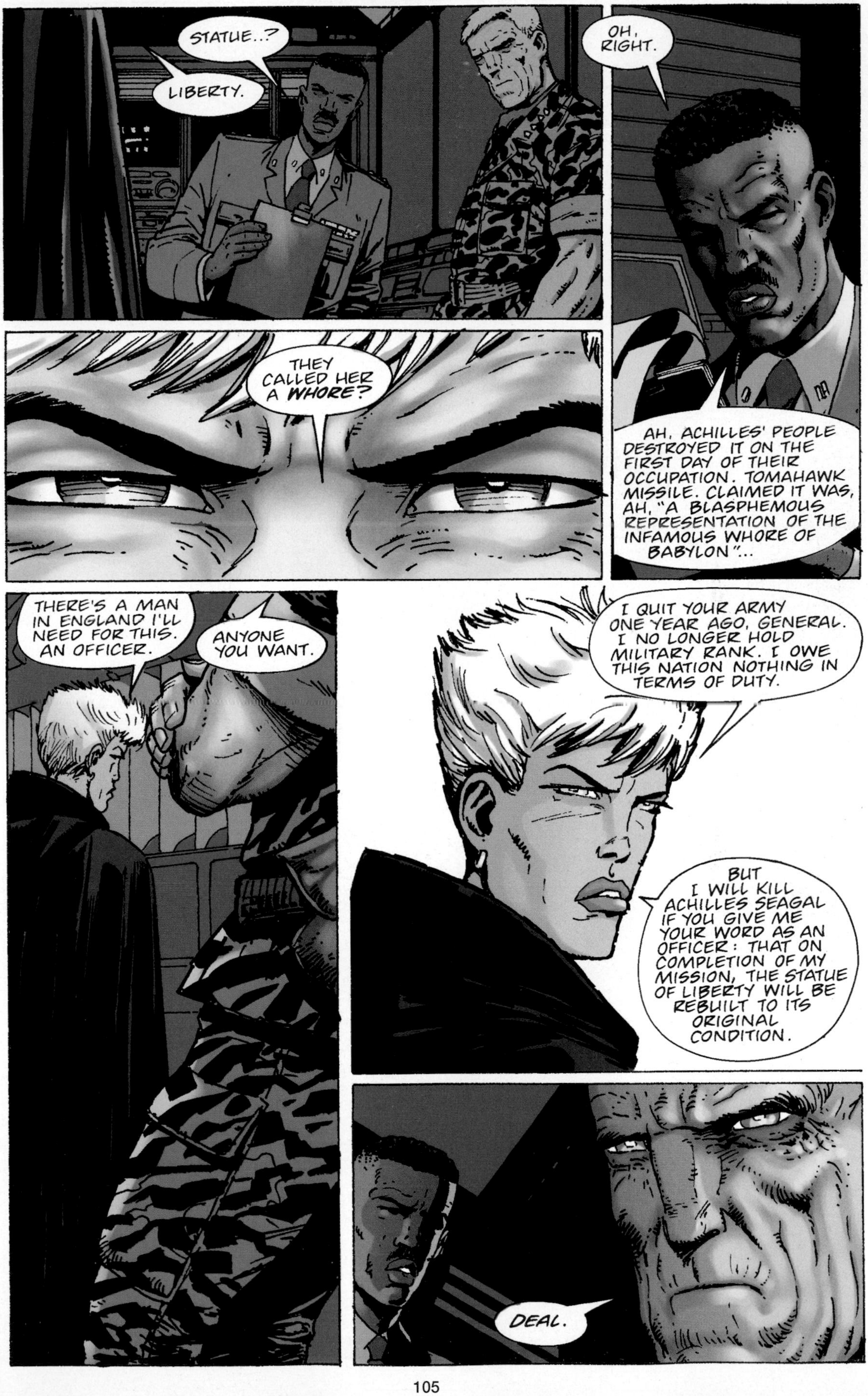
STATUE..?
LIBERTY.
OH, RIGHT.
THEY CALLED HER A WHORE?
AH, ACHILLES' PEOPLE DESTROYED IT ON THE FIRST DAY OF THEIR OCCUPATION. TOMAHAWK MISSILE. CLAIMED IT WAS, AH, "A BLASPHEMOUS REPRESENTATION OF THE INFAMOUS WHORE OF BABYLON"...
THERE'S A MAN IN ENGLAND I'LL NEED FOR THIS. AN OFFICER.
ANYONE YOU WANT.
I QUIT YOUR ARMY ONE YEAR AGO, GENERAL. I NO LONGER HOLD MILITARY RANK. I OWE THIS NATION NOTHING IN TERMS OF DUTY.
BUT I WILL KILL ACHILLES SEAGAL IF YOU GIVE ME YOUR WORD AS AN OFFICER: THAT ON COMPLETION OF MY MISSION, THE STATUE OF LIBERTY WILL BE REBUILT TO ITS ORIGINAL CONDITION.
DEAL.

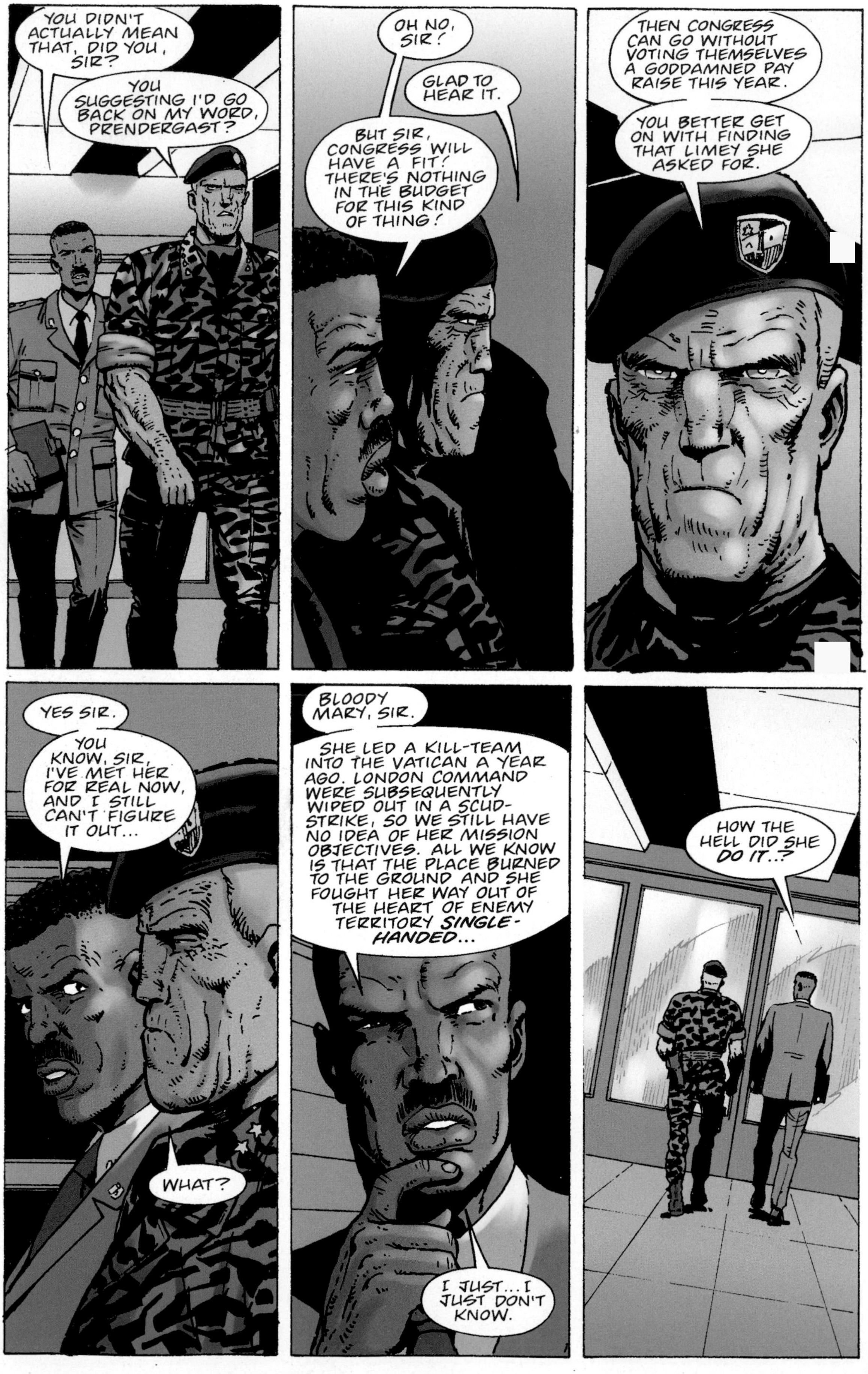
YOU DIDN'T ACTUALLY MEAN THAT, DID YOU, SIR?
YOU SUGGESTING I'D GO BACK ON MY WORD, PRENDERGAST?
OH NO, SIR!
GLAD TO HEAR IT.
BUT SIR, CONGRESS WILL HAVE A FIT! THERE'S NOTHING IN THE BUDGET FOR THIS KIND OF THING!
THEN CONGRESS CAN GO WITHOUT VOTING THEMSELVES A GODDAMNED PAY RAISE THIS YEAR.
YOU BETTER GET ON WITH FINDING THAT LIMEY SHE ASKED FOR.
YES SIR.
YOU KNOW, SIR, I'VE MET HER FOR REAL NOW, AND I STILL CAN'T FIGURE IT OUT...
WHAT?
BLOODY MARY, SIR.
SHE LED A KILL-TEAM INTO THE VATICAN A YEAR AGO. LONDON COMMAND WERE SUBSEQUENTLY WIPED OUT IN A SCUD-STRIKE, SO WE STILL HAVE NO IDEA OF HER MISSION OBJECTIVES. ALL WE KNOW IS THAT THE PLACE BURNED TO THE GROUND AND SHE FOUGHT HER WAY OUT OF THE HEART OF ENEMY TERRITORY *SINGLE-HANDED*...
I JUST... I JUST DON'T KNOW.
HOW THE HELL DID SHE *DO IT*..?

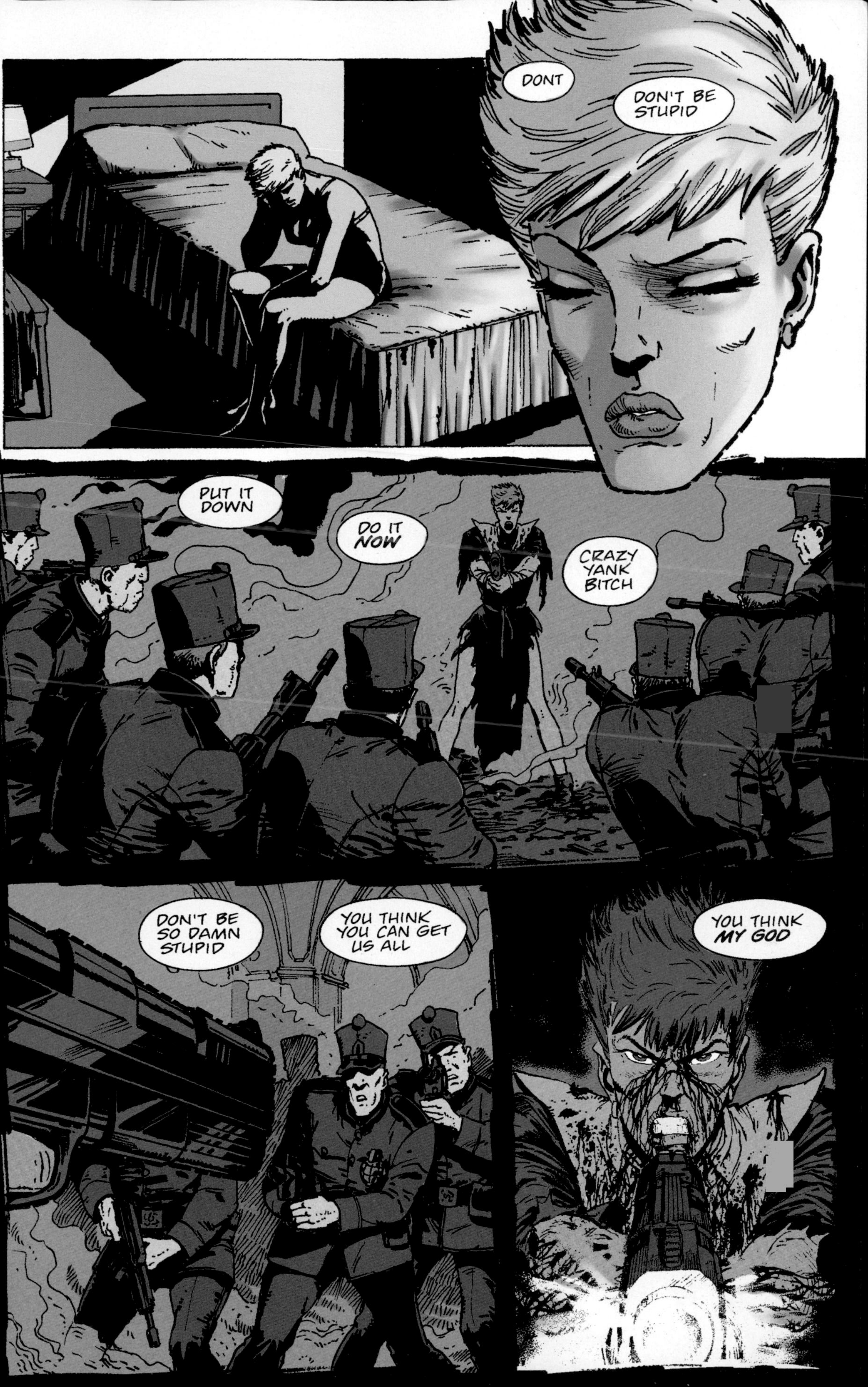
DONT
DON'T BE STUPID
PUT IT DOWN
DO IT NOW
CRAZY YANK BITCH
DON'T BE SO DAMN STUPID
YOU THINK YOU CAN GET US ALL
YOU THINK MY GOD

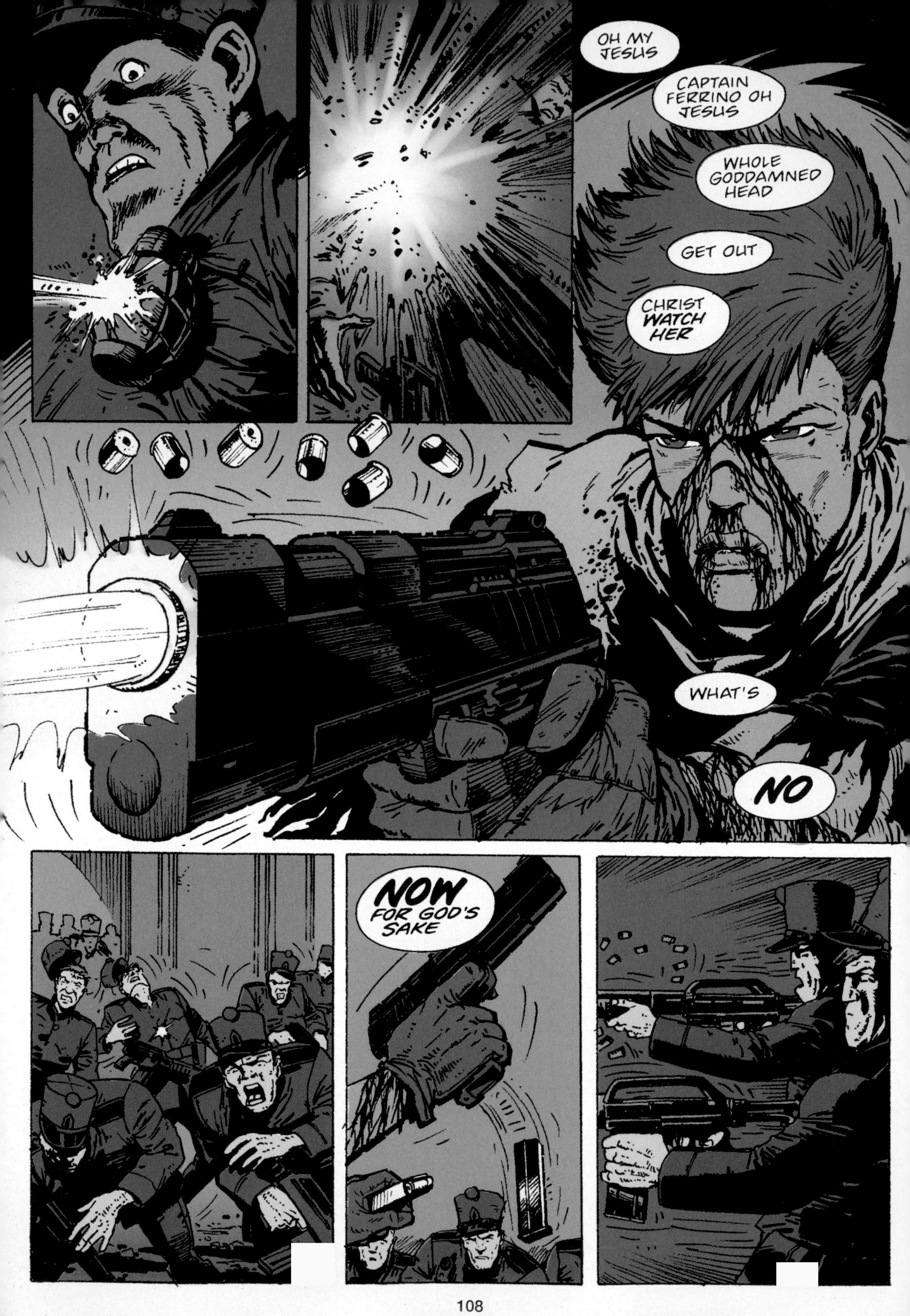
OH MY JESUS
CAPTAIN FERRINO OH JESUS
WHOLE GODDAMNED HEAD
GET OUT
CHRIST WATCH HER
WHAT'S
NO
NOW FOR GOD'S SAKE

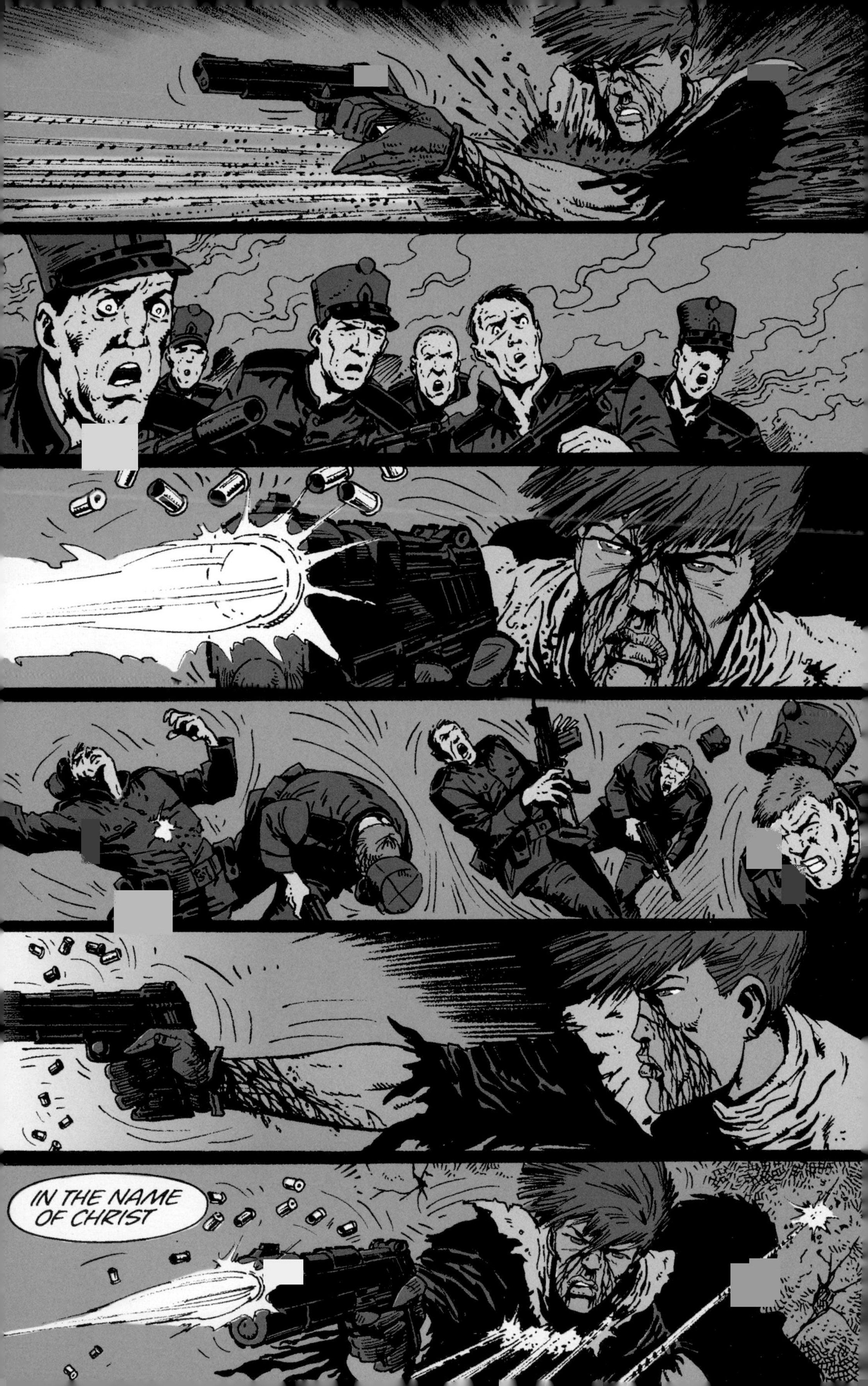
IN THE NAME OF CHRIST

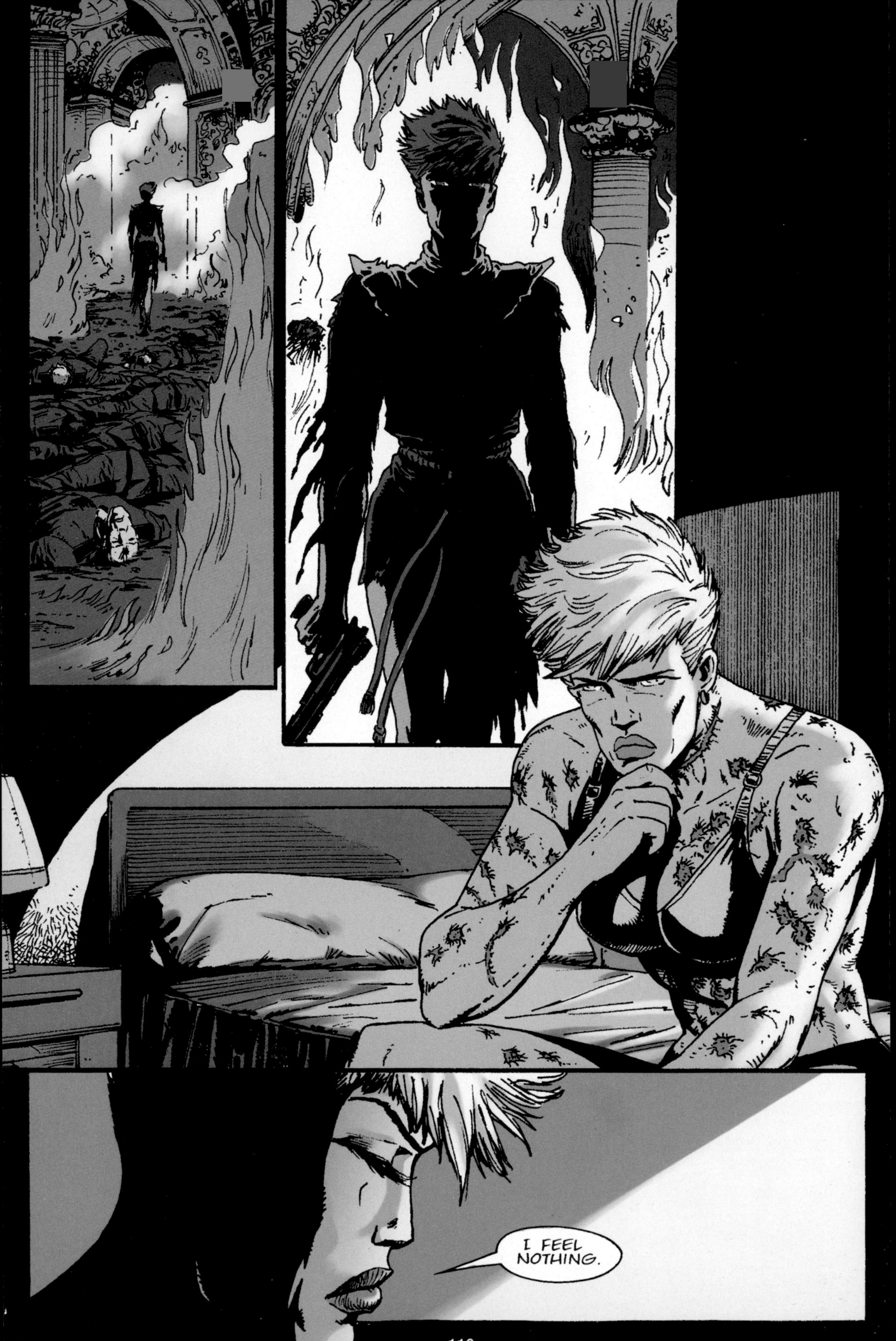
I FEEL NOTHING.

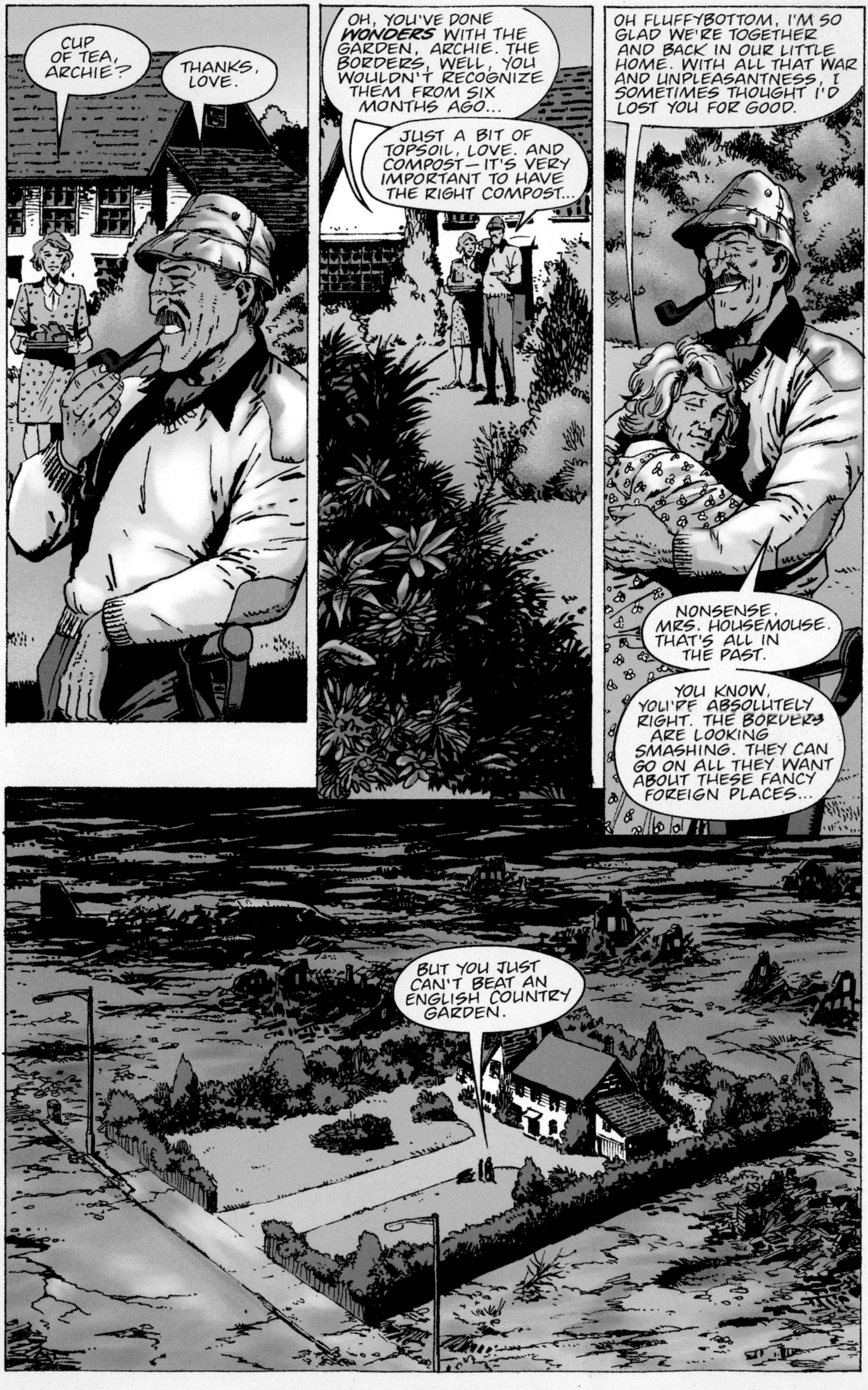
CUP OF TEA, ARCHIE?
THANKS, LOVE.
OH, YOU'VE DONE **WONDERS** WITH THE GARDEN, ARCHIE. THE BORDERS, WELL, YOU WOULDN'T RECOGNIZE THEM FROM SIX MONTHS AGO...
JUST A BIT OF TOPSOIL, LOVE. AND COMPOST—IT'S VERY IMPORTANT TO HAVE THE RIGHT COMPOST...
OH FLUFFYBOTTOM, I'M SO GLAD WE'RE TOGETHER AND BACK IN OUR LITTLE HOME. WITH ALL THAT WAR AND UNPLEASANTNESS, I SOMETIMES THOUGHT I'D LOST YOU FOR GOOD.
NONSENSE, MRS. HOUSEMOUSE. THAT'S ALL IN THE PAST.
YOU KNOW, YOU'RE ABSOLUTELY RIGHT. THE BORDERS ARE LOOKING SMASHING. THEY CAN GO ON ALL THEY WANT ABOUT THESE FANCY FOREIGN PLACES...
BUT YOU JUST CAN'T BEAT AN ENGLISH COUNTRY GARDEN.

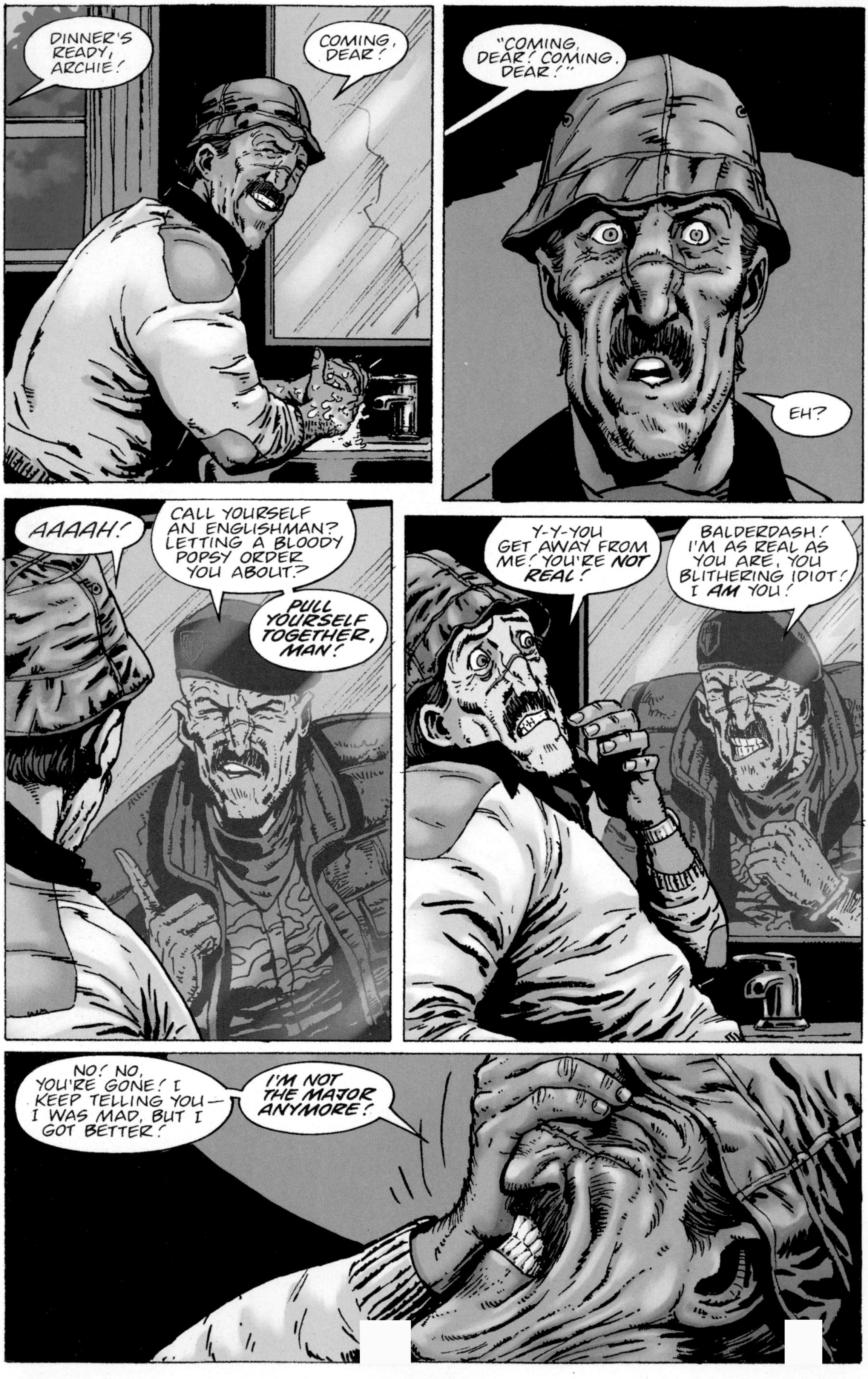
DINNER'S READY, ARCHIE!
COMING, DEAR!
"COMING, DEAR! COMING, DEAR!"
EH?
AAAAH!
CALL YOURSELF AN ENGLISHMAN? LETTING A BLOODY POPSY ORDER YOU ABOUT?
PULL YOURSELF TOGETHER, MAN!
Y-Y-YOU GET AWAY FROM ME! YOU'RE NOT REAL!
BALDERDASH! I'M AS REAL AS YOU ARE, YOU BLITHERING IDIOT! I AM YOU!
NO! NO, YOU'RE GONE! I KEEP TELLING YOU— I WAS MAD, BUT I GOT BETTER!
I'M NOT THE MAJOR ANYMORE!

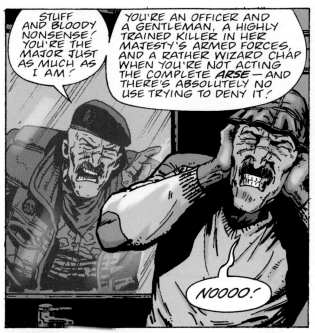

STUFF AND BLOODY NONSENSE! YOU'RE THE MAJOR JUST AS MUCH AS I AM!

YOU'RE AN OFFICER AND A GENTLEMAN, A HIGHLY TRAINED KILLER IN HER MAJESTY'S ARMED FORCES, AND A RATHER WIZARD CHAP WHEN YOU'RE NOT ACTING THE COMPLETE *ARSE*— AND THERE'S ABSOLUTELY NO USE TRYING TO DENY IT!

NOOOO!

WHAT THE BLUE BLAZES DO YOU THINK YOU'RE PLAYING AT? *GARDENING* WHEN THERE'S A WAR TO BE WON? AND *PLANTING FLOWERS*—GOOD GOD, MAN, YOU KNOW THE KIND OF THING THAT CAN LEAD TO, DON'T YOU?

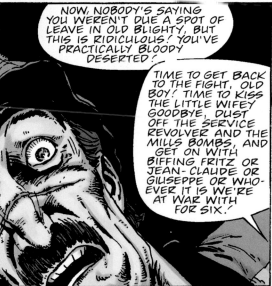

NOW, NOBODY'S SAYING YOU WEREN'T DUE A SPOT OF LEAVE IN OLD BLIGHTY, BUT THIS IS RIDICULOUS! YOU'VE PRACTICALLY BLOODY DESERTED!

TIME TO GET BACK TO THE FIGHT, OLD BOY! TIME TO KISS THE LITTLE WIFEY GOODBYE, DUST OFF THE SERVICE REVOLVER AND THE MILLS BOMBS, AND GET ON WITH BIFFING FRITZ OR JEAN-CLAUDE OR GIUSEPPE OR WHO-EVER IT IS WE'RE AT WAR WITH FOR SIX!

YOU CAN'T DO THIS TO ME! I'M HAPPY HERE! I'M SANE!

FOR THE LAST TIME, LEAVE ME BEEEEE!!

ARCHIE!

ARCHIE, I HEARD YOU SHOUTING! WHAT'S WRONG?

I—I—

I'M STILL HERE, MATEY!

AAAAAAHHH!!!

ARCHIE!

ARCHIE, WHAT'S THE MATTER?

NO! NUH—NUHHH—

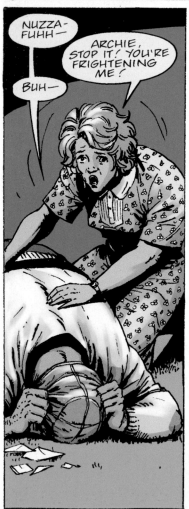

NUZZA-FUHH—

ARCHIE, STOP IT! YOU'RE FRIGHTENING ME!

BUH—

ARCHIE?

BUH—

BUH—

BUH—

BLOODY GOOD SHOW...!

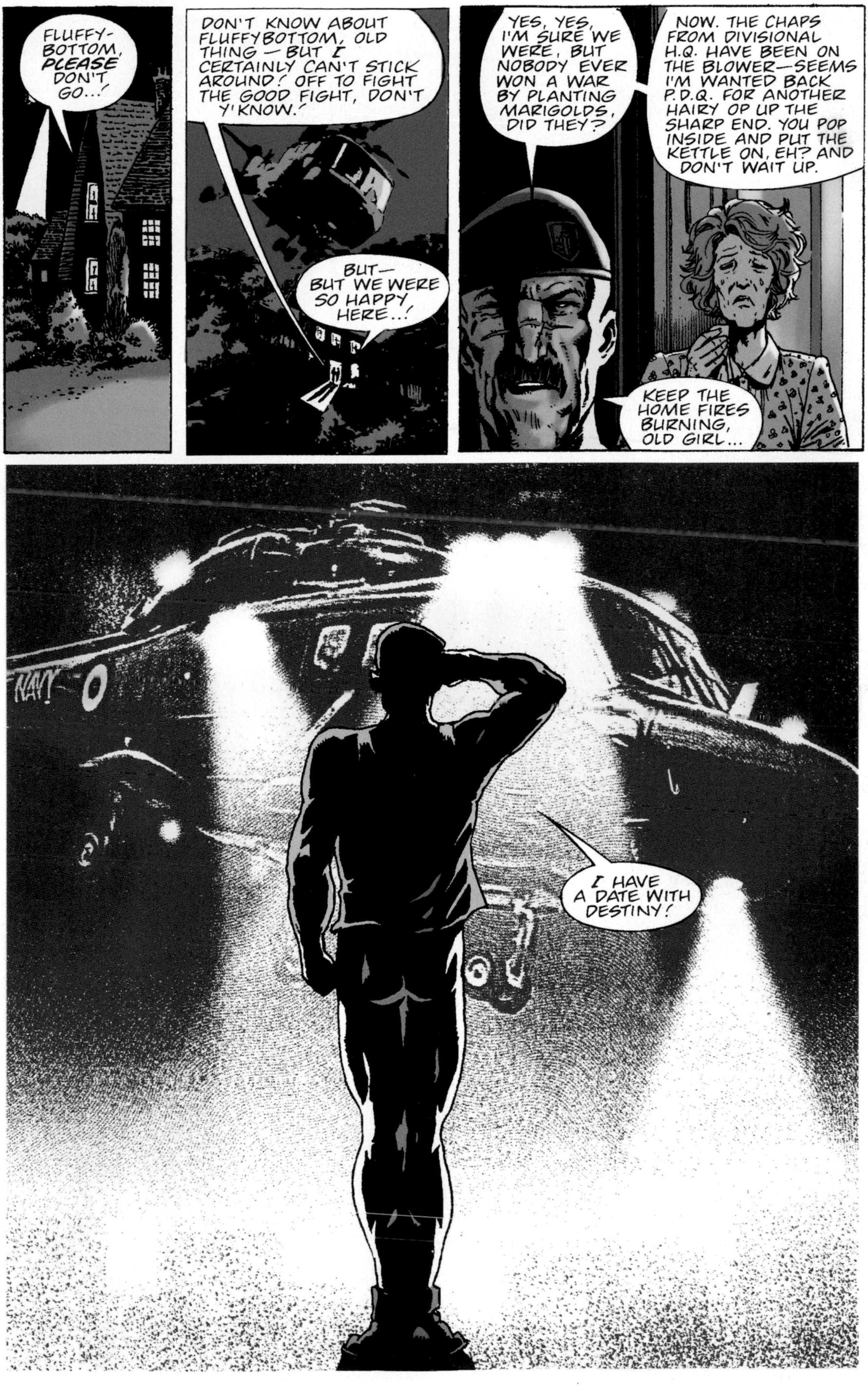
FLUFFY-BOTTOM, PLEASE DON'T GO...!
DON'T KNOW ABOUT FLUFFYBOTTOM, OLD THING — BUT I CERTAINLY CAN'T STICK AROUND! OFF TO FIGHT THE GOOD FIGHT, DON'T Y'KNOW.
BUT— BUT WE WERE SO HAPPY HERE...!
YES, YES, I'M SURE WE WERE, BUT NOBODY EVER WON A WAR BY PLANTING MARIGOLDS, DID THEY?
NOW. THE CHAPS FROM DIVISIONAL H.Q. HAVE BEEN ON THE BLOWER—SEEMS I'M WANTED BACK P.D.Q. FOR ANOTHER HAIRY OP UP THE SHARP END. YOU POP INSIDE AND PUT THE KETTLE ON, EH? AND DON'T WAIT UP.
KEEP THE HOME FIRES BURNING, OLD GIRL...
NAVY
I HAVE A DATE WITH DESTINY!

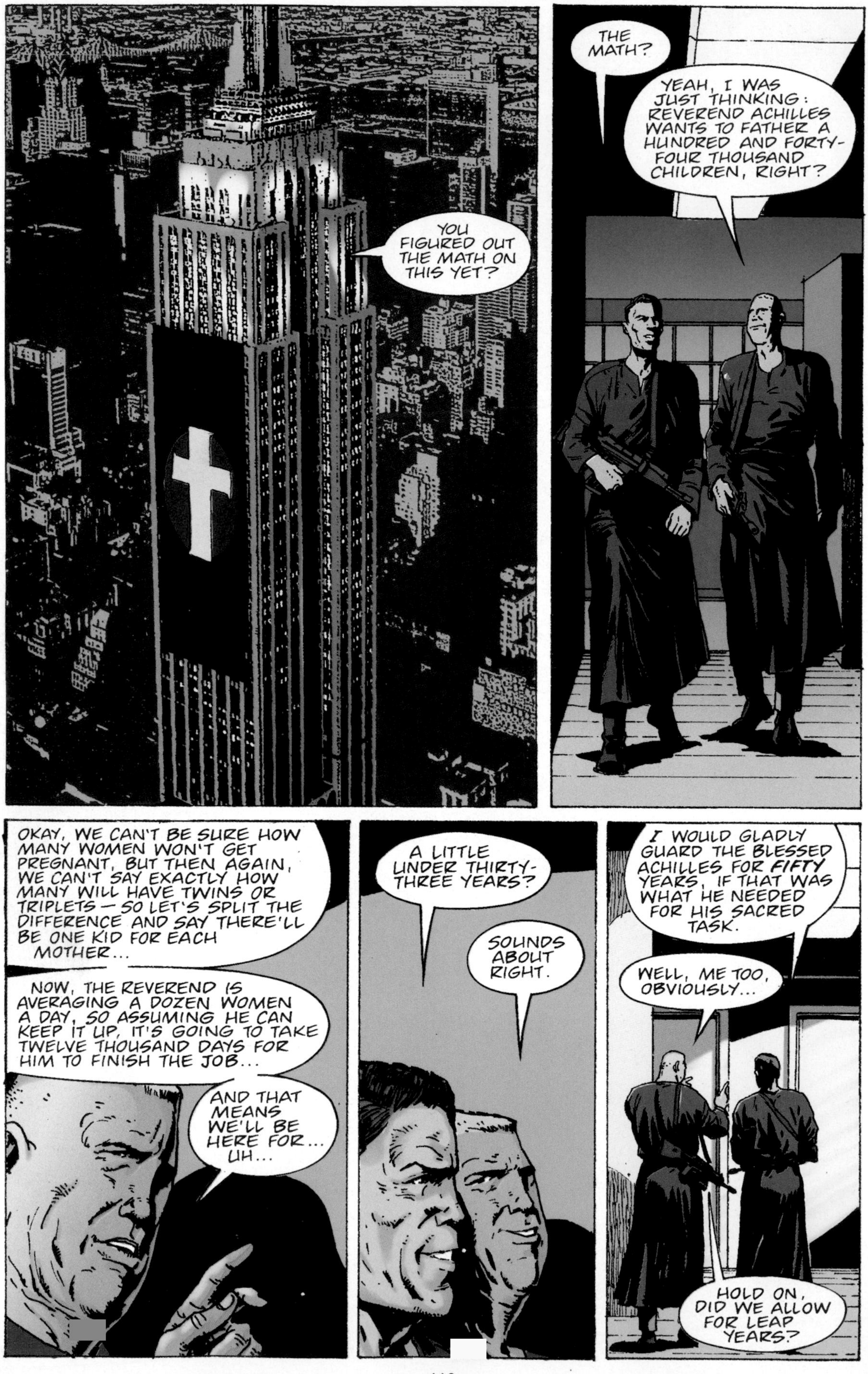
YOU FIGURED OUT THE MATH ON THIS YET?
THE MATH?
YEAH, I WAS JUST THINKING: REVEREND ACHILLES WANTS TO FATHER A HUNDRED AND FORTY-FOUR THOUSAND CHILDREN, RIGHT?
OKAY, WE CAN'T BE SURE HOW MANY WOMEN WON'T GET PREGNANT, BUT THEN AGAIN, WE CAN'T SAY EXACTLY HOW MANY WILL HAVE TWINS OR TRIPLETS — SO LET'S SPLIT THE DIFFERENCE AND SAY THERE'LL BE ONE KID FOR EACH MOTHER...
NOW, THE REVEREND IS AVERAGING A DOZEN WOMEN A DAY, SO ASSUMING HE CAN KEEP IT UP, IT'S GOING TO TAKE TWELVE THOUSAND DAYS FOR HIM TO FINISH THE JOB...
AND THAT MEANS WE'LL BE HERE FOR... UH...
A LITTLE UNDER THIRTY-THREE YEARS?
SOUNDS ABOUT RIGHT.
I WOULD GLADLY GUARD THE BLESSED ACHILLES FOR FIFTY YEARS, IF THAT WAS WHAT HE NEEDED FOR HIS SACRED TASK.
WELL, ME TOO, OBVIOUSLY...
HOLD ON, DID WE ALLOW FOR LEAP YEARS?

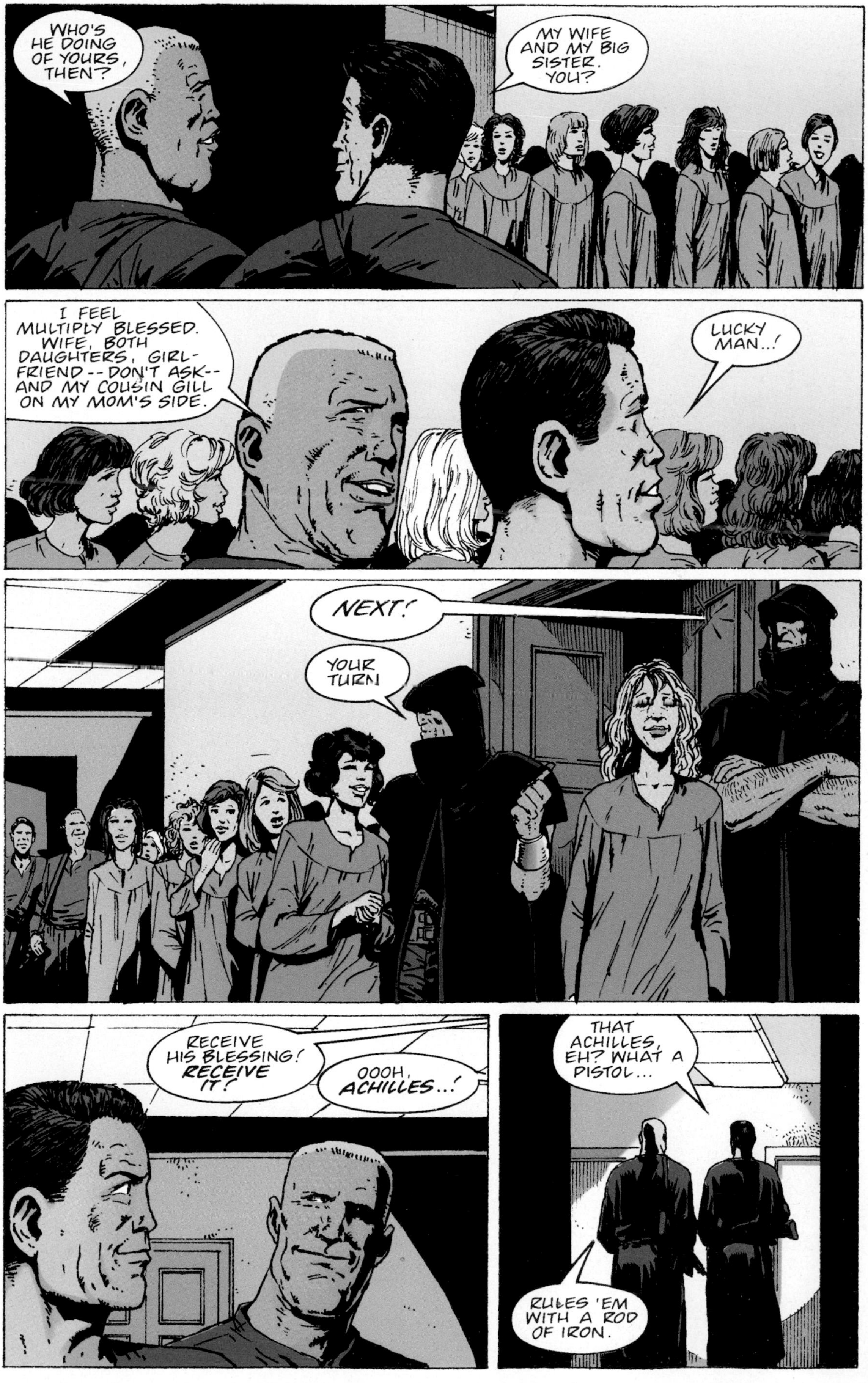
WHO'S HE DOING OF YOURS, THEN?
MY WIFE AND MY BIG SISTER. YOU?
I FEEL MULTIPLY BLESSED. WIFE, BOTH DAUGHTERS, GIRL-FRIEND--DON'T ASK--AND MY COUSIN GILL ON MY MOM'S SIDE.
LUCKY MAN...!
NEXT!
YOUR TURN
RECEIVE HIS BLESSING! RECEIVE IT!
OOOH, ACHILLES...!
THAT ACHILLES, EH? WHAT A PISTOL...
RULES 'EM WITH A ROD OF IRON.

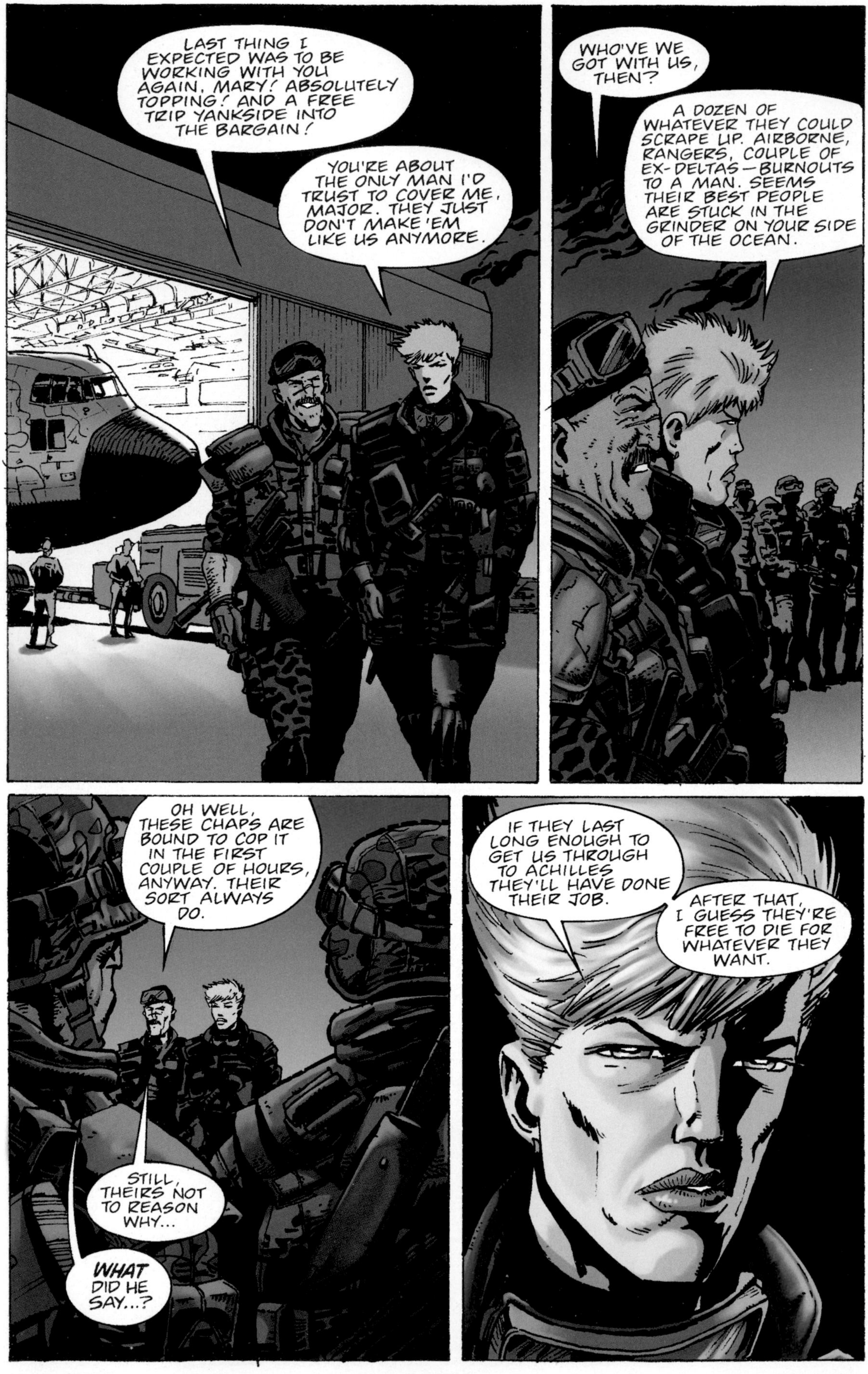
LAST THING I EXPECTED WAS TO BE WORKING WITH YOU AGAIN, MARY! ABSOLUTELY TOPPING! AND A FREE TRIP YANKSIDE INTO THE BARGAIN!
YOU'RE ABOUT THE ONLY MAN I'D TRUST TO COVER ME, MAJOR. THEY JUST DON'T MAKE 'EM LIKE US ANYMORE.
WHO'VE WE GOT WITH US, THEN?
A DOZEN OF WHATEVER THEY COULD SCRAPE UP. AIRBORNE, RANGERS, COUPLE OF EX-DELTAS—BURNOUTS TO A MAN. SEEMS THEIR BEST PEOPLE ARE STUCK IN THE GRINDER ON YOUR SIDE OF THE OCEAN.
OH WELL, THESE CHAPS ARE BOUND TO COP IT IN THE FIRST COUPLE OF HOURS, ANYWAY. THEIR SORT ALWAYS DO.
STILL, THEIRS NOT TO REASON WHY...
WHAT DID HE SAY...?
IF THEY LAST LONG ENOUGH TO GET US THROUGH TO ACHILLES THEY'LL HAVE DONE THEIR JOB.
AFTER THAT, I GUESS THEY'RE FREE TO DIE FOR WHATEVER THEY WANT.

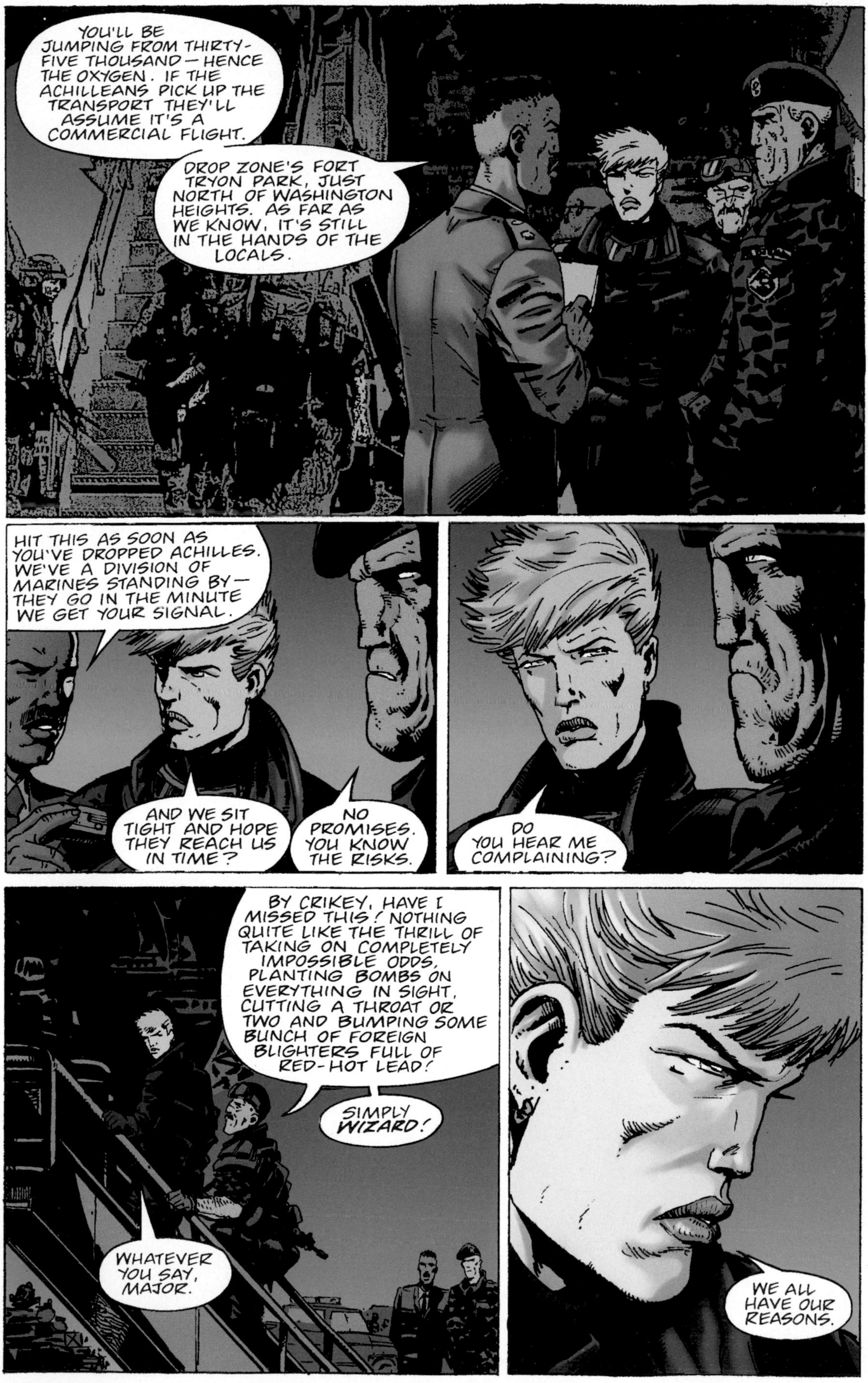
YOU'LL BE JUMPING FROM THIRTY-FIVE THOUSAND — HENCE THE OXYGEN. IF THE ACHILLEANS PICK UP THE TRANSPORT THEY'LL ASSUME IT'S A COMMERCIAL FLIGHT.
DROP ZONE'S FORT TRYON PARK, JUST NORTH OF WASHINGTON HEIGHTS. AS FAR AS WE KNOW, IT'S STILL IN THE HANDS OF THE LOCALS.
HIT THIS AS SOON AS YOU'VE DROPPED ACHILLES. WE'VE A DIVISION OF MARINES STANDING BY— THEY GO IN THE MINUTE WE GET YOUR SIGNAL.
AND WE SIT TIGHT AND HOPE THEY REACH US IN TIME?
NO PROMISES. YOU KNOW THE RISKS.
DO YOU HEAR ME COMPLAINING?
BY CRIKEY, HAVE I MISSED THIS! NOTHING QUITE LIKE THE THRILL OF TAKING ON COMPLETELY IMPOSSIBLE ODDS, PLANTING BOMBS ON EVERYTHING IN SIGHT, CUTTING A THROAT OR TWO AND BUMPING SOME BUNCH OF FOREIGN BLIGHTERS FULL OF RED-HOT LEAD!
SIMPLY WIZARD!
WHATEVER YOU SAY, MAJOR.
WE ALL HAVE OUR REASONS.

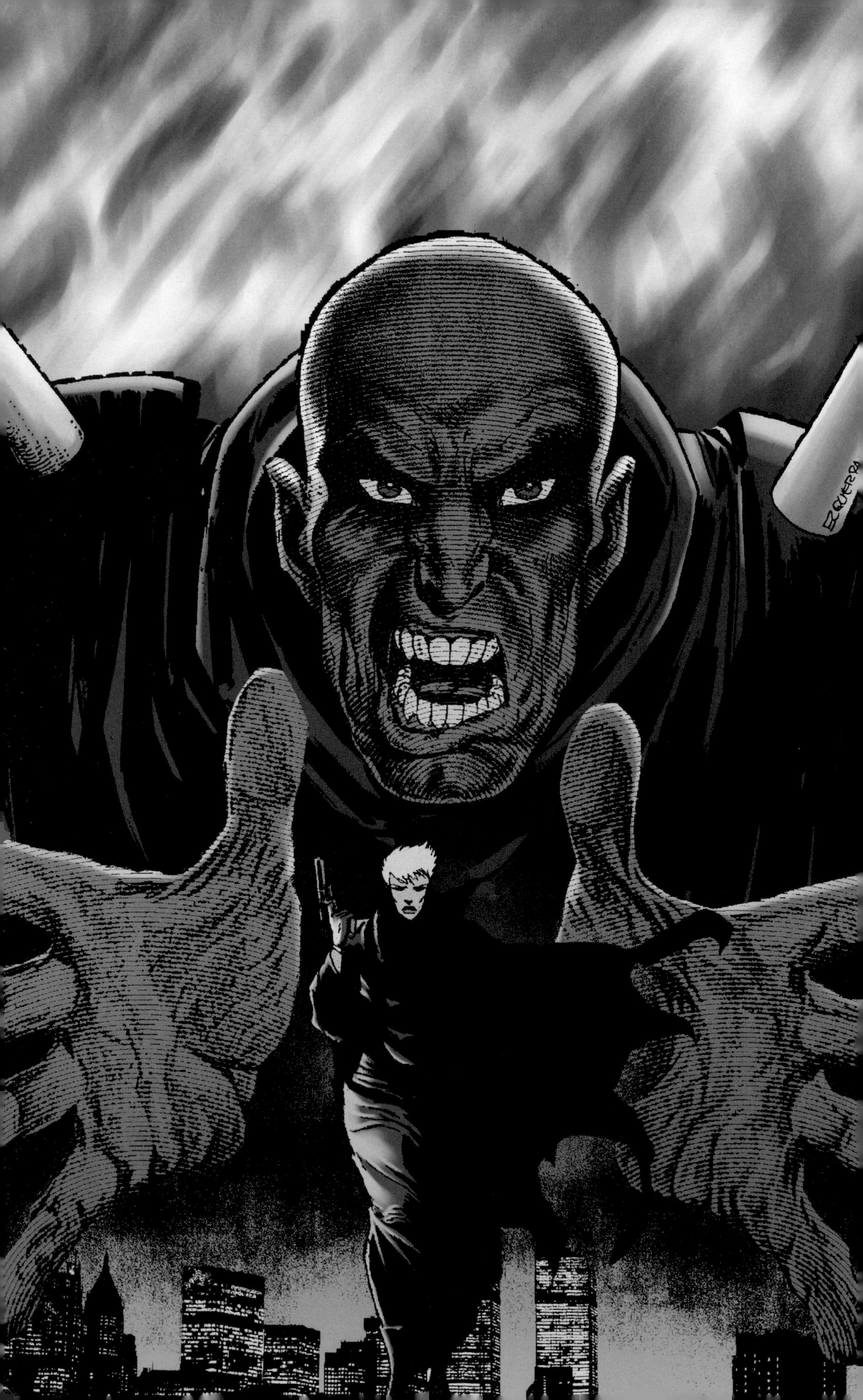
EZQUERRA

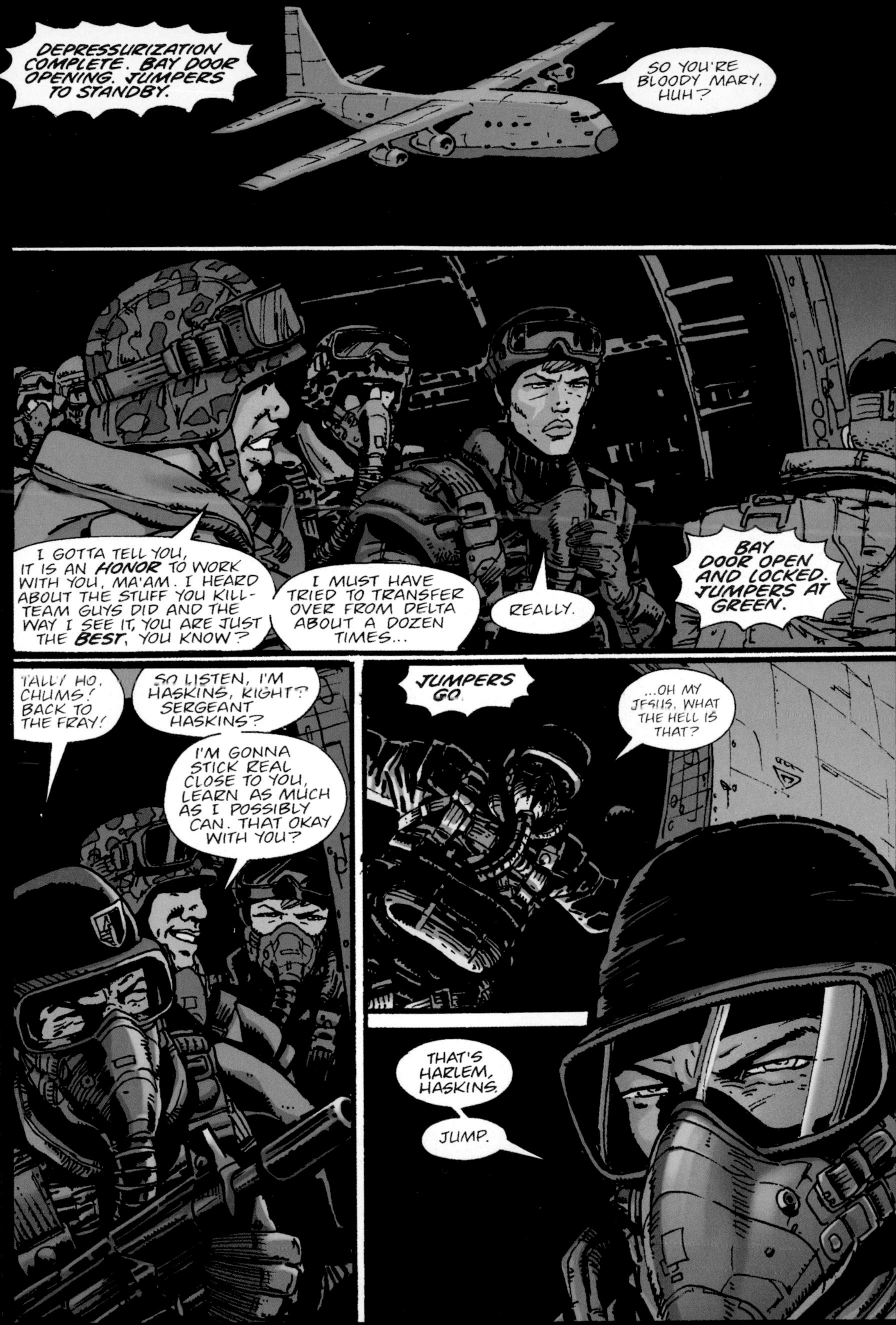
DEPRESSURIZATION COMPLETE. BAY DOOR OPENING. JUMPERS TO STANDBY.
SO YOU'RE BLOODY MARY, HUH?
I GOTTA TELL YOU, IT IS AN HONOR TO WORK WITH YOU, MA'AM. I HEARD ABOUT THE STUFF YOU KILL-TEAM GUYS DID AND THE WAY I SEE IT, YOU ARE JUST THE BEST, YOU KNOW?
I MUST HAVE TRIED TO TRANSFER OVER FROM DELTA ABOUT A DOZEN TIMES...
REALLY.
BAY DOOR OPEN AND LOCKED. JUMPERS AT GREEN.
TALLY HO, CHUMS! BACK TO THE FRAY!
SO LISTEN, I'M HASKINS, RIGHT? SERGEANT HASKINS?
I'M GONNA STICK REAL CLOSE TO YOU, LEARN AS MUCH AS I POSSIBLY CAN. THAT OKAY WITH YOU?
JUMPERS GO.
...OH MY JESUS, WHAT THE HELL IS THAT?
THAT'S HARLEM, HASKINS.
JUMP.

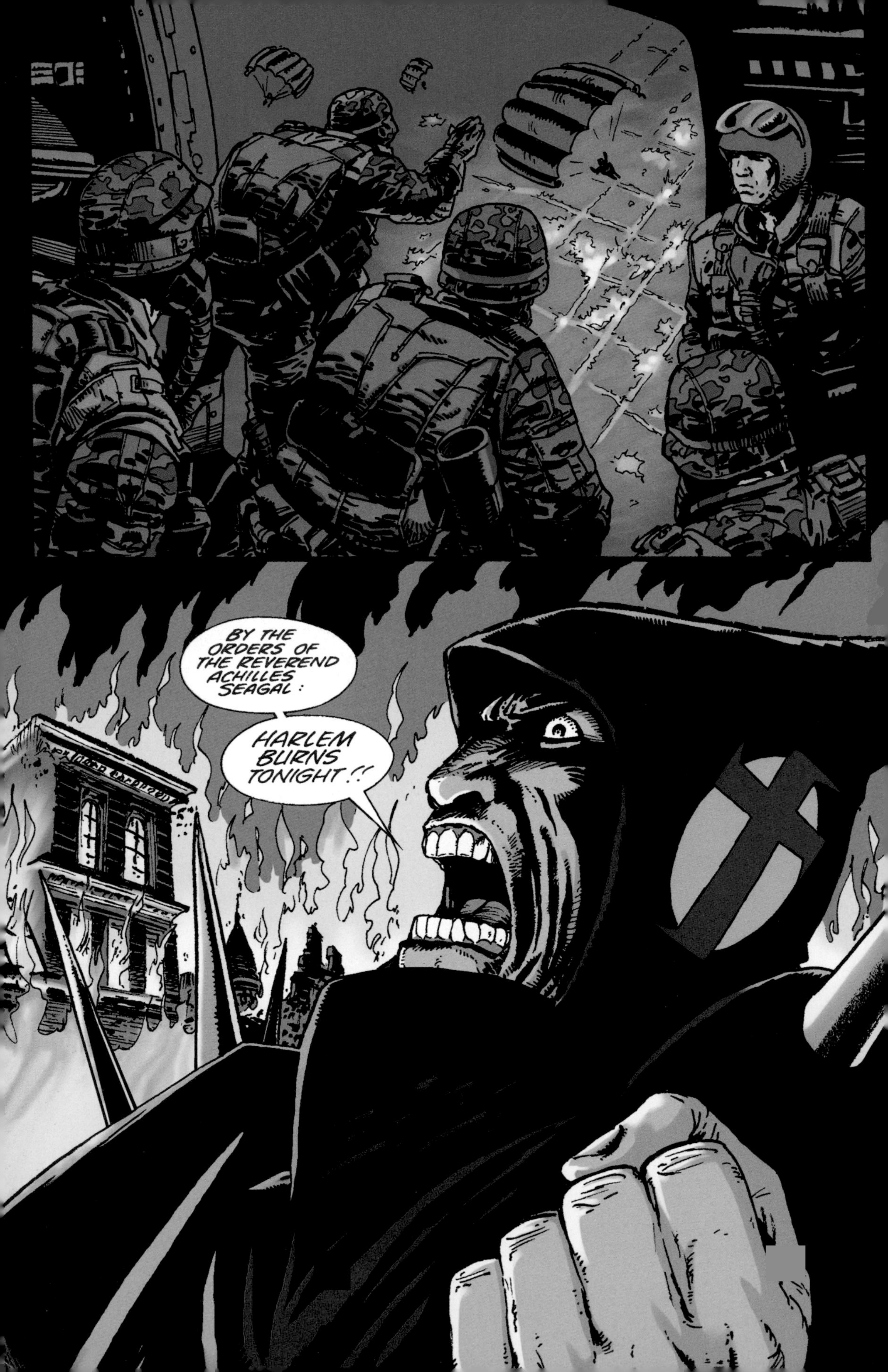
BY THE ORDERS OF THE REVEREND ACHILLES SEAGAL:
HARLEM BURNS TONIGHT!!

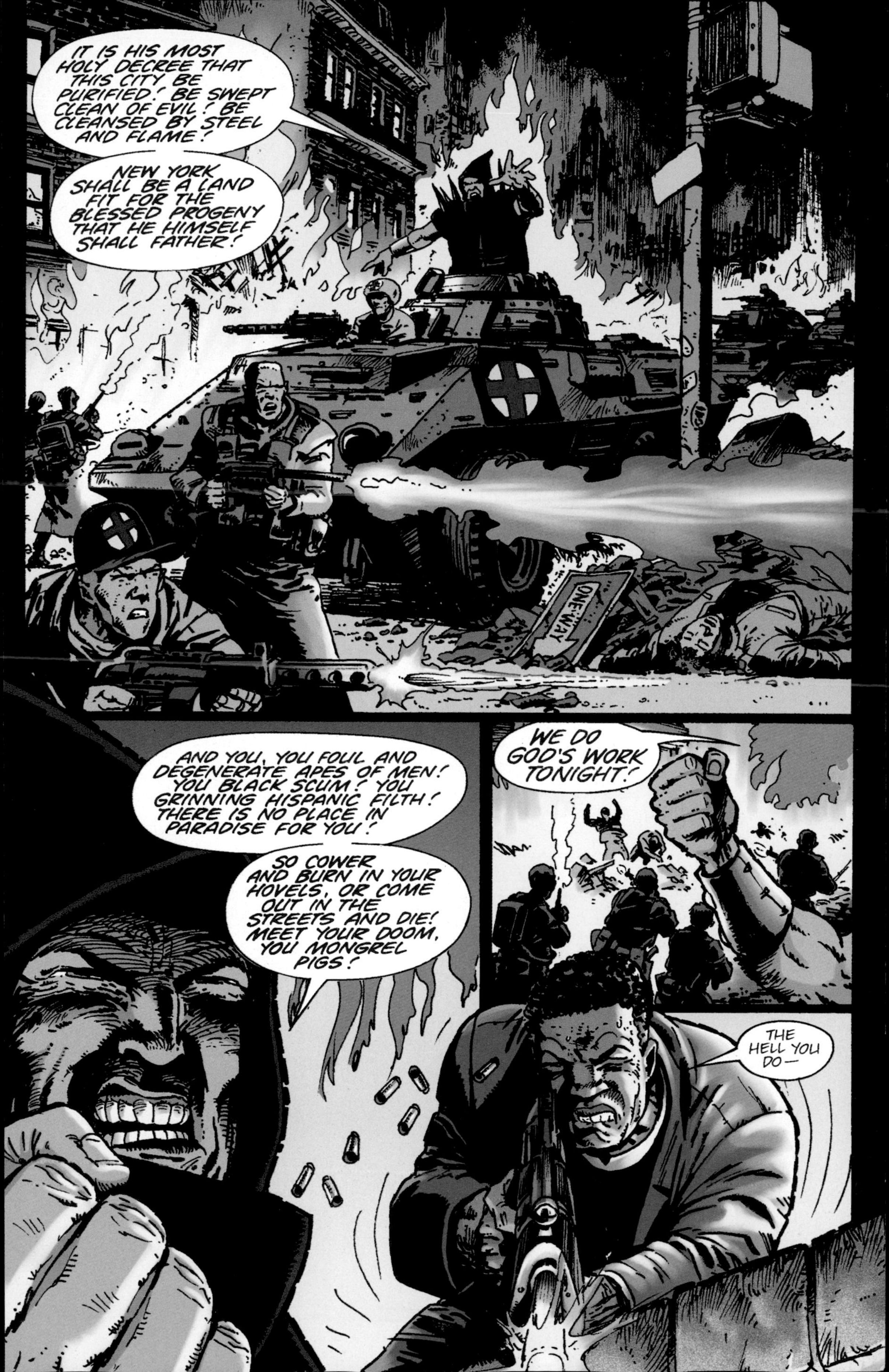
IT IS HIS MOST HOLY DECREE THAT THIS CITY BE PURIFIED! BE SWEPT CLEAN OF EVIL! BE CLEANSED BY STEEL AND FLAME!
NEW YORK SHALL BE A LAND FIT FOR THE BLESSED PROGENY THAT HE HIMSELF SHALL FATHER!
ONE WAY
AND YOU, YOU FOUL AND DEGENERATE APES OF MEN! YOU BLACK SCUM! YOU GRINNING HISPANIC FILTH! THERE IS NO PLACE IN PARADISE FOR YOU!
SO COWER AND BURN IN YOUR HOVELS, OR COME OUT IN THE STREETS AND DIE! MEET YOUR DOOM, YOU MONGREL PIGS!
WE DO GOD'S WORK TONIGHT!
THE HELL YOU DO—

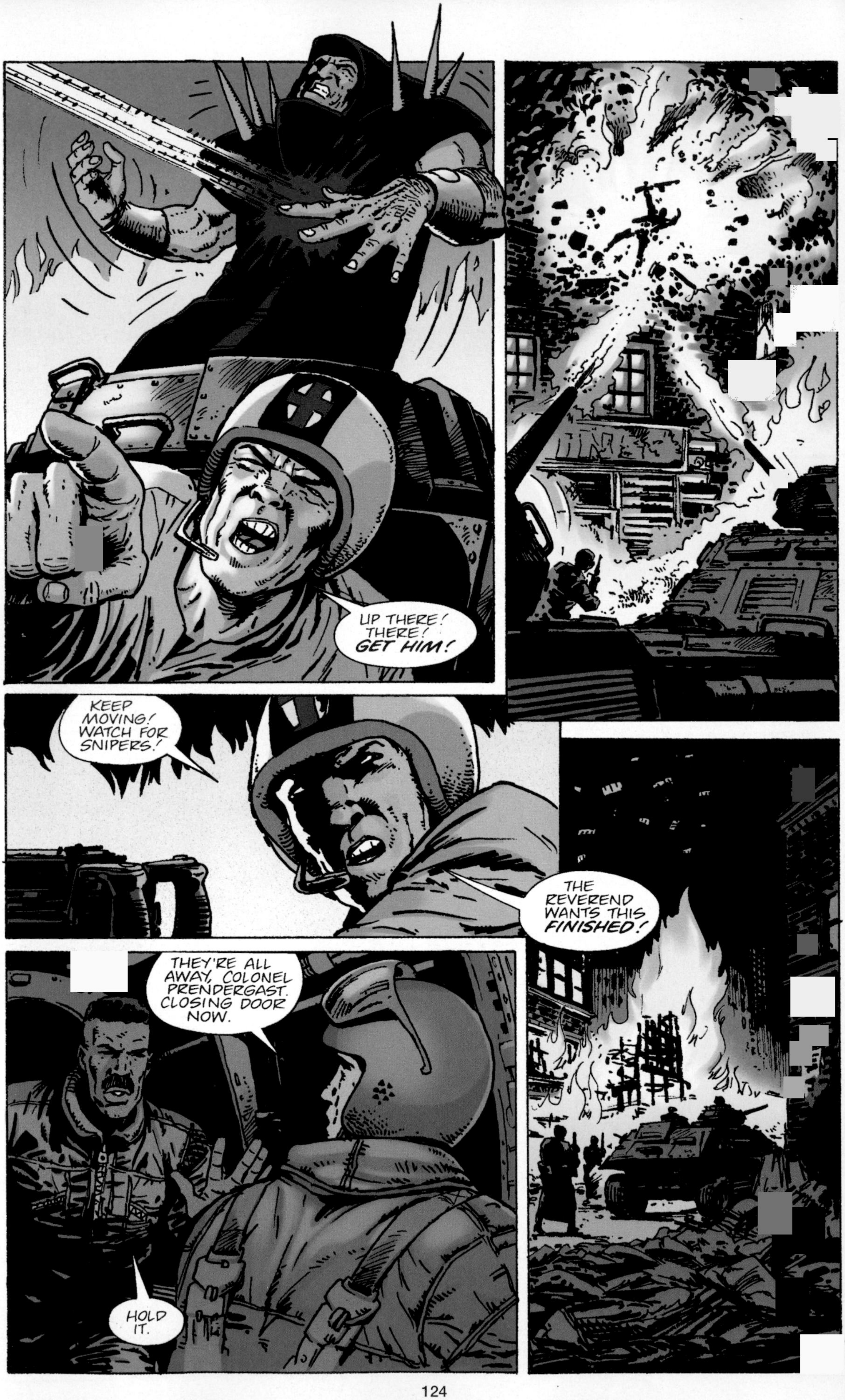
UP THERE! THERE! GET HIM!
KEEP MOVING! WATCH FOR SNIPERS!
THE REVEREND WANTS THIS FINISHED!
THEY'RE ALL AWAY, COLONEL PRENDERGAST. CLOSING DOOR NOW.
HOLD IT.

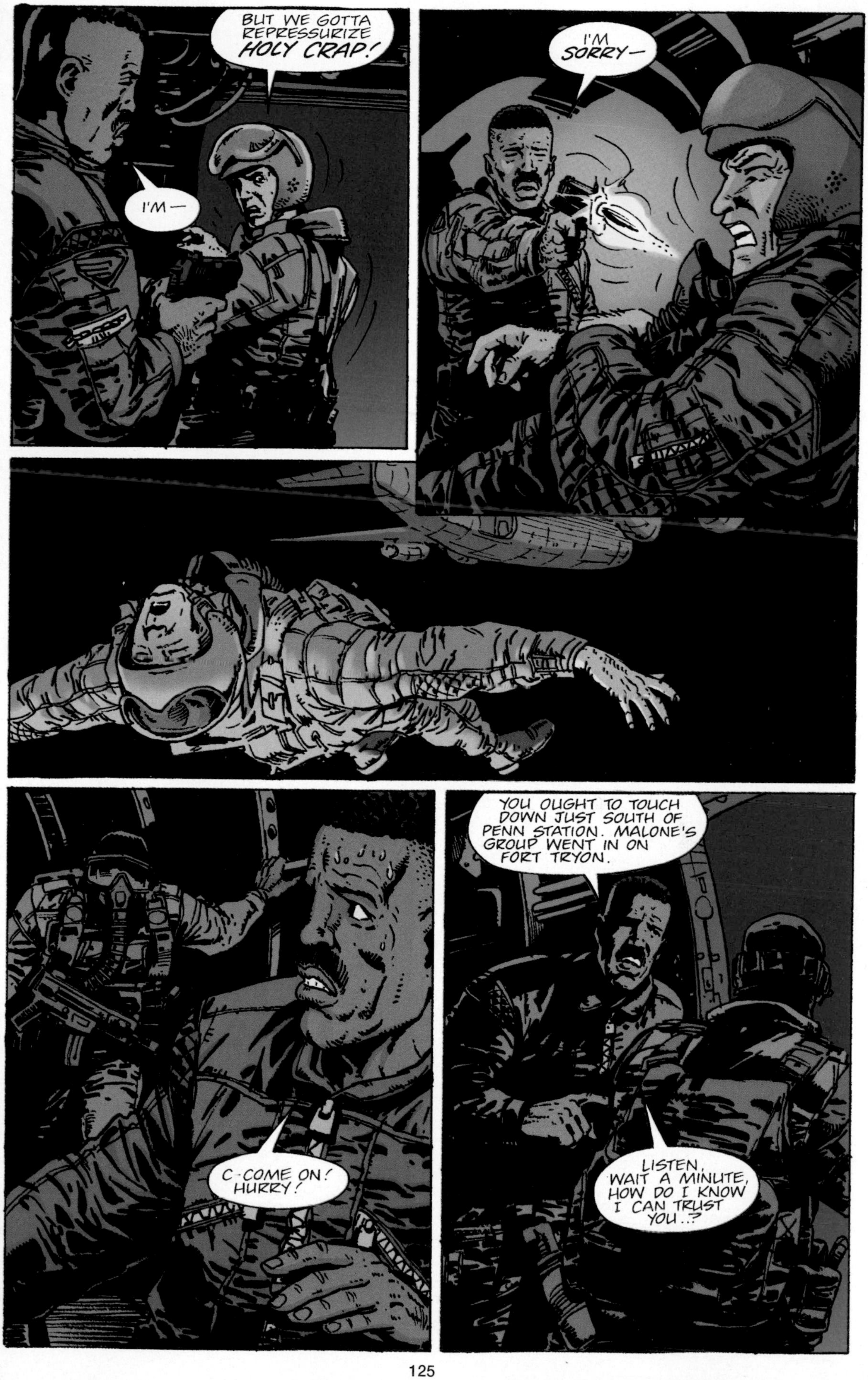
BUT WE GOTTA REPRESSURIZE HOLY CRAP!
I'M—
I'M SORRY—
C-COME ON! HURRY!
YOU OUGHT TO TOUCH DOWN JUST SOUTH OF PENN STATION. MALONE'S GROUP WENT IN ON FORT TRYON.
LISTEN, WAIT A MINUTE, HOW DO I KNOW I CAN TRUST YOU..?

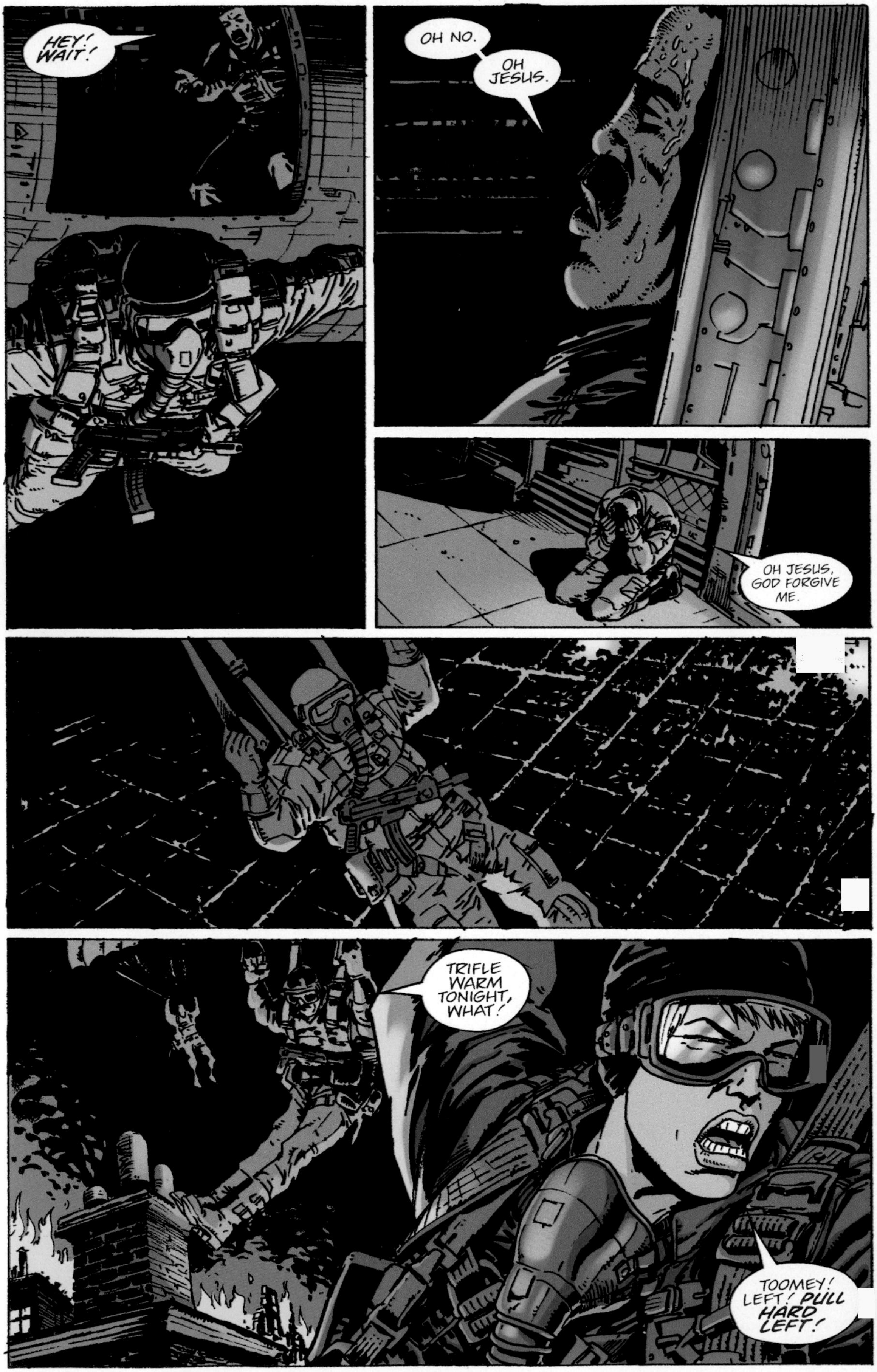
HEY! WAIT!
OH NO.
OH JESUS.
OH JESUS, GOD FORGIVE ME.
TRIFLE WARM TONIGHT, WHAT!
TOOMEY! LEFT! PULL HARD LEFT!

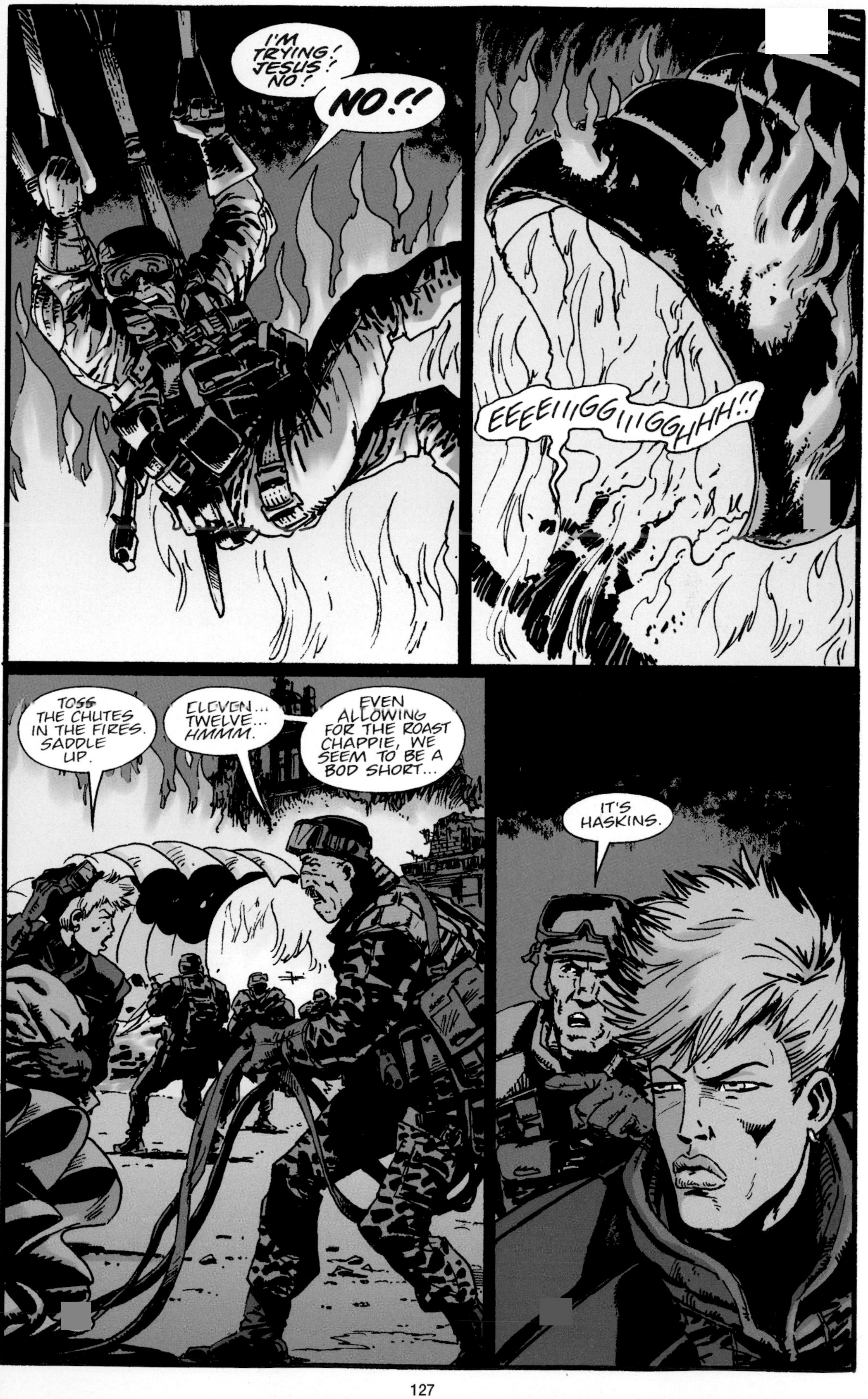
I'M TRYING! JESUS! NO!
NO.?!
EEEEIIIGGIIIIGGHHH!!
TOSS THE CHUTES IN THE FIRES. SADDLE UP.
ELEVEN... TWELVE... HMMM.
EVEN ALLOWING FOR THE ROAST CHAPPIE, WE SEEM TO BE A BOD SHORT...
IT'S HASKINS.

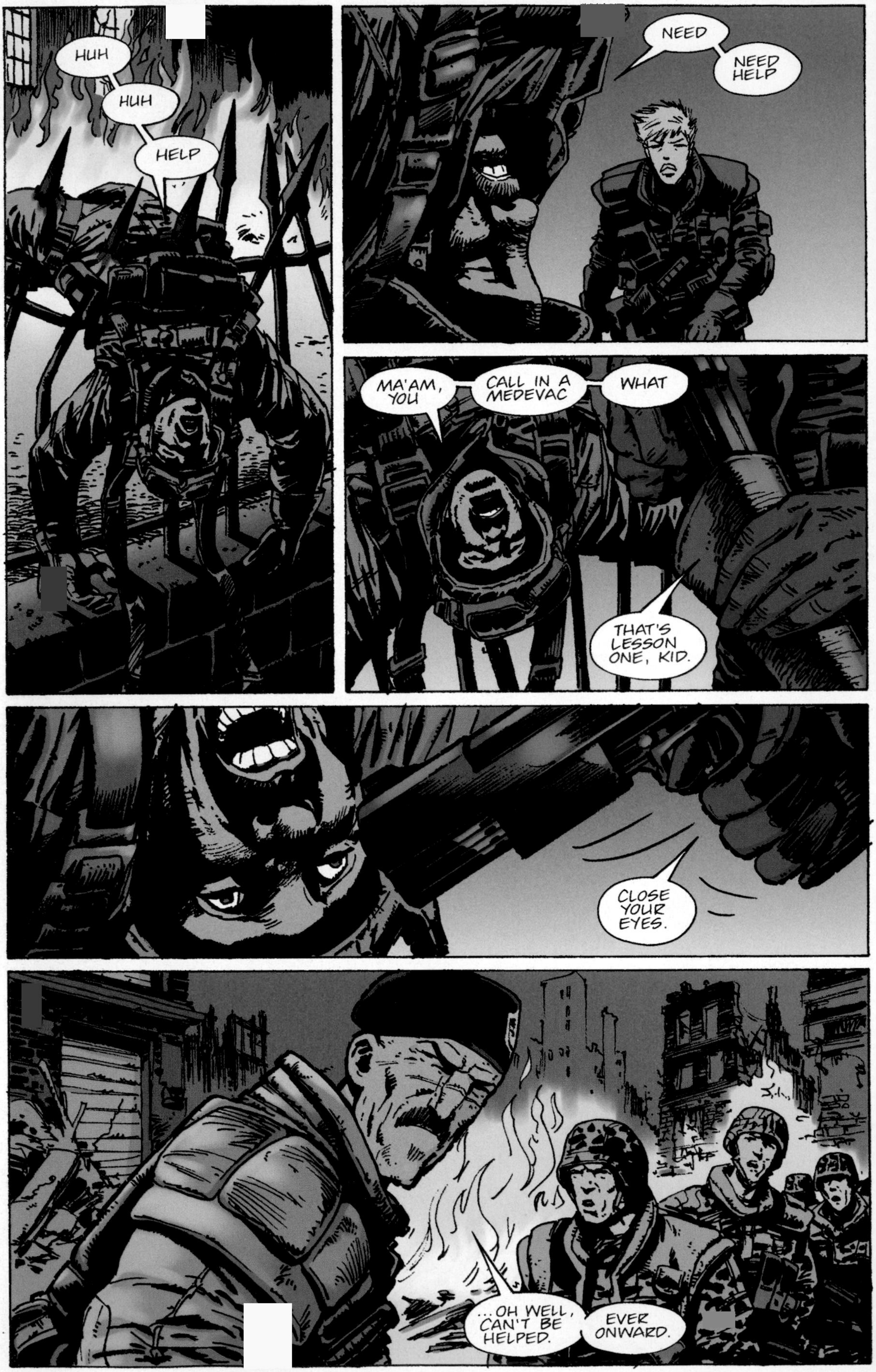
HUH
HUH
HELP
NEED
NEED HELP
MA'AM, YOU
CALL IN A MEDEVAC
WHAT
THAT'S LESSON ONE, KID.
CLOSE YOUR EYES.
...OH WELL, CAN'T BE HELPED.
EVER ONWARD.

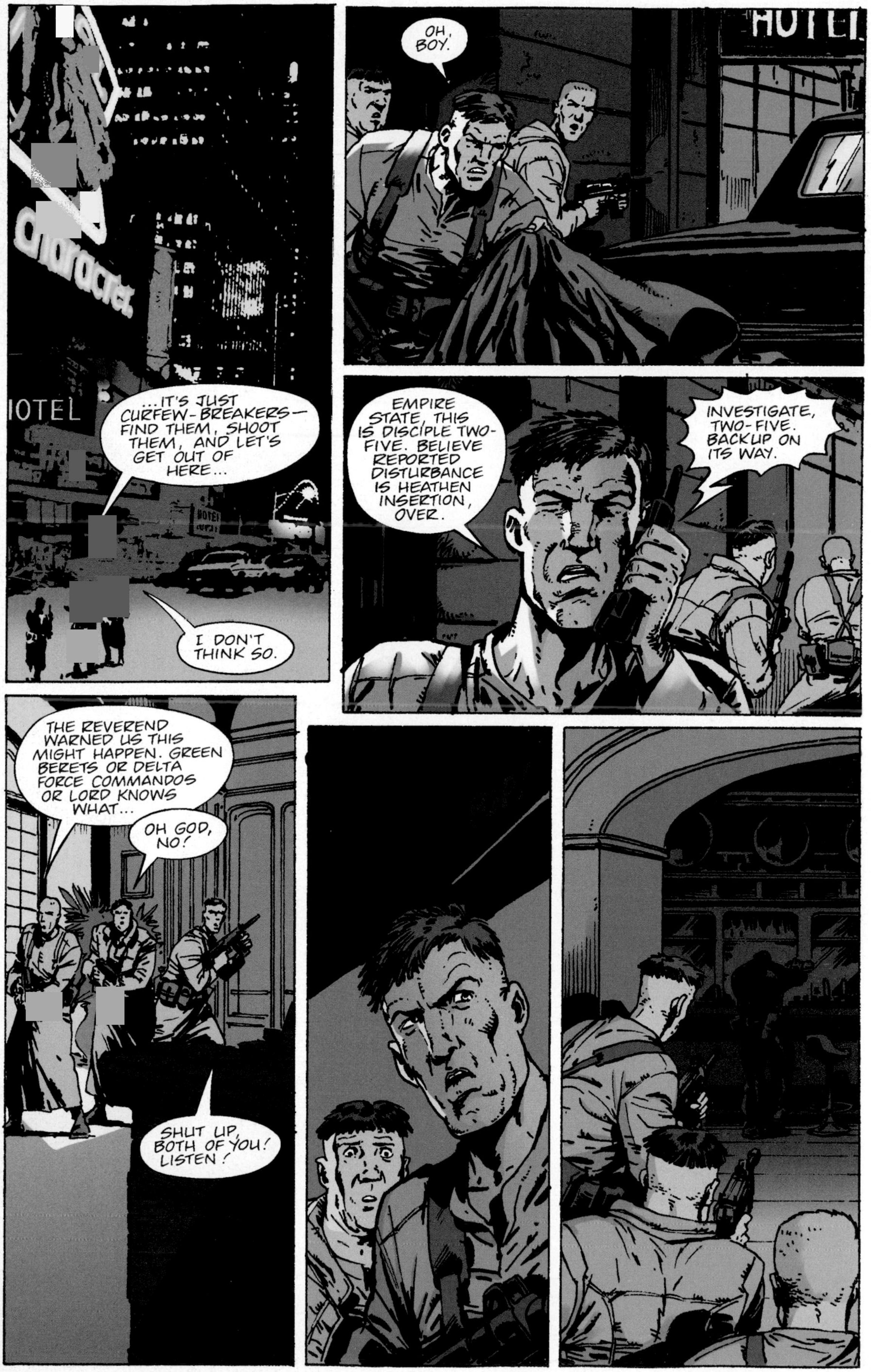
...IT'S JUST CURFEW-BREAKERS— FIND THEM, SHOOT THEM, AND LET'S GET OUT OF HERE...
I DON'T THINK SO.
OH, BOY.
EMPIRE STATE, THIS IS DISCIPLE TWO-FIVE. BELIEVE REPORTED DISTURBANCE IS HEATHEN INSERTION, OVER.
INVESTIGATE, TWO-FIVE. BACKUP ON ITS WAY.
THE REVEREND WARNED US THIS MIGHT HAPPEN. GREEN BERETS OR DELTA FORCE COMMANDOS OR LORD KNOWS WHAT...
OH GOD, NO!
SHUT UP, BOTH OF YOU! LISTEN!

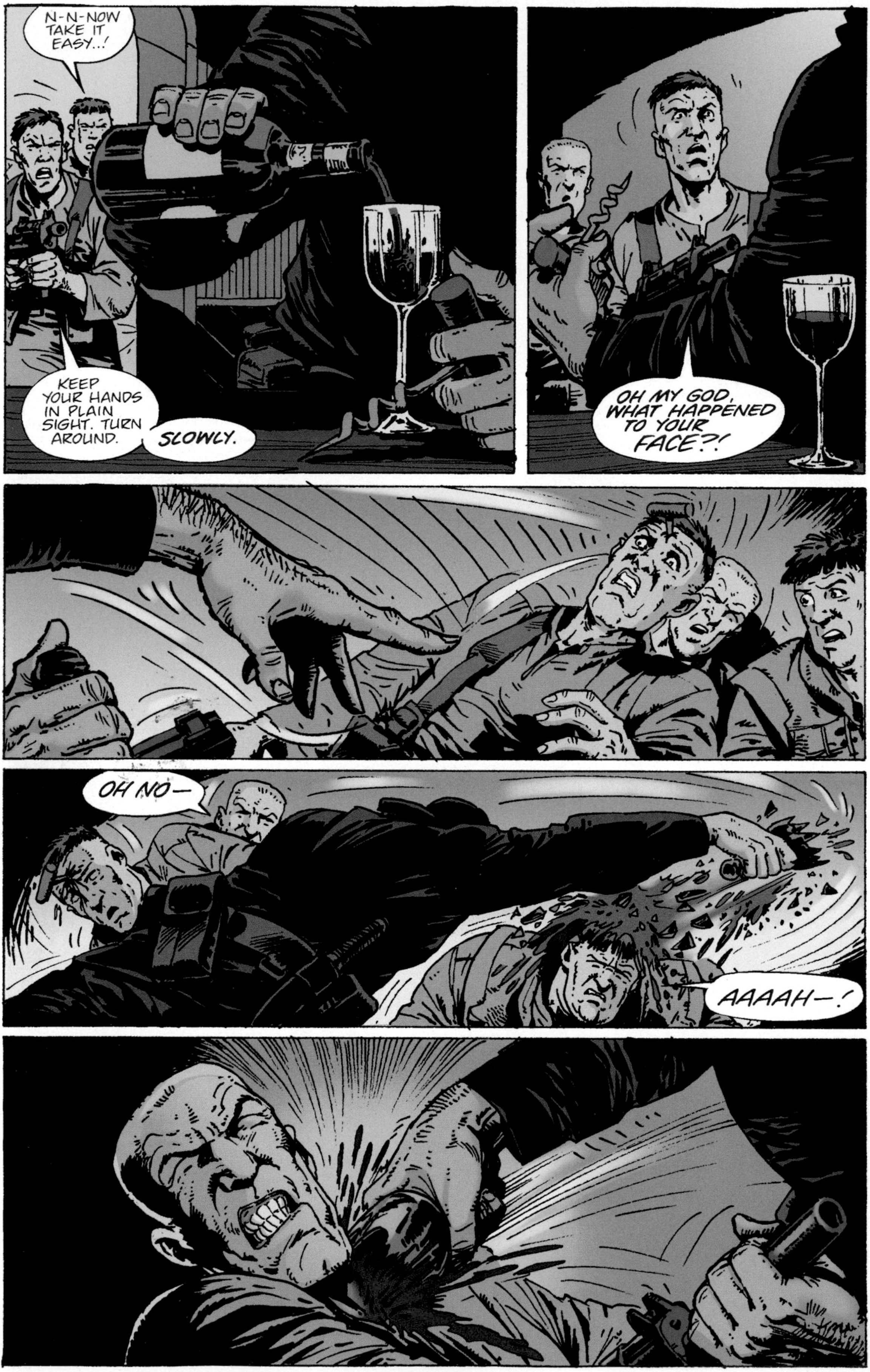
N-N-NOW TAKE IT EASY..!
KEEP YOUR HANDS IN PLAIN SIGHT. TURN AROUND.
SLOWLY.
OH MY GOD, WHAT HAPPENED TO YOUR FACE?!
OH NO—
AAAAH—!

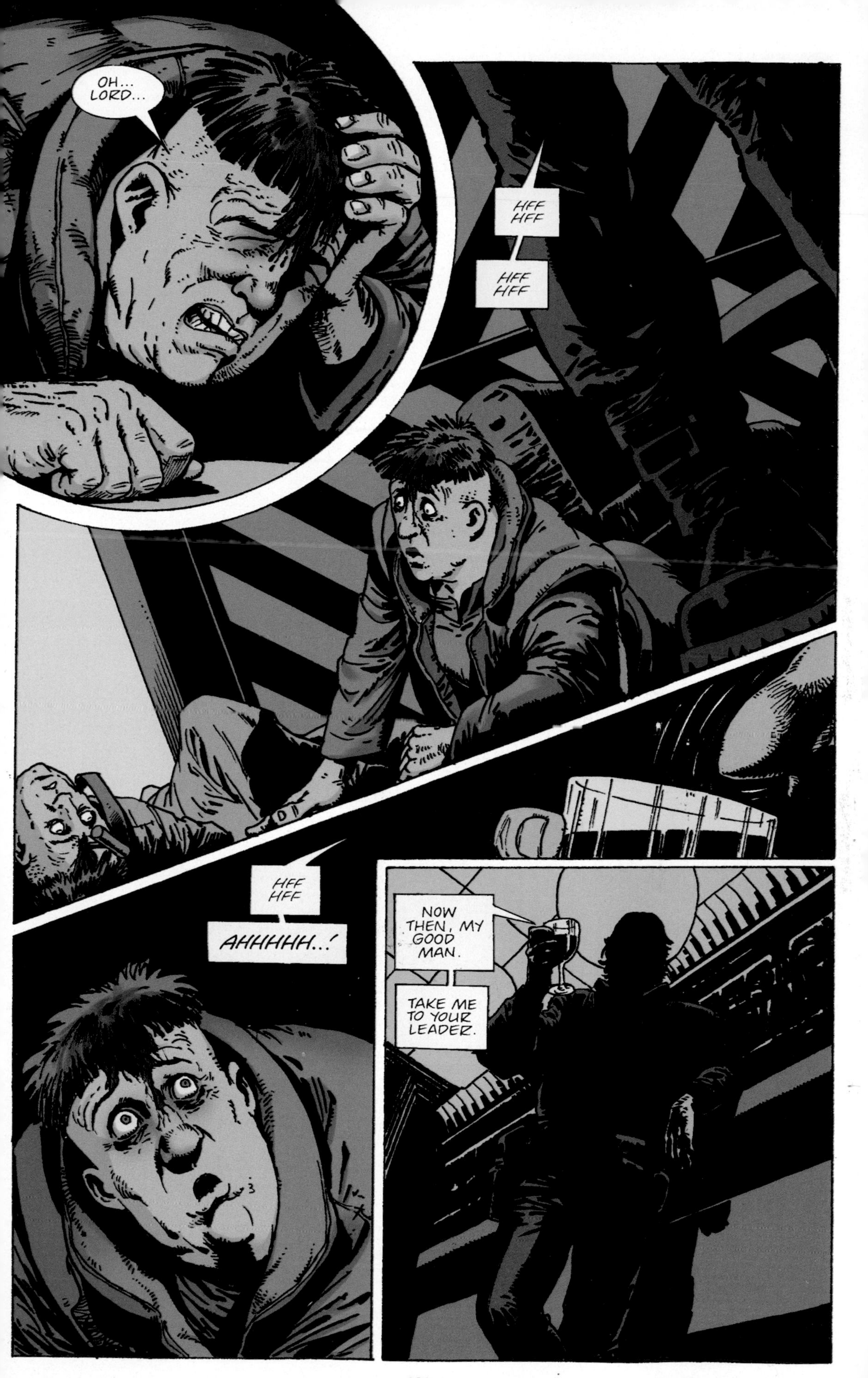
OH... LORD...
HFF HFF
HFF HFF
HFF HFF
AHHHHH...!
NOW THEN, MY GOOD MAN.
TAKE ME TO YOUR LEADER.

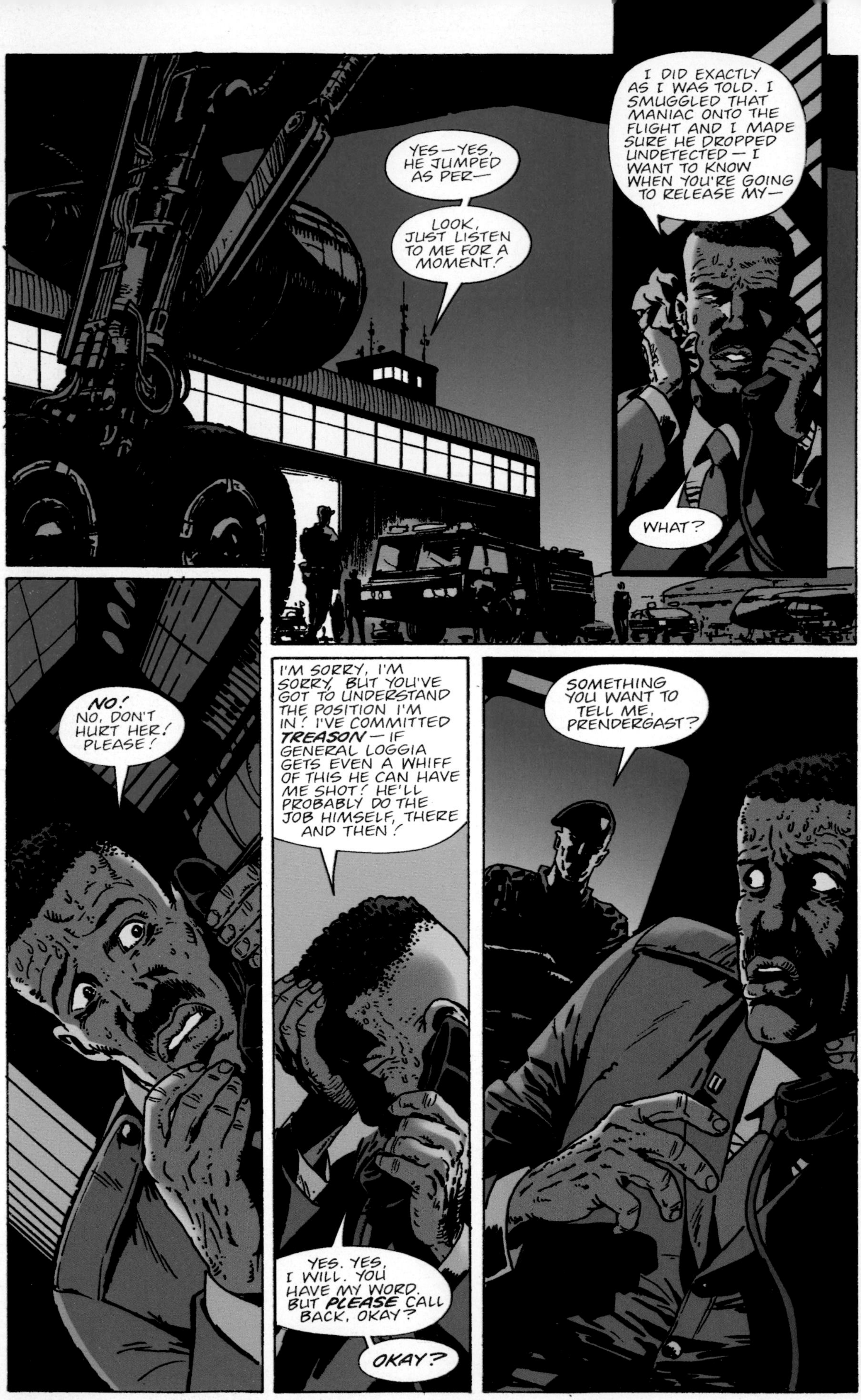
YES—YES, HE JUMPED AS PER—
LOOK, JUST LISTEN TO ME FOR A MOMENT!
I DID EXACTLY AS I WAS TOLD. I SMUGGLED THAT MANIAC ONTO THE FLIGHT AND I MADE SURE HE DROPPED UNDETECTED—I WANT TO KNOW WHEN YOU'RE GOING TO RELEASE MY—
WHAT?
NO! NO, DON'T HURT HER! PLEASE!
I'M SORRY, I'M SORRY, BUT YOU'VE GOT TO UNDERSTAND THE POSITION I'M IN! I'VE COMMITTED TREASON—IF GENERAL LOGGIA GETS EVEN A WHIFF OF THIS HE CAN HAVE ME SHOT! HE'LL PROBABLY DO THE JOB HIMSELF, THERE AND THEN!
YES. YES, I WILL. YOU HAVE MY WORD. BUT PLEASE CALL BACK, OKAY?
OKAY?
SOMETHING YOU WANT TO TELL ME, PRENDERGAST?

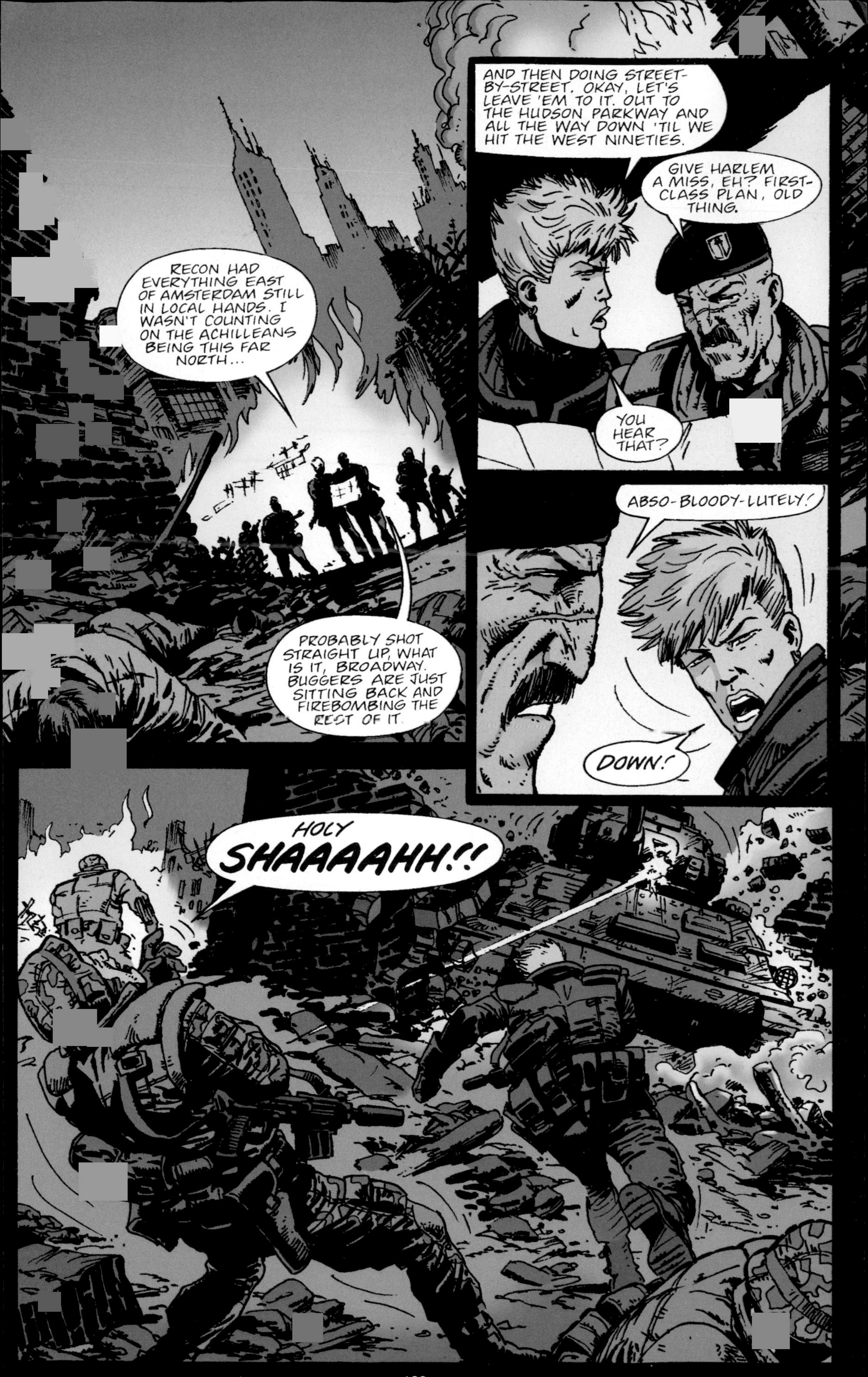
RECON HAD EVERYTHING EAST OF AMSTERDAM STILL IN LOCAL HANDS. I WASN'T COUNTING ON THE ACHILLEANS BEING THIS FAR NORTH...
PROBABLY SHOT STRAIGHT UP, WHAT IS IT, BROADWAY. BUGGERS ARE JUST SITTING BACK AND FIREBOMBING THE REST OF IT.
AND THEN DOING STREET-BY-STREET. OKAY, LET'S LEAVE 'EM TO IT. OUT TO THE HUDSON PARKWAY AND ALL THE WAY DOWN 'TIL WE HIT THE WEST NINETIES.
GIVE HARLEM A MISS, EH? FIRST-CLASS PLAN, OLD THING.
YOU HEAR THAT?
ABSO-BLOODY-LUTELY!
DOWN!
HOLY SHAAAAHH!?!

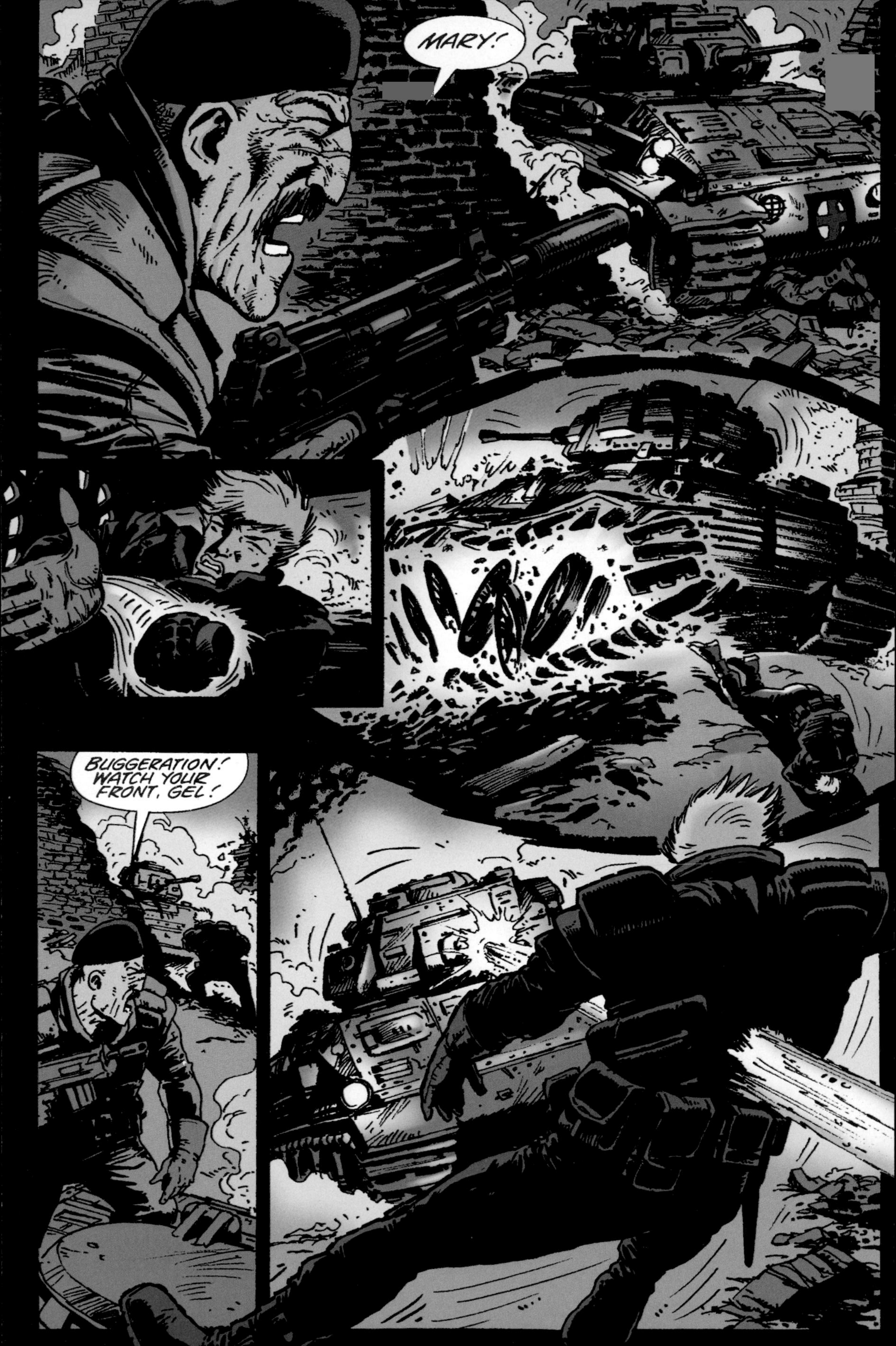
MARY!
BUGGERATION! WATCH YOUR FRONT, GEL!

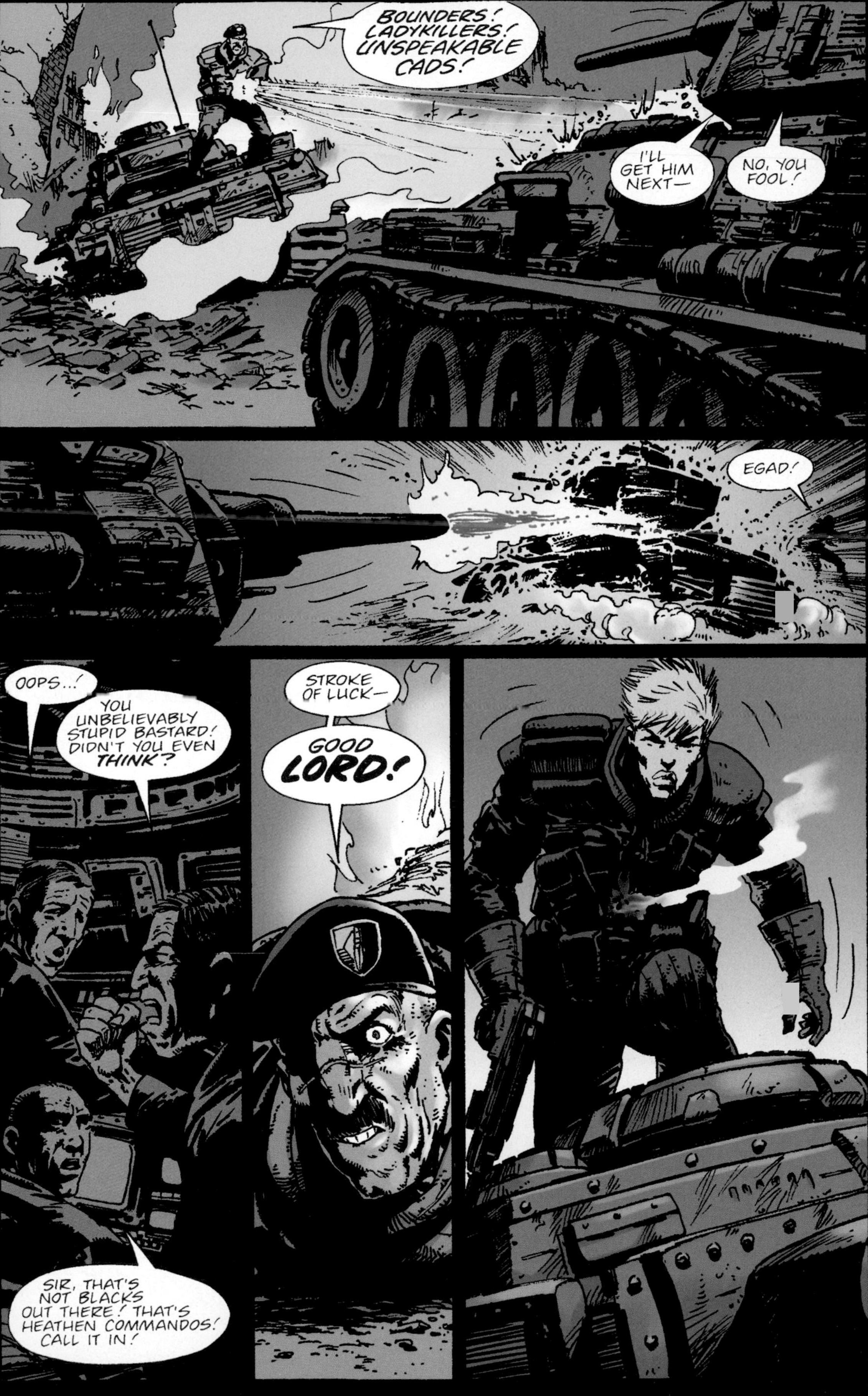
BOUNDERS! LADYKILLERS! UNSPEAKABLE CADS!
I'LL GET HIM NEXT—
NO, YOU FOOL!
EGAD!
OOPS...!
YOU UNBELIEVABLY STUPID BASTARD! DIDN'T YOU EVEN THINK?
SIR, THAT'S NOT BLACKS OUT THERE! THAT'S HEATHEN COMMANDOS! CALL IT IN!
STROKE OF LUCK—
GOOD LORD!

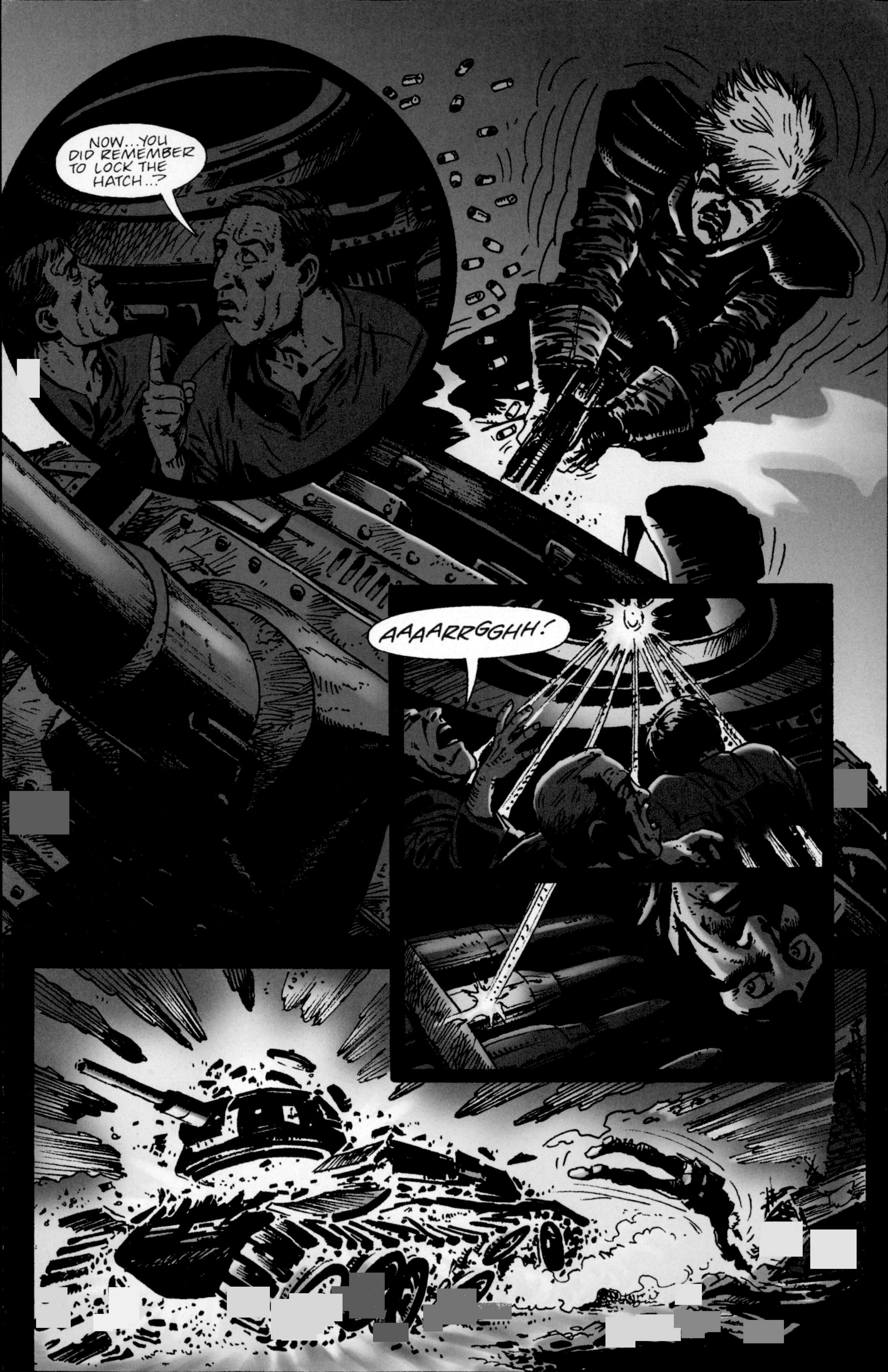
NOW...YOU DID REMEMBER TO LOCK THE HATCH..?
AAAARRGGHH!

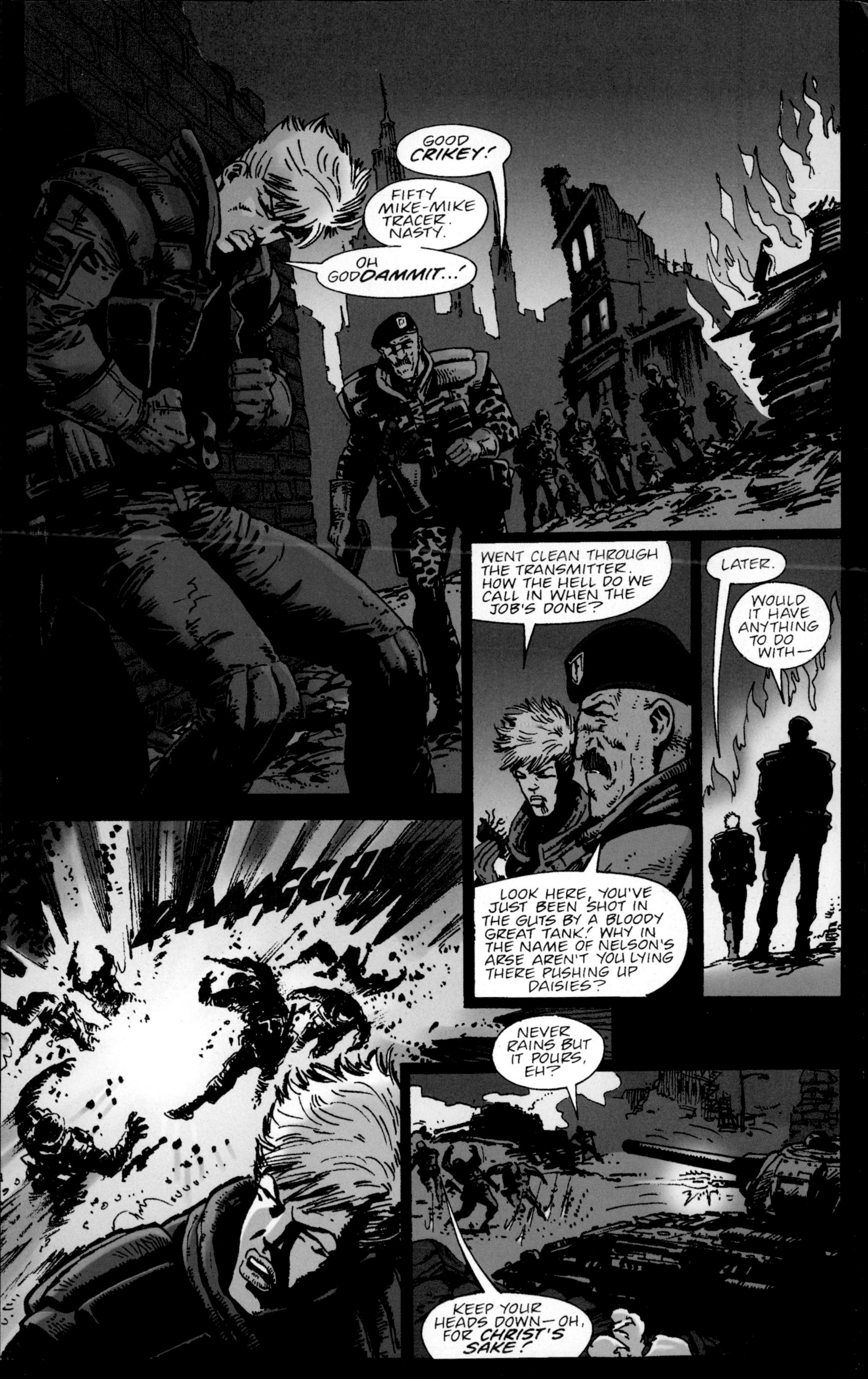
GOOD CRIKEY!
FIFTY MIKE-MIKE TRACER. NASTY.
OH GODDAMMIT...!
WENT CLEAN THROUGH THE TRANSMITTER. HOW THE HELL DO WE CALL IN WHEN THE JOB'S DONE?
LOOK HERE, YOU'VE JUST BEEN SHOT IN THE GUTS BY A BLOODY GREAT TANK! WHY IN THE NAME OF NELSON'S ARSE AREN'T YOU LYING THERE PUSHING UP DAISIES?
LATER.
WOULD IT HAVE ANYTHING TO DO WITH—
NEVER RAINS BUT IT POURS, EH?
KEEP YOUR HEADS DOWN—OH, FOR CHRIST'S SAKE!

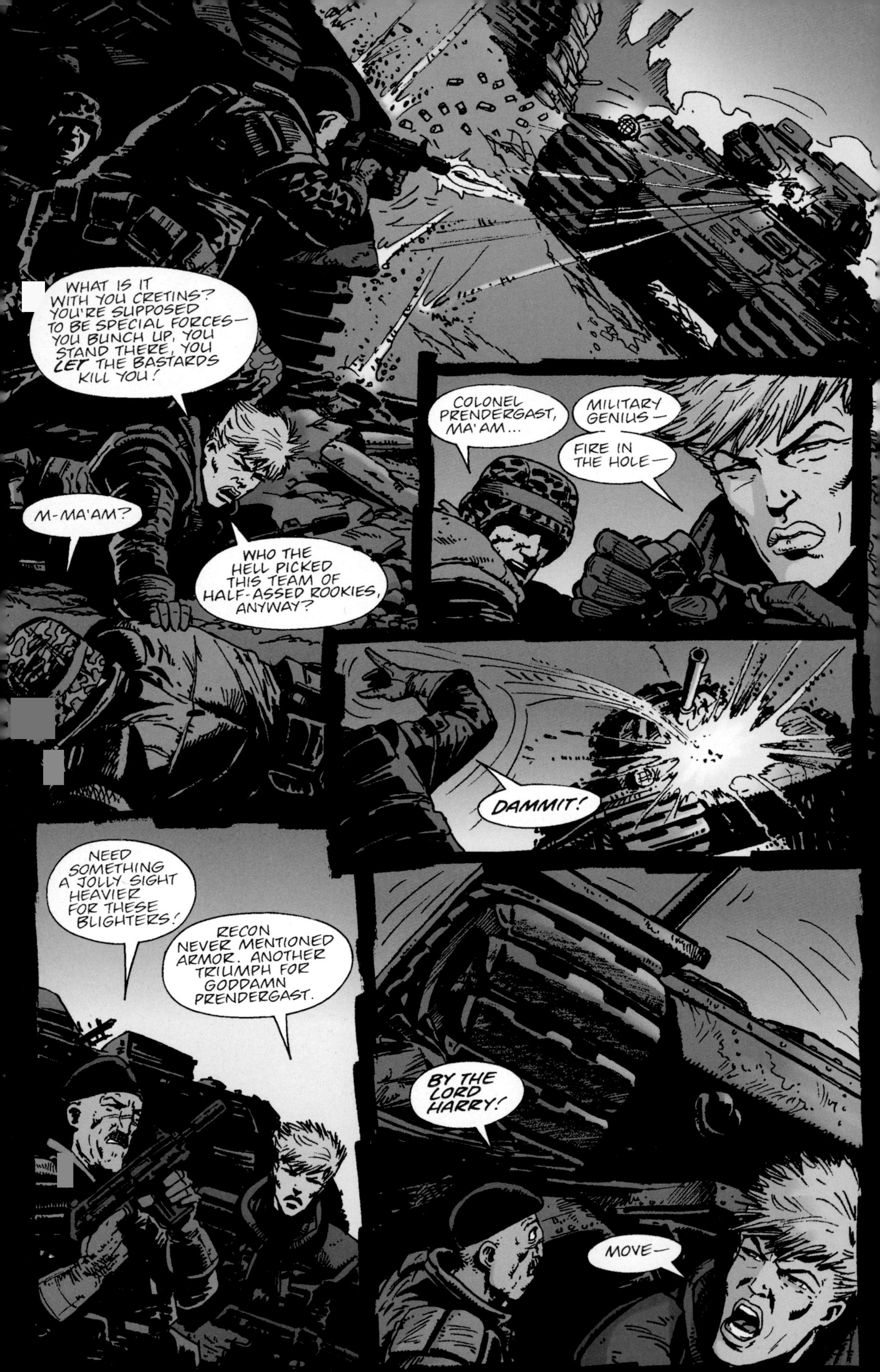

WHAT IS IT WITH YOU CRETINS? YOU'RE SUPPOSED TO BE SPECIAL FORCES— YOU BUNCH UP, YOU STAND THERE, YOU LET THE BASTARDS KILL YOU!
M-MA'AM?
WHO THE HELL PICKED THIS TEAM OF HALF-ASSED ROOKIES, ANYWAY?
COLONEL PRENDERGAST, MA'AM...
MILITARY GENIUS—
FIRE IN THE HOLE—
DAMMIT!
NEED SOMETHING A JOLLY SIGHT HEAVIER FOR THESE BLIGHTERS!
RECON NEVER MENTIONED ARMOR. ANOTHER TRIUMPH FOR GODDAMN PRENDERGAST.
BY THE LORD HARRY!
MOVE—

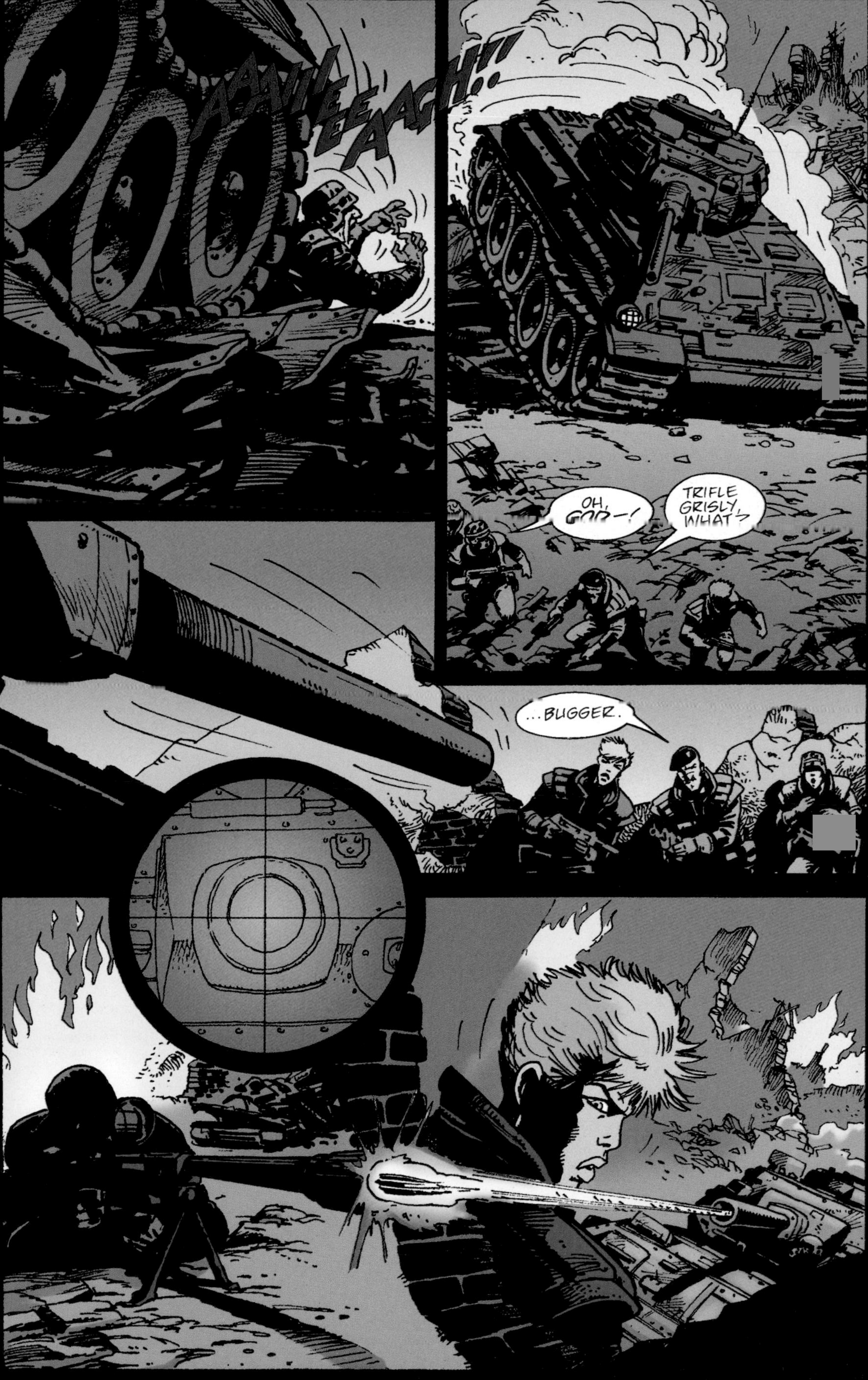
AAAIIIEEEAAAGH!!
OH, GOD--!
TRIFLE GRISLY, WHAT?
...BUGGER.

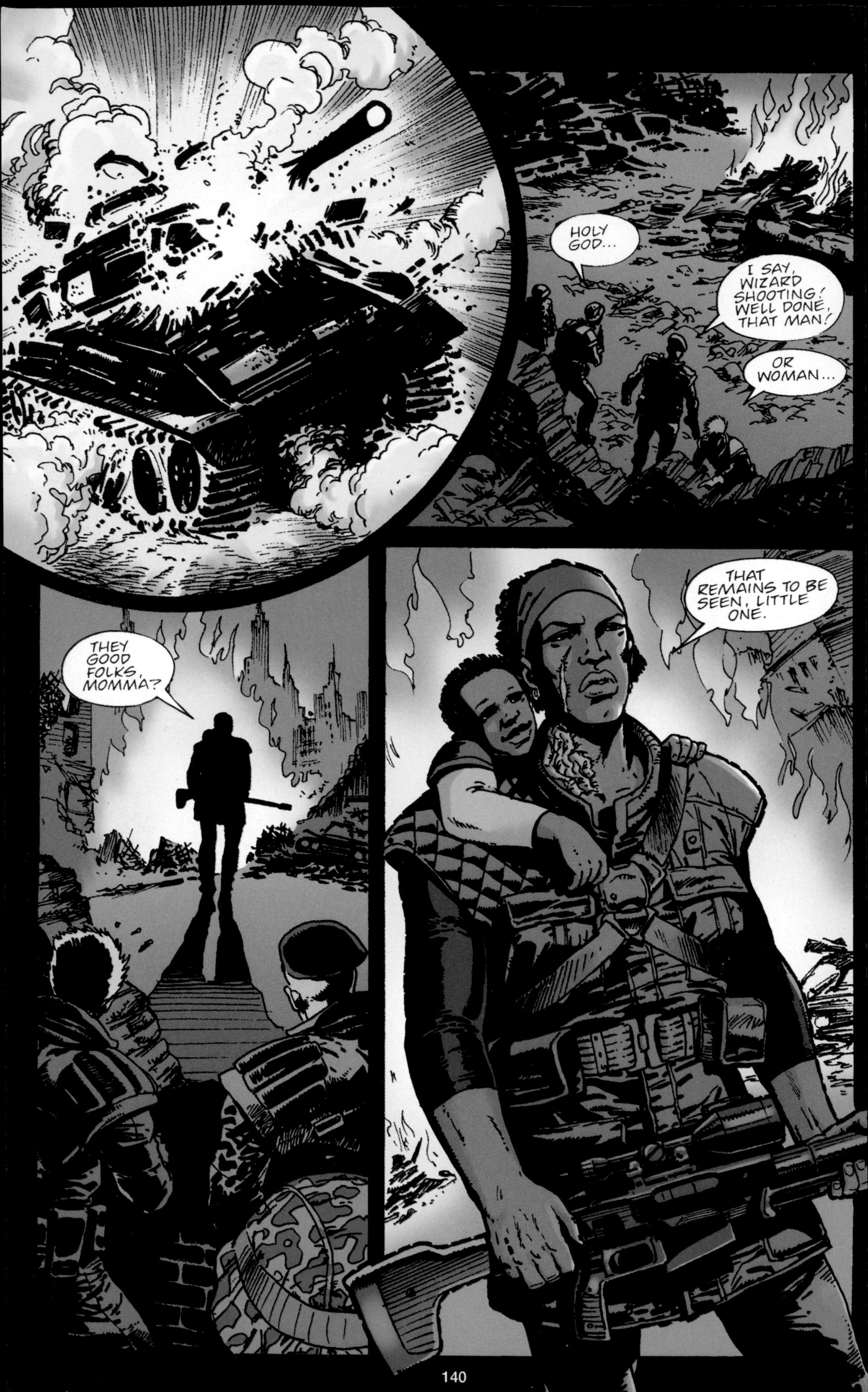
HOLY GOD...
I SAY, WIZARD SHOOTING! WELL DONE, THAT MAN!
OR WOMAN...
THEY GOOD FOLKS, MOMMA?
THAT REMAINS TO BE SEEN, LITTLE ONE.

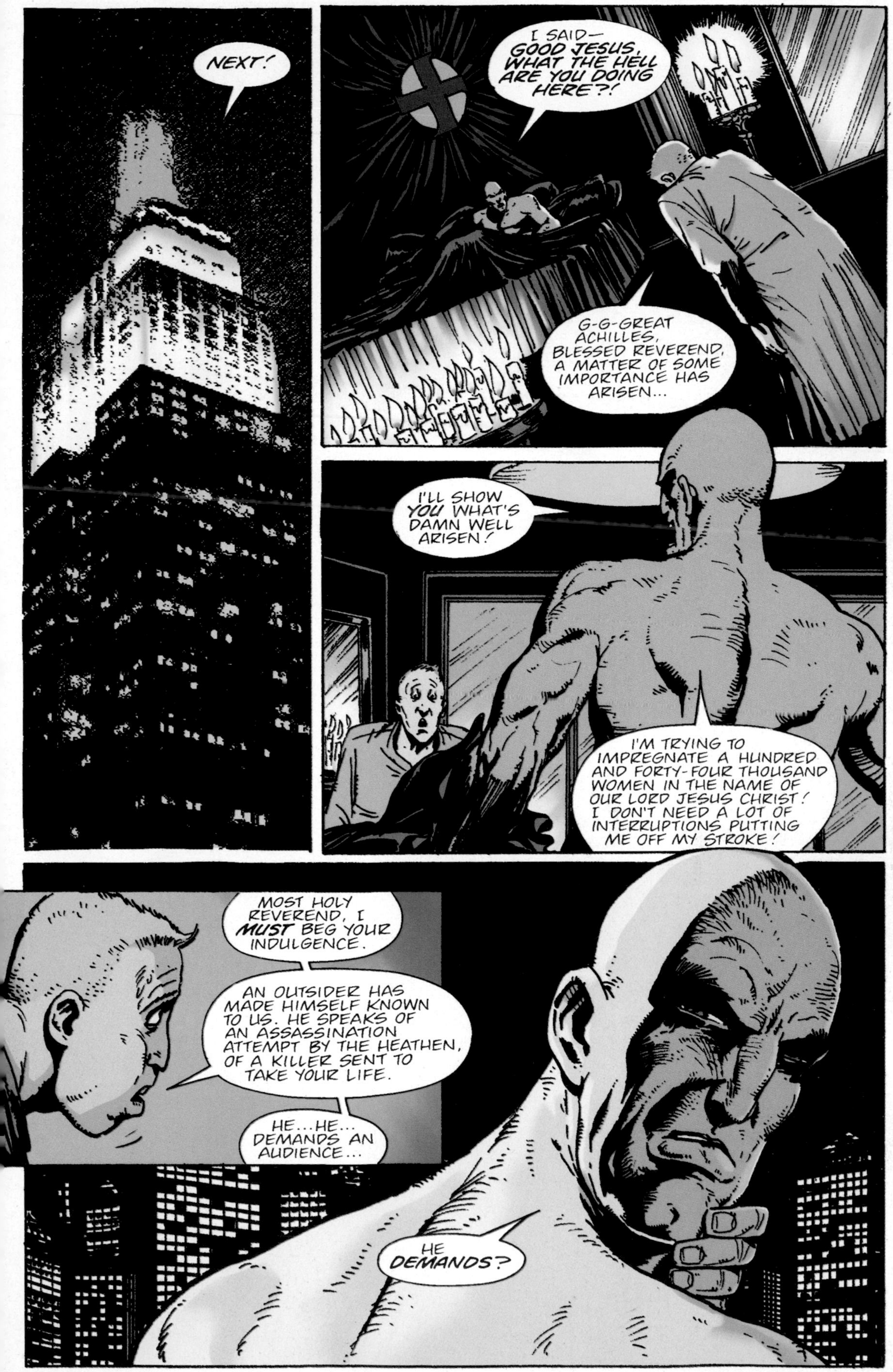
NEXT!
I SAID—
GOOD JESUS, WHAT THE HELL ARE YOU DOING HERE?!
G-G-GREAT ACHILLES, BLESSED REVEREND, A MATTER OF SOME IMPORTANCE HAS ARISEN...
I'LL SHOW YOU WHAT'S DAMN WELL ARISEN!
I'M TRYING TO IMPREGNATE A HUNDRED AND FORTY-FOUR THOUSAND WOMEN IN THE NAME OF OUR LORD JESUS CHRIST! I DON'T NEED A LOT OF INTERRUPTIONS PUTTING ME OFF MY STROKE!
MOST HOLY REVEREND, I MUST BEG YOUR INDULGENCE.
AN OUTSIDER HAS MADE HIMSELF KNOWN TO US. HE SPEAKS OF AN ASSASSINATION ATTEMPT BY THE HEATHEN, OF A KILLER SENT TO TAKE YOUR LIFE.
HE...HE... DEMANDS AN AUDIENCE...
HE DEMANDS?

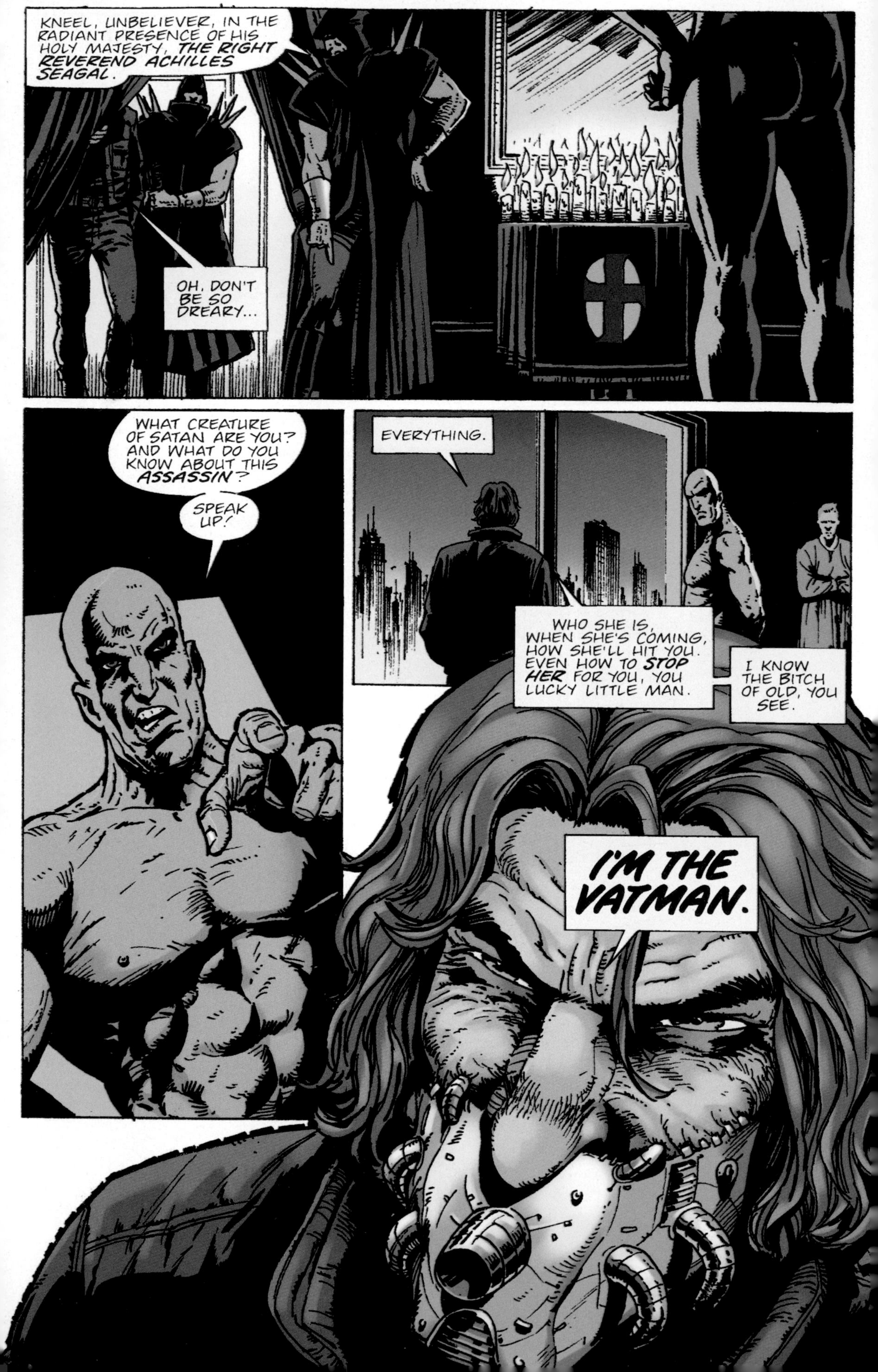

KNEEL, UNBELIEVER, IN THE RADIANT PRESENCE OF HIS HOLY MAJESTY, THE RIGHT REVEREND ACHILLES SEAGAL.
OH. DON'T BE SO DREARY...
WHAT CREATURE OF SATAN ARE YOU? AND WHAT DO YOU KNOW ABOUT THIS ASSASSIN?
SPEAK UP!
EVERYTHING.
WHO SHE IS, WHEN SHE'S COMING, HOW SHE'LL HIT YOU. EVEN HOW TO STOP HER FOR YOU, YOU LUCKY LITTLE MAN.
I KNOW THE BITCH OF OLD, YOU SEE.
I'M THE VATMAN.

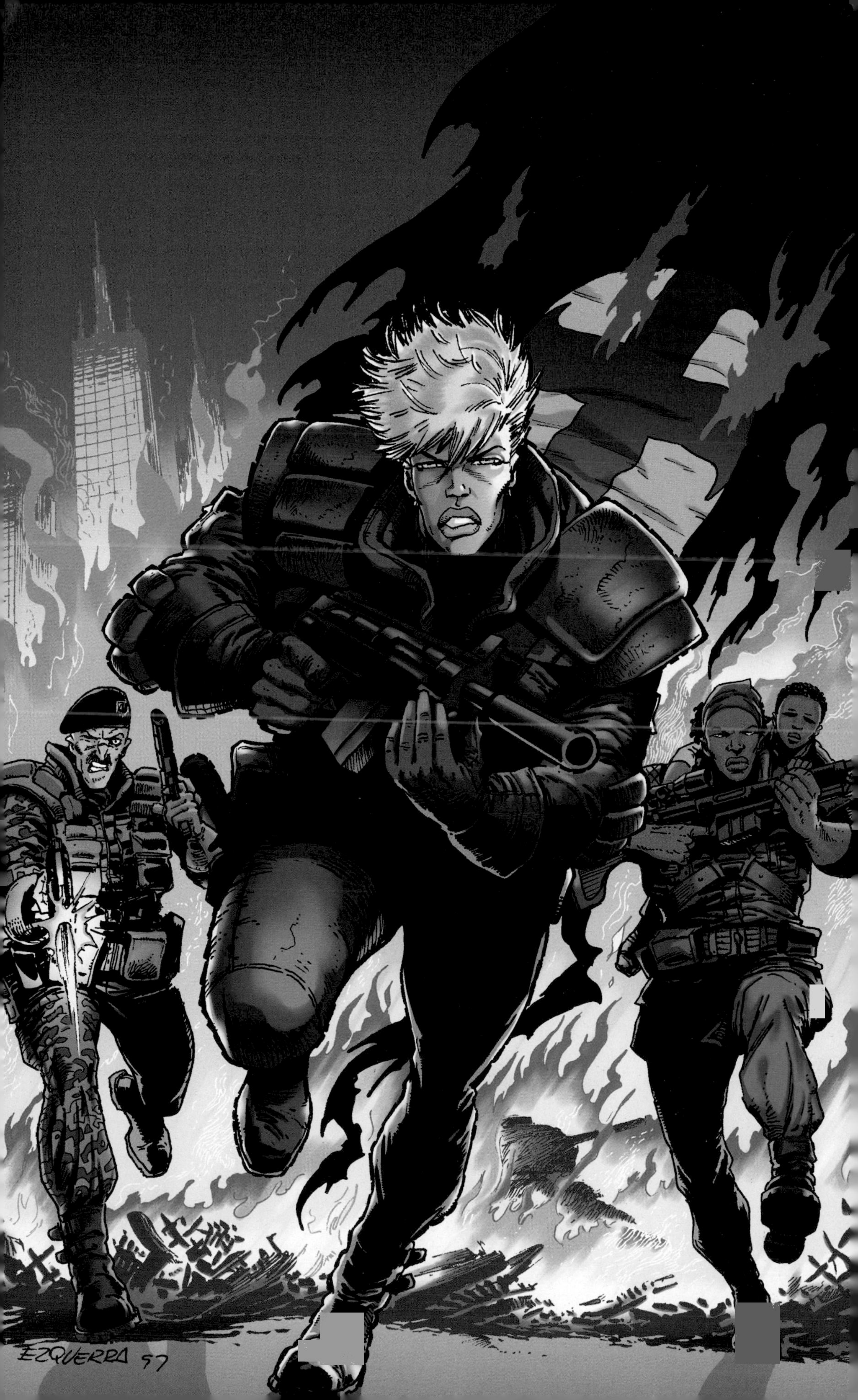
EZQUERRA 97

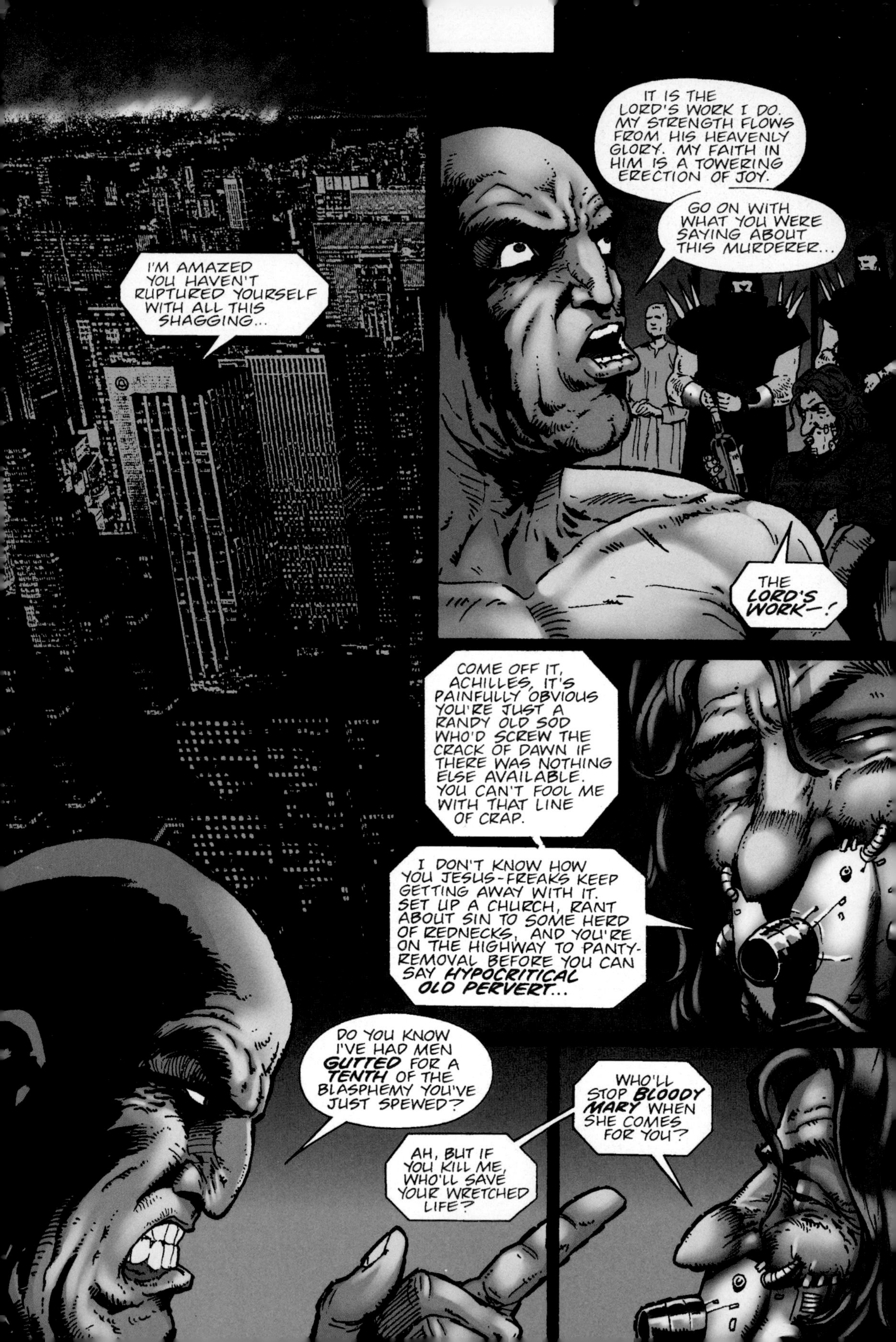

I'M AMAZED YOU HAVEN'T RUPTURED YOURSELF WITH ALL THIS SHAGGING...
IT IS THE LORD'S WORK I DO. MY STRENGTH FLOWS FROM HIS HEAVENLY GLORY. MY FAITH IN HIM IS A TOWERING ERECTION OF JOY.
GO ON WITH WHAT YOU WERE SAYING ABOUT THIS MURDERER...
THE LORD'S WORK--!
COME OFF IT, ACHILLES, IT'S PAINFULLY OBVIOUS YOU'RE JUST A RANDY OLD SOD WHO'D SCREW THE CRACK OF DAWN IF THERE WAS NOTHING ELSE AVAILABLE. YOU CAN'T FOOL ME WITH THAT LINE OF CRAP.
I DON'T KNOW HOW YOU JESUS-FREAKS KEEP GETTING AWAY WITH IT. SET UP A CHURCH, RANT ABOUT SIN TO SOME HERD OF REDNECKS, AND YOU'RE ON THE HIGHWAY TO PANTY-REMOVAL BEFORE YOU CAN SAY HYPOCRITICAL OLD PERVERT...
DO YOU KNOW I'VE HAD MEN GUTTED FOR A TENTH OF THE BLASPHEMY YOU'VE JUST SPEWED?
AH, BUT IF YOU KILL ME, WHO'LL SAVE YOUR WRETCHED LIFE?
WHO'LL STOP BLOODY MARY WHEN SHE COMES FOR YOU?

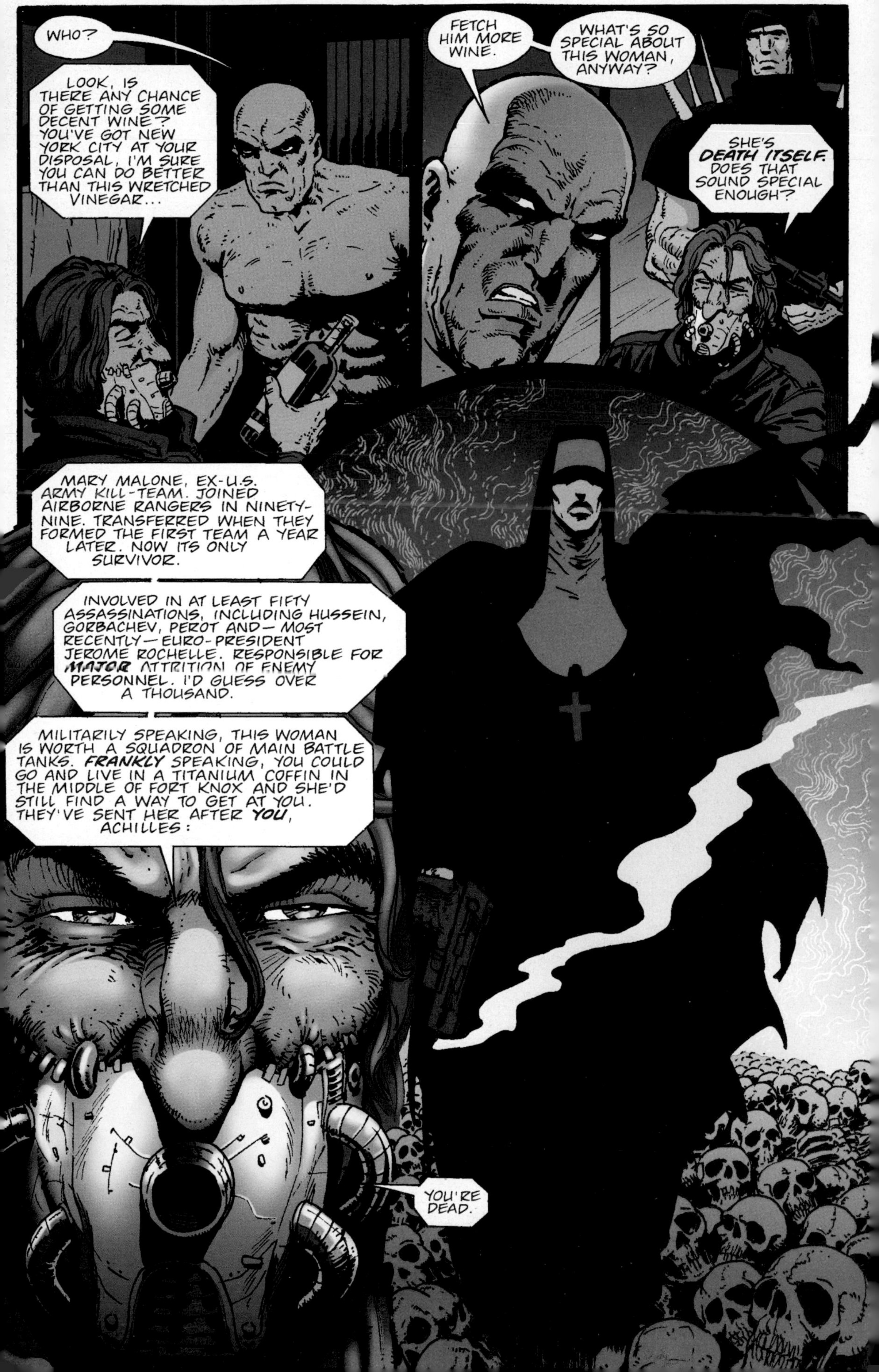
WHO?
LOOK, IS THERE ANY CHANCE OF GETTING SOME DECENT WINE? YOU'VE GOT NEW YORK CITY AT YOUR DISPOSAL, I'M SURE YOU CAN DO BETTER THAN THIS WRETCHED VINEGAR...
FETCH HIM MORE WINE.
WHAT'S SO SPECIAL ABOUT THIS WOMAN, ANYWAY?
SHE'S DEATH ITSELF. DOES THAT SOUND SPECIAL ENOUGH?
MARY MALONE, EX-U.S. ARMY KILL-TEAM. JOINED AIRBORNE RANGERS IN NINETY-NINE. TRANSFERRED WHEN THEY FORMED THE FIRST TEAM A YEAR LATER. NOW ITS ONLY SURVIVOR.
INVOLVED IN AT LEAST FIFTY ASSASSINATIONS, INCLUDING HUSSEIN, GORBACHEV, PEROT AND— MOST RECENTLY— EURO-PRESIDENT JEROME ROCHELLE. RESPONSIBLE FOR MAJOR ATTRITION OF ENEMY PERSONNEL. I'D GUESS OVER A THOUSAND.
MILITARILY SPEAKING, THIS WOMAN IS WORTH A SQUADRON OF MAIN BATTLE TANKS. FRANKLY SPEAKING, YOU COULD GO AND LIVE IN A TITANIUM COFFIN IN THE MIDDLE OF FORT KNOX AND SHE'D STILL FIND A WAY TO GET AT YOU. THEY'VE SENT HER AFTER YOU, ACHILLES:
YOU'RE DEAD.

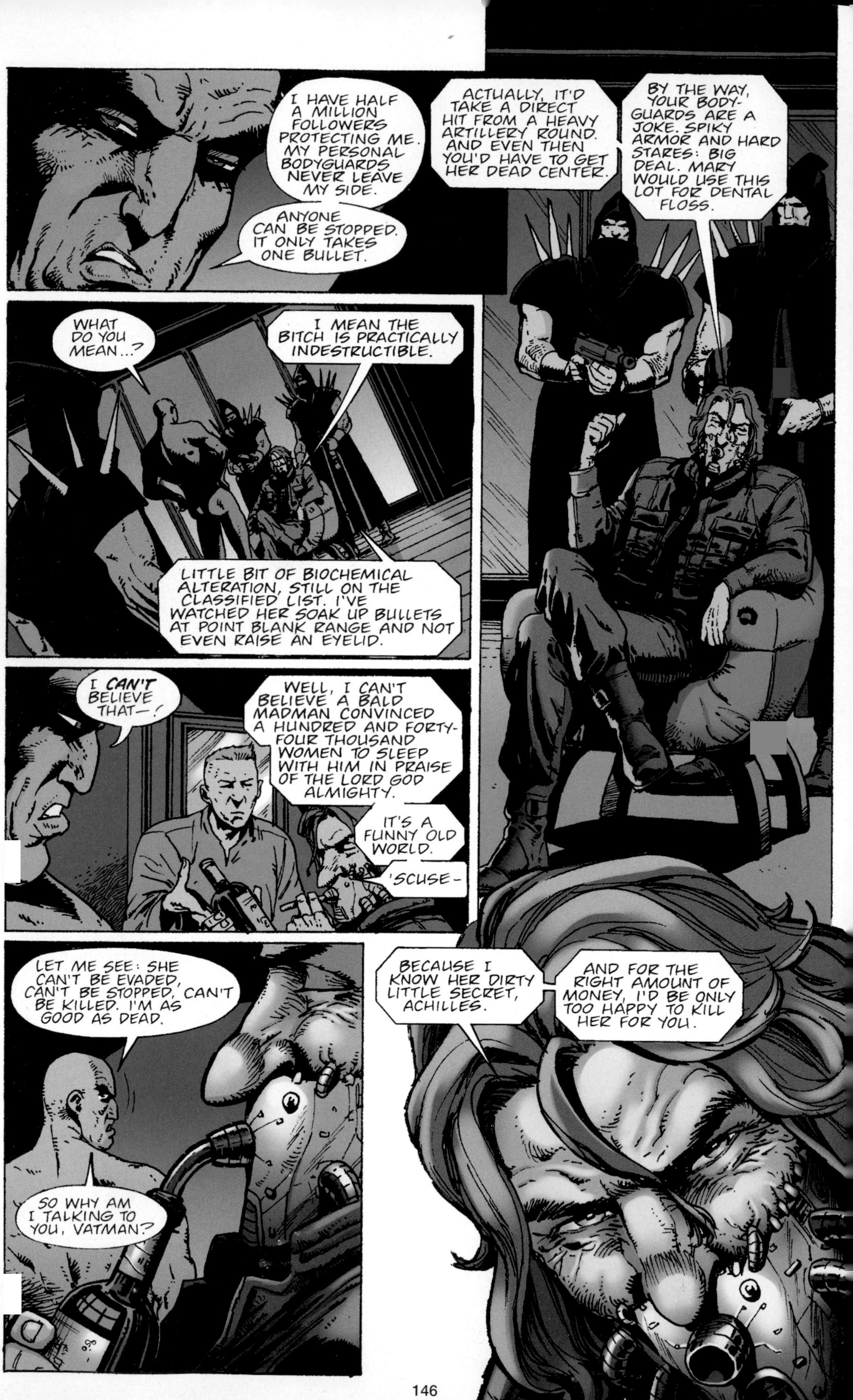
I HAVE HALF A MILLION FOLLOWERS PROTECTING ME. MY PERSONAL BODYGUARDS NEVER LEAVE MY SIDE.
ANYONE CAN BE STOPPED. IT ONLY TAKES ONE BULLET.
ACTUALLY, IT'D TAKE A DIRECT HIT FROM A HEAVY ARTILLERY ROUND. AND EVEN THEN YOU'D HAVE TO GET HER DEAD CENTER.
BY THE WAY, YOUR BODY-GUARDS ARE A JOKE. SPIKY ARMOR AND HARD STARES: BIG DEAL. MARY WOULD USE THIS LOT FOR DENTAL FLOSS.
WHAT DO YOU MEAN...?
I MEAN THE BITCH IS PRACTICALLY INDESTRUCTIBLE.
LITTLE BIT OF BIOCHEMICAL ALTERATION, STILL ON THE CLASSIFIED LIST. I'VE WATCHED HER SOAK UP BULLETS AT POINT BLANK RANGE AND NOT EVEN RAISE AN EYELID.
I CAN'T BELIEVE THAT--!
WELL, I CAN'T BELIEVE A BALD MADMAN CONVINCED A HUNDRED AND FORTY-FOUR THOUSAND WOMEN TO SLEEP WITH HIM IN PRAISE OF THE LORD GOD ALMIGHTY.
IT'S A FUNNY OLD WORLD.
'SCUSE-
LET ME SEE: SHE CAN'T BE EVADED, CAN'T BE STOPPED, CAN'T BE KILLED. I'M AS GOOD AS DEAD.
SO WHY AM I TALKING TO YOU, VATMAN?
BECAUSE I KNOW HER DIRTY LITTLE SECRET, ACHILLES.
AND FOR THE RIGHT AMOUNT OF MONEY, I'D BE ONLY TOO HAPPY TO KILL HER FOR YOU.

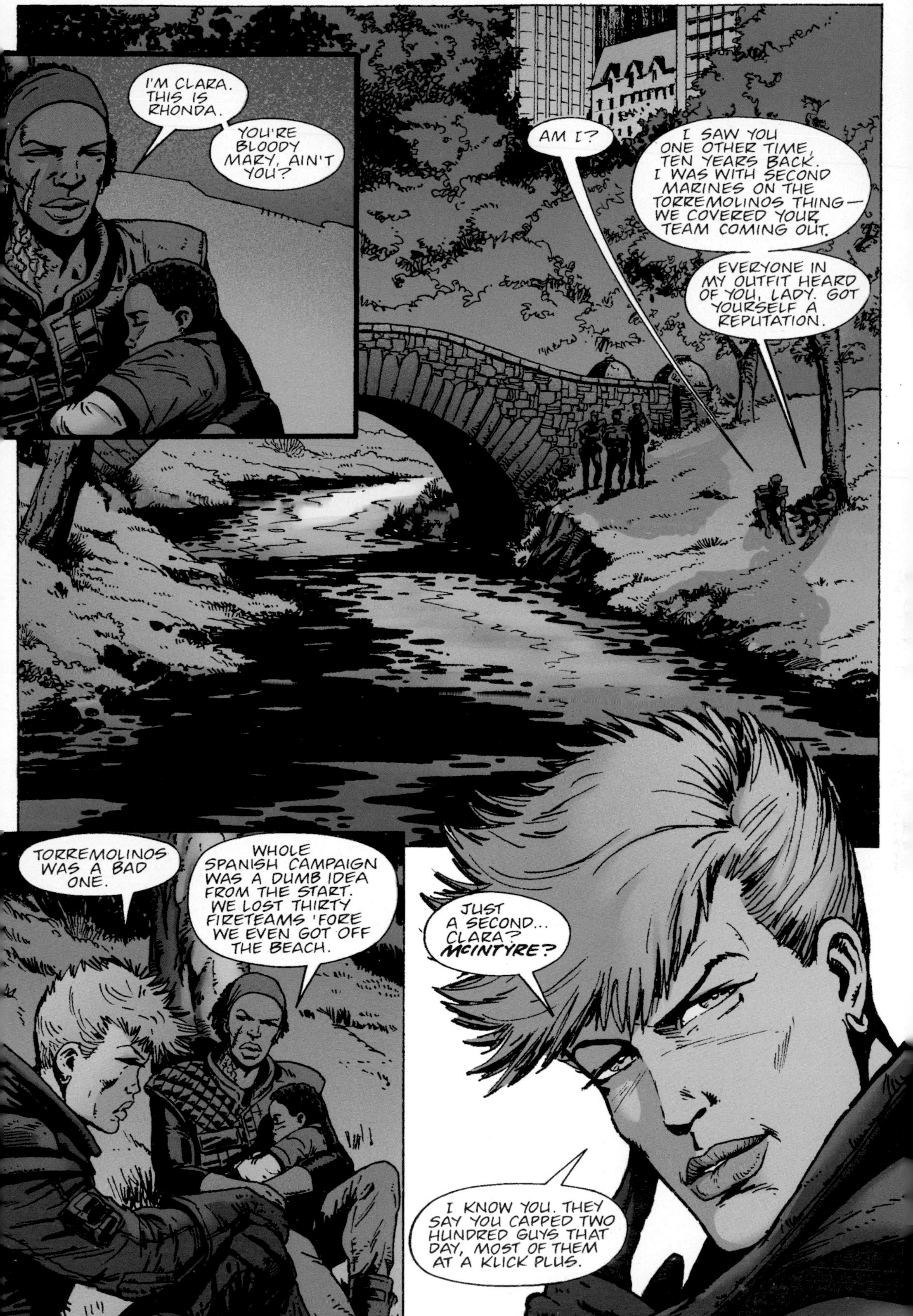
I'M CLARA. THIS IS RHONDA.
YOU'RE BLOODY MARY, AIN'T YOU?
AM I?
I SAW YOU ONE OTHER TIME, TEN YEARS BACK. I WAS WITH SECOND MARINES ON THE TORREMOLINOS THING— WE COVERED YOUR TEAM COMING OUT.
EVERYONE IN MY OUTFIT HEARD OF YOU, LADY. GOT YOURSELF A REPUTATION.
TORREMOLINOS WAS A BAD ONE.
WHOLE SPANISH CAMPAIGN WAS A DUMB IDEA FROM THE START. WE LOST THIRTY FIRETEAMS 'FORE WE EVEN GOT OFF THE BEACH.
JUST A SECOND... CLARA? MCINTYRE?
I KNOW YOU. THEY SAY YOU CAPPED TWO HUNDRED GUYS THAT DAY, MOST OF THEM AT A KLICK PLUS.

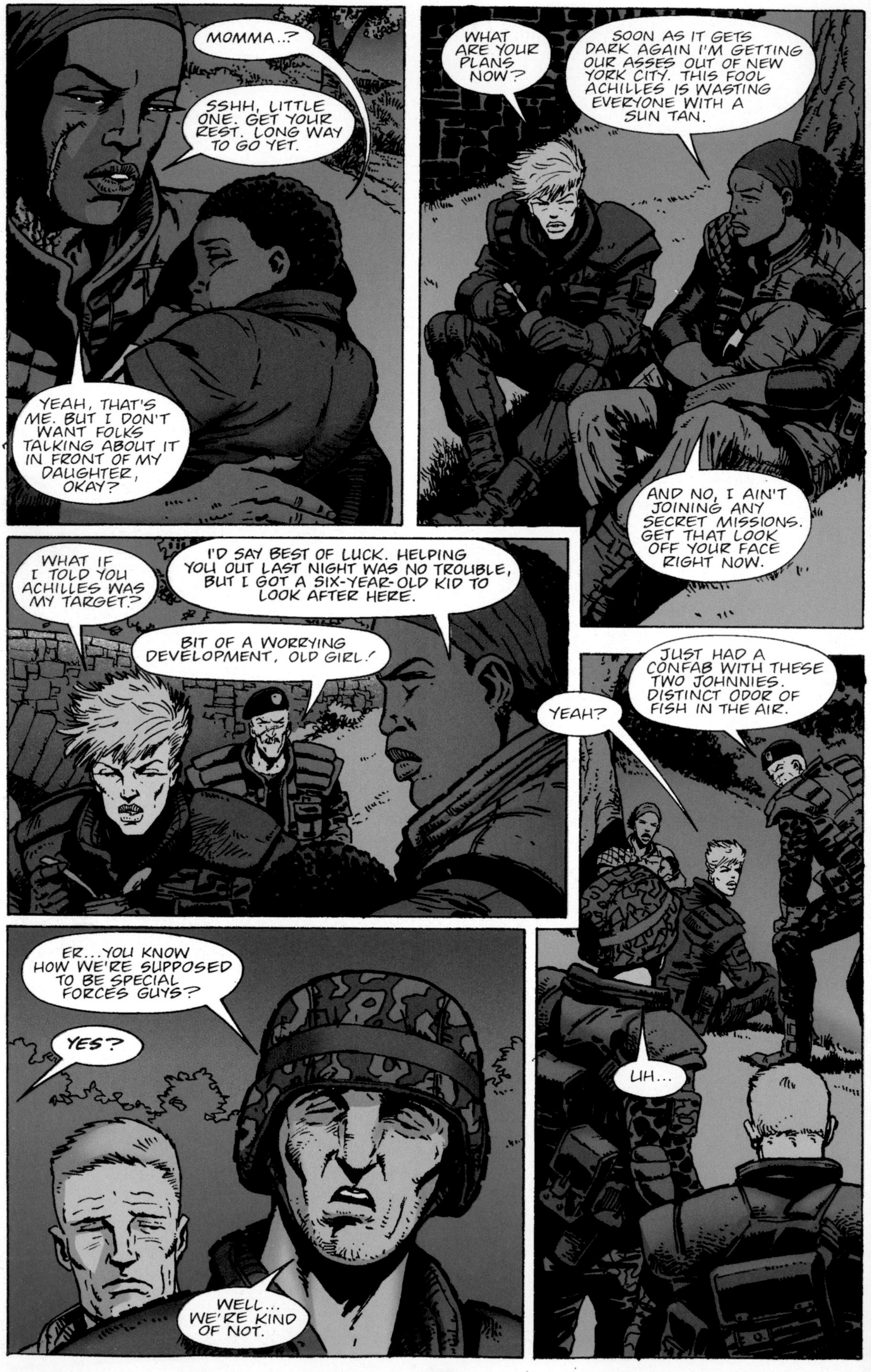
MOMMA..?
SSHH, LITTLE ONE. GET YOUR REST. LONG WAY TO GO YET.
YEAH, THAT'S ME. BUT I DON'T WANT FOLKS TALKING ABOUT IT IN FRONT OF MY DAUGHTER, OKAY?
WHAT ARE YOUR PLANS NOW?
SOON AS IT GETS DARK AGAIN I'M GETTING OUR ASSES OUT OF NEW YORK CITY. THIS FOOL ACHILLES IS WASTING EVERYONE WITH A SUN TAN.
AND NO, I AIN'T JOINING ANY SECRET MISSIONS. GET THAT LOOK OFF YOUR FACE RIGHT NOW.
WHAT IF I TOLD YOU ACHILLES WAS MY TARGET?
I'D SAY BEST OF LUCK. HELPING YOU OUT LAST NIGHT WAS NO TROUBLE, BUT I GOT A SIX-YEAR-OLD KID TO LOOK AFTER HERE.
BIT OF A WORRYING DEVELOPMENT, OLD GIRL!
YEAH?
JUST HAD A CONFAB WITH THESE TWO JOHNNIES. DISTINCT ODOR OF FISH IN THE AIR.
ER...YOU KNOW HOW WE'RE SUPPOSED TO BE SPECIAL FORCES GUYS?
YES?
WELL... WE'RE KIND OF NOT.
UH...

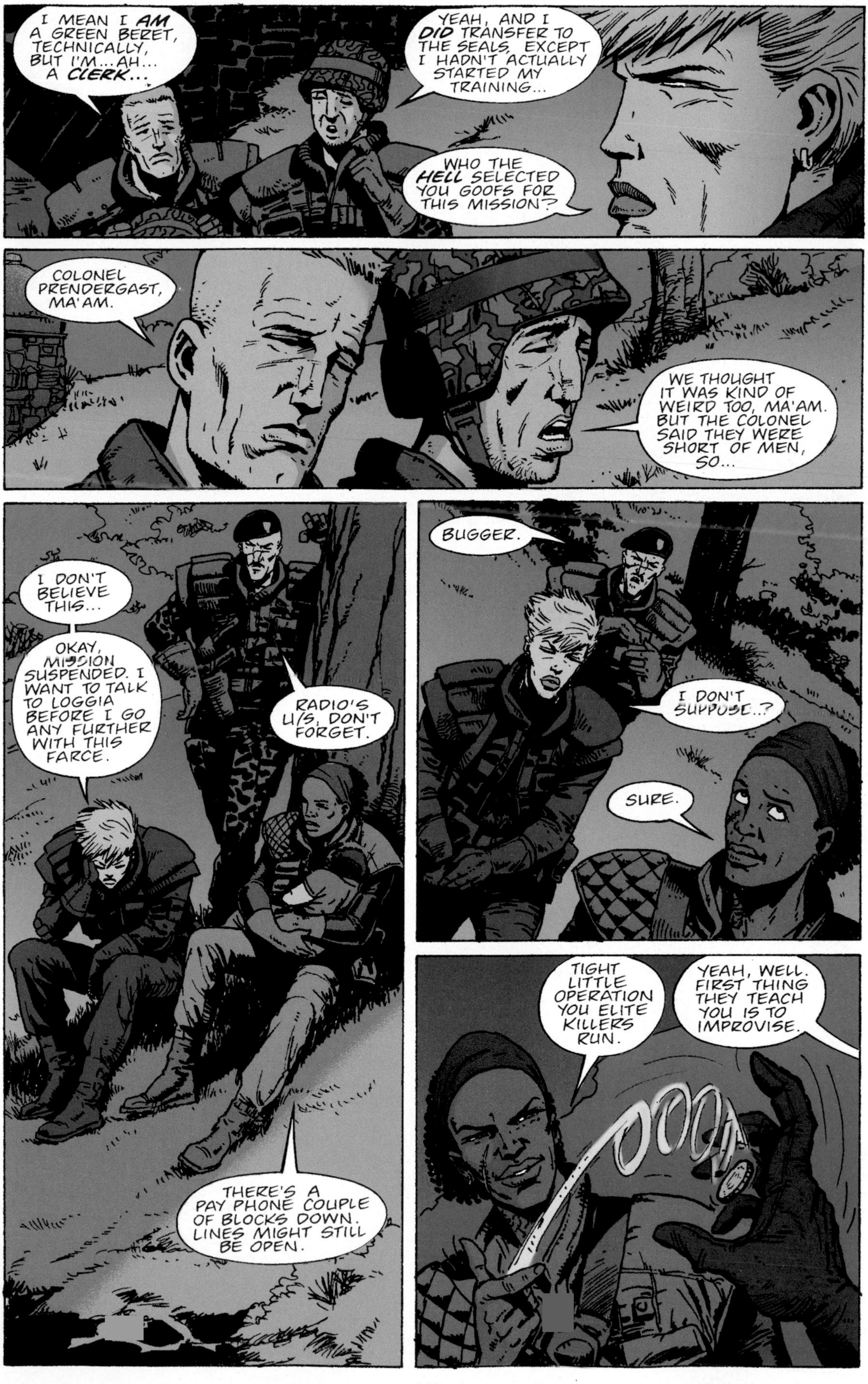
I MEAN I AM A GREEN BERET, TECHNICALLY, BUT I'M... AH... A CLERK...
YEAH, AND I DID TRANSFER TO THE SEALS, EXCEPT I HADN'T ACTUALLY STARTED MY TRAINING...
WHO THE HELL SELECTED YOU GOOFS FOR THIS MISSION?
COLONEL PRENDERGAST, MA'AM.
WE THOUGHT IT WAS KIND OF WEIRD TOO, MA'AM. BUT THE COLONEL SAID THEY WERE SHORT OF MEN, SO...
I DON'T BELIEVE THIS...
OKAY, MISSION SUSPENDED. I WANT TO TALK TO LOGGIA BEFORE I GO ANY FURTHER WITH THIS FARCE.
RADIO'S U/S, DON'T FORGET.
THERE'S A PAY PHONE COUPLE OF BLOCKS DOWN. LINES MIGHT STILL BE OPEN.
BUGGER.
I DON'T SUPPOSE..?
SURE.
TIGHT LITTLE OPERATION YOU ELITE KILLERS RUN.
YEAH, WELL. FIRST THING THEY TEACH YOU IS TO IMPROVISE.

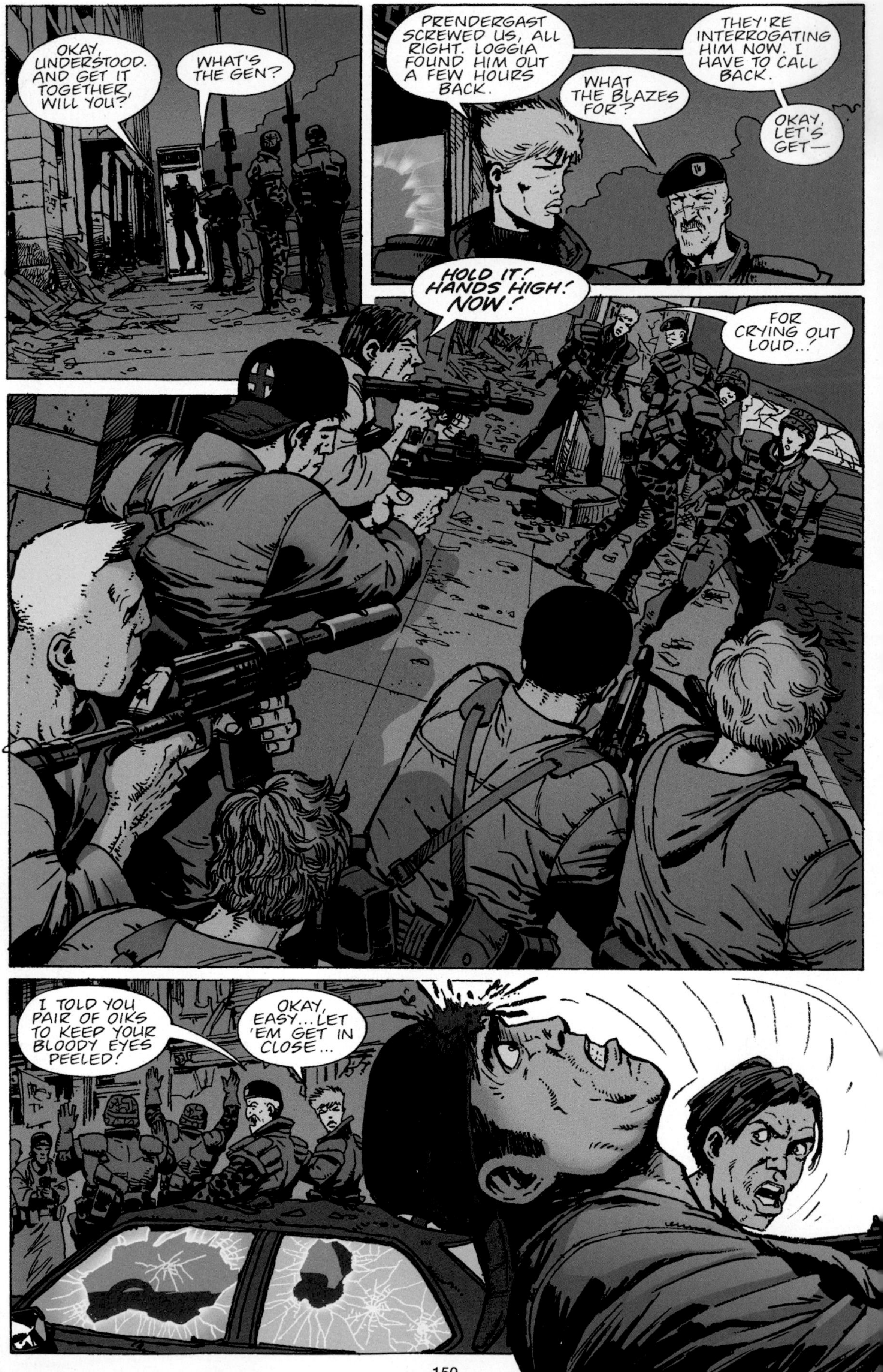
OKAY, UNDERSTOOD. AND GET IT TOGETHER, WILL YOU?'
WHAT'S THE GEN?
PRENDERGAST SCREWED US, ALL RIGHT. LOGGIA FOUND HIM OUT A FEW HOURS BACK.
THEY'RE INTERROGATING HIM NOW. I HAVE TO CALL BACK.
WHAT THE BLAZES FOR?
OKAY, LET'S GET—
HOLD IT! HANDS HIGH! NOW!
FOR CRYING OUT LOUD...!
I TOLD YOU PAIR OF OIKS TO KEEP YOUR BLOODY EYES PEELED!
OKAY, EASY... LET 'EM GET IN CLOSE...

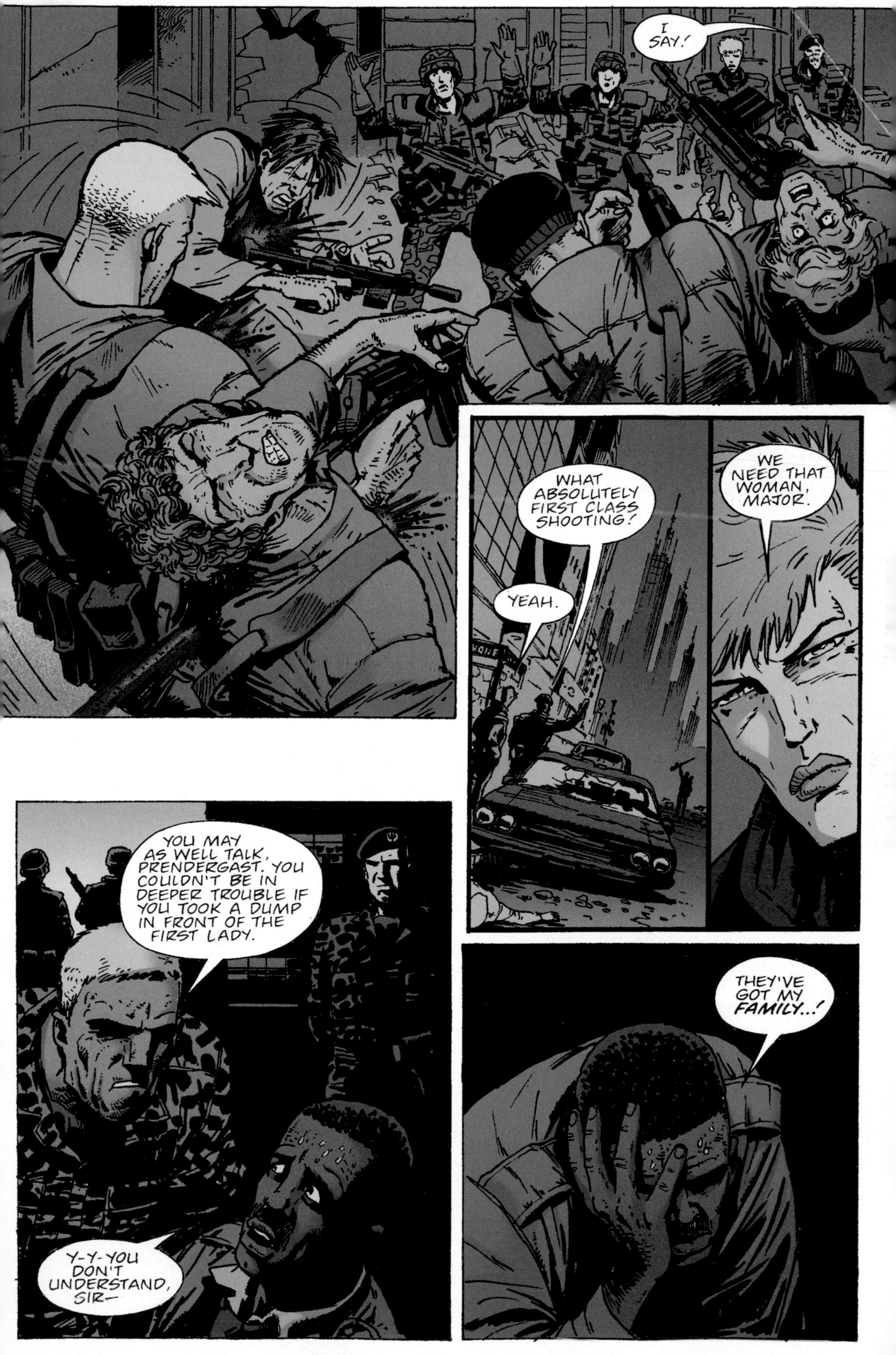
I SAY!
WHAT ABSOLUTELY FIRST CLASS SHOOTING!
YEAH.
WE NEED THAT WOMAN, MAJOR.
YOU MAY AS WELL TALK, PRENDERGAST. YOU COULDN'T BE IN DEEPER TROUBLE IF YOU TOOK A DUMP IN FRONT OF THE FIRST LADY.
Y-Y-YOU DON'T UNDERSTAND, SIR—
THEY'VE GOT MY *FAMILY*...!

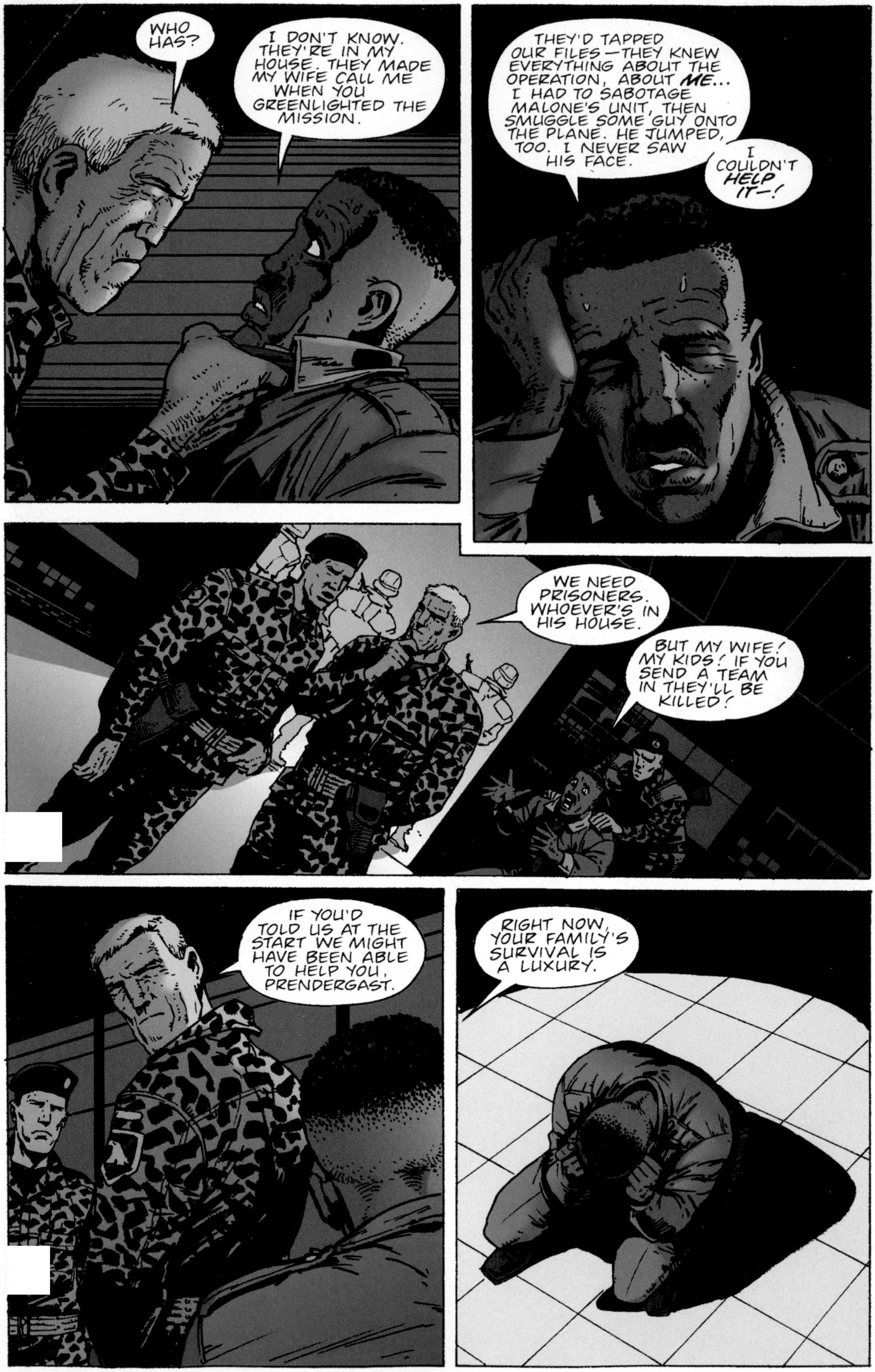
WHO HAS?
I DON'T KNOW. THEY'RE IN MY HOUSE. THEY MADE MY WIFE CALL ME WHEN YOU GREENLIGHTED THE MISSION.
THEY'D TAPPED OUR FILES—THEY KNEW EVERYTHING ABOUT THE OPERATION, ABOUT ME... I HAD TO SABOTAGE MALONE'S UNIT, THEN SMUGGLE SOME GUY ONTO THE PLANE. HE JUMPED, TOO. I NEVER SAW HIS FACE.
I COULDN'T HELP IT—!
WE NEED PRISONERS. WHOEVER'S IN HIS HOUSE.
BUT MY WIFE! MY KIDS! IF YOU SEND A TEAM IN THEY'LL BE KILLED!
IF YOU'D TOLD US AT THE START WE MIGHT HAVE BEEN ABLE TO HELP YOU, PRENDERGAST.
RIGHT NOW, YOUR FAMILY'S SURVIVAL IS A LUXURY.

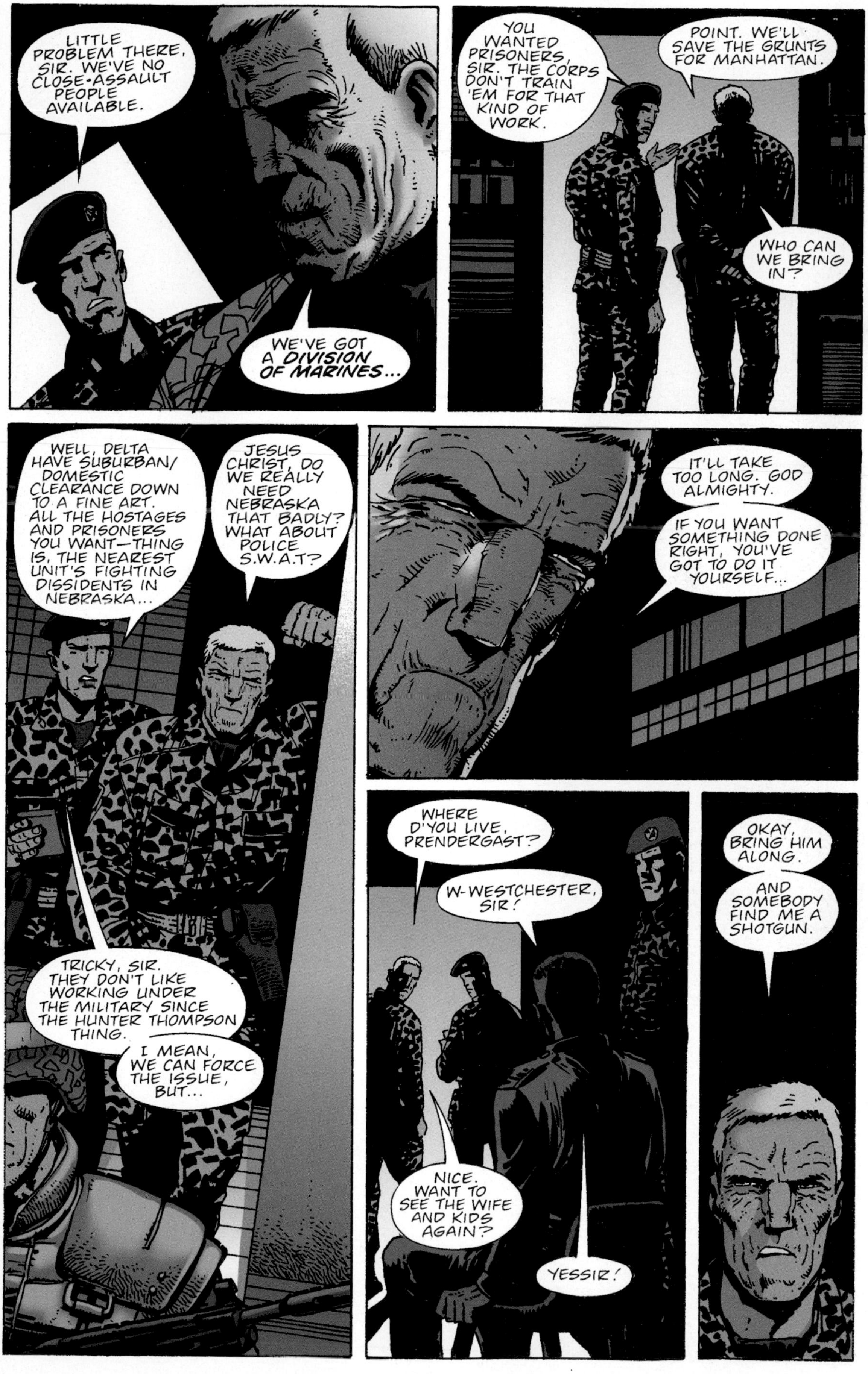
LITTLE PROBLEM THERE, SIR. WE'VE NO CLOSE-ASSAULT PEOPLE AVAILABLE.
WE'VE GOT A DIVISION OF MARINES...
YOU WANTED PRISONERS, SIR. THE CORPS DON'T TRAIN 'EM FOR THAT KIND OF WORK.
POINT. WE'LL SAVE THE GRUNTS FOR MANHATTAN.
WHO CAN WE BRING IN?
WELL, DELTA HAVE SUBURBAN/ DOMESTIC CLEARANCE DOWN TO A FINE ART. ALL THE HOSTAGES AND PRISONERS YOU WANT—THING IS, THE NEAREST UNIT'S FIGHTING DISSIDENTS IN NEBRASKA...
JESUS CHRIST, DO WE REALLY NEED NEBRASKA THAT BADLY? WHAT ABOUT POLICE S.W.A.T?
TRICKY, SIR. THEY DON'T LIKE WORKING UNDER THE MILITARY SINCE THE HUNTER THOMPSON THING.
I MEAN, WE CAN FORCE THE ISSUE, BUT...
IT'LL TAKE TOO LONG. GOD ALMIGHTY.
IF YOU WANT SOMETHING DONE RIGHT, YOU'VE GOT TO DO IT YOURSELF...
WHERE D'YOU LIVE, PRENDERGAST?
W-WESTCHESTER, SIR!
NICE. WANT TO SEE THE WIFE AND KIDS AGAIN?
YESSIR!
OKAY, BRING HIM ALONG.
AND SOMEBODY FIND ME A SHOTGUN.

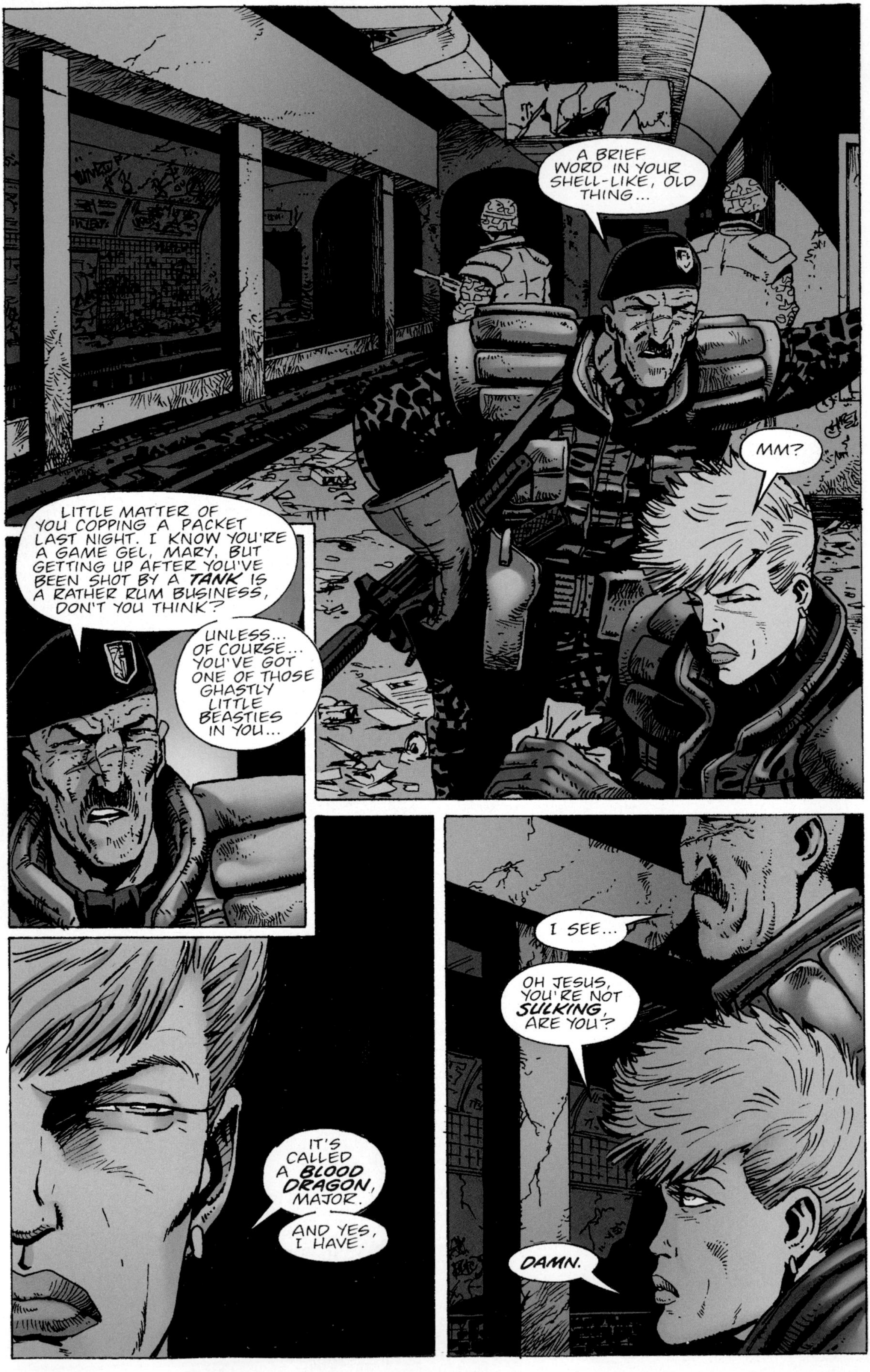
A BRIEF WORD IN YOUR SHELL-LIKE, OLD THING...
MM?
LITTLE MATTER OF YOU COPPING A PACKET LAST NIGHT. I KNOW YOU'RE A GAME GEL, MARY, BUT GETTING UP AFTER YOU'VE BEEN SHOT BY A TANK IS A RATHER RUM BUSINESS, DON'T YOU THINK?
UNLESS... OF COURSE... YOU'VE GOT ONE OF THOSE GHASTLY LITTLE BEASTIES IN YOU...
IT'S CALLED A BLOOD DRAGON, MAJOR.
AND YES, I HAVE.
I SEE...
OH JESUS, YOU'RE NOT SULKING, ARE YOU?
DAMN.

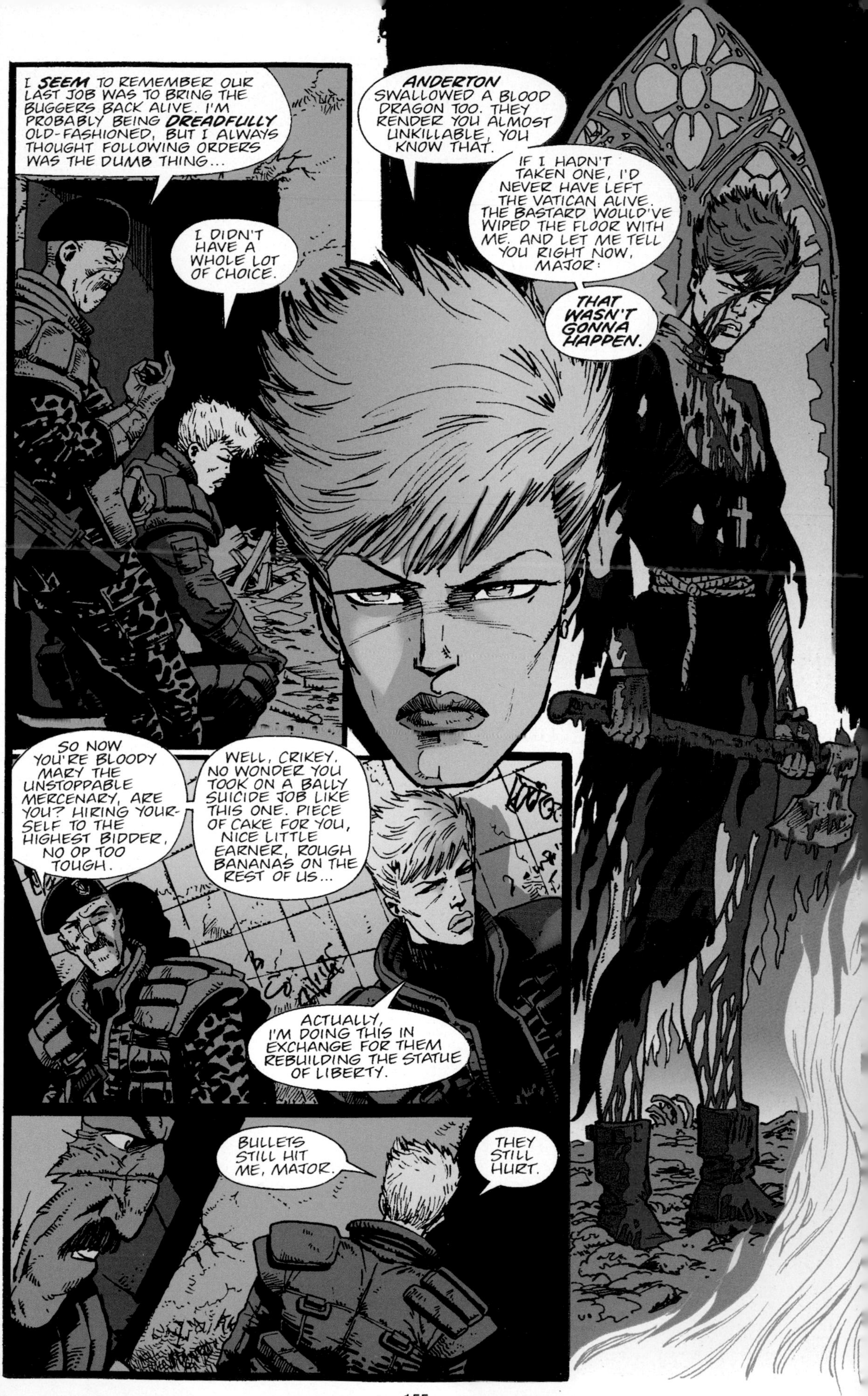
I SEEM TO REMEMBER OUR LAST JOB WAS TO BRING THE BUGGERS BACK ALIVE. I'M PROBABLY BEING DREADFULLY OLD-FASHIONED, BUT I ALWAYS THOUGHT FOLLOWING ORDERS WAS THE DUMB THING...
I DIDN'T HAVE A WHOLE LOT OF CHOICE.
ANDERTON SWALLOWED A BLOOD DRAGON TOO. THEY RENDER YOU ALMOST UNKILLABLE, YOU KNOW THAT.
IF I HADN'T TAKEN ONE, I'D NEVER HAVE LEFT THE VATICAN ALIVE. THE BASTARD WOULD'VE WIPED THE FLOOR WITH ME. AND LET ME TELL YOU RIGHT NOW, MAJOR:
THAT WASN'T GONNA HAPPEN.
SO NOW YOU'RE BLOODY MARY THE UNSTOPPABLE MERCENARY, ARE YOU? HIRING YOURSELF TO THE HIGHEST BIDDER, NO OP TOO TOUGH.
WELL, CRIKEY. NO WONDER YOU TOOK ON A BALLY SUICIDE JOB LIKE THIS ONE. PIECE OF CAKE FOR YOU, NICE LITTLE EARNER, ROUGH BANANAS ON THE REST OF US...
ACTUALLY, I'M DOING THIS IN EXCHANGE FOR THEM REBUILDING THE STATUE OF LIBERTY.
BULLETS STILL HIT ME, MAJOR.
THEY STILL HURT.

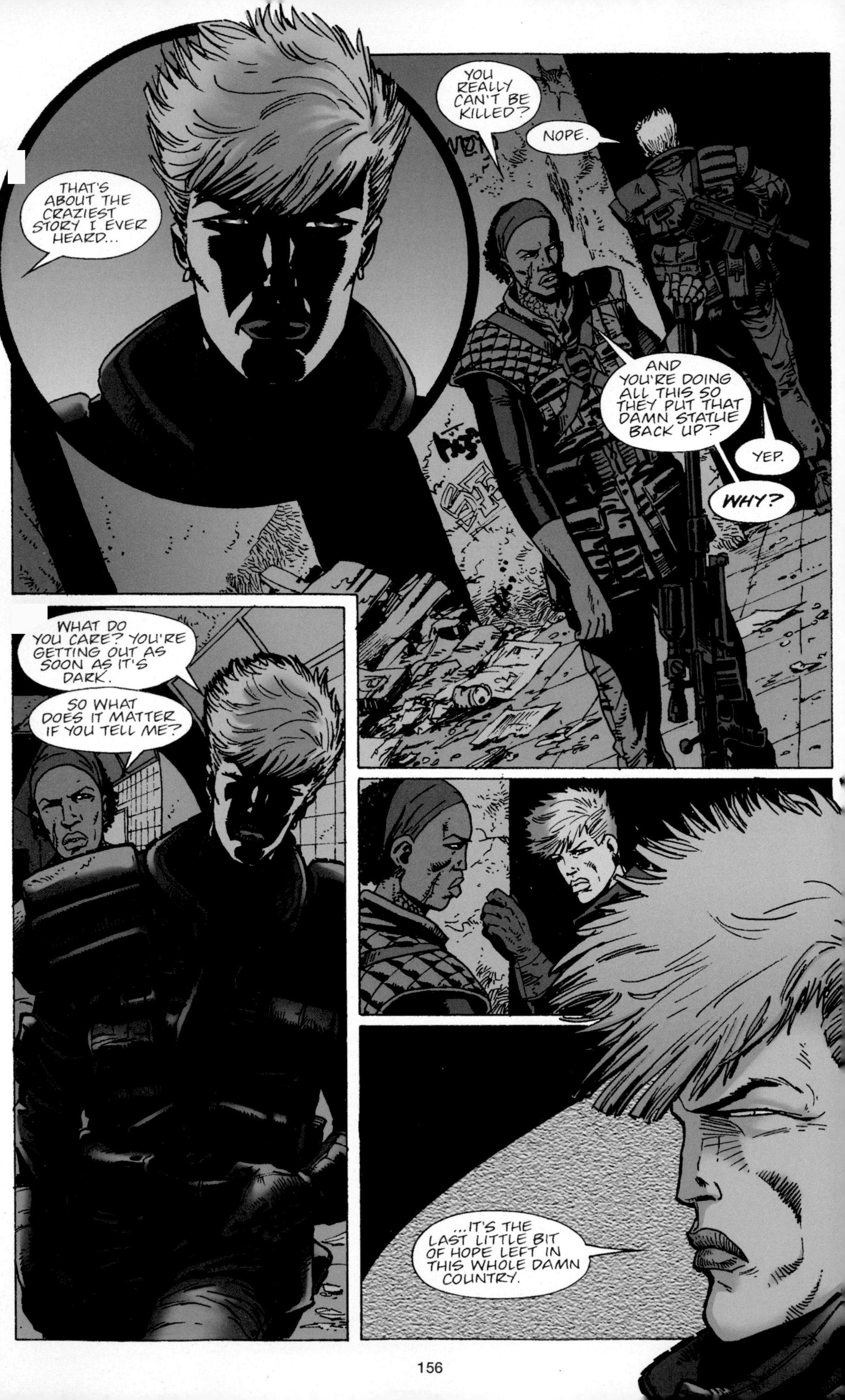

THAT'S ABOUT THE CRAZIEST STORY I EVER HEARD...
YOU REALLY CAN'T BE KILLED?
NOPE.
AND YOU'RE DOING ALL THIS SO THEY PUT THAT DAMN STATUE BACK UP?
YEP.
WHY?
WHAT DO YOU CARE? YOU'RE GETTING OUT AS SOON AS IT'S DARK.
SO WHAT DOES IT MATTER IF YOU TELL ME?
...IT'S THE LAST LITTLE BIT OF HOPE LEFT IN THIS WHOLE DAMN COUNTRY.

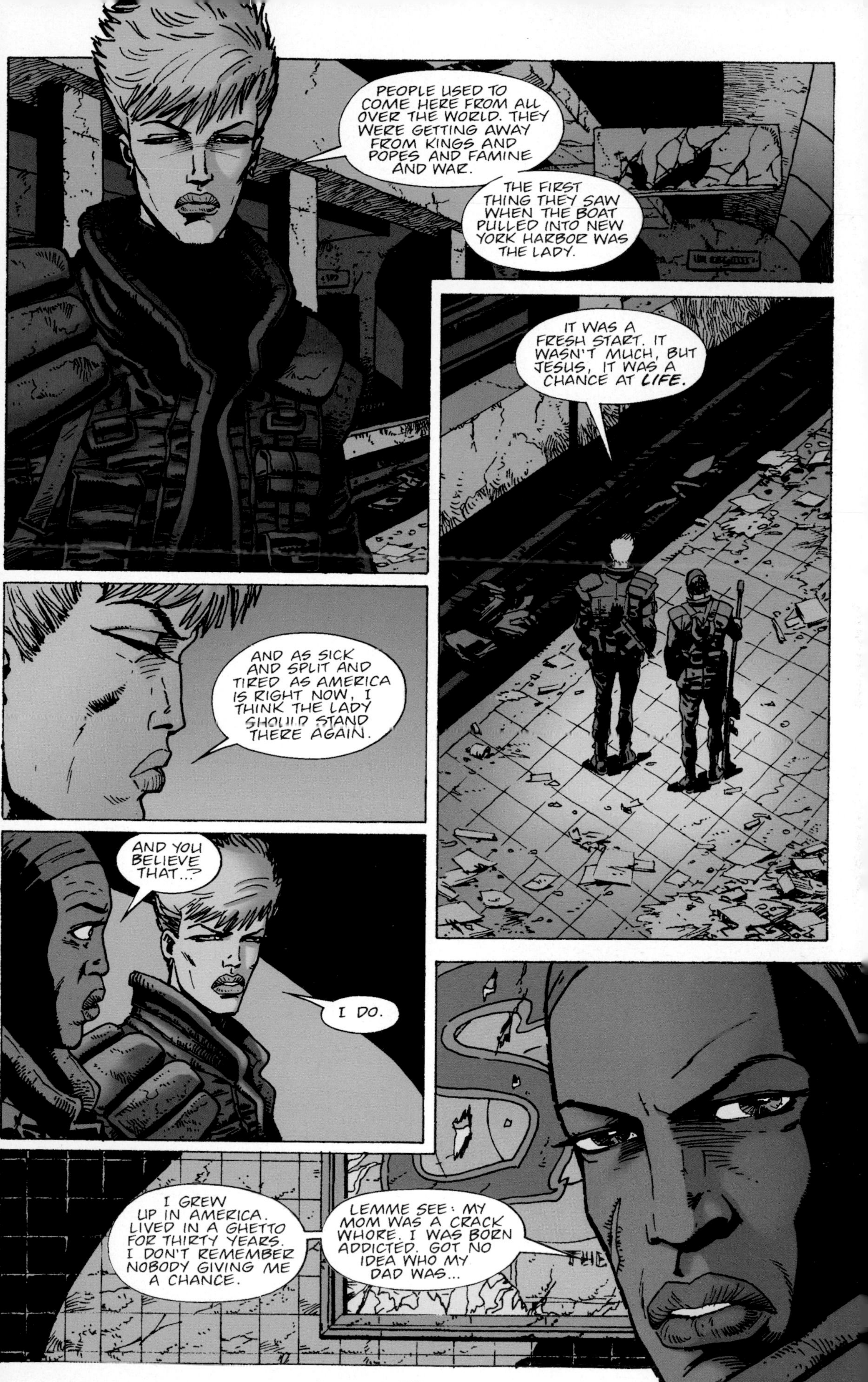
PEOPLE USED TO COME HERE FROM ALL OVER THE WORLD. THEY WERE GETTING AWAY FROM KINGS AND POPES AND FAMINE AND WAR.
THE FIRST THING THEY SAW WHEN THE BOAT PULLED INTO NEW YORK HARBOR WAS THE LADY.
IT WAS A FRESH START. IT WASN'T MUCH, BUT JESUS, IT WAS A CHANCE AT LIFE.
AND AS SICK AND SPLIT AND TIRED AS AMERICA IS RIGHT NOW, I THINK THE LADY SHOULD STAND THERE AGAIN.
AND YOU BELIEVE THAT...?
I DO.
LEMME SEE: MY MOM WAS A CRACK WHORE. I WAS BORN ADDICTED. GOT NO IDEA WHO MY DAD WAS...
I GREW UP IN AMERICA. LIVED IN A GHETTO FOR THIRTY YEARS. I DON'T REMEMBER NOBODY GIVING ME A CHANCE.

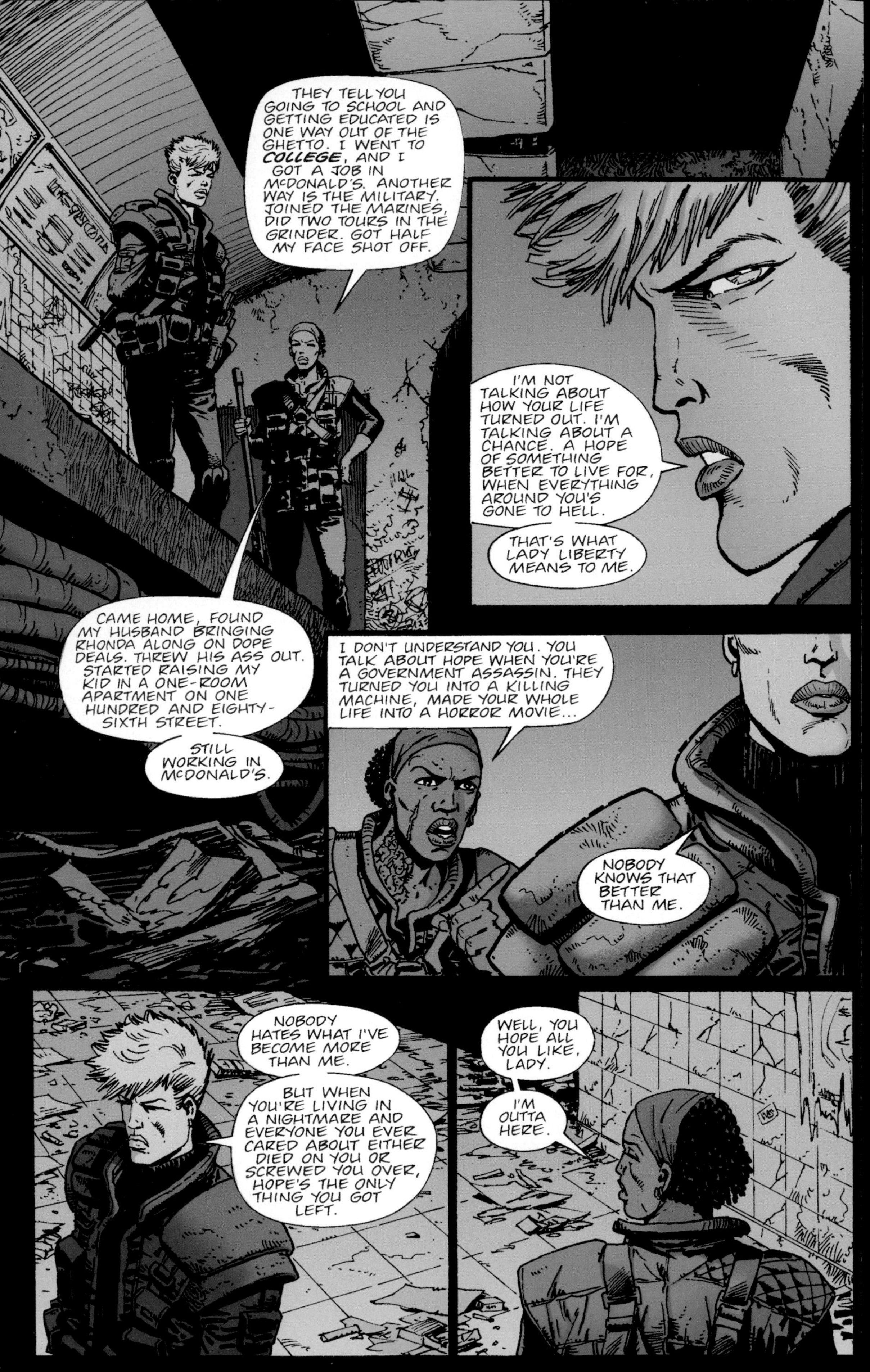
THEY TELL YOU GOING TO SCHOOL AND GETTING EDUCATED IS ONE WAY OUT OF THE GHETTO. I WENT TO **COLLEGE**, AND I GOT A JOB IN McDONALD'S. ANOTHER WAY IS THE MILITARY. JOINED THE MARINES, DID TWO TOURS IN THE GRINDER. GOT HALF MY FACE SHOT OFF.
CAME HOME, FOUND MY HUSBAND BRINGING RHONDA ALONG ON DOPE DEALS. THREW HIS ASS OUT. STARTED RAISING MY KID IN A ONE-ROOM APARTMENT ON ONE HUNDRED AND EIGHTY-SIXTH STREET.
STILL WORKING IN McDONALD'S.
I'M NOT TALKING ABOUT HOW YOUR LIFE TURNED OUT. I'M TALKING ABOUT A CHANCE. A HOPE OF SOMETHING BETTER TO LIVE FOR, WHEN EVERYTHING AROUND YOU'S GONE TO HELL.
THAT'S WHAT LADY LIBERTY MEANS TO ME.
I DON'T UNDERSTAND YOU. YOU TALK ABOUT HOPE WHEN YOU'RE A GOVERNMENT ASSASSIN. THEY TURNED YOU INTO A KILLING MACHINE, MADE YOUR WHOLE LIFE INTO A HORROR MOVIE...
NOBODY KNOWS THAT BETTER THAN ME.
NOBODY HATES WHAT I'VE BECOME MORE THAN ME.
BUT WHEN YOU'RE LIVING IN A NIGHTMARE AND EVERYONE YOU EVER CARED ABOUT EITHER DIED ON YOU OR SCREWED YOU OVER, HOPE'S THE ONLY THING YOU GOT LEFT.
WELL, YOU HOPE ALL YOU LIKE, LADY.
I'M OUTTA HERE.

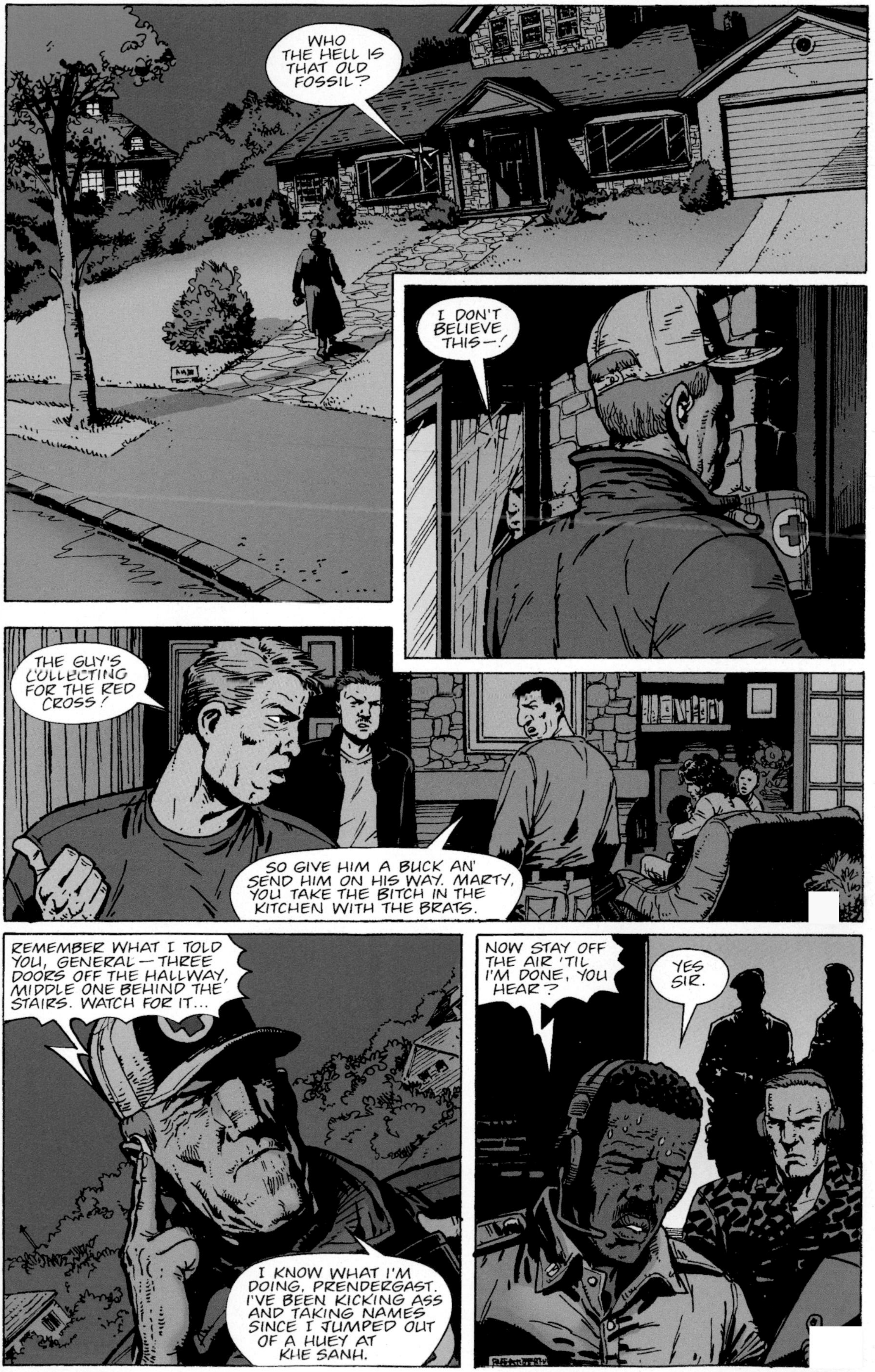
WHO THE HELL IS THAT OLD FOSSIL?
I DON'T BELIEVE THIS—!
THE GUY'S COLLECTING FOR THE RED CROSS!
SO GIVE HIM A BUCK AN' SEND HIM ON HIS WAY. MARTY, YOU TAKE THE BITCH IN THE KITCHEN WITH THE BRATS.
REMEMBER WHAT I TOLD YOU, GENERAL—THREE DOORS OFF THE HALLWAY, MIDDLE ONE BEHIND THE STAIRS. WATCH FOR IT...
I KNOW WHAT I'M DOING, PRENDERGAST. I'VE BEEN KICKING ASS AND TAKING NAMES SINCE I JUMPED OUT OF A HUEY AT KHE SANH.
NOW STAY OFF THE AIR 'TIL I'M DONE, YOU HEAR?
YES SIR.

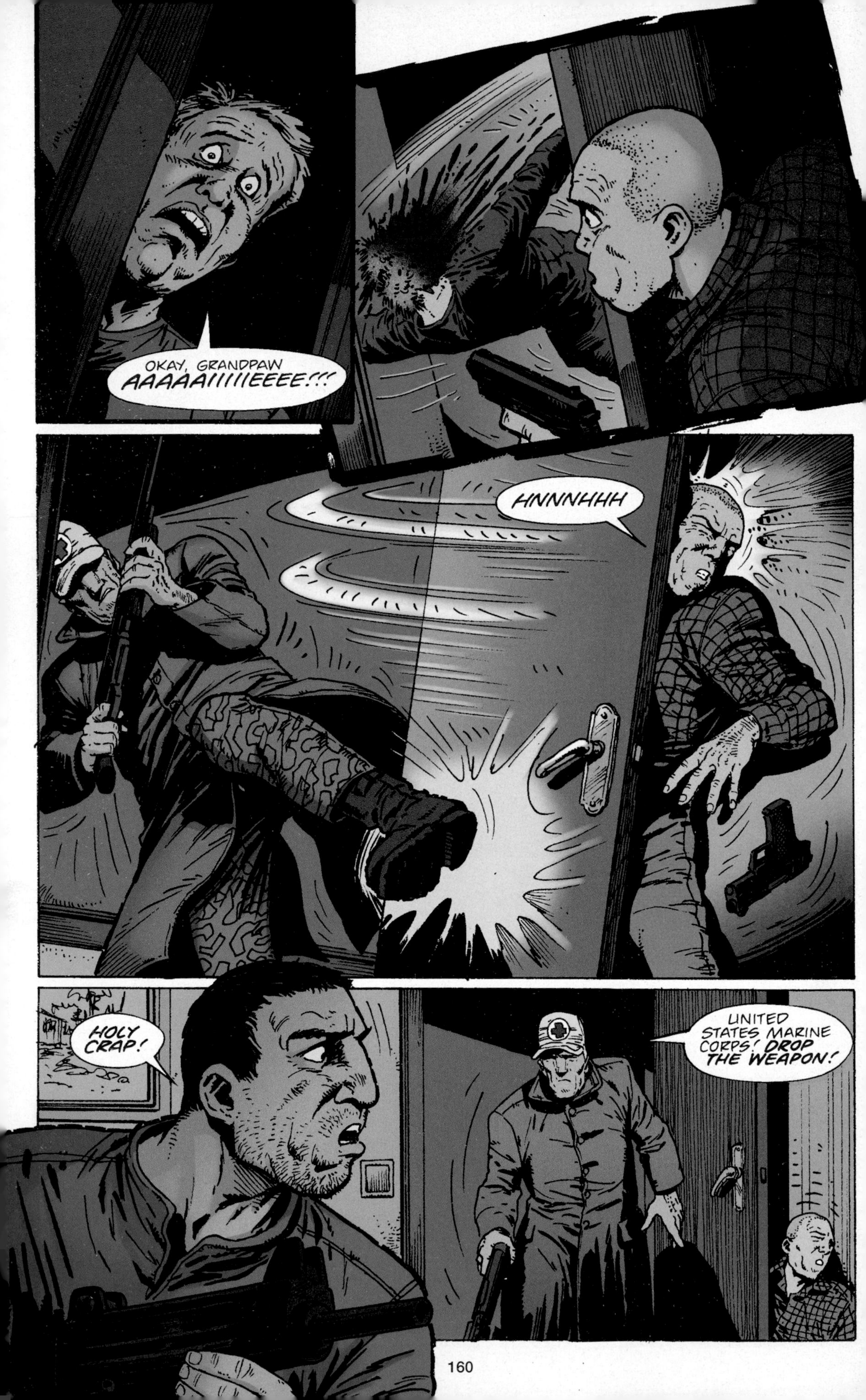
OKAY, GRANDPAW AAAAAIIIIIIEEEE!!!
HNNNHHH
HOLY CRAP!
UNITED STATES MARINE CORPS! DROP THE WEAPON!

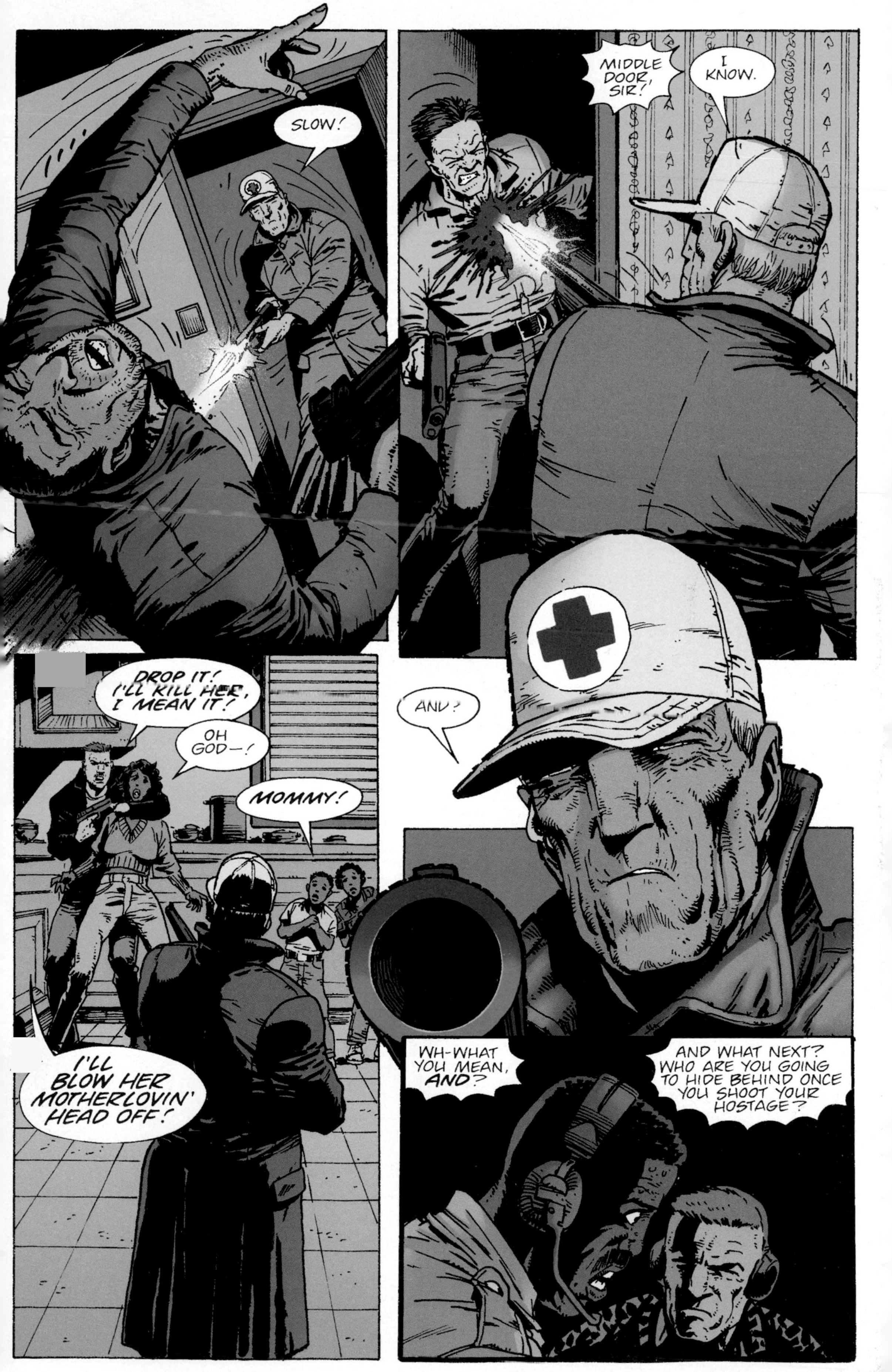
SLOW!
MIDDLE DOOR, SIR!
I KNOW.
DROP IT! I'LL KILL HER, I MEAN IT!
OH GOD--!
MOMMY!
I'LL BLOW HER MOTHERLOVIN' HEAD OFF!
AND?
WH-WHAT YOU MEAN, AND?
AND WHAT NEXT? WHO ARE YOU GOING TO HIDE BEHIND ONCE YOU SHOOT YOUR HOSTAGE?

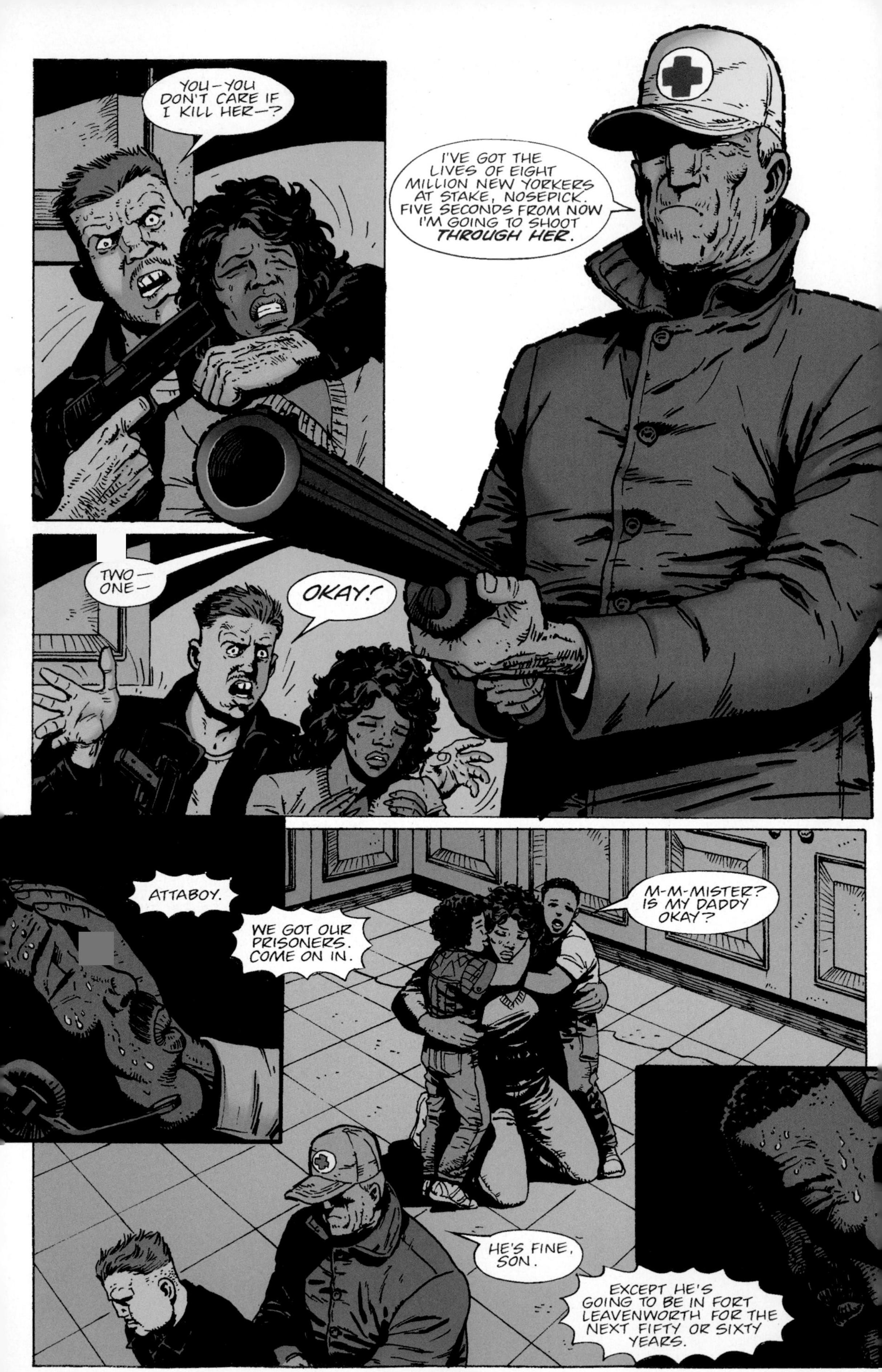
YOU—YOU DON'T CARE IF I KILL HER—?
I'VE GOT THE LIVES OF EIGHT MILLION NEW YORKERS AT STAKE, NOSEPICK. FIVE SECONDS FROM NOW I'M GOING TO SHOOT THROUGH HER.
TWO— ONE—
OKAY!
ATTABOY.
WE GOT OUR PRISONERS. COME ON IN.
M-M-MISTER? IS MY DADDY OKAY?
HE'S FINE, SON.
EXCEPT HE'S GOING TO BE IN FORT LEAVENWORTH FOR THE NEXT FIFTY OR SIXTY YEARS.

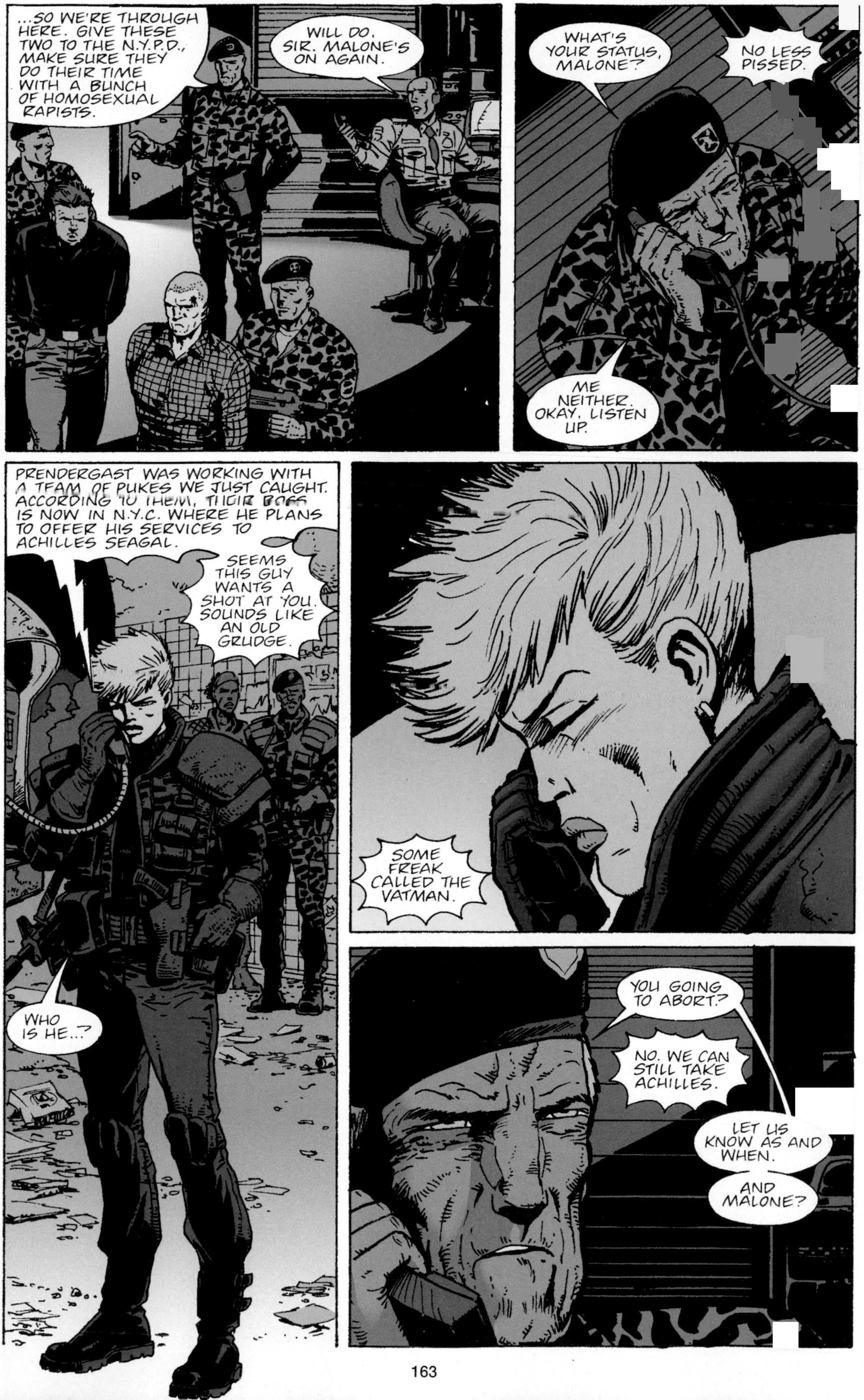
...SO WE'RE THROUGH HERE. GIVE THESE TWO TO THE N.Y.P.D., MAKE SURE THEY DO THEIR TIME WITH A BUNCH OF HOMOSEXUAL RAPISTS.
WILL DO, SIR. MALONE'S ON AGAIN.
WHAT'S YOUR STATUS, MALONE?
NO LESS PISSED.
ME NEITHER. OKAY, LISTEN UP.
PRENDERGAST WAS WORKING WITH A TEAM OF PUKES WE JUST CAUGHT. ACCORDING TO THEM, THEIR BOSS IS NOW IN N.Y.C. WHERE HE PLANS TO OFFER HIS SERVICES TO ACHILLES SEAGAL.
SEEMS THIS GUY WANTS A SHOT AT YOU. SOUNDS LIKE AN OLD GRUDGE.
WHO IS HE...?
SOME FREAK CALLED THE VATMAN.
YOU GOING TO ABORT?
NO. WE CAN STILL TAKE ACHILLES.
LET US KNOW AS AND WHEN.
AND MALONE?

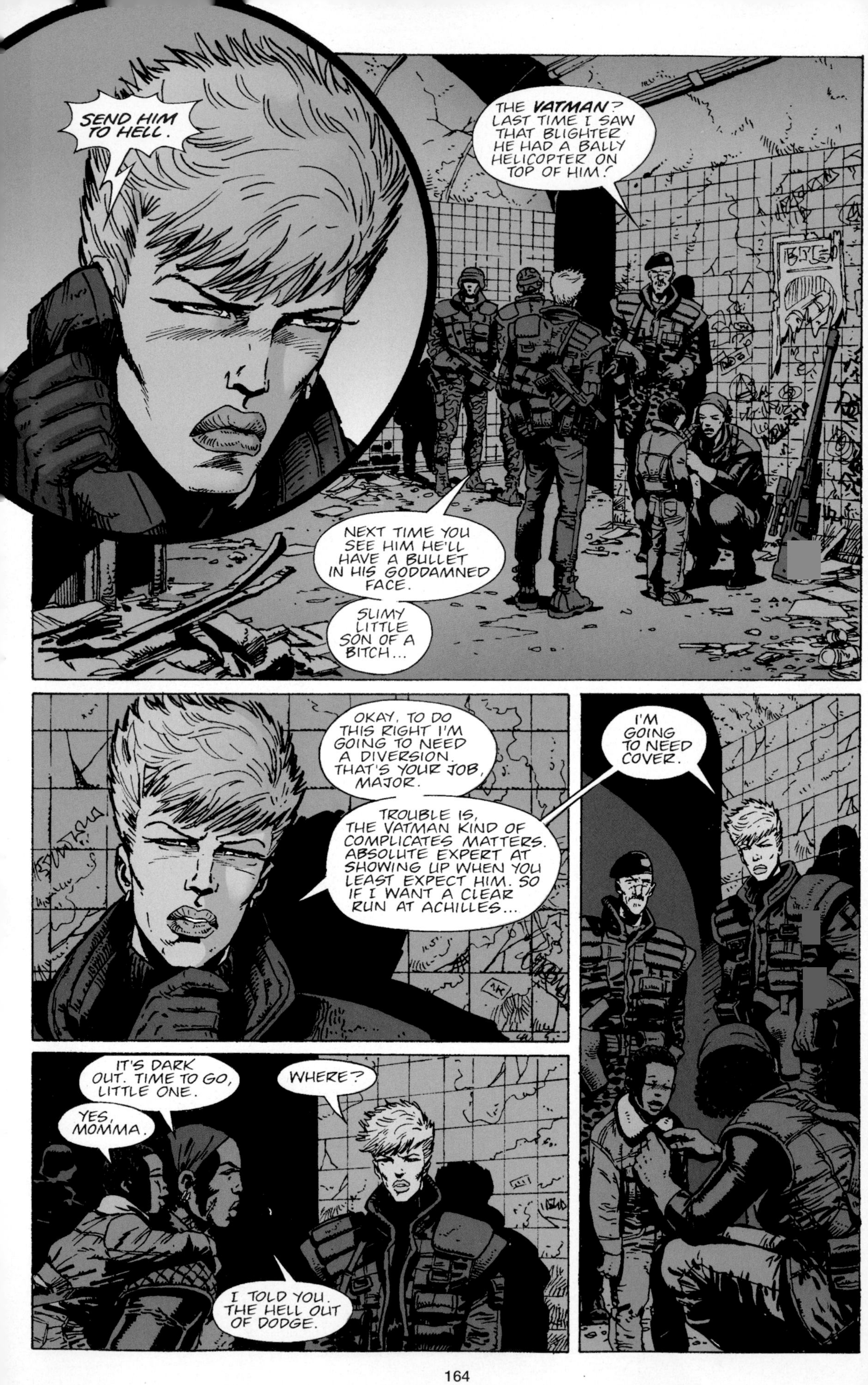

SEND HIM TO HELL.
THE VATMAN? LAST TIME I SAW THAT BLIGHTER HE HAD A BALLY HELICOPTER ON TOP OF HIM!
NEXT TIME YOU SEE HIM HE'LL HAVE A BULLET IN HIS GODDAMNED FACE.
SLIMY LITTLE SON OF A BITCH...
OKAY, TO DO THIS RIGHT I'M GOING TO NEED A DIVERSION. THAT'S YOUR JOB, MAJOR.
TROUBLE IS, THE VATMAN KIND OF COMPLICATES MATTERS. ABSOLUTE EXPERT AT SHOWING UP WHEN YOU LEAST EXPECT HIM. SO IF I WANT A CLEAR RUN AT ACHILLES...
I'M GOING TO NEED COVER.
IT'S DARK OUT. TIME TO GO, LITTLE ONE.
YES, MOMMA.
WHERE?
I TOLD YOU. THE HELL OUT OF DODGE.

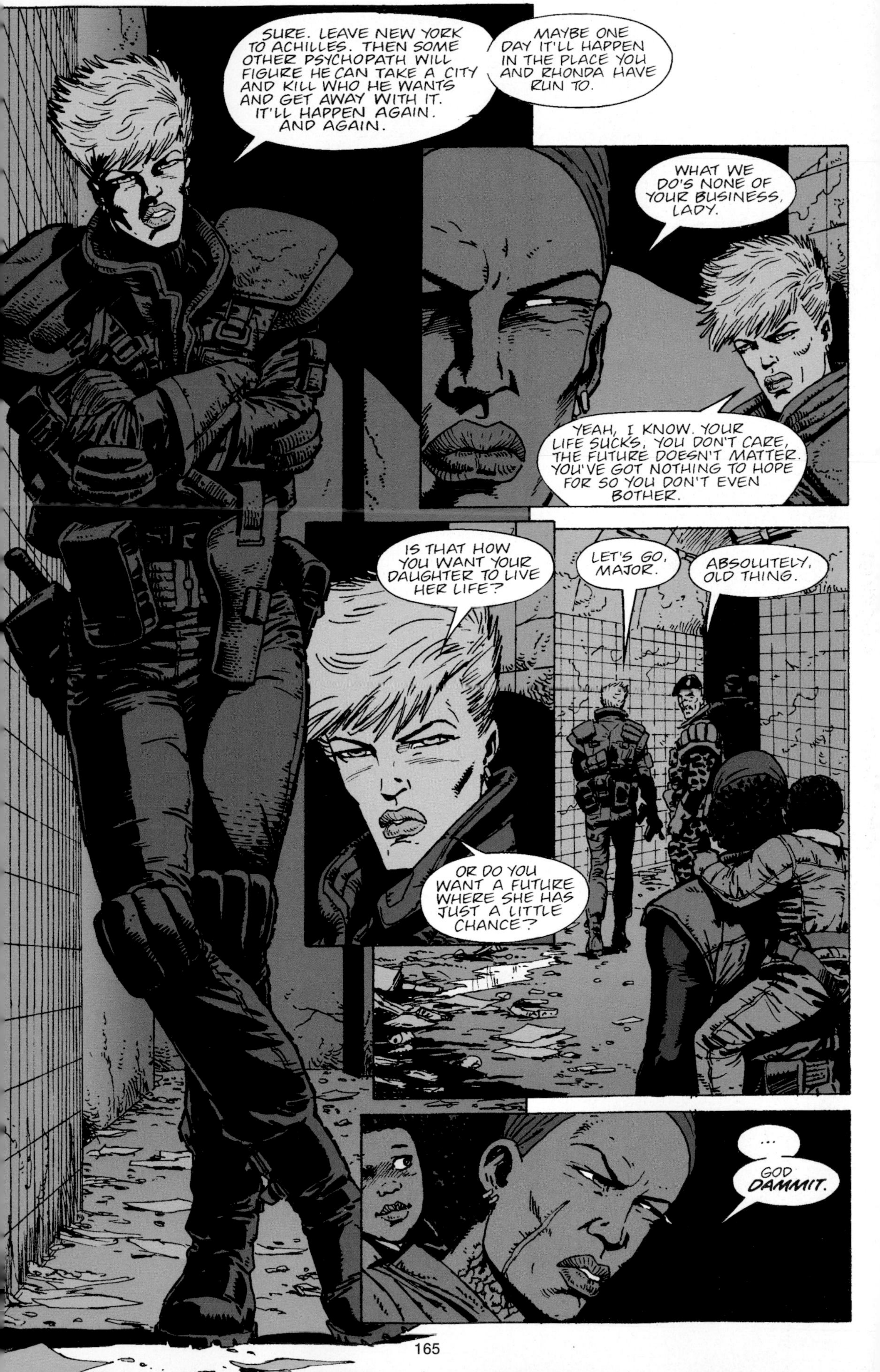
SURE. LEAVE NEW YORK TO ACHILLES. THEN SOME OTHER PSYCHOPATH WILL FIGURE HE CAN TAKE A CITY AND KILL WHO HE WANTS AND GET AWAY WITH IT. IT'LL HAPPEN AGAIN. AND AGAIN.
MAYBE ONE DAY IT'LL HAPPEN IN THE PLACE YOU AND RHONDA HAVE RUN TO.
WHAT WE DO'S NONE OF YOUR BUSINESS, LADY.
YEAH, I KNOW. YOUR LIFE SUCKS, YOU DON'T CARE, THE FUTURE DOESN'T MATTER. YOU'VE GOT NOTHING TO HOPE FOR SO YOU DON'T EVEN BOTHER.
IS THAT HOW YOU WANT YOUR DAUGHTER TO LIVE HER LIFE?
OR DO YOU WANT A FUTURE WHERE SHE HAS JUST A LITTLE CHANCE?
LET'S GO, MAJOR.
ABSOLUTELY, OLD THING.
...
GOD *DAMMIT.*

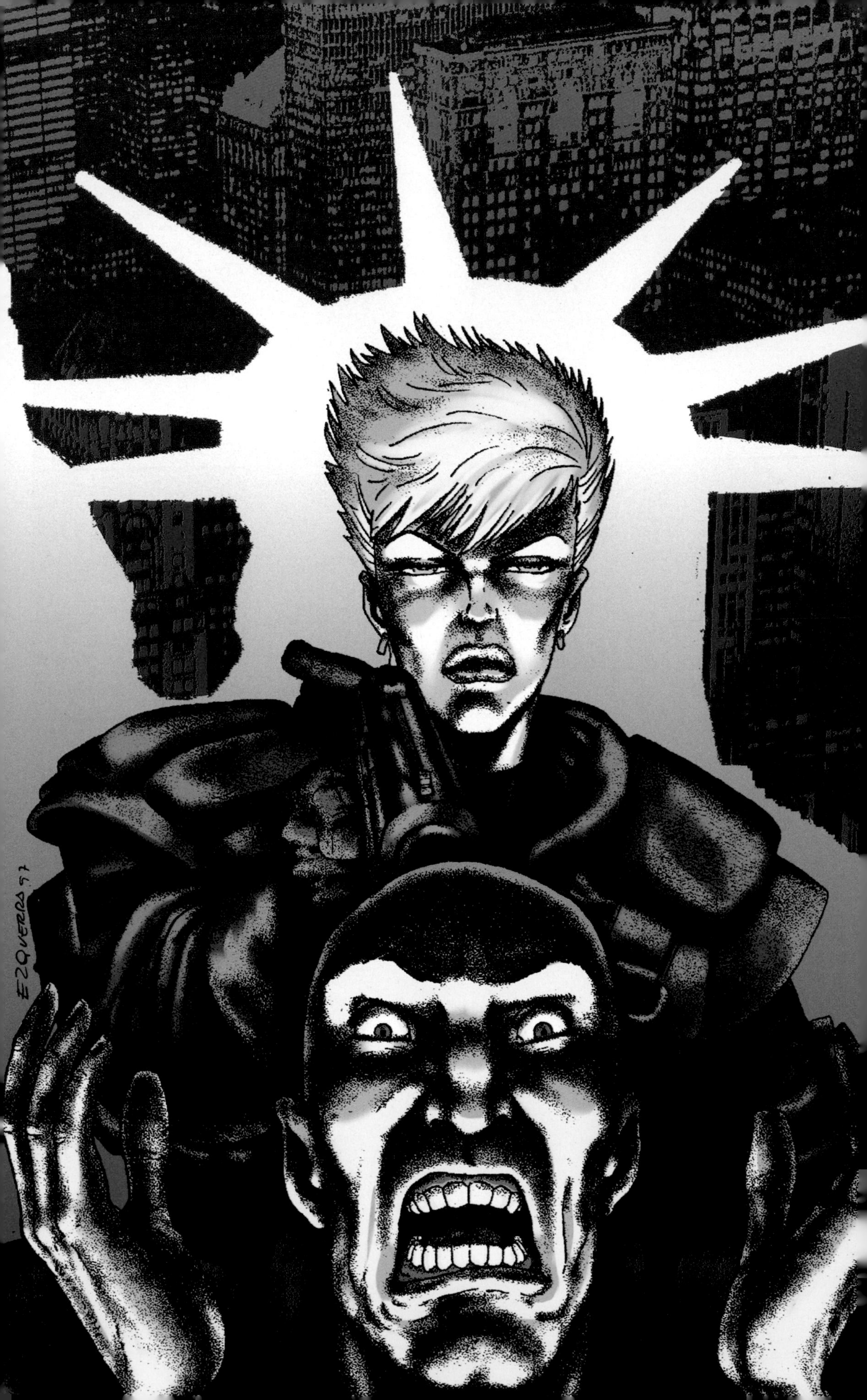

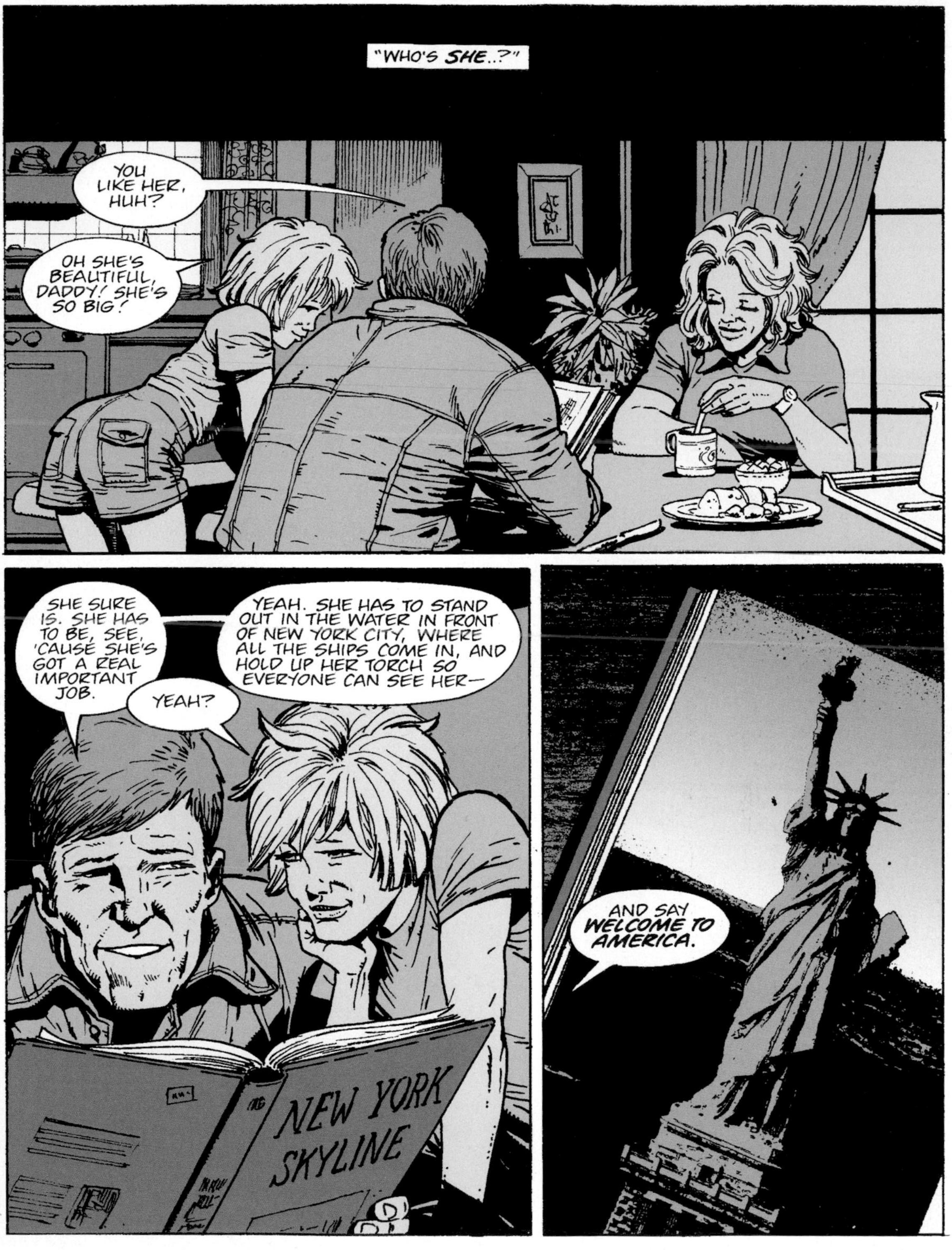
"WHO'S SHE..?"
YOU LIKE HER, HUH?
OH SHE'S BEAUTIFUL, DADDY! SHE'S SO BIG!
SHE SURE IS. SHE HAS TO BE, SEE, 'CAUSE SHE'S GOT A REAL IMPORTANT JOB.
YEAH?
YEAH. SHE HAS TO STAND OUT IN THE WATER IN FRONT OF NEW YORK CITY, WHERE ALL THE SHIPS COME IN, AND HOLD UP HER TORCH SO EVERYONE CAN SEE HER—
NEW YORK SKYLINE
AND SAY WELCOME TO AMERICA.

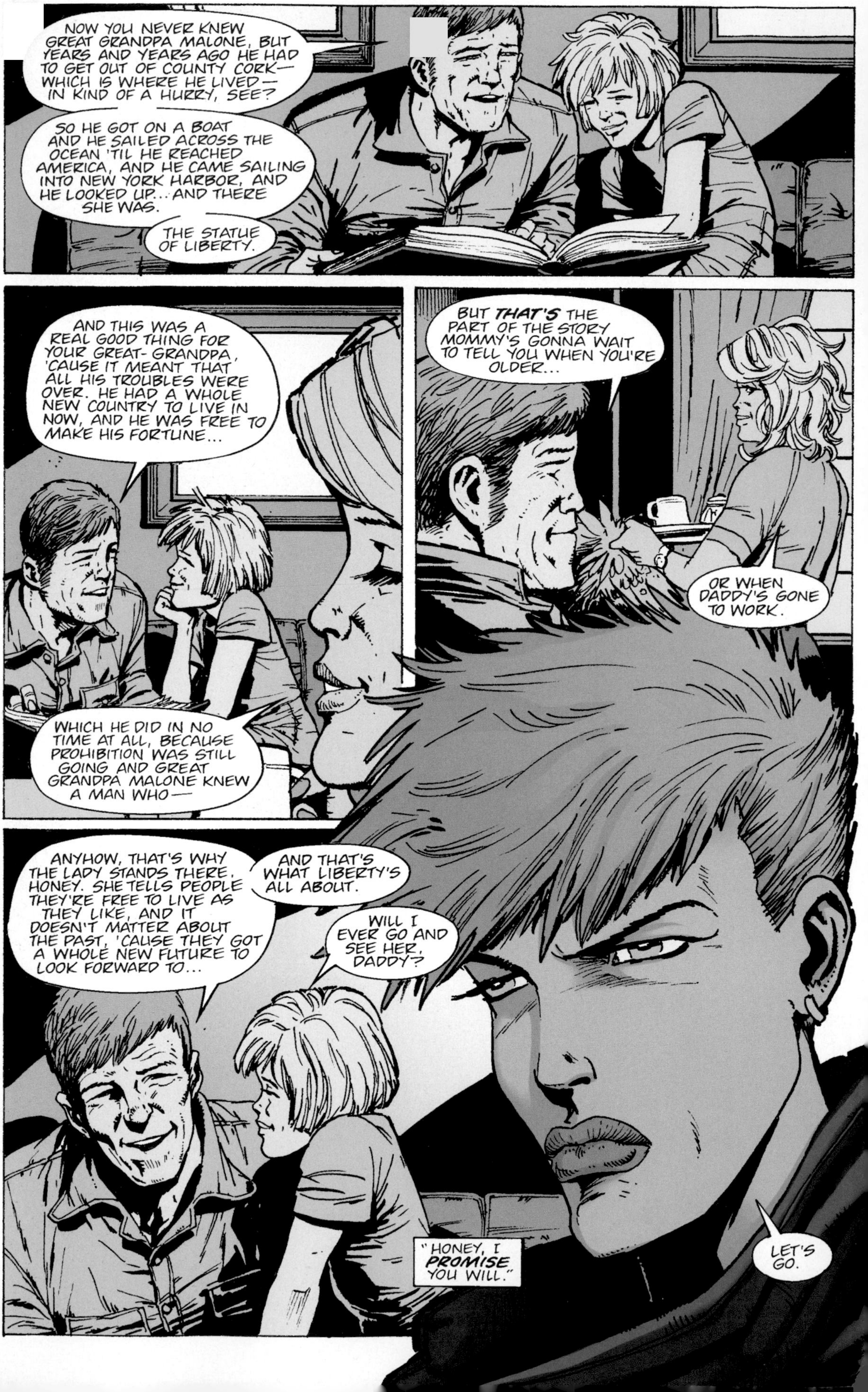
NOW YOU NEVER KNEW GREAT GRANDPA MALONE, BUT YEARS AND YEARS AGO HE HAD TO GET OUT OF COUNTY CORK— WHICH IS WHERE HE LIVED— IN KIND OF A HURRY, SEE?
SO HE GOT ON A BOAT AND HE SAILED ACROSS THE OCEAN 'TIL HE REACHED AMERICA, AND HE CAME SAILING INTO NEW YORK HARBOR, AND HE LOOKED UP... AND THERE SHE WAS.
THE STATUE OF LIBERTY.
AND THIS WAS A REAL GOOD THING FOR YOUR GREAT- GRANDPA, 'CAUSE IT MEANT THAT ALL HIS TROUBLES WERE OVER. HE HAD A WHOLE NEW COUNTRY TO LIVE IN NOW, AND HE WAS FREE TO MAKE HIS FORTUNE...
WHICH HE DID IN NO TIME AT ALL, BECAUSE PROHIBITION WAS STILL GOING AND GREAT GRANDPA MALONE KNEW A MAN WHO—
BUT THAT'S THE PART OF THE STORY MOMMY'S GONNA WAIT TO TELL YOU WHEN YOU'RE OLDER...
OR WHEN DADDY'S GONE TO WORK.
ANYHOW, THAT'S WHY THE LADY STANDS THERE, HONEY. SHE TELLS PEOPLE THEY'RE FREE TO LIVE AS THEY LIKE, AND IT DOESN'T MATTER ABOUT THE PAST, 'CAUSE THEY GOT A WHOLE NEW FUTURE TO LOOK FORWARD TO...
AND THAT'S WHAT LIBERTY'S ALL ABOUT.
WILL I EVER GO AND SEE HER, DADDY?
"HONEY, I PROMISE YOU WILL."
LET'S GO.

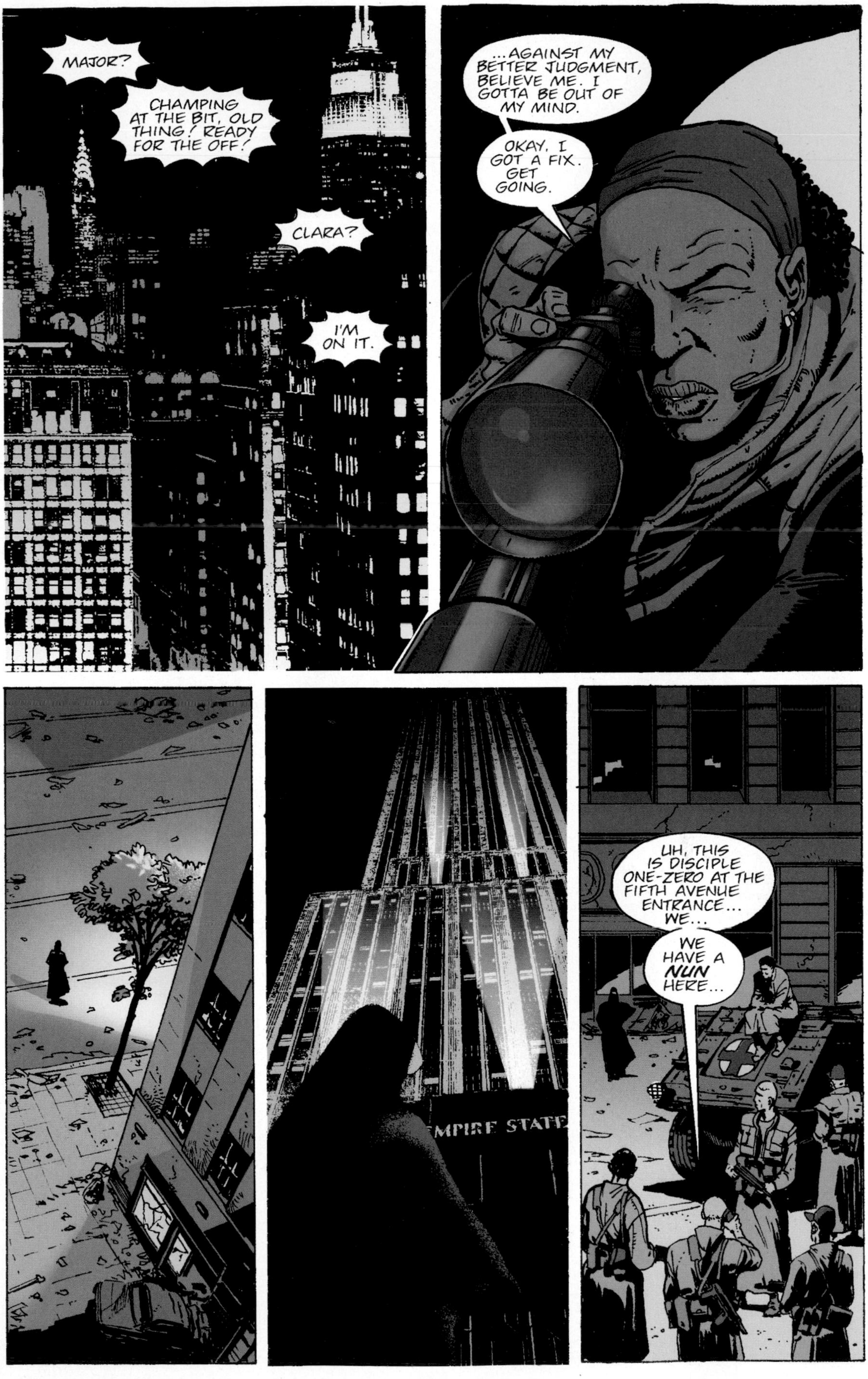
MAJOR?
CHAMPING AT THE BIT, OLD THING! READY FOR THE OFF!
CLARA?
I'M ON IT.
...AGAINST MY BETTER JUDGMENT, BELIEVE ME. I GOTTA BE OUT OF MY MIND.
OKAY, I GOT A FIX. GET GOING.
EMPIRE STATE
UH, THIS IS DISCIPLE ONE-ZERO AT THE FIFTH AVENUE ENTRANCE... WE...
WE HAVE A NUN HERE...

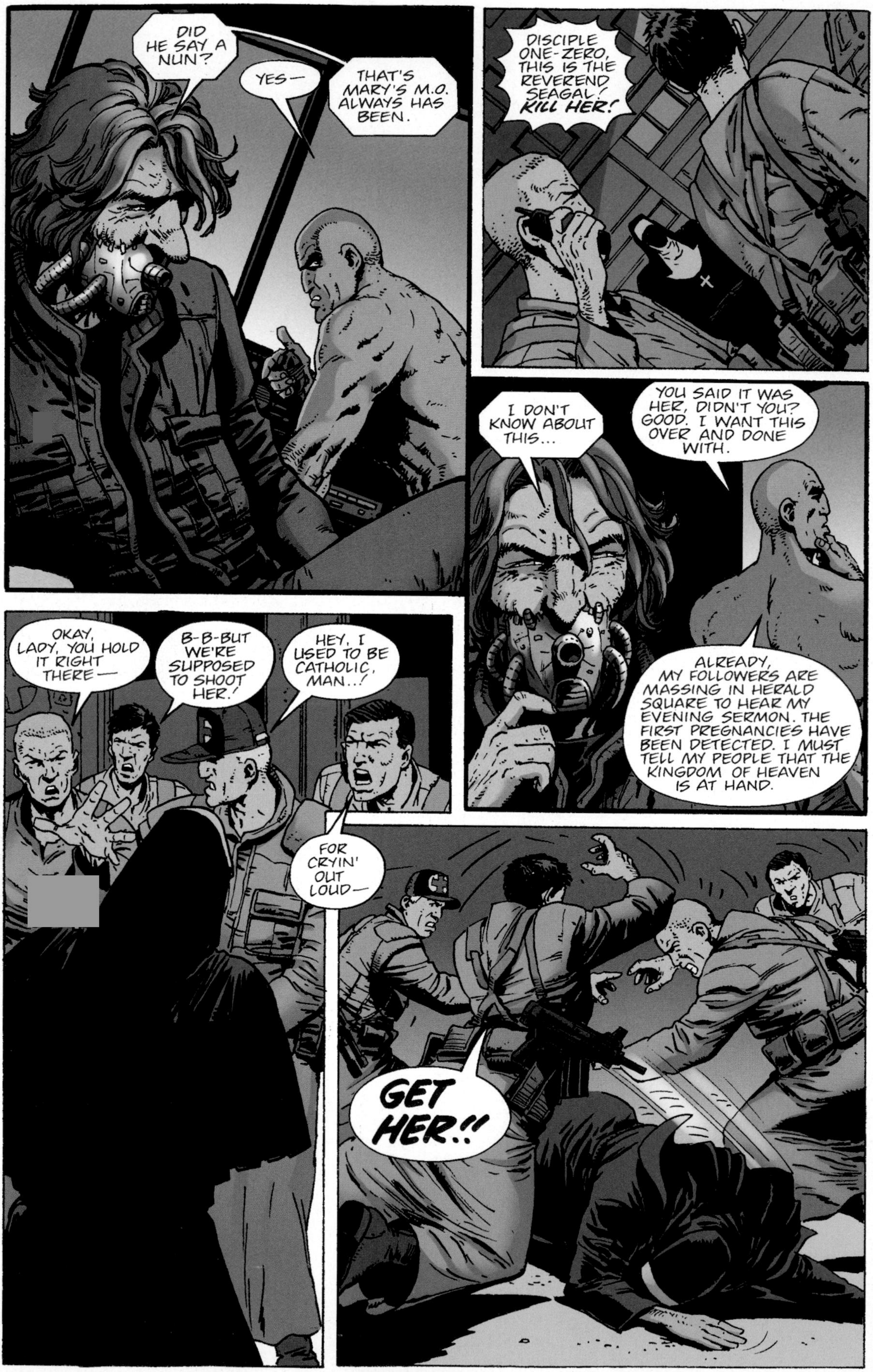
DID HE SAY A NUN?
YES—
THAT'S MARY'S M.O. ALWAYS HAS BEEN.
DISCIPLE ONE-ZERO, THIS IS THE REVEREND SEAGAL! KILL HER!
I DON'T KNOW ABOUT THIS...
YOU SAID IT WAS HER, DIDN'T YOU? GOOD. I WANT THIS OVER AND DONE WITH.
ALREADY, MY FOLLOWERS ARE MASSING IN HERALD SQUARE TO HEAR MY EVENING SERMON. THE FIRST PREGNANCIES HAVE BEEN DETECTED. I MUST TELL MY PEOPLE THAT THE KINGDOM OF HEAVEN IS AT HAND.
OKAY, LADY, YOU HOLD IT RIGHT THERE—
B-B-BUT WE'RE SUPPOSED TO SHOOT HER!
HEY, I USED TO BE CATHOLIC, MAN...!
FOR CRYIN' OUT LOUD—
GET HER!!

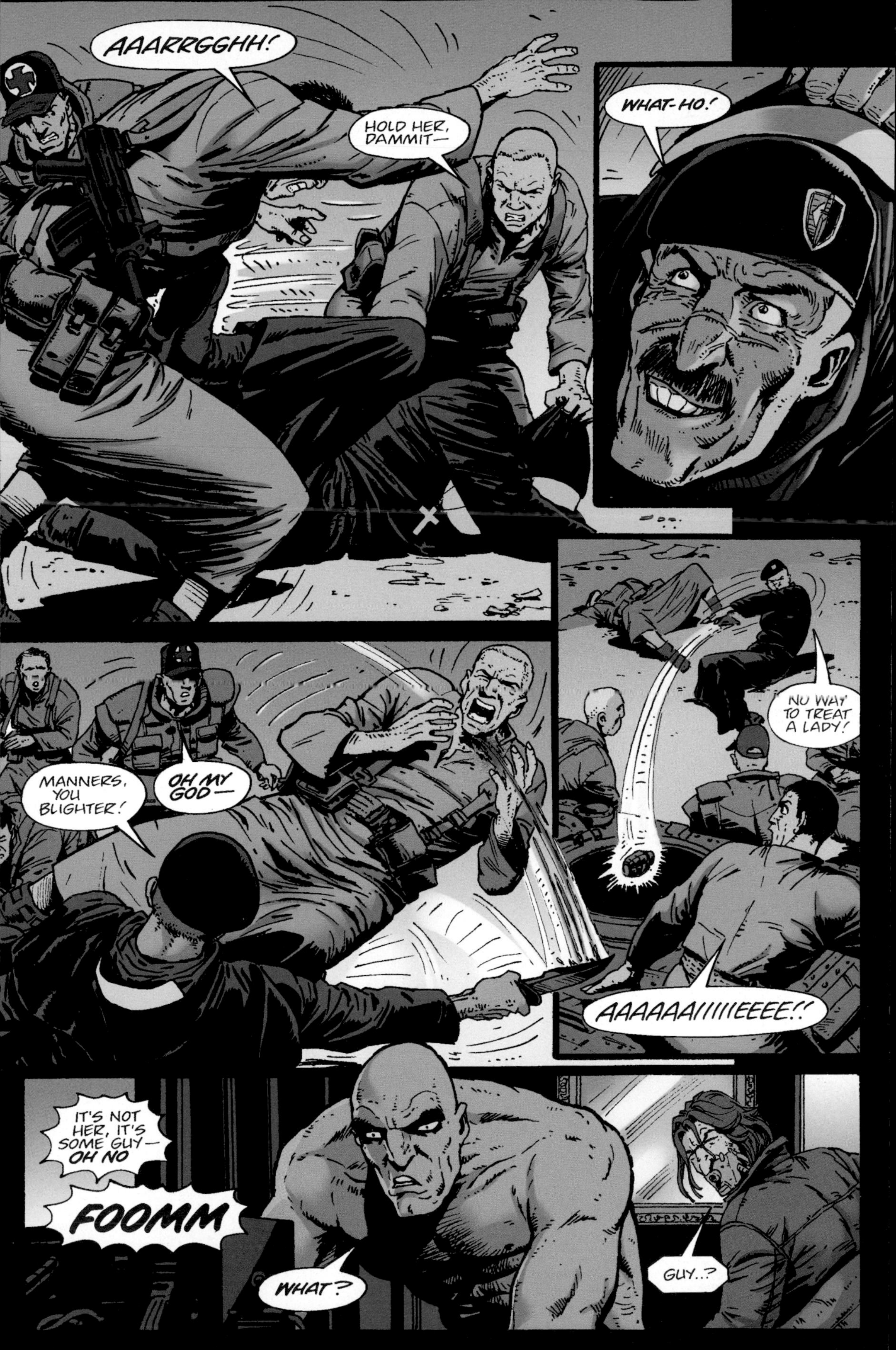
AAARRGGHH!
HOLD HER, DAMMIT—
WHAT-HO!
MANNERS, YOU BLIGHTER!
OH MY GOD—
NO WAY TO TREAT A LADY!
AAAAAAIIIIIEEEE!!
IT'S NOT HER, IT'S SOME GUY— OH NO
FOOMM
WHAT?
GUY..?

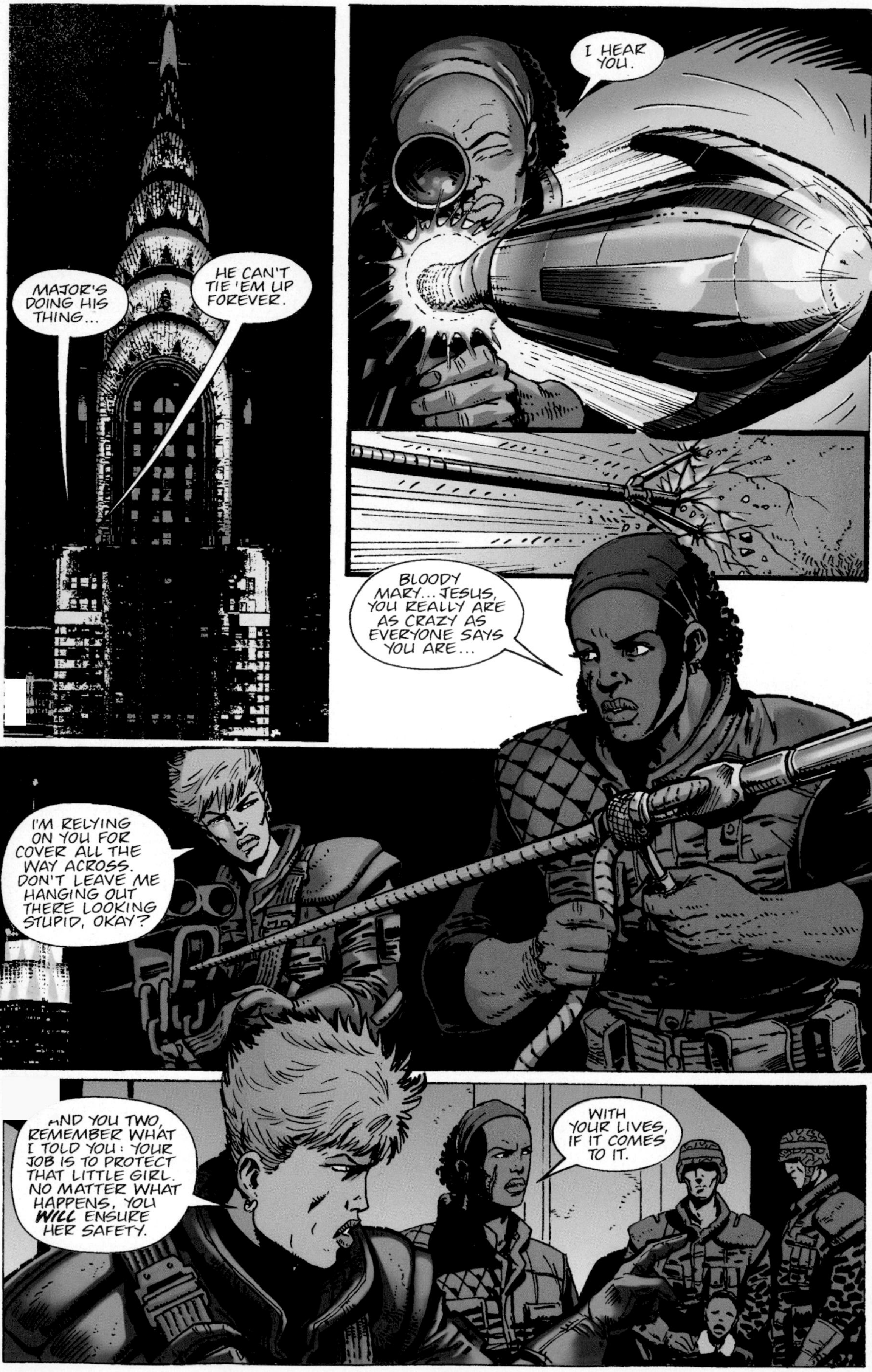
MAJOR'S DOING HIS THING...
HE CAN'T TIE 'EM UP FOREVER.
I HEAR YOU.
BLOODY MARY... JESUS, YOU REALLY ARE AS CRAZY AS EVERYONE SAYS YOU ARE...
I'M RELYING ON YOU FOR COVER ALL THE WAY ACROSS. DON'T LEAVE ME HANGING OUT THERE LOOKING STUPID, OKAY?
AND YOU TWO, REMEMBER WHAT I TOLD YOU: YOUR JOB IS TO PROTECT THAT LITTLE GIRL. NO MATTER WHAT HAPPENS, YOU WILL ENSURE HER SAFETY.
WITH YOUR LIVES, IF IT COMES TO IT.

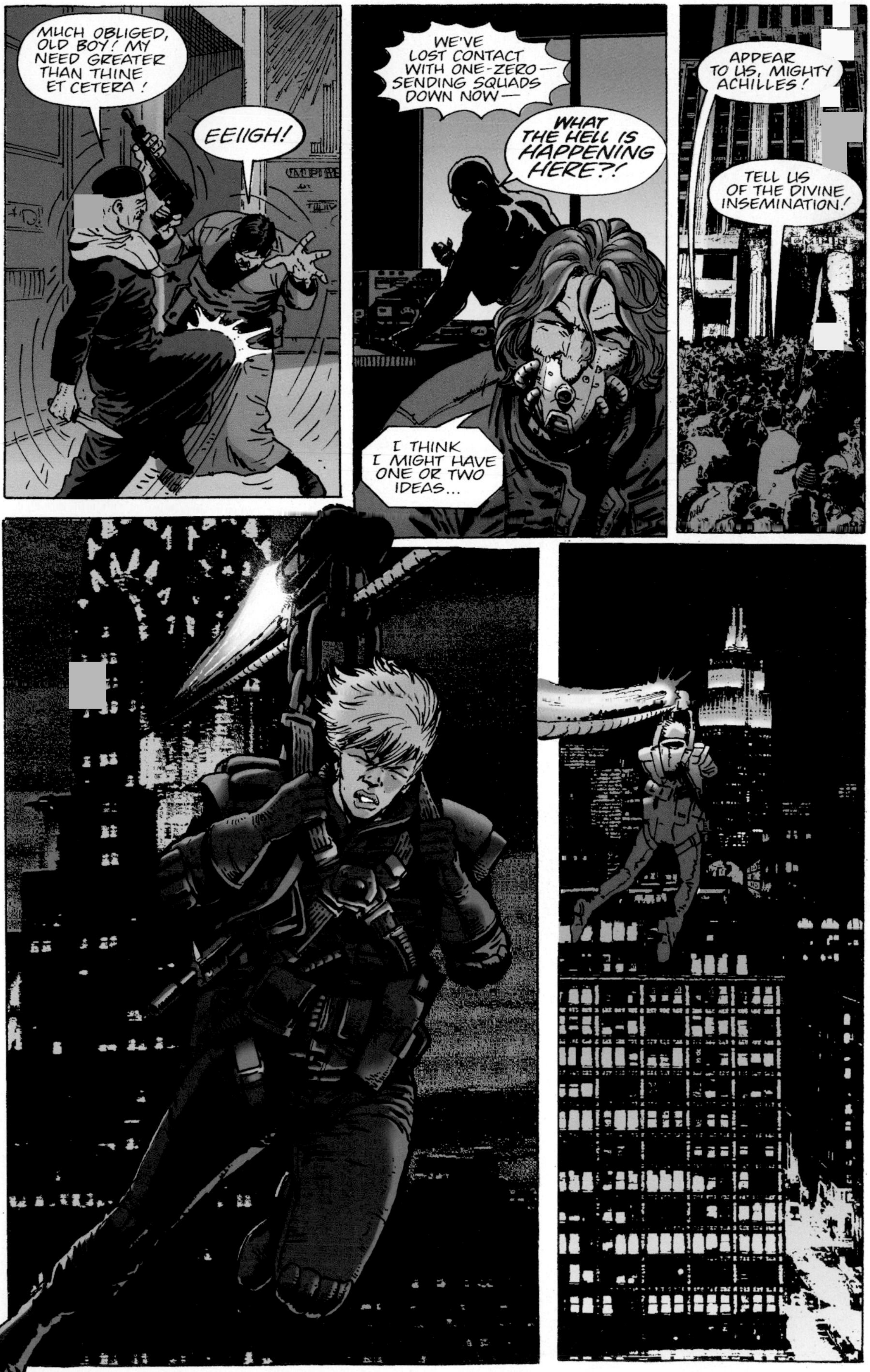
MUCH OBLIGED, OLD BOY! MY NEED GREATER THAN THINE ET CETERA!
EEIIGH!
WE'VE LOST CONTACT WITH ONE-ZERO— SENDING SQUADS DOWN NOW—
WHAT THE HELL IS HAPPENING HERE?!
I THINK I MIGHT HAVE ONE OR TWO IDEAS...
APPEAR TO US, MIGHTY ACHILLES!
TELL US OF THE DIVINE INSEMINATION!

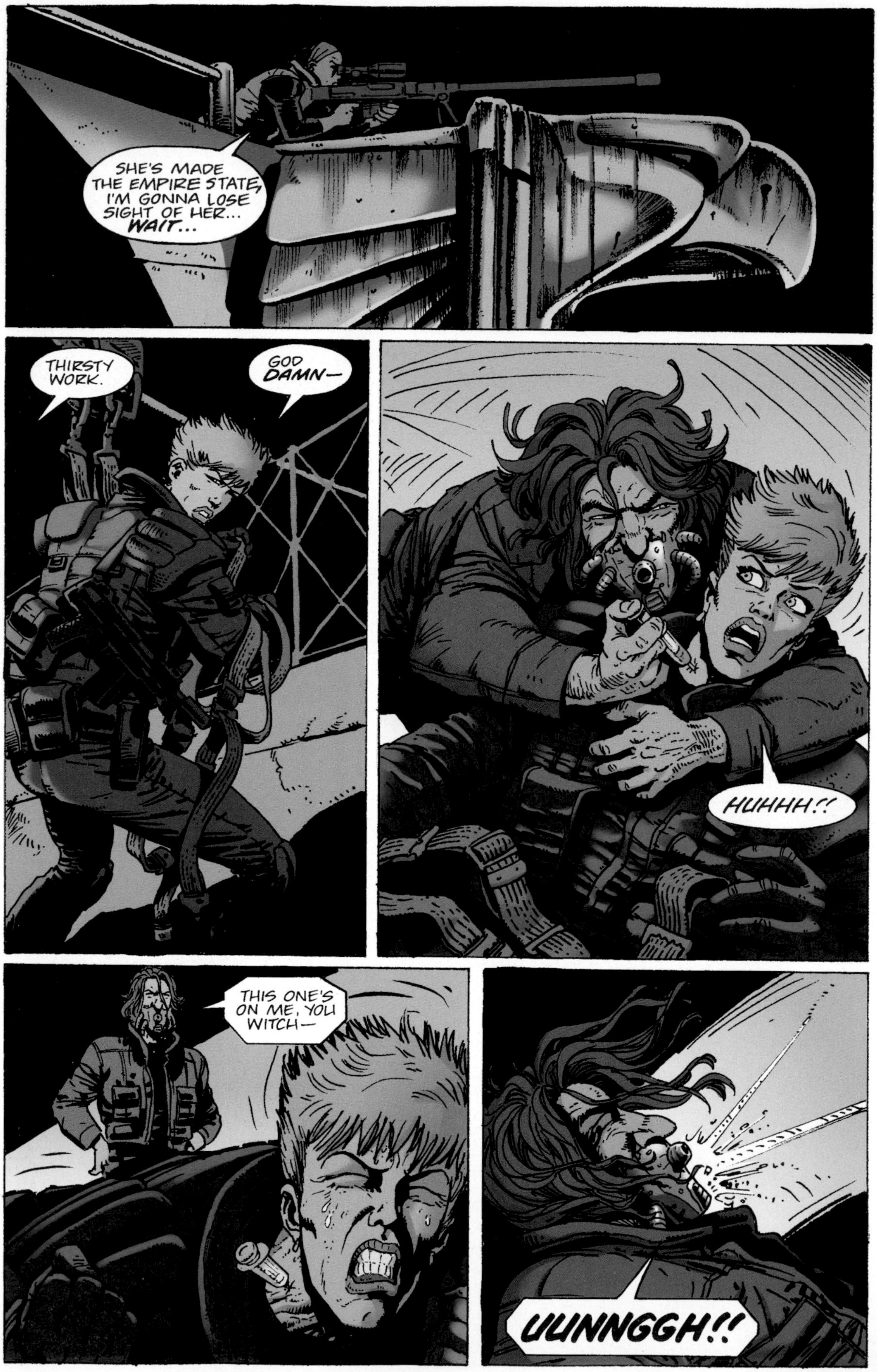
SHE'S MADE THE EMPIRE STATE, I'M GONNA LOSE SIGHT OF HER... WAIT...
THIRSTY WORK.
GOD DAMN—
HUHHH!!
THIS ONE'S ON ME, YOU WITCH—
UUNNGGH!!

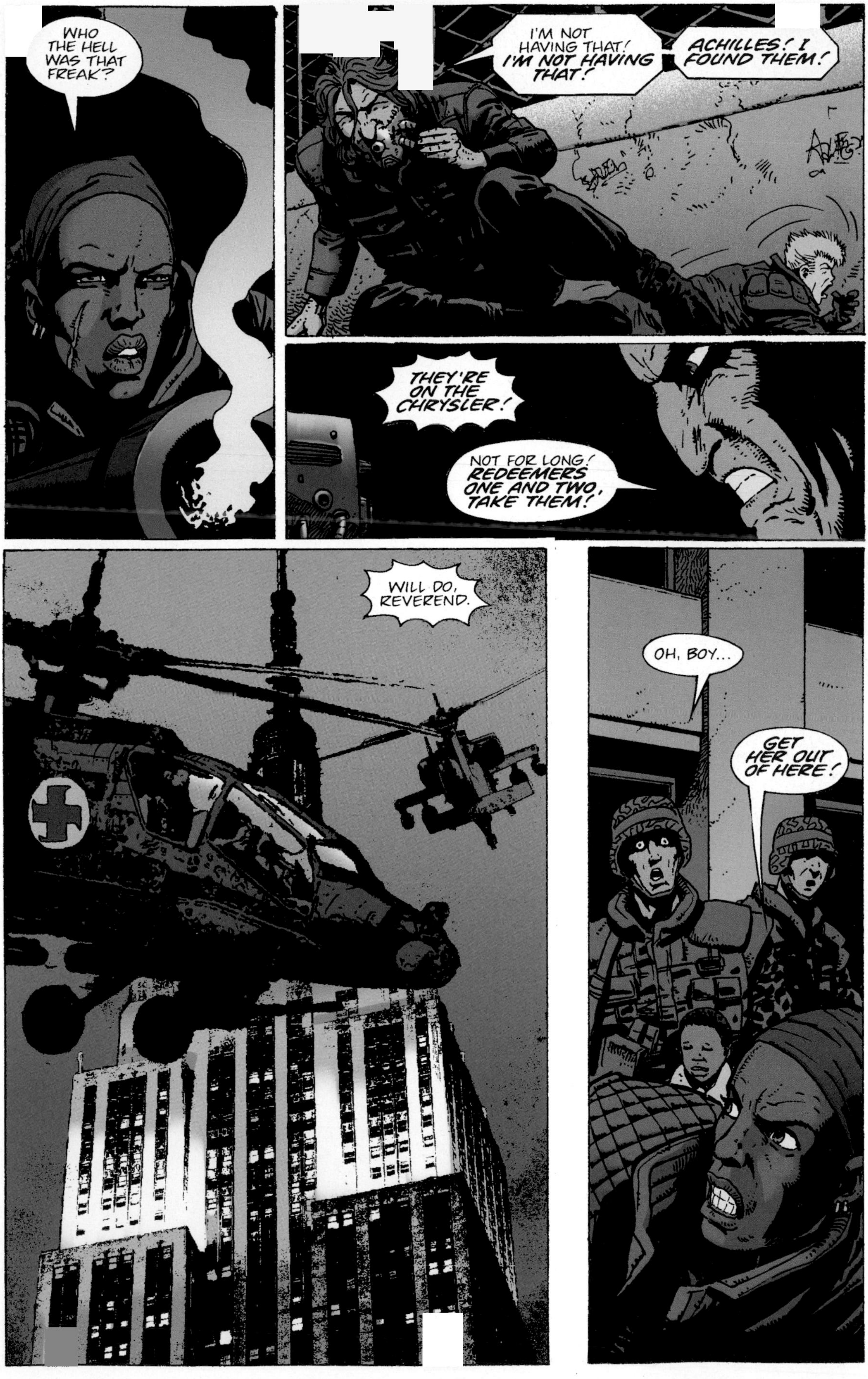
WHO THE HELL WAS THAT FREAK?
I'M NOT HAVING THAT! I'M NOT HAVING THAT!
ACHILLES! I FOUND THEM!
THEY'RE ON THE CHRYSLER!
NOT FOR LONG! REDEEMERS ONE AND TWO, TAKE THEM!
WILL DO, REVEREND.
OH, BOY...
GET HER OUT OF HERE!

LOOKS LIKE A CONTACT ON THE *CHRYSLER GENERAL.* GUNSHIPS GOING IN.

MALONE.

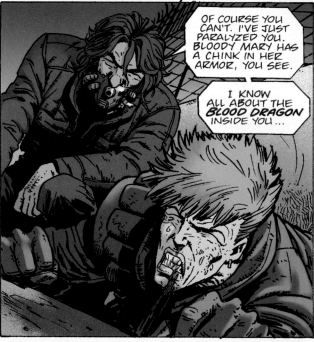

OF COURSE YOU CAN'T. I'VE JUST PARALYZED YOU. BLOODY MARY HAS A CHINK IN HER ARMOR, YOU SEE.

I KNOW ALL ABOUT THE *BLOOD DRAGON* INSIDE YOU...

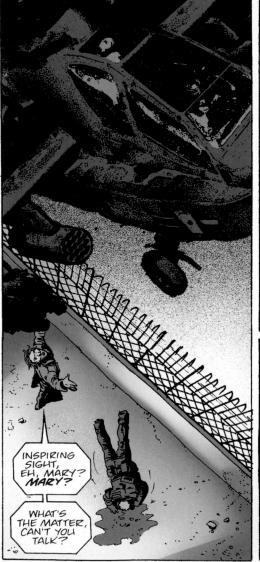

INSPIRING SIGHT, EH, MARY? *MARY?*

WHAT'S THE MATTER, CAN'T YOU TALK?

AND I'VE JUST KILLED IT STONE DEAD.

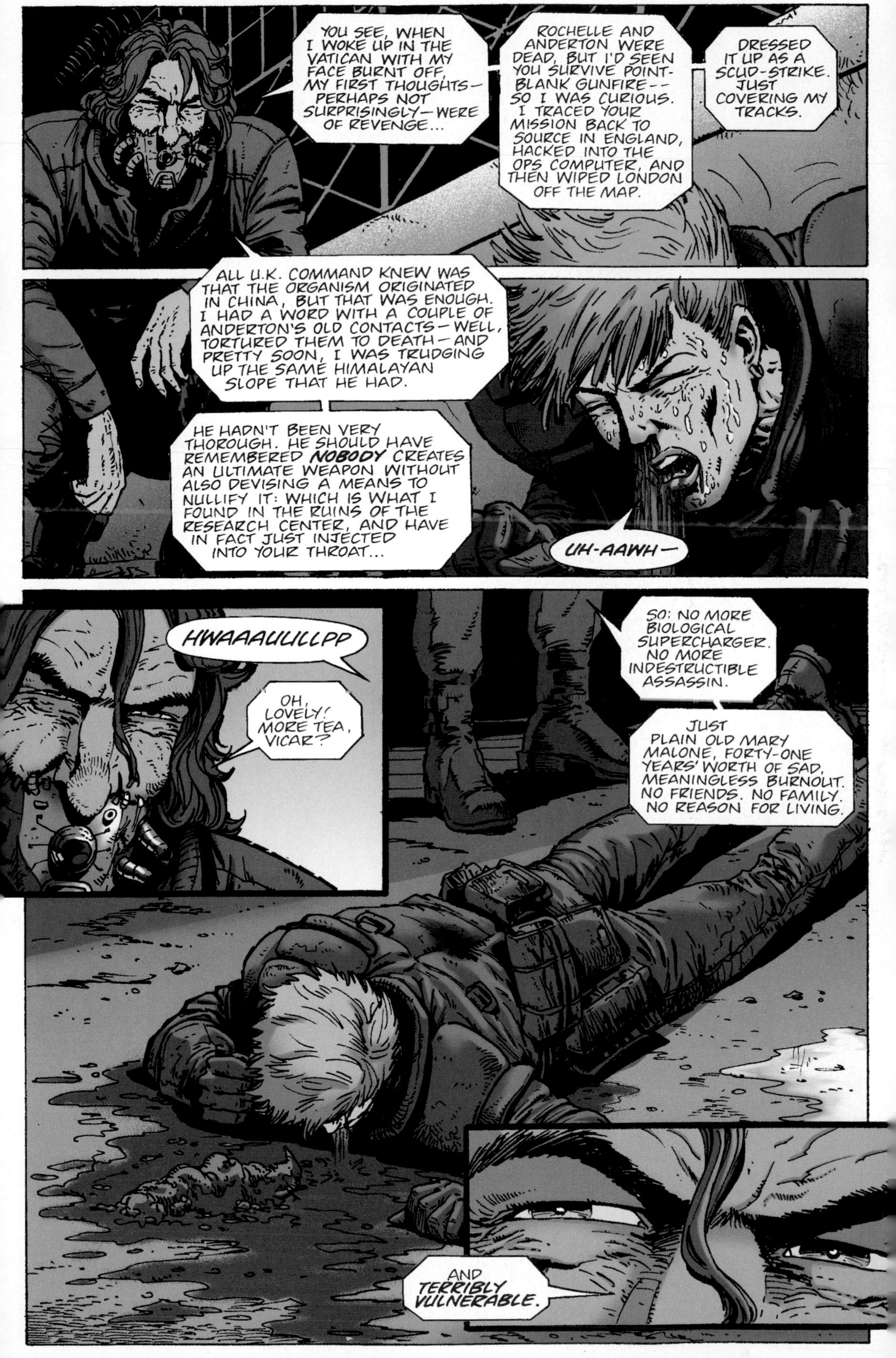
YOU SEE, WHEN I WOKE UP IN THE VATICAN WITH MY FACE BURNT OFF, MY FIRST THOUGHTS—PERHAPS NOT SURPRISINGLY—WERE OF REVENGE...
ROCHELLE AND ANDERTON WERE DEAD, BUT I'D SEEN YOU SURVIVE POINT-BLANK GUNFIRE--SO I WAS CURIOUS. I TRACED YOUR MISSION BACK TO SOURCE IN ENGLAND, HACKED INTO THE OPS COMPUTER, AND THEN WIPED LONDON OFF THE MAP.
DRESSED IT UP AS A SCUD-STRIKE. JUST COVERING MY TRACKS.
ALL U.K. COMMAND KNEW WAS THAT THE ORGANISM ORIGINATED IN CHINA, BUT THAT WAS ENOUGH. I HAD A WORD WITH A COUPLE OF ANDERTON'S OLD CONTACTS—WELL, TORTURED THEM TO DEATH—AND PRETTY SOON, I WAS TRUDGING UP THE SAME HIMALAYAN SLOPE THAT HE HAD.
HE HADN'T BEEN VERY THOROUGH. HE SHOULD HAVE REMEMBERED ***NOBODY*** CREATES AN ULTIMATE WEAPON WITHOUT ALSO DEVISING A MEANS TO NULLIFY IT: WHICH IS WHAT I FOUND IN THE RUINS OF THE RESEARCH CENTER, AND HAVE IN FACT JUST INJECTED INTO YOUR THROAT...
UH-AAWH—
HWAAAAULLLPP
OH, LOVELY! MORE TEA, VICAR?
SO: NO MORE BIOLOGICAL SUPERCHARGER. NO MORE INDESTRUCTIBLE ASSASSIN.
JUST PLAIN OLD MARY MALONE, FORTY-ONE YEARS' WORTH OF SAD, MEANINGLESS BURNOUT. NO FRIENDS. NO FAMILY. NO REASON FOR LIVING.
AND ***TERRIBLY VULNERABLE.***

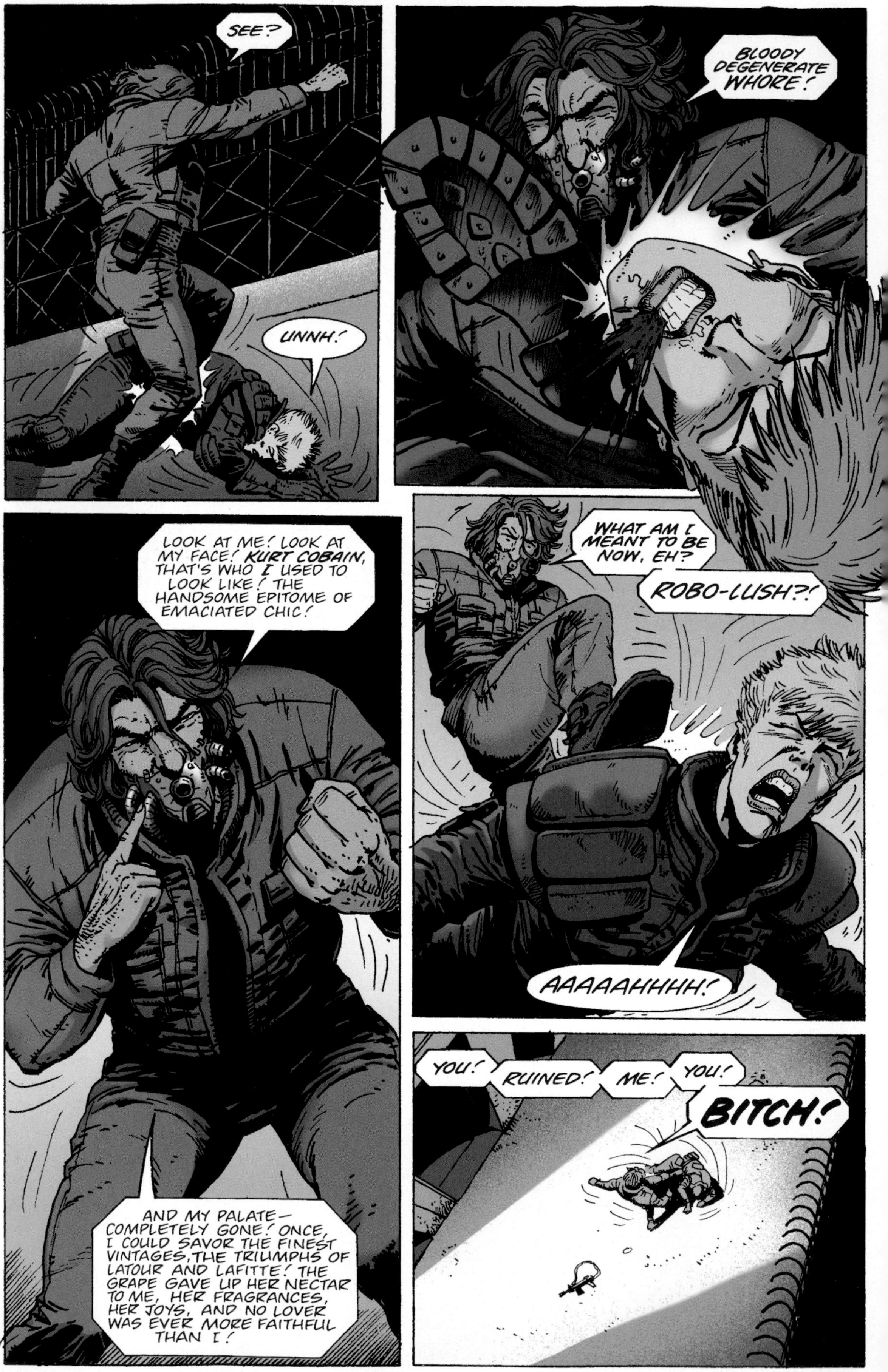
SEE?
UNNH!
BLOODY DEGENERATE WHORE!
LOOK AT ME! LOOK AT MY FACE! KURT COBAIN, THAT'S WHO I USED TO LOOK LIKE! THE HANDSOME EPITOME OF EMACIATED CHIC!
AND MY PALATE— COMPLETELY GONE! ONCE, I COULD SAVOR THE FINEST VINTAGES, THE TRIUMPHS OF LATOUR AND LAFITTE! THE GRAPE GAVE UP HER NECTAR TO ME, HER FRAGRANCES, HER JOYS, AND NO LOVER WAS EVER MORE FAITHFUL THAN I!
WHAT AM I MEANT TO BE NOW, EH?
ROBO-LUSH?!
AAAAAHHHH!
YOU!
RUINED!
ME!
YOU!
BITCH!

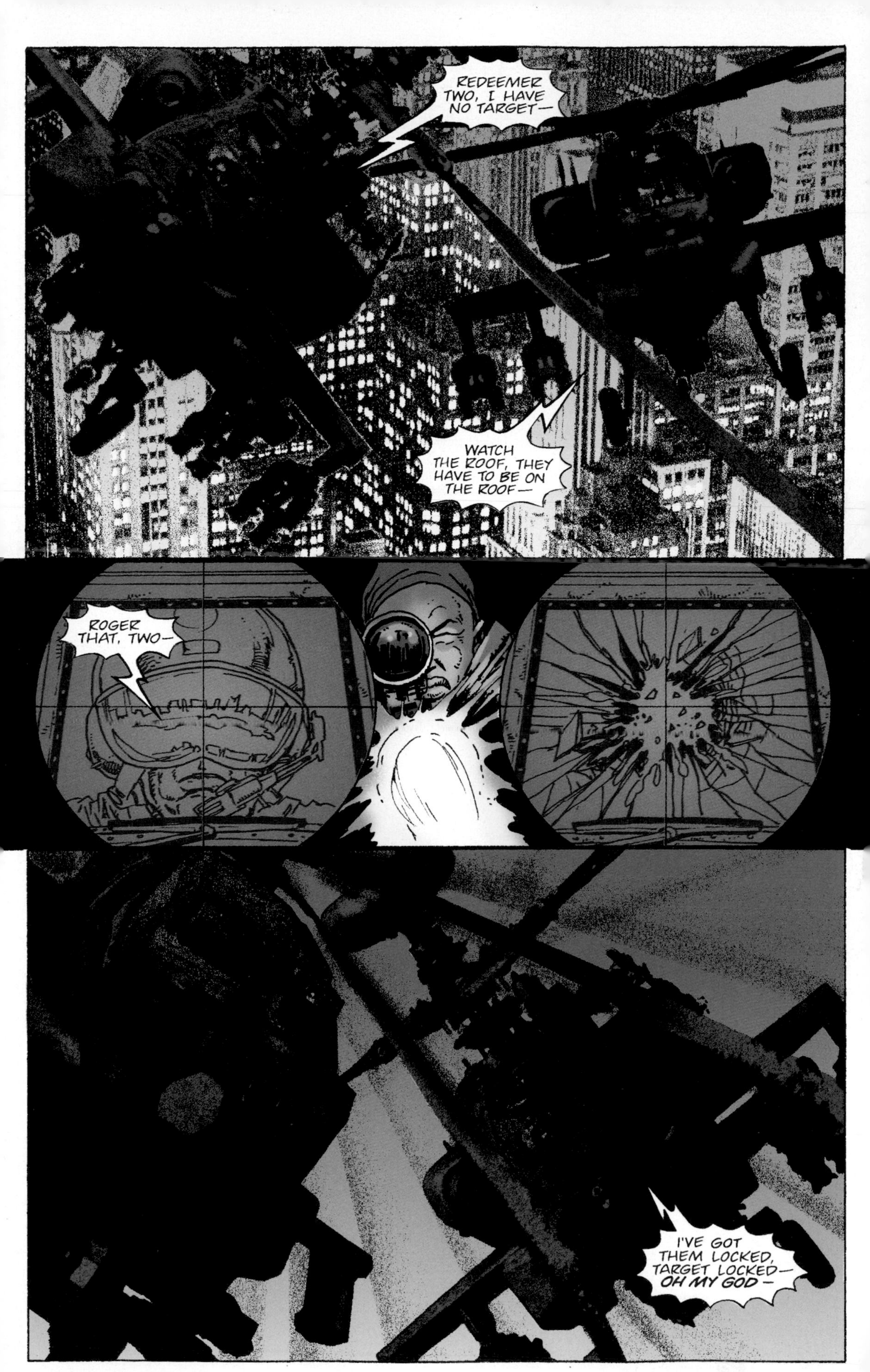
REDEEMER TWO, I HAVE NO TARGET—
WATCH THE ROOF, THEY HAVE TO BE ON THE ROOF—
ROGER THAT, TWO—
I'VE GOT THEM LOCKED, TARGET LOCKED— OH MY GOD—

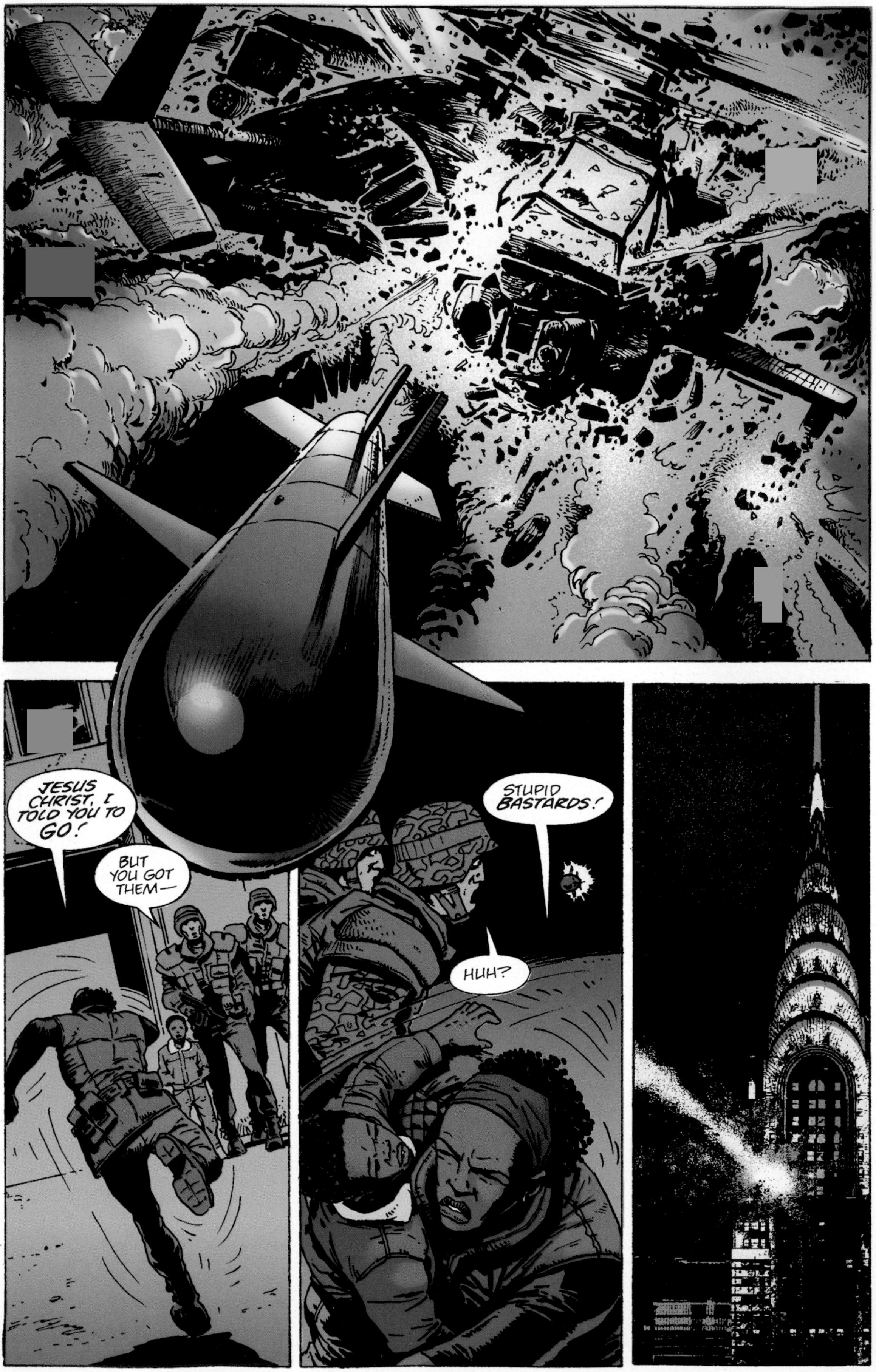
JESUS CHRIST, I TOLD YOU TO GO!
BUT YOU GOT THEM—
STUPID BASTARDS!
HUH?

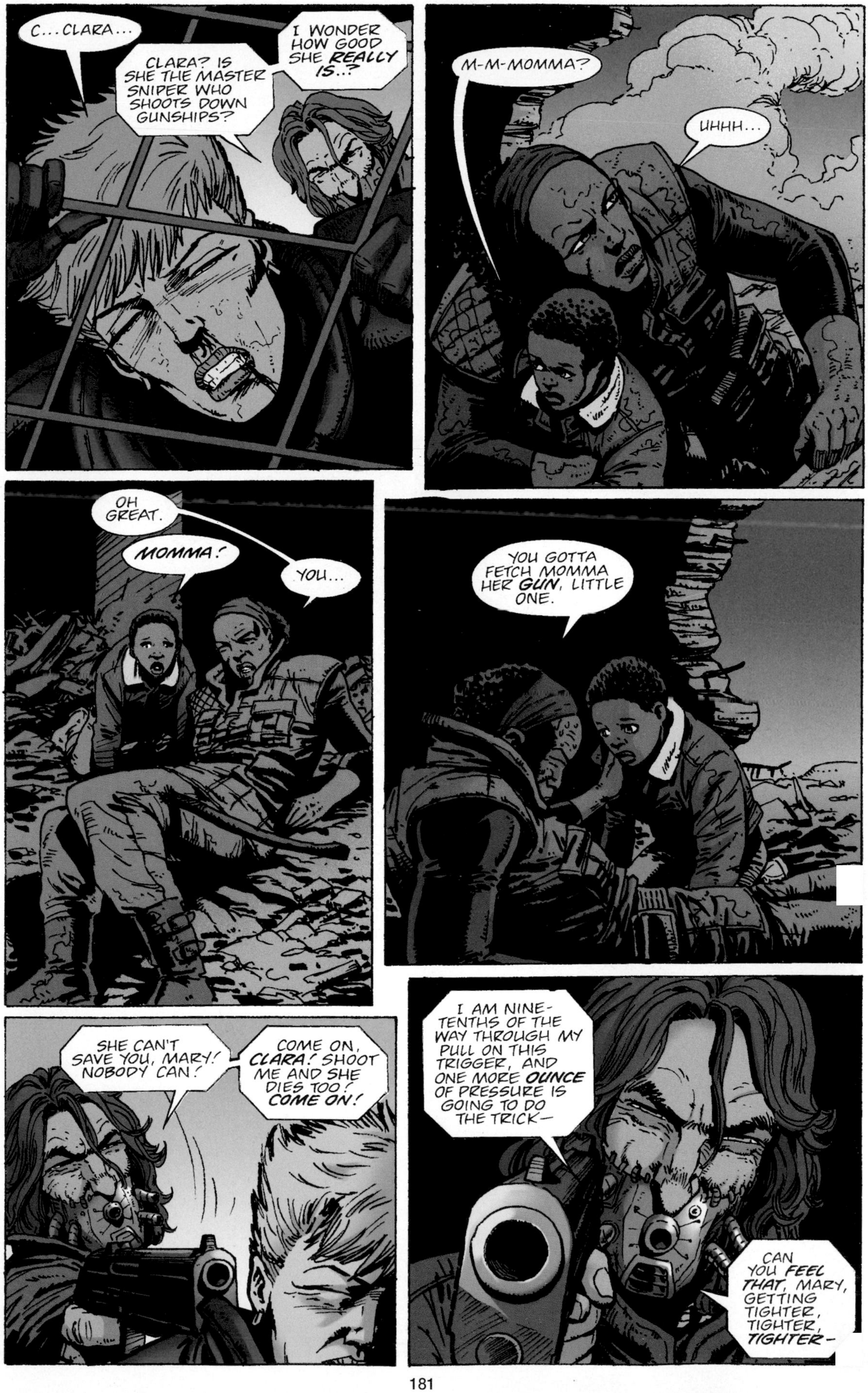
C... CLARA...
CLARA? IS SHE THE MASTER SNIPER WHO SHOOTS DOWN GUNSHIPS?
I WONDER HOW GOOD SHE REALLY IS..?
M-M-MOMMA?
UHHH...
OH GREAT.
MOMMA!
YOU...
YOU GOTTA FETCH MOMMA HER GUN, LITTLE ONE.
SHE CAN'T SAVE YOU, MARY! NOBODY CAN!
COME ON, CLARA! SHOOT ME AND SHE DIES TOO! COME ON!
I AM NINE-TENTHS OF THE WAY THROUGH MY PULL ON THIS TRIGGER, AND ONE MORE OUNCE OF PRESSURE IS GOING TO DO THE TRICK—
CAN YOU FEEL THAT, MARY, GETTING TIGHTER, TIGHTER, TIGHTER—

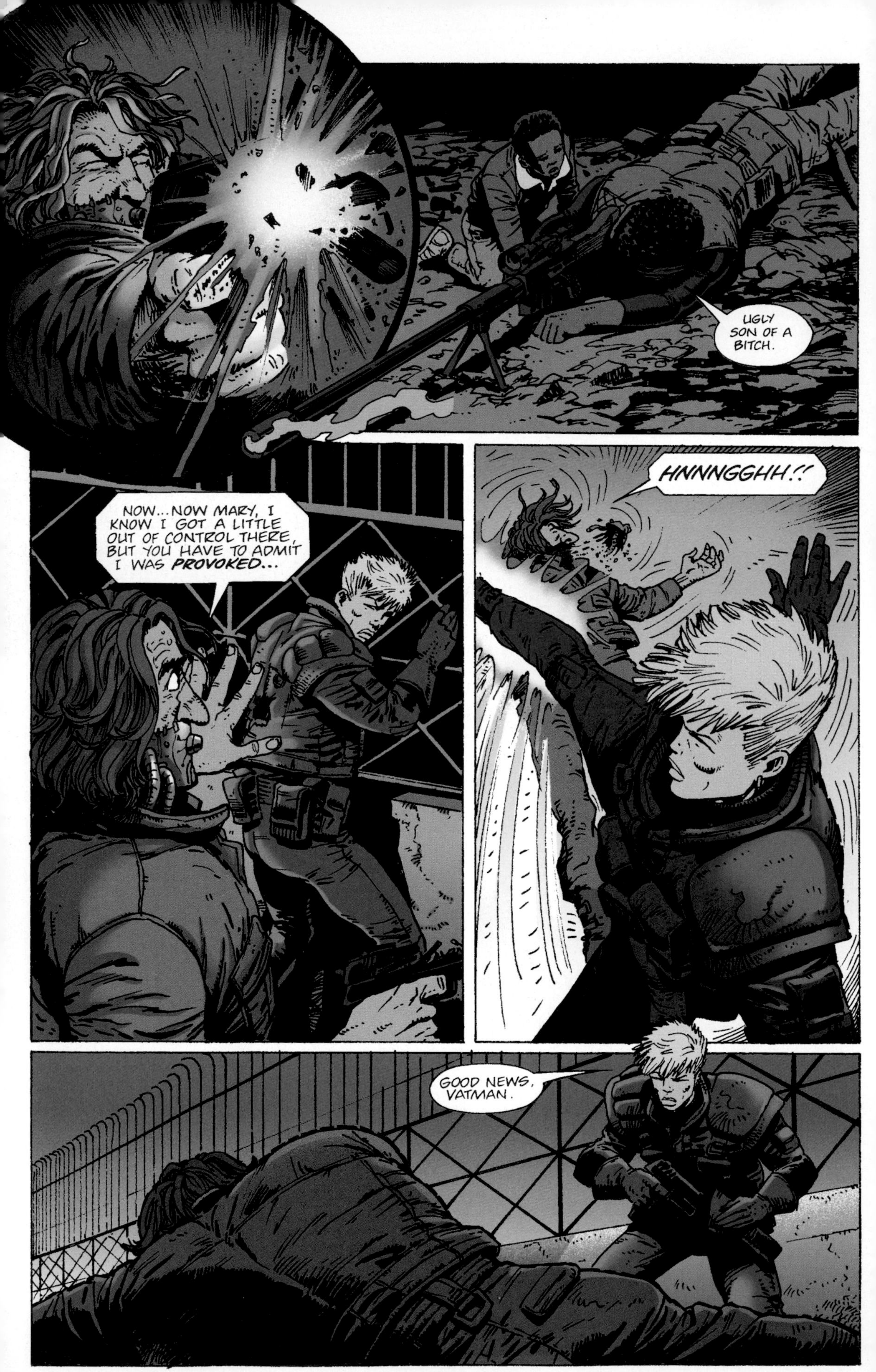
UGLY SON OF A BITCH.
NOW...NOW MARY, I KNOW I GOT A LITTLE OUT OF CONTROL THERE, BUT YOU HAVE TO ADMIT I WAS PROVOKED...
HNNNGGHH!!
GOOD NEWS, VATMAN.

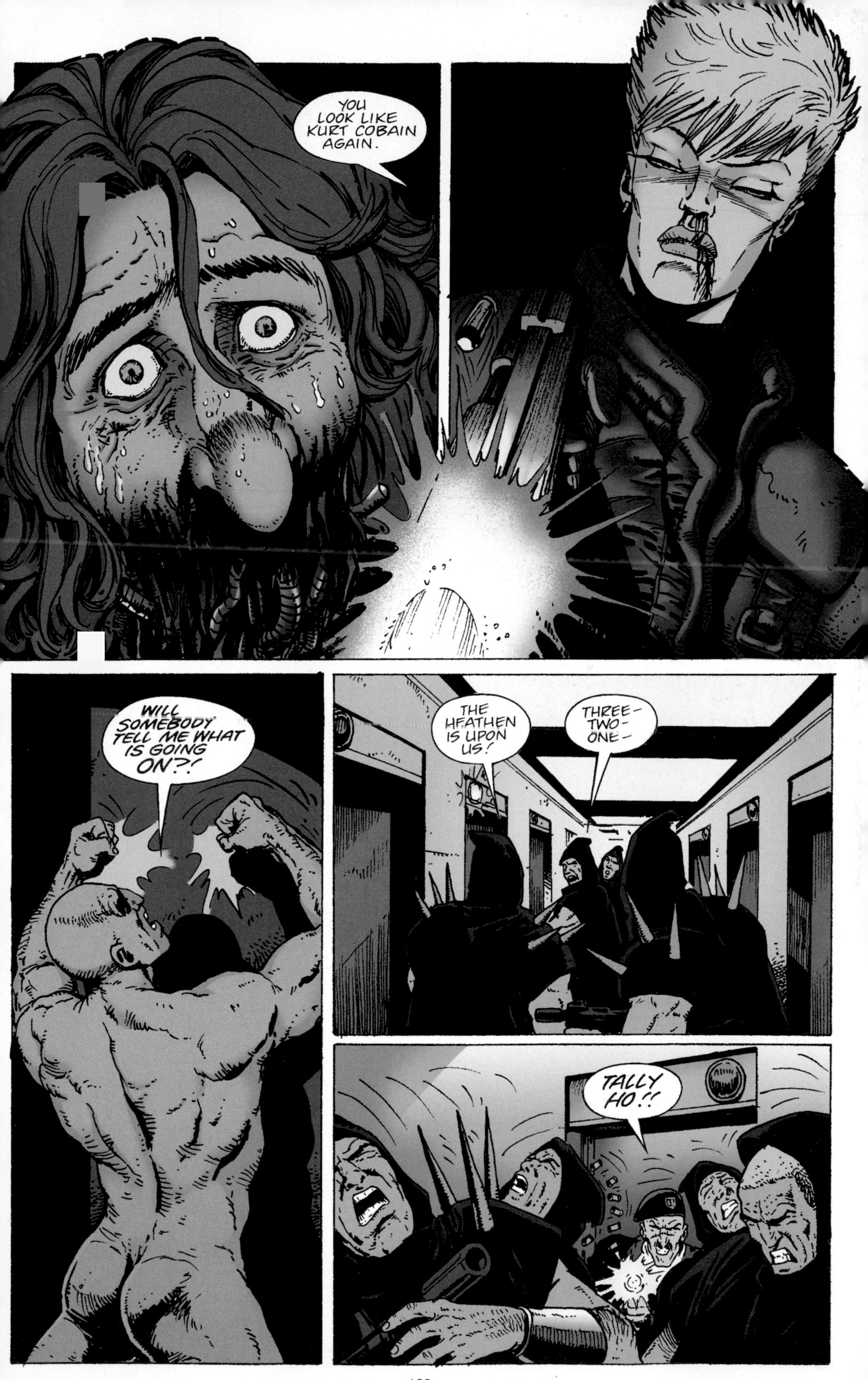
YOU LOOK LIKE KURT COBAIN AGAIN.
WILL SOMEBODY TELL ME WHAT IS GOING ON?!
THE HEATHEN IS UPON US!
THREE-TWO-ONE-
TALLY HO!!

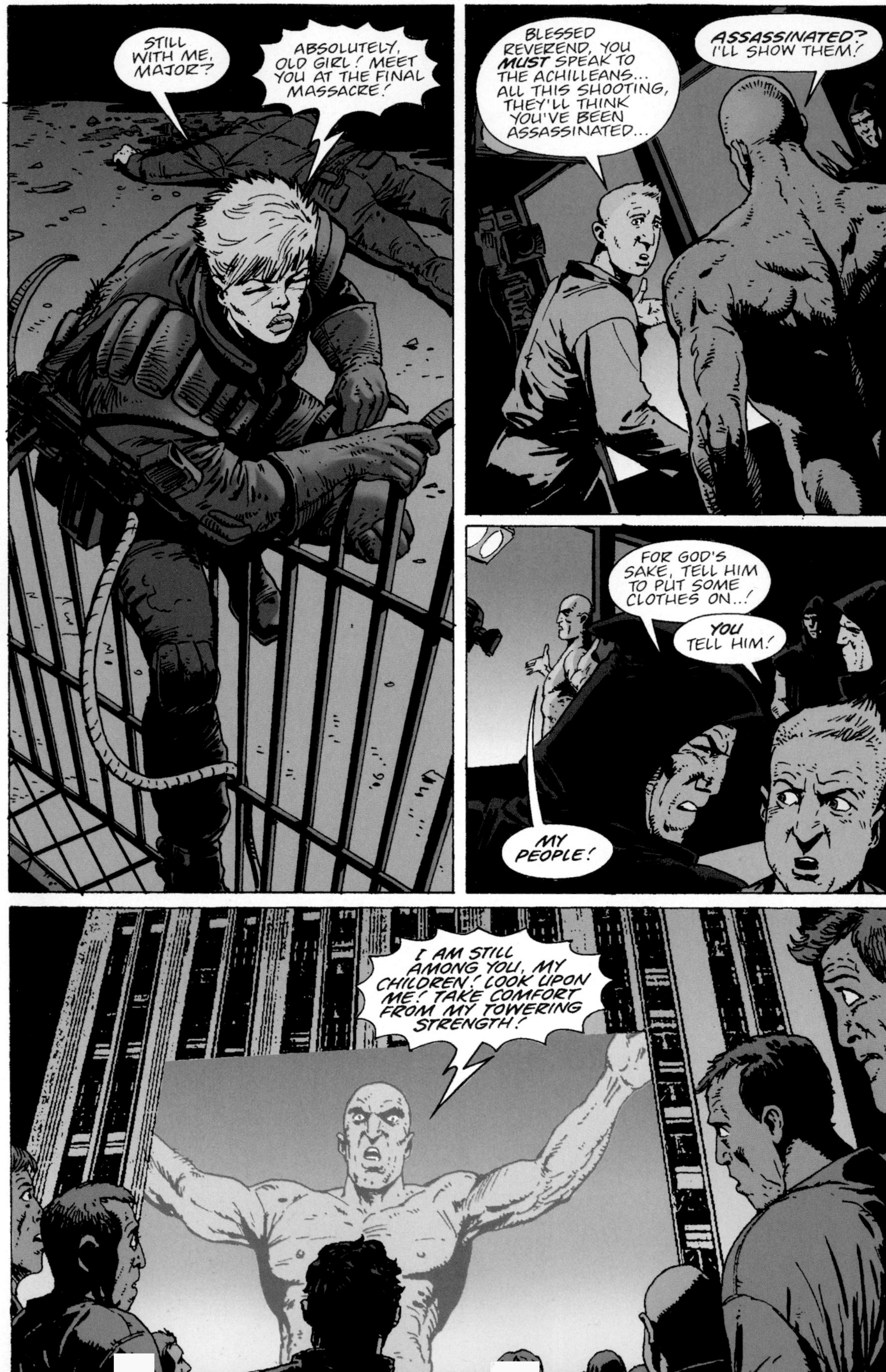
STILL WITH ME, MAJOR?
ABSOLUTELY, OLD GIRL! MEET YOU AT THE FINAL MASSACRE!
BLESSED REVEREND, YOU MUST SPEAK TO THE ACHILLEANS... ALL THIS SHOOTING, THEY'LL THINK YOU'VE BEEN ASSASSINATED...
ASSASSINATED? I'LL SHOW THEM!
FOR GOD'S SAKE, TELL HIM TO PUT SOME CLOTHES ON...!
YOU TELL HIM!
MY PEOPLE!
I AM STILL AMONG YOU, MY CHILDREN! LOOK UPON ME! TAKE COMFORT FROM MY TOWERING STRENGTH!

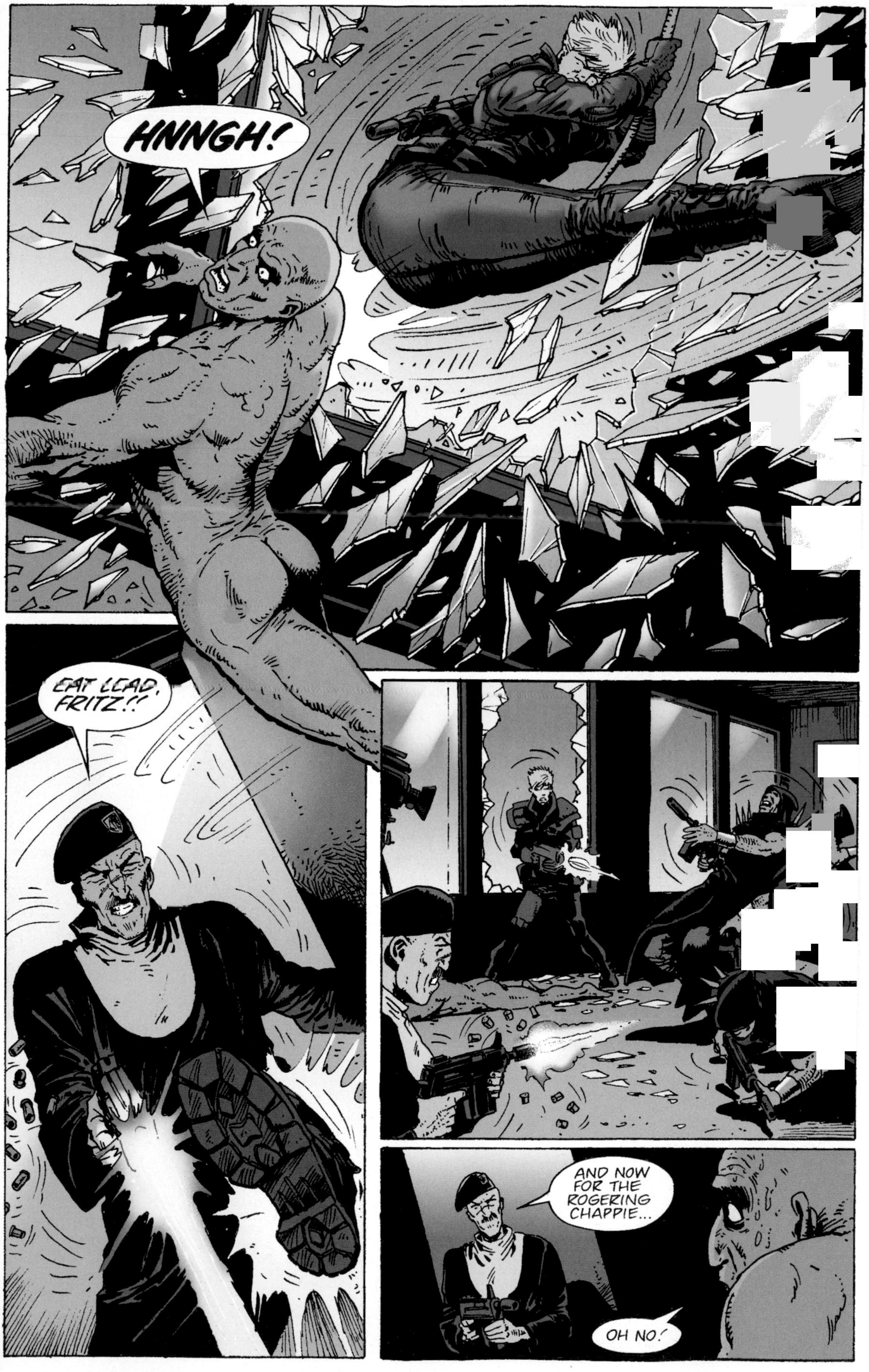
HNNGH!
EAT LEAD, FRITZ!!
AND NOW FOR THE ROGERING CHAPPIE...
OH NO!

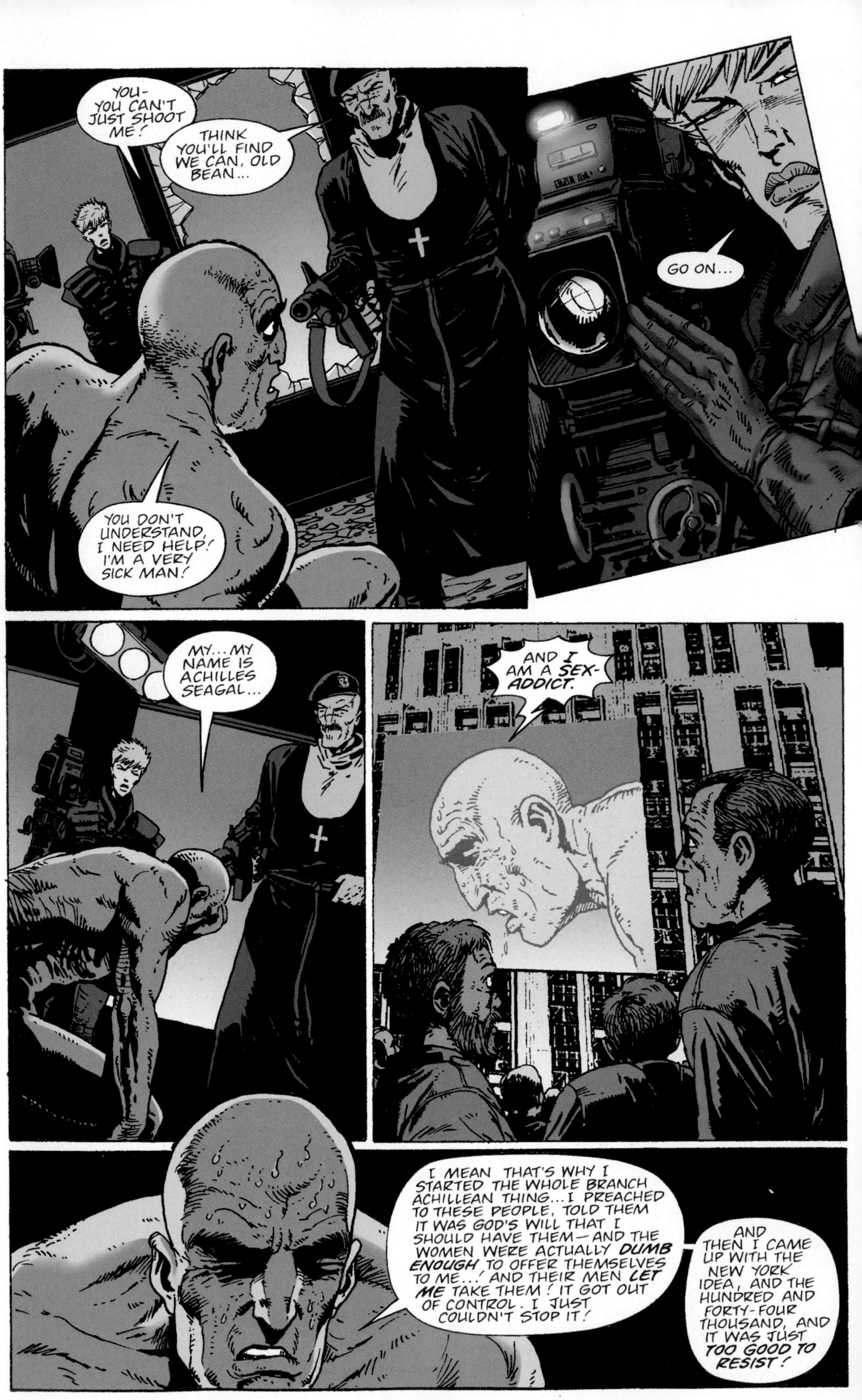
YOU- YOU CAN'T JUST SHOOT ME!
THINK YOU'LL FIND WE CAN, OLD BEAN...
YOU DON'T UNDERSTAND, I NEED HELP! I'M A VERY SICK MAN!
GO ON...
MY... MY NAME IS ACHILLES SEAGAL...
AND I AM A SEX-ADDICT.
I MEAN THAT'S WHY I STARTED THE WHOLE BRANCH ACHILLEAN THING... I PREACHED TO THESE PEOPLE, TOLD THEM IT WAS GOD'S WILL THAT I SHOULD HAVE THEM— AND THE WOMEN WERE ACTUALLY DUMB ENOUGH TO OFFER THEMSELVES TO ME...! AND THEIR MEN LET ME TAKE THEM! IT GOT OUT OF CONTROL. I JUST COULDN'T STOP IT!
AND THEN I CAME UP WITH THE NEW YORK IDEA, AND THE HUNDRED AND FORTY-FOUR THOUSAND, AND IT WAS JUST TOO GOOD TO RESIST!

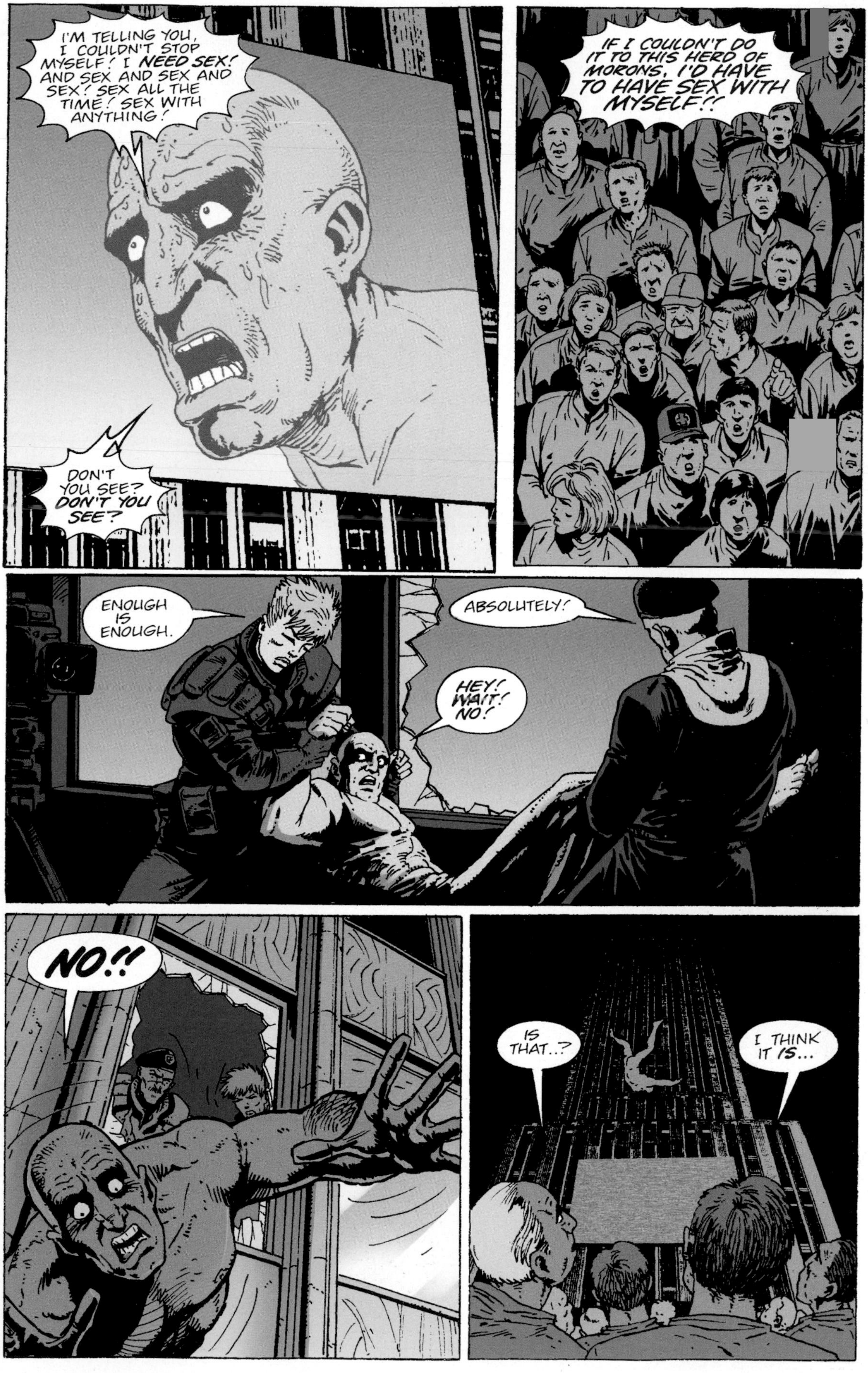
I'M TELLING YOU, I COULDN'T STOP MYSELF! I NEED SEX! AND SEX AND SEX AND SEX! SEX ALL THE TIME! SEX WITH ANYTHING!
DON'T YOU SEE? DON'T YOU SEE?
IF I COULDN'T DO IT TO THIS HERD OF MORONS, I'D HAVE TO HAVE SEX WITH MYSELF!!
ENOUGH IS ENOUGH.
ABSOLUTELY!
HEY! WAIT! NO!
NO!!
IS THAT..?
I THINK IT IS...

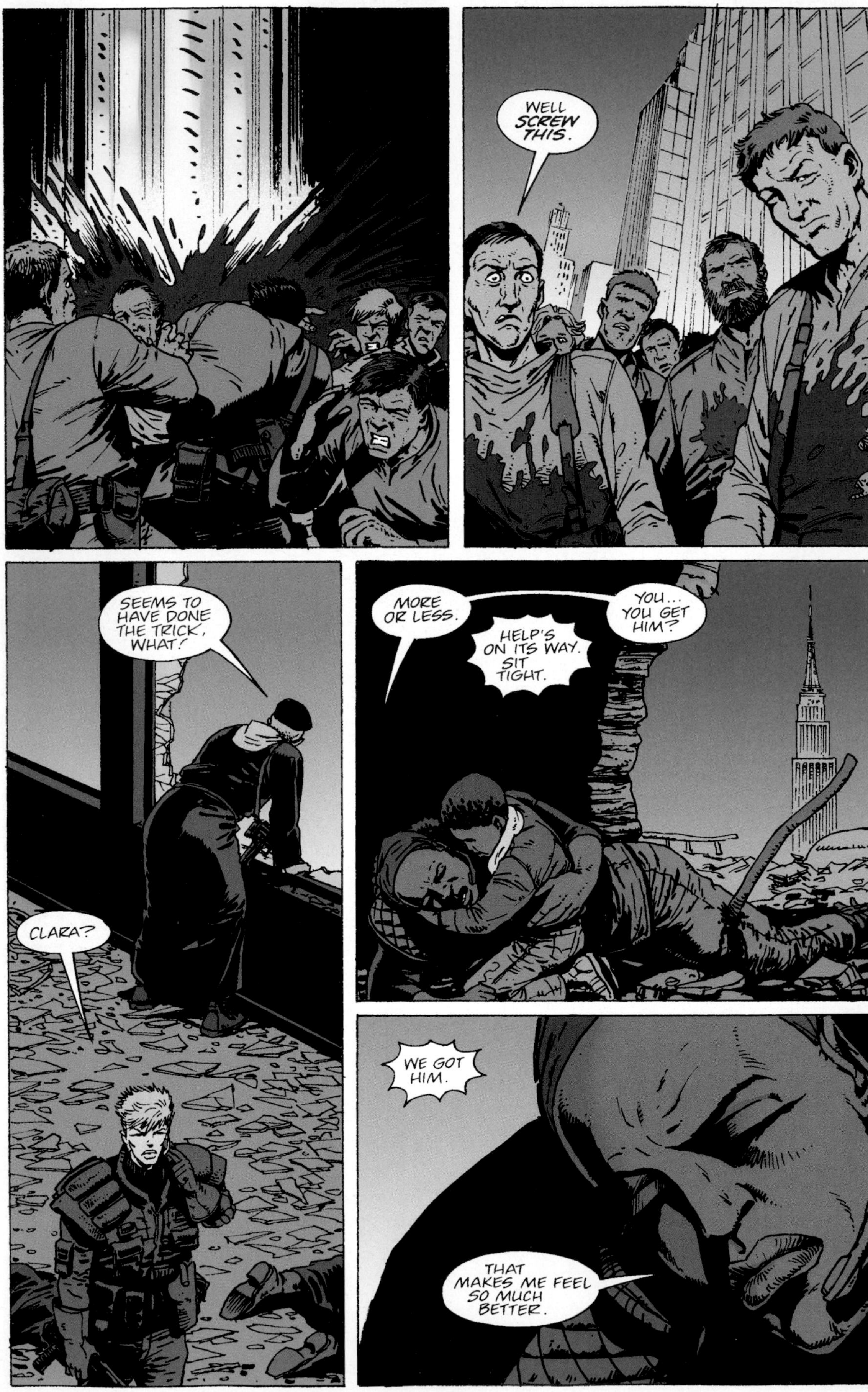
WELL SCREW THIS.
SEEMS TO HAVE DONE THE TRICK, WHAT?
CLARA?
MORE OR LESS.
YOU... YOU GET HIM?
HELP'S ON ITS WAY. SIT TIGHT.
WE GOT HIM.
THAT MAKES ME FEEL SO MUCH BETTER.

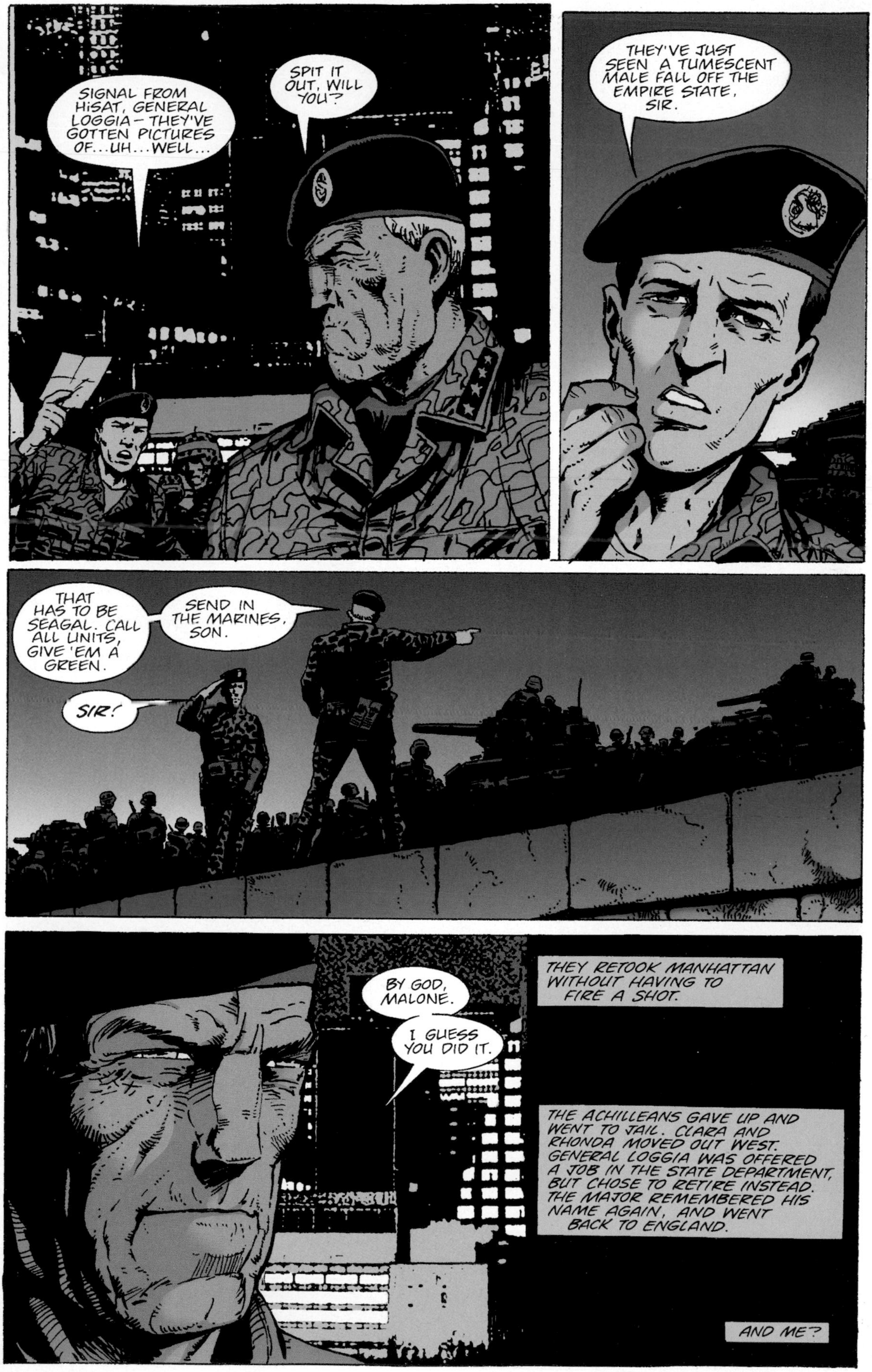
SIGNAL FROM HiSAT, GENERAL LOGGIA - THEY'VE GOTTEN PICTURES OF...UH...WELL...
SPIT IT OUT, WILL YOU?
THEY'VE JUST SEEN A TUMESCENT MALE FALL OFF THE EMPIRE STATE, SIR.
THAT HAS TO BE SEAGAL. CALL ALL UNITS, GIVE 'EM A GREEN.
SEND IN THE MARINES, SON.
SIR!
BY GOD, MALONE.
I GUESS YOU DID IT.
THEY RETOOK MANHATTAN WITHOUT HAVING TO FIRE A SHOT.
THE ACHILLEANS GAVE UP AND WENT TO JAIL. CLARA AND RHONDA MOVED OUT WEST. GENERAL LOGGIA WAS OFFERED A JOB IN THE STATE DEPARTMENT, BUT CHOSE TO RETIRE INSTEAD. THE MAJOR REMEMBERED HIS NAME AGAIN, AND WENT BACK TO ENGLAND.
AND ME?

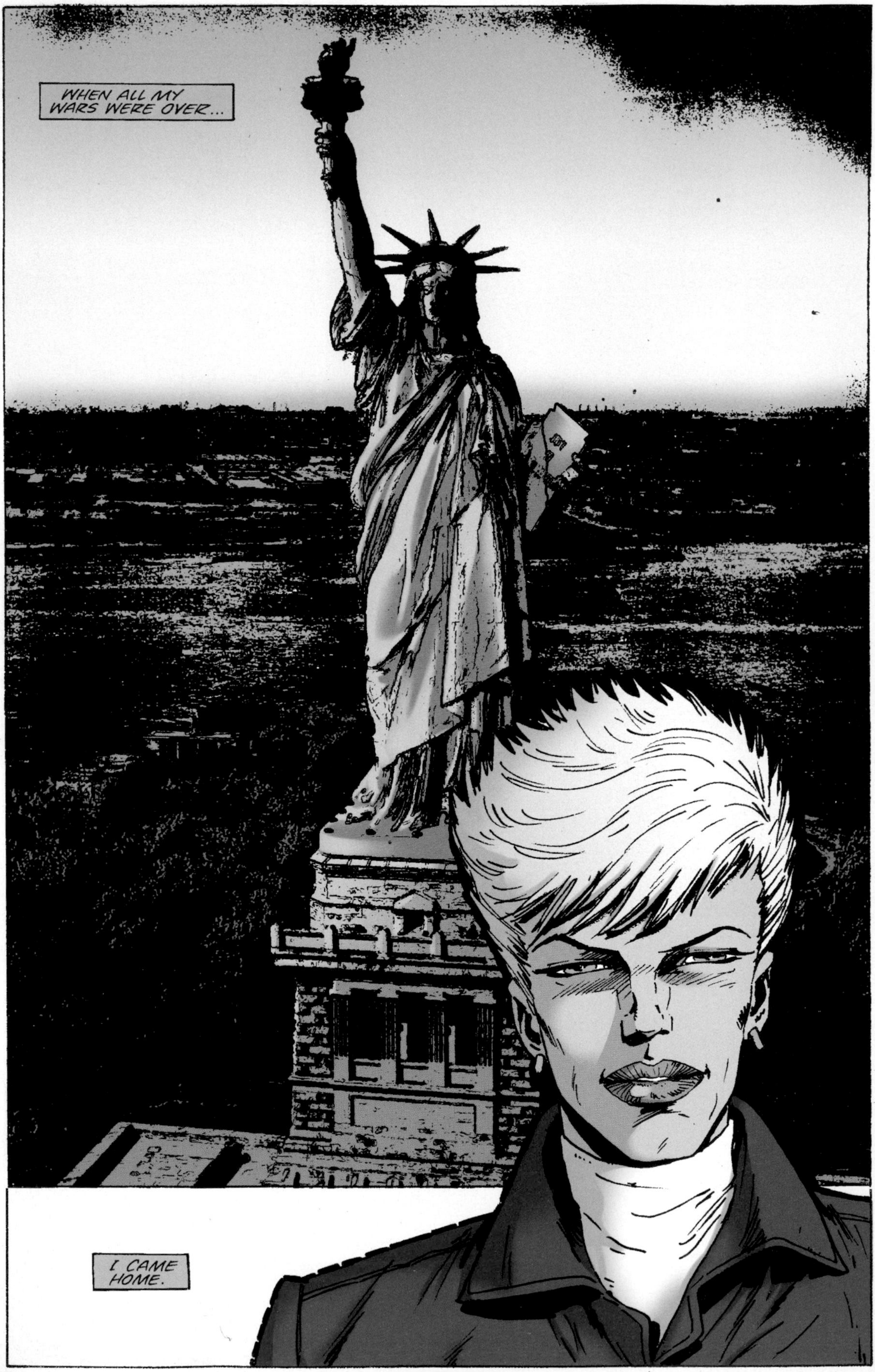
WHEN ALL MY WARS WERE OVER...
I CAME HOME.

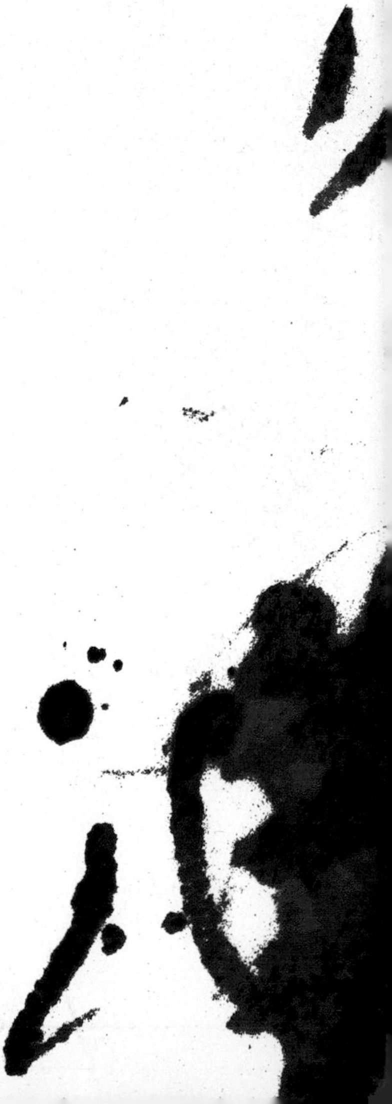

Garth Ennis

has been writing comics for over twenty-five years. His credits include *Preacher*, *The Boys*, *Hitman*, *Red Team*, *Caliban*, *Rover Red Charlie*, *Battlefields* and *War Stories*. Originally from Belfast, Northern Ireland, Ennis now lives in New York City with his wife, Ruth.

Carlos Ezquerra

has been drawing comics for forty-five years. He is the creator and designer of *Judge Dredd*, *Strontium Dog*, *Major Eazy*, *Just a Pilgrim*, *Cursed Earth Koburn*, *Adventures in the Rifle Brigade*, *Rat Pack*, *Al's Baby*, and many more. Born in Spain, he currently lives in Andorra, right in the heart of the Pyrenees.